Online Gaming in India

This book offers a comprehensive overview from diverse perspectives of online gaming technology, policy, and experiments to understand and review the Indian approach. It starts with the technological viewpoint on the governance and regulation of online gaming and includes the Indian experiment in governing and regulating it. The book brings a nuanced approach related to the perspectives of various stakeholders, the players, the developers, the gamers, the regulators, the law enforcement agencies, the industry and most importantly, the consumers, who are also the intended audience of the work.

Features:

- Presents a holistic view of the online gaming industry from technical, legal, and policymaking perspectives.
- Offers critical technical highlights, including online transactions, online games ecosystem, online games varied platforms, web3, metaverse, Artificial Intelligence (AI), and fantasy games.
- Includes a comparative analysis to evaluate better the laws, rules, and regulations and the governance of online gaming in India.
- Encapsulates the Indian experience in intervening and streamlining the online gaming industry.

The book is for professionals and scholars in the fields of online gaming in Computer Science, law, and other related disciplines. It also serves as a textbook for students for online gaming courses.

Online Gaming in India

Technology, Policy, and Challenges

Edited by
Lovely Dasgupta and Shameek Sen

CRC Press
Taylor & Francis Group
Boca Raton London New York

CRC Press is an imprint of the
Taylor & Francis Group, an **informa** business
A CHAPMAN & HALL BOOK

Designed cover image: sezer66/Shutterstock

First edition published 2025
by CRC Press
2385 NW Executive Center Drive, Suite 320, Boca Raton FL 33431

and by CRC Press
4 Park Square, Milton Park, Abingdon, Oxon, OX14 4RN

CRC Press is an imprint of Taylor & Francis Group, LLC

Library of Congress Cataloging-in-Publication Data
Names: Dasgupta, Lovely, editor. | Sen, Shameek, editor.
Title: Online gaming in India : technology, policy, and challenges /
edited by Lovely Dasgupta and Shameek Sen.
Description: First edition. | Boca Raton : C&H/ CRC Press, 2025. |
Includes bibliographical references and index. |
Identifiers: LCCN 2024029013 (print) | LCCN 2024029014 (ebook) |
ISBN 9781032619194 (hbk) | ISBN 9781032624167 (pbk) | ISBN 9781032624204 (ebk)
Subjects: LCSH: Video games–Social aspects–India. |
Video games–Economic aspects–India. | Video games industry–India.
Classification: LCC GV1469.34.S52 O55 2025 (print) | LCC GV1469.34.S52 (ebook) |
DDC 794.8/146780954–dc23/eng/20240819
LC record available at https://lccn.loc.gov/2024029013
LC ebook record available at https://lccn.loc.gov/2024029014

ISBN: 9781032619194 (hbk)
ISBN: 9781032624167 (pbk)
ISBN: 9781032624204 (ebk)

DOI: 10.1201/9781032624204

Typeset in Times
by Newgen Publishing UK

Contents

Acknowledgment

The book is the outcome of a process that began with a conversation. The conversation was about the interface between law, tech, policy, and gaming. The concerned individuals were Rajesh Dey, Lovely Dasgupta, and Shameek Sen. Consequently, Dasgupta and Sen decided to collaborate and edit, which resulted in this book. Thus, the first person to be acknowledged has to be Rajesh Dey, the Senior Commissioning Editor of CRC Press, Taylor and Francis Group. While Rajesh set the ball rolling, as editors, we had to pool the resources and ensure that the work was done on time. Editing is quite an ask, and it would not have been smooth without the immense help we received from our student assistants, Mr. Sharbadeb Biswas and Mr. Budhaditya Ghosh. These two helped us with our editorial work. Whenever required, they were there and always ready to chip in. We also acknowledge the immense support received from each contributor, without which this book would have ended with the conversation. Lastly, we acknowledge the support and guidance of our Publisher, CRC Press, Taylor and Francis Group.

Editors' Biography

Lovely Dasgupta has been in the teaching profession for the last eighteen years. She is an alumnus of the West Bengal National University of Juridical Sciences, where she has completed her L.L.M., M.Phil., and Ph.D. She primarily teaches Contract and Commercial law at the Undergraduate level and Competition Law at the Postgraduate level. She is one of the founding Indian academics to introduce a taught course on Sports Law. In the past sixteen years, she has been writing about and researching issues within the field of sports law. In addition, she has also published in competition law. To date, she has published four books on Sports Law and Competition Law. In addition, she has also published on Legal Education, which has been one of her highly cited works. Among others, Prof. Werner Menski in 'Shah Bano, Narendra Modi and reality checks about global understandings of Indian law,' *Nirma University Law Journal* (Ahmedabad), Volume 1, Issue 1(2011), has cited pp. 7-26 of 'Reforming Indian Legal education: Linking Research and Teaching, *Journal of Legal Education*, Volume 59, Number 3' (see Footnote No. 15 of Menski). She is heading the Centre for Sports Law and Policy at NUJS. She is the only Indian to be a member of the International Network of Doping Research, Department of Public Health, Aarhus University, Denmark.

Shameek Sen is Associate Professor at the West Bengal National University of Juridical Sciences, Kolkata, India. He specializes in public law disciplines such as constitutional law and media law. He has several publications as books, book chapters, and articles in peer-reviewed journals and newspaper op-ed articles. His book titled *Sports Law in India: Policy, Regulation and Commercialisation*, co-edited with Dr. Lovely Dasgupta, is considered to be one of the leading Indian books on the subject. He has also presented several papers at international conferences and symposia, including the Asian Law Institute (ASLI) Annual Conferences and the Biennial Conferences organized by the Asian Constitutional Law Forum. His article titled 'Constitutional Crisis, Autocratic Legalism and the Indian Constitution: Constitutionalism at Crossroads?' was selected as the sole Indian entry at a project on Constitutional Struggles in Asia and was presented at an International Webinar organized by the Australian National University and the National University of Singapore Centre for Asian Legal Studies Faculty of Law. He currently holds the position of Director at the Centre for Technology, Entertainment and Sports Laws, a Research Centre that was set up at WBNUJS with financial support from M/S Gameskraft Technologies Pvt. Ltd., one of India's largest skill-based online gaming platforms. The Center is a pioneer academic contributor in India to the scholarship in these niche areas of study, organizing lectures, symposia, workshops, and training programs dealing with the latest domain knowledge on the nuances of these subject matters.

Contributors

Anuj Berry
Trilegal
New Delhi, India

Sudipta Bhattacharjee
Khaitan & Co
India

Animesh Anand Bordoloi
O.P. Jindal Global University
Sonipat, India

Soumitra Bose
Senior Journalist
India

Agniva Chakrabarti
Trilegal
New Delhi, India

Atish Chakraborty
The West Bengal University of Juridical Sciences
Kolkata, India

Subhrajit Chanda
O.P. Jindal Global University
Sonipat, India

Ashiv Choudhary
O.P. Jindal Global University
Sonipat, India

V.S. Gigimon
Maharashtra National Law University
Mumbai, India

Mili Gupta
Presidency University
Bangalore, India

Megha Janakiraman
Trilegal
New Delhi, India

Kuldeep Kaur
NLIU
Bhopal, India

Sachin Kumar
O.P. Jindal Global University
Sonipat, India

Prakhar Maheshwari
Board of Control for Cricket in India
Mumbai, India

Sarath Ninan Mathew
University of Oxford
Oxford, UK

Ananya S. Menon
LawNK
India

Meyyappan Nagappan
Trilegal
New Delhi, India

Angesh A. Panchal
GLS University
Ahmedabad, India

Niyati Pandey
Gujarat National Law University
Gandhinagar, India

Arup Poddar
The West Bengal National University of Juridical Sciences
Kolkata, India

Eshwar Ramachandran
LawNK
Bengaluru, India

Varun Ramdas
Koan Advisory
New Delhi, India

Suhasini Rao
Vinayaka Mission's Law School
Chennai, India

Sourabh Rath
Trilegal
New Delhi, India

Sanjay Ravi
LawNK
India

Saranya Ravindran
NALSAR University of Law
Hyderabad, India

Kazim Rizvi
The Dialogue
New Delhi, India

Arjyadeep Roy
Khaitan & Co
India

Bissheesh Roy
Board of Control for Cricket in India
India

Jay Sayta
Technology & Gaming Lawyer
India

Vidhi Shah
GLS University
Ahmedabad, India

Narayana Sharma
Maharashtra National Law University
Mumbai, India

Nishant Sheokand
Vinayaka Mission's Law School
Chennai, India

Abhinav Shrivastava
LawNK

Saloni Tyagi Shrivastava
Kalinga University
Raipur, India

Gagneet Singh
Presidency University
Bangalore, India

Kriti Singh
The Dialogue
New Delhi, India

Vidushpat Singhania
KRIDA LEGAL
New Delhi, India

Eeshan Sonak
NALSAR University of Law
Hyderabad, India

V.J.S. Srivastav
Skill Online Games Institute (SOGI)
Gurgaon, India

Shirin Suri
NLIU
Bhopal, India

Pujaarchana Talukdar
KRIDA LEGAL
New Delhi, India

S. Tarun
Gujarat National Law University
Koba, India

Gyan Tripathi
Technology Law and Policy Researcher
India

Ananya Giri Upadhya
NLU
Delhi, India

Ishaan Vohra
The West Bengal University of Juridical Sciences
Kolkata, India

Anjali Yadav
VSL VIT-AP University
Vijayawada, India

Introduction

Lovely Dasgupta and Shameek Sen

Mr. X is a prudent investor. He decides to make a substantial investment into mutual funds. Cognizant of the disclaimers about the market risk and the need to read the offer documents, he does some market research before investing and lets market forces take their course thereafter.

Ms. Y is an avid chess player. She likes to sit down for a game of chess whenever she gets an opportunity. In the process, she sometimes loses track of time and her usual chores get delayed, which she does not seem to mind ever. In fact, she often takes part in the open chess tournaments (occasionally paying small entry fees) organized in her city where chess players from all over come to compete for the coveted monetary awards.

In both these situations, despite the obvious difference in the nature of the exercises, certain commonalities exist. In both, there is an element of monetary risk. In both, there is some degree of addictiveness. And in both, there is definitely a substantial requirement of skill.

A recent Public Interest Litigation filed before the Delhi High Court challenges the Information Technology (Intermediary Guidelines and Digital Media Ethics Code) Amendment Rules, 2023 as being ultra vires the Constitution of India and the Information Technology Act, 2000, insofar as the rules seek to regulate the online gaming industry, a 'sunrise sector' in which India is aggressively trying to create a footprint. The primary grounds of challenge are two-fold. One, the petitioner argues that online games which are played by making a deposit with the expectation of earning gains ('Real Money Games' in short) fall within the broader realm of 'betting and gambling' and the legislative competence to regulate this subject matter lies with the State Legislatures, under Entry 34 of List II (State List) of Schedule VII to the Constitution of India. The other substantive ground of challenge is that online gaming platforms have been wrongly brought within the ambit of the expression 'intermediaries'.

With regards to the first question as to whether online games can fall within the definition of 'betting and gambling', one has to turn backward in history and look at the catena of decisive determinations both by the Supreme Courts and High Courts where a clear distinction has been made between a 'game of skill' and a 'game of chance'. While betting and gambling would fall within the ambit of a 'game of chance', Courts

DOI: 10.1201/9781032624204-1

have held with absolute certainty that games like rummy and poker do involve a substantial degree of skill and have to be treated differently from games of chance like betting and gambling. For example, in the 2021 case of *Junglee Games India Pvt Ltd v. State of Tamil Nadu*, the Madras High Court drew upon this difference to strike down certain amendments to the Tamil Nadu Gaming and Police Laws (Amendment) Act, 2021 to state that a complete ban on games of skill involving money is an unreasonable restriction to a citizen's Right to Freedom of Trade, Occupation and Business guaranteed under Article 19(1)(g) of the Constitution. By virtue of the consistent line of determinations by the Courts, it is quite obvious that games of skill, whether they involve money or not, fall within the contours of this Right, and therefore, any attempt to impose restrictions that are disproportionate and overbearing would be considered unreasonable and would be liable to be struck down.

To further illustrate the skill vs chance divide, let us consider the example of fantasy cricket. When one is building a team of eleven players, the eventual composition of the team is contingent on several factors – pitch, weather, players' current form, etc., each of which play a key role in the selection of players of specific expertise over others. To obviate this skill requirement and to conflate the 'skill vs chance' divide is an oversimplification of the discourse and an absolute disregard of decades of settled jurisprudence on the subject.

This is a malaise that even the GST Council led by the Union Finance Minister Nirmala Sitharaman has been afflicted by, when on 11th July 2023, the Council decided to levy 28% GST on the proceeds from Online Real Money Games. This move, apart from having a seriously debilitating impact on the online gaming industry, also leads to a significant jurisprudential dichotomy. The moment the 'skill vs chance' question is rendered insignificant, the Union Parliament loses legislative competence over the real money online gaming industry, because the Entry 34 List II issue gets opened up. Thus, it becomes a regulatory conundrum when the Ministry of Information Technology is steadfastly trying to bring the online gaming industry within its regulatory purview, and the GST Council, shepherded by the Union Finance Minister, is in a way giving up the regulation in favor of the States by ignoring the 'skill vs chance' question.

Quite obviously, there is a Federalism question that opens up as a result. If Entry 34 List II is inapplicable, then which legislative body should have competence in regulating online gaming? Will it be the State Legislature again, by virtue of Entry 33 List II that *inter alia* deals with sports, entertainments, and amusements? Or will it be the Union Parliament by virtue of Entry 31 List I that deals with 'Posts and telegraphs; telephones, wireless, broadcasting and other like forms of communication'? It is argued that since online games are played predominantly through smartphone-reliant platforms, the Union should have regulatory authority in view of Entry 31 List I, read with the *non-obstante* clauses in Article 246 that clearly underscore a parliamentary predominance in matters involving legislative competence.

In arguendo, one can always argue that if Entry 31 List I seems untenable, then the legislative history of the Information Technology Act 2000 provides a clear insight into why the Parliament should exercise legislative prerogative in regulating the online gaming sector. The Information Technology Act was enacted to effectuate the vision of an United Nations General Assembly Resolution that had adopted the

Model Law on Electronic Commerce adopted by the United Nations Commission on International Trade Law. The Act did not however confine itself to only Electronic Commerce. It became the omnibus source of regulation of all activities that require the use of an electronic communicating device. Thus, cyber frauds and cyber pornography are also issues that are dealt with under the provisions of this Act. By virtue of Article 253 of the Constitution of India, the Parliament assumes competence to legislate even on out-and-out State List Entries, if this legislation is brought about to implement any international treaty, agreement, decision, etc. Hence, there should be no problems whatsoever in a parliamentary regulation of online gaming.

The other issue raised in the petition however deserves some thoughtful considerations. Bringing all online gaming activities within the larger definition of 'intermediaries' is a 'one-size-that-fits-all' measure. Quite obviously, a strategy game like fantasy cricket or chess cannot be compared with an action game like Call of Duty or Ninja Action. In a recently published article in the Economic and Political Weekly, the authors classify online games into the following broad categories – adventure/action games, first-person shooter games, sports-based games, online board games, arcade-based games, online fantasy sports, and online casino sports. The challenges toward regulating each category are very different from the other one. Adventure/action games and first-person shooter games have the potential of involving a considerable degree of violence, and the impression on the adolescent minds becomes a relevant consideration for regulation. The other categories of games have varying degrees of skill prerequisite in each and require focused regulation for each category rather than bludgeoning all of them under the umbrella of 'intermediaries'. A standard-form identical regulation of any form that does not consider their inherent specificities will not only be logically inappropriate, they would also be constitutionally untenable because the Right to Equality is premised on the idea of reasonable classification that only equals are treated equally.

One of the regulatory measures that had been initially proposed by the MEITY was regulation by means of self-regulatory organizations (SROs), also referred to as self-regulatory bodies (SRBs) occasionally. This organization was supposed to be the industry self-regulation of the industry rather than a command-and-control top-down regulation from the state. Recent reports have however suggested that the Central Government has, at least for the time being, rejected the idea of an SRO and have decided to take up regulations by themselves. This is a typical instance of the dynamic nature of the industry and how quickly the legal and regulatory landscape goes through abrupt upheavals. On a functional plane, it also posits obvious editorial challenges for compiling a book like this. However, as editors, we have gone ahead with the chapters analyzing the viabilities of the SROs simply because as legal critiques, we do not wish to foreclose any avenue for exploration. And the sheer pace at which the regulatory preferences are undergoing thorough transformations, one can never say the final words on such issues.

Mr. X and Ms. Y can be found all around us. The activities carried out by both of them have widespread societal acceptance. It is absolutely necessary that in a country that has the highest youth population (between ages 15 and 35), a significantly high smartphone penetration of almost 80% and an estimated 90 million people playing fantasy sports in 2019 as per the NITI Aayog Report in 2020, we normalize online gaming activities by bringing it out of the shadow of betting and gambling. This book is an attempt toward normalization of the discourse on online gaming by discussing the gaming jurisprudence through an interdisciplinary and comparative lens. The contributors to this book are leading names from the industry and the academia who have looked into the multifarious facets of the issue and associated complexities, both functional and legal.

The first chapter titled "Online Games in India: Ancient Legacy, Modern Challenges" by VJS Srivastav traces the history of gaming in India to its ancient roots in games like *Chaturanga* and *Pachisi* to the modern gaming paradigms. This chapter serves as an introduction of sorts to exploring the keys to human behavior and preferences, through a study of the evolution of their gaming preferences, and explores the ways forward from an industry insider's perspective.

In the chapter titled "Evolution of Jurisprudence on Online Games of Skill", Jay Sayta articulates on the historical journey on regulation of the industry. Starting from the Public Gambling Act of 1867 to the Intermediary Guidelines of 2023, the author succinctly traces the regulatory journey where gaming has emerged out of the shadows of gambling and how the courts have decisively used the preponderance of skill test to highlight the difference between the two.

The chapter titled "In Regulatory Purgatory: How many lives left before mission success for the Indian gaming industry?" by Vidushpat Singhania and Pujaarchana Talukdar highlights the regulatory conundrum involving the online gaming industry. The authors analyze the 'command-and-control' regulatory models involving the MEITY as the key player, regulatory recommendations by the Law Commission of India, and the proposed regulatory models involving SRBs (self-regulatory bodies). They also explore the regulatory models through a comparative perspective in looking at regulatory models of other jurisdictions like the United Kingdom, Germany, Denmark, etc.

The chapter titled "Pathways to Stakeholder-Led Regulation in Online Gaming" by Abhinav Shrivastava, Eshwar Ramachandran, Ananya S. Menon, and Sanjay Ravi focuses on the nuances of the self-regulatory models. The chapter highlights the pros and cons of self-regulation in the online gaming sector and critically looks at the challenges that these regulatory models would possibly encounter.

The chapter titled "Of Monopolistic Attitude, Power Mongering and Trust Deficit" by Dr. Soumitra Bose offers a counter-narrative. Shorn of commendations and adulations on the online gaming sector, this chapter offers a journalistic dissection of what the author calls "a rather reckless industry". He articulates on the lack of trust between leading gaming operators and the deepening fault lines attributable according to him to the regulatory efforts by the government.

The chapter titled "Regulatory Progress and Challenges in India's Booming Online Gaming Market" by Niyati Pandey articulates on psychological issues like addiction to online gaming and offers a cross-jurisdictional prism toward regulating such problems. The authors explore regulations such as age gating and lootboxes from across jurisdictions as probable mechanisms as to how children and adolescents can be protected from the apparently pernicious impacts of online games.

The chapter titled "Regulating Online Gaming: Centre Versus State Competence" by Gyan Tripathi and Ananya Giri Upadhya delves into the Federalism question which is equally pivotal to online gaming regulations. The authors point out how location-specific socio-cultural mores often determine levels of tolerance toward games involving money and explores the scope of the interplay between Entry 31 of List I and Entries 33 and 34 of List II. They also look into the Constituent Assembly Debates leading up to the delineation of the subject matters of legislative competence.

In the chapter titled "Walking on Eggshells: Prospects of Self-Regulating Online Gaming in India" by Shirin Suri and Kuldeep Kaur, the authors analyze the MEITY guidelines and seek to critique it in terms of its loopholes, leading up to a conclusion that the guidelines undermine the goals of self-regulation. Subsequently, the authors propose a viable self-regulation model by making references to global best practices.

The chapter titled "Challenges and Prospects: An Analysis of Fantasy Sports Regulation in India" by Sachin Kumar and Animesh Bordoloi explores the regulation of the Fantasy Gaming landscape. While the jurisprudence appeared to be largely settled on the issue that fantasy games are games of skill, there are still threshold regulatory issues that require jurisprudential resolution. The authors of this chapter purport to offer some solutions to these normative complexities.

The chapter titled "Online Gambling through an Anti-Money Laundering Perspective: A Cross-Jurisdictional Analysis" by Anuj Berry, Sourabh Rath, Megha Janakiraman, and Agniva Chakrabarti critically analyzes the legal framework dealing with issues pertaining to money laundering in the online gambling landscape. In this chapter, the authors discuss the applicability of the Prevention of Money Laundering Act, 2002 and the Prevention of Money Laundering (Maintenance of Records) Rules, 2005 to the online gaming sector and articulate on the challenges faced by the anti-money laundering regulatory apparatus while dealing with online gambling intermediaries. The chapter traverses through the global regulatory landscape and offers pragmatic policy reform solutions for India.

The chapter titled "Cyber-Security and Data Privacy Challenges in Online Gaming: Analyzing the Cyber-Security Risks and Challenges Faced by Online Gaming Platforms in India" by Saloni Tyagi Shrivastava analyzes the cyber-security risks and challenges faced by online gaming platforms in India, with a specific focus on data privacy. The author in this chapter explores the challenges associated with data privacy, including issues of consent, transparency, and user control, and explores into the extent of compliance of online gaming platforms with existing data protection laws and regulations in India, such as the Personal Data Protection Bill.

The chapter titled "Blockchain in Online Gaming: Navigating the Legal Landscape for India and the World" by Prof. Subhrajit Chanda and Prof. Ashiv Choudhary seeks to discuss the way blockchain is contributing toward online gaming from the legal landscape for India and the world. The chapter investigates the national strategies adopted by India and the global community to facilitate the secure and responsible use of blockchain in online gaming and sheds light on the legal considerations and possible pathways for integrating blockchain technology into the online gaming ecosystem while addressing concerns of security, privacy, and consumer protection.

In the chapter titled "A Study on the Legal Challenges in Online Gaming with Special Reference to Network, Accessibility, and Piracy", the authors Angesh A. Panchal and Dr. Vidhi Shah analyze issues like the impact of the country's network infrastructure on the online gaming industry. The authors examine how the digital divide, particularly between urban and rural areas, affects accessibility and user experience. The chapter also analyzes issues of accessibility and inclusivity in terms of economic barriers, social perceptions, linguistic diversity, and cultural relevance in the context of Indian gaming.

The chapter titled "Innovation and Policy: Balancing Technological Advancements with Regulatory Frameworks in Indian Online Gaming" by Prof. Arup Kumar Poddar examines the current landscape of technology in the industry, from the meteoric rise of mobile gaming to the implementation of AI/ML/blockchain and discusses the importance of striking a balance between encouraging innovation, protecting consumers' rights, and being ethical in business practices. It examines regulatory practices around the world and offers recommendations for a nuanced strategy in policymaking alongside illuminating case examples.

The chapter titled "Dark Patterns in the Gaming Industry: Legal Implications and Safeguarding User Rights" by Prof. VS Gigimon and Narayana Sharma illustrates the complex wave of dark patterns – deceptive design techniques, subtly embedded in-game interfaces, and mechanics that manipulate player's choices often leading to unintended consequences detrimental to their interests and rights. The chapter critically analyzes issues of user rights, including financial exploitation, addiction, and privacy breaches and sheds light on the ethical dilemmas and moral responsibilities of game developers and publishers, highlighting the fine line between engaging game design and manipulative practices.

The chapter titled "Navigating the Legal Landscape of Online Gaming in India: Precedence, Regulations, and Future Perspectives" by Nishant Sheokand And Suhasini Rao provides a comprehensive overview of the legal regime on online gaming and deals with constitutional issues as well issues pertaining to taxation.

In the chapter titled "Do E-Sports Broadcasts Infringe Videogame Copyright?", the author Sarath Ninan Mathew delves into the area of E-Sports within the larger online gaming ecosystem and explores the question as to whether unauthorized E-Sports broadcasts infringe videogame copyrights.

The chapter titled "Player Image Rights and Online Gaming: Decoding the Game" by Prakhar Maheshwari and Bissheesh Roy embarks on a comprehensive exploration of the legal framework surrounding player image rights in India in the context of online gaming, given the growing commercial significance of such rights in modern sports. It evaluates the lack of statutory recognition for a sportsperson to protect their image rights and explores the possible policy choices on a need for a specific statute for governing and regulating player image rights.

In the chapter titled "Copyrightability of Digital Player Cards in Online Fantasy Sports: A Conundrum in the Indian Copyright Law", the authors Atish Chakraborty and Ishaan Vohra critically evaluate issues pertaining to leveraging of digital collectibles – unique and limited edition virtual items that use blockchain technology to generate non-fungible tokens whose ownership is freely transferable, which has now become the new currency of trade in this arena.

The chapter titled "Navigating Legal and Operational Uncertainty Around Advertisement of Online Games" by Varun Ramdas explores the issue of advertisement of online games and engages with issues like the distinction between advertisements for legal Real Money Games and surrogate advertisements of offshore betting entities in the absence of a clear legal demarcation between the two. It proposes a comparative overview of different jurisdictions and makes pertinent policy recommendations.

The chapter titled "Gender Dynamics in Online Gaming: Exploring Participation and Representation in India" by Anjali Yadav delves into the need for a more inclusive gaming environment by exploring women's participation patterns and representation in gaming communities, highlighting their challenges and potential strategies for fostering inclusivity and gender equality in the online gaming industry.

The chapter titled "Child's Consent in Online Gaming Click-Wrap Agreements and its Intersection with Privacy" by Mili Gupta and Gagneet Singh looks at the regulatory complexities arising out of a situation when a minor misrepresents his age and clicks on the "I agree" button for playing online games by making the gaming platform believe that the game is being played by an adult only. In doing so, the authors analyze issues pertaining to protection of personal data of minors and the need for parental consent, in light of the inherently ineffective age verification mechanisms.

The chapter titled "Responsible & Ethical Framework in Online Gaming: A Shared Responsibility" by Kriti Singh and Kazim Rizvi explores the need for responsible gaming principles to safeguard user well-being, financial integrity, and transparency. The authors explore the possibilities toward a standardized mechanism that acknowledges the heterogeneity of business models and services within the online gaming sector while emphasizing the collective responsibility of all stakeholders to prioritize user protection and economic growth.

The penultimate chapter titled "A Comparative Study of the GGR and Turnover Models of Taxing Online Gaming" by Meyyappan Nagappan, Eeshan Sonak, and Saranya Ravindran articulates on the slew of changes brought about in the real money online gaming sector in 2023 through the application of a 28% turnover tax on the industry, replacing the existing practice of defining online gaming as an OIDAR service and taxing it at 18% on the commissions earned by gaming platforms under a gross gaming revenue ("GGR") taxation model. The chapter provides a comparative overview of the two models.

The final chapter titled "GST and Online Gaming Sector – A Taxing Saga" by Sudipta Bhattacharjee and Arjyadeep Roy provides a holistic and comprehensive overview of the GST architecture with regards to real money online gaming. The authors in this chapter provide a chronological account of the indirect taxation structure before and after the 101st Constitutional Amendment Act, 2016 that introduced the GST as a single levy for taxing goods and services, and it subsumed various other indirect levies.

As editors of this book which can be safely called a first-of-its-kind omnibus on issues pertaining to online gaming in India, it has been our privilege and honor to go through each chapter and the treasure-trove of ideas that each of them has to offer. The book has contributions by academicians, journalists, policy activists as well as litigators and solicitors who inject their wealth of expertise into their respective chapters. We owe the success of this book to each one of them.

1 Online Games in India
Ancient Legacy, Modern Challenges

V.J.S. Srivastav

1.1 INTRODUCTION

The tapestry of Indian culture is rich with various forms of entertainment that have not only served as leisure activities but also played significant roles in the social, cultural, and educational spheres of life. Among these, indoor games like card games, chess (chaturanga), and gambling stand out for their historical roots, widespread appeal, and deep-seated significance in the traditions of India. This chapter aims to uncover the layers of historical, cultural, and social importance of these games, tracing their evolution and examining their role in the contemporary cultural landscape of India.

The historical roots and evolution of indoor games in India, particularly card games, chess (chaturanga), and gambling, weave through the annals of Indian civilization, reflecting the cultural dynamism and intellectual vibrancy of the subcontinent. These games, embedded within the societal fabric, not only served as entertainment but also mirrored the philosophical, moral, and educational ethos of their times. Tracing their evolution offers insight into how these pastimes have shaped and been shaped by Indian culture through millennia.

1.2 ANCIENT BEGINNINGS

The genesis of card games and gambling in India can be traced back to ancient texts and archaeological findings, suggesting their existence as far back as the Indus Valley Civilization (around 3300–1300 BCE). Artifacts such as dice made from terracotta and ivory found in the ruins of Mohenjo-Daro and Harappa bear testament to the prevalence of gambling and board games among the ancient Indians. The Rigveda, one of the oldest known texts, mentions dice games, highlighting their significance in Vedic society.

Chess, or chaturanga, is believed to have originated in India during the Gupta Empire (circa 5th–6th centuries CE). The name itself, meaning 'four divisions of the military'—infantry, cavalry, elephantry, and chariotry—suggests its conceptualization from Indian military strategy. Chaturanga is thus not just a game but a representation of the battlefield, demonstrating the deep intellectual and strategic thinking of ancient Indian society (Saletore, 1985).

 DOI: 10.1201/9781032624204-2

1.3 CULTURAL INTEGRATION AND SIGNIFICANCE

Over the centuries, these games evolved, integrating into the cultural and social life of India. The Mahabharata, an epic narrative from the 8th-century BCE, illustrates the pivotal role of dice games in Indian mythology and history. The fateful game of dice between the Pandavas and the Kauravas, leading to the exile of the Pandavas, underscores the game's potential impact on destiny and morality.

The evolution of chess from chaturanga to its current form is a journey that reflects India's cultural exchanges with the outside world. As Indian traders and scholars interacted with their Persian and Arab counterparts, chaturanga spread westward, evolving into shatranj in Persia by the 7th-century CE. This iteration of the game would later lay the foundation for modern chess, spreading to Europe in the Middle Ages (Saletore, 1985).

1.4 SOCIO-ECONOMIC DIMENSIONS

Gambling, with its roots in ancient pastimes, evolved into a complex socio-economic activity. Manusmriti and other Dharmashastra texts, dating back to between 200 BCE and 200 CE, delineate strict regulations for gambling, indicating its prevalence and the societal attempts to control its consequences (Saletore, 1985). The existence of state-controlled gambling houses in later periods, as documented by Kautilya in the Arthashastra (circa 4th-century BCE), points toward its recognition as both a source of royal revenue and a potential cause of social discord.

1.5 RENAISSANCE IN MEDIEVAL INDIA

The medieval period saw a renaissance of these games, with the Islamic conquests introducing new forms and variations. Chess and card games, enriched by Islamic cultural elements, became popular in royal courts. The Mughal era, in particular, was notable for its patronage of art, culture, and intellect, with emperors like Akbar and Shah Jahan being avid patrons of chess and gambling games, often depicted in miniatures of the time (Saletore, 1985).

The game of cards, known as Ganjifa, was introduced to the Indian subcontinent by the Mughals. Made from precious materials and beautifully hand-painted, these cards were not just for play but also a form of art, collected and treasured by the nobility.

1.6 COLONIAL INFLUENCE AND MODERN ADAPTATIONS

The arrival of European colonizers introduced new card games and gambling practices, further diversifying the Indian gaming tradition. The British influence on card games was particularly pronounced, with games like Bridge and Poker becoming popular among the Indian elite.

The 20th and 21st centuries have seen these traditional games adapt to the digital era, with online platforms enabling their resurgence among younger generations. Online chess platforms and digital versions of traditional card games have revitalized interest, ensuring these ancient games continue to be part of India's living cultural heritage.

The historical roots and evolution of card games, chess, and gambling in India are a testament to the subcontinent's rich cultural tapestry. From ancient pastimes embedded with societal norms and values, these games have traversed through epochs, embodying the shifts in cultural, social, and intellectual paradigms. As they continue to evolve in the modern digital landscape, these games remain a bridge connecting the past with the present, celebrating the enduring legacy of India's cultural diversity and intellectual prowess.

1.7 ADVENT OF ONLINE GAMES

From time to time, Indian start-ups have built on the rich legacy of games in India to introduce digital and online variations of popular existing Indian games, some common examples are Ludo and the card game Rummy (Figure 1.1).

1.8 FANTASY SPORTS: DREAM11 AS AN EXAMPLE

Dream11 is a prominent fantasy sports platform based in India, which allows users to play fantasy cricket, football, kabaddi, and other sports. Fantasy sports are online games where participants assemble imaginary teams of real players from a professional sport and compete based on the statistical performances of those players in actual games.

Dream11 was co-founded by Harsh Jain and Bhavit Sheth in 2008 (Thaker, 2022). Initially, it started as a platform for fantasy cricket and later expanded to include other sports. The platform saw significant growth in its user base over the years. By 2012, Dream11 introduced a freemium model of gameplay, which significantly boosted its popularity. Users could join free contests with virtual points or enter paid contests to win real money. Fantasy sports often face legal scrutiny due to their resemblance to gambling. However, Dream11 was declared a game of skill by the Indian judiciary,

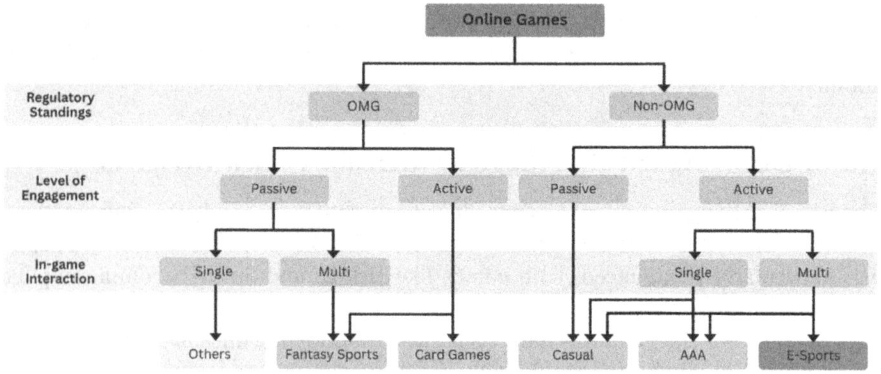

FIGURE 1.1 A classification of online games in India. (Author's original work.)

which helped it operate within the legal frameworks of most Indian states. This legal recognition was crucial for its operation and growth.

Dream11 attracted substantial investment from multiple venture capitalists and private equity firms. In 2019, it became India's first gaming unicorn, achieving a valuation of over $1 billion (Russell, 2019). This was followed by further investment rounds that increased its valuation significantly. Dream11 has partnered with various sports leagues and associations. It became the title sponsor of the Indian Premier League (IPL) in 2020 and continues to be featured on team jerseys into the IPL of 2024, this significantly enhances its visibility and user engagement (Thaker, 2022).

Over the years, Dream11 has invested in technology to improve user experience, including better prediction algorithms, user-friendly interfaces, and secure payment gateways. Apart from fantasy sports, Dream11's parent company, Dream Sports, has ventured into other areas such as sports technology, merchandise, and sports experiences.

1.9 CARD GAMES: ONLINE RUMMY

The history of online rummy in India is a fascinating story of cultural adaptation and technological innovation. Rummy, a popular card game globally, has found a special niche in India, albeit in an indigenized variant, both in its traditional form and its online variant.

Rummy has been a popular card game in India for decades, arriving first sometime during European colonialism. Traditionally played in social settings and during festivals, it involves skills in drawing and discarding cards to form sequences and sets.

The early 2000s saw the digital transformation of various traditional games, and rummy was no exception. The first online platforms began appearing around the mid-2000s. Websites like Ace2Three (Meghani, 2018), launched in 2007, were pioneers in this space, offering players the chance to play rummy online with real money stakes.

The introduction of online rummy coincided with increasing internet penetration and the rise of smartphone usage in India. This allowed the game to reach a wider audience. Several platforms emerged, including RummyCulture, RummyCircle, Junglee Rummy, and Adda52 (Saha, 2022), which further popularized the game. The COVID-19 pandemic saw a surge in online gaming, including rummy, as people looked for entertainment options during lockdowns. This led to increased user engagement and boosted the growth of the sector.

Online rummy platforms have incorporated sophisticated technology to enhance user experience. This includes secure payment systems, random number generators for card dealing, and advanced user interfaces that work well even on mobile devices. They have also employed aggressive marketing strategies. They have sponsored major sporting events, used celebrity endorsements, and offered significant bonuses and promotions to attract and retain players.

Some Indian rummy platforms have also targeted international markets, allowing them to compete globally, taking what is an Indian innovation to the world.

1.10 CASUAL GAMES: FROM PACHISI TO LUDO

Ludo, originally derived from the ancient Indian game of Pachisi, has been a popular household board game for generations. Its transition to the online world marks a significant shift in how traditional games are being consumed in the digital age.

The board game Ludo is a simplified version of Pachisi, a game that dates back to at least the 6th century in India. Ludo as it is known today was patented in England in 1896 as "Ludo" and has been a popular family board game across the world ever since. The adaptation of Ludo to an online platform began in earnest in the late 2000s and early 2010s, as smartphones became widespread and mobile gaming started gaining traction in India. Developers saw an opportunity to digitize traditional games that were already familiar to a large segment of the population.

Online Ludo games started becoming popular in India around the mid-2010s. Apps like Ludo King (Varshney, 2020), launched by Indian studio Gametion Technologies Pvt Ltd in 2016, played a significant role in popularizing online Ludo. Ludo King, in particular, became a massive hit, quickly rising to become one of the top downloaded games in India and a hit internationally as well.

The online versions of Ludo include various features that are not possible in the physical game, such as playing with random people online, connecting with friends and family in private games, and various gameplay enhancements like multiple modes, tournaments, and in-app purchases that enhance the gaming experience.

The popularity of online Ludo games surged dramatically during the COVID-19 lockdowns. With people confined to their homes and looking for ways to connect and entertain themselves, Ludo King and similar apps saw their usage numbers skyrocket. The game provided an easy way for friends and families to stay connected in a socially distant manner.

The success of online Ludo games has also opened up new avenues for monetization through in-app purchases and advertisements. Developers have been able to generate significant revenue, which in turn has helped fund further development and marketing, creating a virtuous cycle of growth.

Online Ludo has made a cultural impact, reinvigorating interest in traditional board games through a modern digital format. It has become a part of popular culture, reflecting broader trends in digital consumption and the social dynamics of gaming. Online Ludo exemplifies how traditional games can be transformed through technology, gaining new life and becoming even more entrenched in the cultural fabric. The digital version continues to evolve, with developers constantly updating and improving the game to keep the global audience engaged.

It is said that the game of Ludo was originally developed alongside the game of Snakes and Ladders as a way to teach morality in ancient India. Not only have the online versions adapted what is an ancient cultural artifact to the modern world, but they also made it a significant export to other countries.

1.11 ESPORTS IN INDIA: A NEW AVENUE FOR COMPETITION

Over the years, the esports scene in India has evolved from a niche interest to a major competitive field, attracting significant investment and producing players who have gained international acclaim.

The foundation of esports in India can be traced back to the early 2000s with the rise of internet cafés. Young gamers gathered in these cafés to play popular AAA games (a high-budget, high-quality video game typically developed by a major studio with extensive resources and significant marketing efforts) like Counter-Strike and Dota. Informal competitions organized in these spaces laid the groundwork for a structured esports environment.

By the late 2000s and early 2010s, formal tournaments began to take shape. Organizations like NODWIN Gaming started to host national competitions (Ghosal, 2016). This period saw the establishment of dedicated gaming lounges and arenas, providing a professional environment for esports athletes. The mid-2010s marked a significant uptick in the popularity of esports in India, thanks in part to the increasing availability of high-speed internet and the proliferation of smartphones. Games like PUBG Mobile (PUBG was later banned by the Government of India) and Call of Duty became immensely popular, leading to organized leagues and tournaments with substantial prize pools.

Indian esports athletes began gaining international recognition in the late 2010s. Teams like Entity Gaming and Global Esports started competing in international tournaments, winning accolades and establishing India on the global esports map. Recognizing the potential of esports as a legitimate sport, the Indian government and various sports institutions began to support and regulate esports. This included initiatives to standardize competitions and ensure fair play and ethics in gaming.

A significant milestone for Indian esports was the inclusion of esports as a pilot event at the 2022 Commonwealth Games held in Birmingham (Olympics, 2022). Indian players showcased their skills on an international stage, competing in games like Dota 2 and Rocket League. This inclusion highlighted the growing acceptance and legitimacy of esports as a competitive sport. Indian teams and players have also made their mark in other international esports tournaments, bringing home medals and trophies. These successes have not only boosted the profile of Indian esports globally but also inspired a younger generation of gamers in India.

In 2024, esports in India is characterized by its vibrant community, professional leagues, and increasing corporate sponsorships. The market is also seeing a rise in streaming and content creation around gaming, further promoting esports as a career option. The future of esports in India looks promising with continuous growth expected in both participation and viewership.

1.12 WAY FORWARD

Games are a pervasive part of culture, offering more than just entertainment. They fulfill deep psychological needs, playing a significant role in motivation, learning, and social interaction. The underlying psychological needs that games, especially online games, satisfy are varied:

1.13 NEED FOR MASTERY AND CONTROL

One of the most compelling psychological needs that video games fulfill is the need for mastery and control. According to Deci and Ryan's Self-Determination Theory (Deci,

2012), humans have an innate drive to be agents of their own lives and to achieve mastery over their environment. Video games are intricately designed to satisfy this need, providing structured environments where players can learn, adapt, and eventually master complex systems and challenges. Each level or challenge overcome serves as a step toward achieving a sense of competency. Games often reward this mastery with in-game achievements, further reinforcing the player's sense of accomplishment and skill.

1.14 AUTONOMY

Autonomy, another core component of Self-Determination Theory, is extensively catered to in the gaming world. Players are frequently given the freedom to make choices that affect the outcome of the game, allowing them to exert a unique influence over their virtual environments. This can range from customizing a character's appearance to making decisions that influence the narrative or gameplay. This ability to influence the game environment not only enhances engagement but also gives players a personal stake in their gaming experience, fostering a deeper connection with the content.

1.15 RELATEDNESS

Video games also meet the need for relatedness—the desire to interact with others and to feel connected to a community. Multiplayer games and online gaming communities provide social platforms where players can engage in cooperative or competitive play. These interactions can lead to the formation of meaningful relationships and a sense of belonging to a community, which is especially important in a world where traditional social structures are often disrupted by modern life's demands. For many, gaming communities become a primary social circle and a key source of social support.

1.16 ESCAPISM AND COPING

Games also serve as a powerful tool for escapism, allowing players to step away from the stresses of real life and immerse themselves in different worlds. This psychological break can be vital for mental health, providing a space to decompress, relax, and manage stress. Furthermore, games can offer safe environments to experiment with different responses to challenges, which can be a form of coping mechanism, allowing individuals to develop resilience in a controlled, low-risk setting.

1.17 IDENTITY FORMATION AND EXPLORATION

Finally, video games offer unique opportunities for identity formation and exploration. In the virtual world, players can adopt identities vastly different from their real-world selves. This can be particularly important during adolescence and early adulthood but remains relevant throughout life. Through role-playing games, players explore various aspects of their personality, experiment with different ethical and moral choices, and discover personal preferences and aversions in a manner that is often not possible in the real world.

While these theories address the complex motivations for playing online games, perhaps the ancient Indians had an intuitive sense of these already. Ancient Indian literature is filled with numerous examples of games, as discussed in this essay. It is only natural therefore that as a format evolves a new system of ethics, law, practices, and systems will need to evolve along with it; the remaining essays in this book is one such attempt by some of India's finest scholars.

REFERENCES

Deci, E. L. (2012). *Intrinsic Motivation*. Springer Science & Business Media.

Ghosal, K. (2016). *eSports in India- then and now: Nodwin Gaming CEO Akshat Rathee shares his views -*. www.animationxpress.com/latest-news/esports-india-now-nodwin-gaming-ceo-akshat-rathee-shares-views/

Meghani, V. (2018). *Head Infotech: Acing the Game*. Forbes India. www.forbesindia.com/article/hidden-gems-2018/head-infotech-acing-the-game/50811/1

Olympics. (2022, August 8). *Commonwealth esports championships 2022: Know all medal winners*. Olympics.Com. https://olympics.com/en/news/commonwealth-esports-championships-birmingham-2022-india-medal-winners

Russell, J. (2019, April 9). Fantasy sports platform Dream11 nets $1 billion valuation following new investment. *TechCrunch*. https://techcrunch.com/2019/04/09/dream11-1-billion/

Saha, S. (2022, September 8). *Gameskraft quietly built a bootstrapped giant, but the game is changing*. The Ken. https://the-ken.com/story/gameskraft-quietly-built-a-bootstrapped-giant-but-the-game-is-changing/

Saletore, R. N. (1985). *Indian Entertainment*. Munshiram Manoharlal.

Thaker, N. (2022). *Dream11 Turned Fantasy (Gaming) into Reality. Now It's Eyeing a Diversified Sports Tech Future*. Forbes India. www.forbesindia.com/article/sports-tech-special/dream11-turned-fantasy-(gaming)-into-reality-now-its-eyeing-a-diversified-sports-tech-future/77065/1

Varshney, R. (2020). *Meet the man behind Ludo King, which has smashed mobile gaming records in India*. https://yourstory.com/2020/05/ludo-king-mobile-gaming-india-android-coronavirus-lockdown

2 Evolution of Jurisprudence on Online Games of Skill

Jay Sayta

2.1 INTRODUCTION

Gambling and betting have traditionally been viewed by both society as well as lawmakers as a vice and a pernicious activity that ought to be prohibited or be discouraged. While most forms of gambling and betting have been banned, gambling legislations from pre-independence era have distinguished between games of skill and games of chance.

The Public Gambling Act, 1867 (**'PGA'**), one of the earliest codified legislations to provide for "the *punishment of public gambling and keeping of common gaming-houses*" in certain British-ruled provinces of India mentions the exemption granted for *'games of mere skill'* in Section 12, in the following terms:

> **Act not to apply to certain games** - Nothing in the foregoing provisions of this Act contained shall apply to any game of mere skill wherever played.

Subsequently, legislations prohibiting gambling and betting enacted by several other provinces and states such as Bombay (now Maharashtra and Gujarat), Delhi, West Bengal, Jammu & Kashmir, etc. have also included a provision similar to Section 12 of the PGA exempting 'games of mere skill' from the ambit of penal provisions prohibiting gaming in general or gaming in common house.

While the watershed exemption of games of mere skill is well enshrined in legislative provisions from pre-independence times, the issue of what categories of games falls within the term 'games of mere skill' and whether such games can be played for stakes or money has been the subject matter of litigation for the past several decades.

Further, after the advent of the internet, and more particularly after rapid penetration of smartphones and access to inexpensive data, the question of whether digital games played through the internet would qualify as games of skill, particularly if participants stake their money in anticipation of winnings in cash or kind, and if the platform or company operating such online game portals earn a platform fee or commission out of such games, has been the matter of several cases in various High Courts in India.

This chapter will aim to analyze the evolution of the interpretation of the judiciary of this exemption granted to games of skill, first in the case of physical games or contests and later in the case of games played in the online or digital format.

 DOI: 10.1201/9781032624204-3

Subsequently, this chapter will also point out certain issues pending for consideration, both at a legislative and judicial level, which once decided will conclusively settle the legal position of online games of skill in India.

2.2 JUDICIAL PRECEDENTS ON GAMES OF SKILL IN THE PRE-INTERNET ERA

The PGA or most provincial gaming legislations as they existed before independence or in the early years after independence, while exempting games of mere skill from the ambit of anti-gambling legislations, did not enumerate the kind of games that would fall within this category, and thus this question was left to be interpreted by the judiciary.

In one of the earliest reported cases on this issue, in 1907, the Calcutta High Court had occasion to consider the question of whether a game known as the ring game falls within the ambit of a games of skill and whether a conviction can be sustained for playing such a game in *Hari Singh v. Emperor* (1907). The Calcutta High Court after analyzing the *modus operandi* of the said game came to the conclusion that although there is an element of chance in throwing a ring over the pins in the game, the overall element of the game is one of skill. The court therefore set aside the conviction of the petitioner.

The Allahabad High Court, however, took a divergent view and held that the ring game is not a game of mere skill and is liable to attract penal provisions under the PGA (*Emperor v. Ahmad Khan*, 1928).

In another subsequent ruling in 1933, the Calcutta High Court noted that although the word '*mere skill*' in the statute would mean pure skill, it would be difficult to construe the term to be conceived to include any game which is absolutely devoid of all possibilities of some fortuitous elements entering into the playing of it (*Saligram Khettry v.Emperor*, 1933). The court therefore while holding that the game of dart does not amount to gambling, noted that it is very difficult to construe the word 'mere' to mean 'pure' in the strict and scientific sense, and that the term game of 'mere skill' should be taken to mean one in which a person playing it, as far as possible in any human affairs, has complete control over the result which he sets out to attain, provided he is sufficiently expert in performance (*Saligram Khettry v.Emperor*, 1933).

Post-independence, the constitution bench of the Supreme Court had occasion to examine the difference between games of skill and chance while deciding on the constitutional validity of the Prize Competition Act, 1955 (R.M.D. Chamarbaugwala v. Union of India, 1957). The court observed as follows:

> As regards competitions which involve substantial skill, however, different considerations arise. They are business activities, the protection of which is guaranteed by Art. 19(1)(g), and the question would have to be determined with reference to those competitions whether Sections 4 and 5 and Rules 11 and 12 are reasonable restrictions enacted in public interest...
>
> Applying these principles to the present Act, it will not be questioned that competitions in which success depends to a substantial extent on skill and

> competitions in which it does not so depend, form two distinct and separate categories. The difference between the two classes of competitions is as clear-cut as that between commercial and wagering contracts. On the facts, there might be difficulty in deciding whether a given competition falls within one category or not; but when its true character is determined, it must fall either under the one or the other.
>
> (R.M.D. Chamarbaugwala v. Union of India, 1957)

In 1967, a division bench of the Supreme Court held that any game is bound to have certain elements of chance or luck, and ultimately, it has to be examined whether the game is one involving a preponderant element of skill (*State of Andhra Pradesh v. K. Satyanarayana*, 1968). While ruling that the game of rummy played in a club would fall within the category of game of mere skill, the apex court noted as follows:

> The game of rummy is not a game entirely of chance like the "three-card" game mentioned in the Madras case to which we were referred. The "three cards" game which goes under different names such as "flush", "brag" etc. is a game of pure chance. Rummy, on the other hand, requires certain amount of skill because the fall of the cards has to be memorised and the building up of Rummy requires considerable skill in holding and discarding cards. We cannot, therefore, say that the game of rummy is a game of entire chance. It is mainly and preponderantly a game of skill… Of course, if there is evidence of gambling in some other way or that the owner of the house or the club is making a profit or gain from the game of Rummy or any other game played for stakes, the offence may be brought home.
>
> (State of Andhra Pradesh v. K. Satyanarayana, 1968)

In 1996, while examining the constitutional validity of the legislation allowing the state government to take over the Madras Race Club and whether wagering or betting on horse-racing would be a game of 'mere skill' and exempt from the provisions of the Madras City Police Act, 1888, and the Madras (now Tamil Nadu) Gaming Act, 1930, a three-judge bench of the Supreme Court held that games that substantially and preponderantly depend on skill would fall within the ambit of 'mere skill' under the Tamil Nadu gaming legislation. The apex court observed as follows (emphasis supplied):

> The expression "gaming" in the two Acts has to be interpreted in the light of the law laid-down by this Court in the two Chamarbaugwala cases, wherein it has been authoritatively held that a competition which substantially depends on skill is not gambling. Gaming is the act or practice of gambling on a game of chance. It is staking on chance where chance is the controlling factor. "Gaming" in the two Acts would, therefore, mean wagering or betting on games of chance… We, therefore, hold that wagering or betting on horse-racing – a game of skill – does not come within the definition of `gaming' under the two Acts.
>
> (Dr. KR Lakshmanan v. State of Tamil Nadu, 1996)

Per contra, however, a year prior to the *Lakshmanan* (*Dr. KR Lakshmanan v. State of Tamil Nadu*, 1996) judgment, in *MJ Sivani v. State of Karnataka* (*MJ Sivani v. State of Karnataka & Others*, 1995), a division bench of the Supreme Court in the context of orders framed by the Tamil Nadu and Karnataka police for regulation of video games, without referring to the *Chamarbaugwala* (*R.M.D. Chamarbaugwala v. Union of India*, 1957) and *Satyanarayana* (*State of Andhra Pradesh v. K. Satyanarayana,* 1968) cases, noted that the word gaming has a wider sense and includes playing any game, whether of skill or chance for money or money's worth. However, even in *Sivani's* case (*MJ Sivani v. State of Karnataka & Others*, 1995), the apex court noted that the determination of whether a particular video game is a game of skill or mixed game of skill and chance would depend on the facts of each case (*MJ Sivani v. State of Karnataka & Others*, 1995).

The court further also noted that in case of rejecting a video game license based on some adverse material, Commissioner or District Magistrate needs to record reasons in writing, and if such material is gathered behind the back of the applicant, then the licensing authority needs to be given an opportunity to meet the grounds of such material (*MJ Sivani v. State of Karnataka & Others*, 1995).

An analysis of the *Chamarbaugwala* (*R.M.D. Chamarbaugwala v. Union of India*, 1957), *Satyanarayana* (*State of Andhra Pradesh v. K. Satyanarayana,* 1968) and *Lakshmanan* (*Dr. KR Lakshmanan v. State of Tamil Nadu*, 1996) judgments would indicate that the Supreme Court conclusively laid down the principle that a game involving substantial or preponderant degree of skill falls in an entirely different category from games involving betting and gambling. The Supreme Court in *Satyanarayana* has laid down that a game, once held to be one involving substantial degree of skill, would not fall foul of the anti-gambling legislation. This view has been further ratified in the *Lakshmanan* (*Dr. KR Lakshmanan v. State of Tamil Nadu*, 1996) judgment wherein even betting or wagering on horse-racing, a game of skill, with the club earning commission out of the activity was held to be outside the ambit of 'gaming' under the Tamil Nadu legislations.

Following the principles laid down by the Supreme Court, various High Courts, including the Madras (*Gugai Palam Makkal Narpani Mandram v. The Commissioner of Police, Salem*, 2002; *Periyampatti Friends Recreation Club v. Superintendent of Police*, 2010), Andhra Pradesh (*Executive Club, Formed by Lalitha Estates Pvt. Ltd., Vijayawada v. State of Andhra Pradesh,* 1998; *Friends Cultural & Sports Society Club, Hyderabad v. Principal Secretary, Home Department, Hyderabad & Others*, 2014; *Patamata Cultural & Recreation Society v. Commissioner of Police & Others*, 2005) and Karnataka (*GS Ananthswamy Iyer & Ors v. State of Karnataka*, 1982; *Kirana S v. State of Karnataka*, 2013; *DVR Recreation Club v. State of Karnataka*, 2016) High Courts, have protected club owners organizing the game of rummy from interference by the police or quashed criminal proceedings instituted under the State Gaming Acts for clubs organizing the game of rummy.

2.3 RECENT JUDICIAL PRECEDENTS ON ONLINE GAMES OF SKILL

With the advent of internet, newer kinds of games and formats started to become increasingly popular online ('Online Gaming in India: Reaching a new pinnacle', 2017) and issues of whether particular formats of online games amount to be being a game of skill arose for consideration before various High Courts.

In one of the earliest detailed decisions on online games played for stakes, a single-judge bench of the Punjab and Haryana High Court (*Varun Gumber v. UT of Chandigarh & Others*, 2017) had occasion to consider whether daily fantasy sports, where a user pays an entry fee to play to compete against other players by selecting a virtual team of sports persons of a real-world sporting event, amounts to be being a game of skill. The single-judge bench of the Punjab and Haryana High Court observed as under:

> The respondent company's website and success in Dream 11's fantasy sports basically arises out of users exercise, superior knowledge, judgment and attention. I am of the further view that the element of skill and predominant influence on the outcome of the Dream11 fantasy than any other incidents are and therefore, I do not have any hesitation in holding the any sports game to constitute the game of "mere skill" and not falling within the activity of gambling for the invocation of 1867 Act and thus, the respondent company is therefore, exempt from the application of provisions, including the penal provisions, in view of Section 18 of 1867 Act. Equally so, before I conclude, I must express that gambling is not a trade and thus, is not protected by Article 19(1)(g) of Constitution of India and thus, the fantasy games of the respondent-company cannot said to be falling within the gambling activities as the same involves the substantial skills which is nothing but is a business activity with due registration and paying the service tax and income tax, thus, they have protection granted by Article 19(1)(g) of Constitution of India.
>
> (Varun Gumber v. UT of Chandigarh & Others, 2017)

The decision of the Punjab and Haryana High Court has been cited and affirmed by the Bombay High Court (*Gurdeep Singh Sachar v. Union of India & Others*, 2019) and Rajasthan (Jaipur Bench) High Court (*Chandresh Sankhla v. State of Rajasthan & Others*, 2020; *Ravindra Singh Chaudhary v. Union of India & Others*, 2020). Further, a Special Leave Petition against the *Varun Gumber* decision was also dismissed by the Supreme Court (*Varun Gumber v. Union of India & Others*, 2019). A review petition filed against the said dismissal was also dismissed by the apex court both on grounds of delay as well as merit (*Varun Gumber v. Union Territory of Chandigarh & Others*, 2022).

Similarly, a Special Leave Petition filed against the *Chandresh Sankhla* (*Chandresh Sankhla v. State of Rajasthan & Others*, 2020) judgment has also been dismissed by the Supreme Court on 30th July, 2021, with the observation that the issue of whether fantasy sports amounts to gambling is no longer *res integra* (*Avinash Mehrotra v. Union of India & Others*, 2020).

The decision of the Bombay High Court in *Gurdeep Singh Sachar* (*Gurdeep Singh Sachar v. Union of India & Others*, 2019), which involved questions of both interpretation of Goods and Services Tax (GST) rules for online fantasy sports and the issue of whether it amounts to gambling under the state gaming legislation, has however been stayed by the Supreme Court (*Gurdeep Singh Sachar v. Union of India & Others*, 2019) and is pending further hearing.

Besides the issue of online fantasy sports, High Courts have also had the occasion to decide on the constitutional validity of amendments passed by state legislatures to ban online games played for stakes, without differentiating between games of skill and chance. Such amendments also deleted exemption granted for games of mere skill from state gaming legislations.

In a landmark decision in 2021, the Madras High Court struck down Part II of the Tamil Nadu Gaming and Police Laws (Amendment) Act, 2021, as unconstitutional that prohibited all forms of as being capricious, disproportionate, capricious and irrational (*Junglee Games India Private Limited v. State of Tamil Nadu & Others*, 2021).

The court while referring extensively to the *Chamarbaugwala* (*R.M.D. Chamarbaugwala v. Union of India*, 1957), *Satyanarayana* (*State of Andhra Pradesh v. K. Satyanarayana,* 1968) and *Lakshmanan* (*Dr. KR Lakshmanan v. State of Tamil Nadu*, 1996) decisions noted that card games or board games or games such as chess and scrabble played online, i.e., in the cyberspace for stakes also involve exercise, and there is no difference in games like poker and rummy, whether played virtually or physically (*Junglee Games India Private Limited v. State of Tamil Nadu & Others*, 2021).

The court while striking down the Tamil Nadu Gaming and Police Laws (Amendment) Act, 2021 observed as follows:

> The wording of the amending Act is so crass and overbearing that it smacks of unreasonableness in its every clause and can be seen to be manifestly arbitrary. Whatever may have been the pious intention of the legislature, the reading of the impugned statute and how it may operate amounts to a baby being thrown out with the bathwater and more. And, irrespective of the noblest of intentions, the effect of the provisions of the impugned statute is the primary consideration for assessing the validity thereof…
>
> There appears to be a little doubt that both rummy and poker are games of skill as they involve considerable memory, working out of percentages, the ability to follow the cards on the table and constantly adjust to the changing possibilities of the unseen cards…
>
> The absurdity of the amended provisions has more to do with all forms of games – where games must be understood to be distinct from gaming, whether in the ordinary parlance or as per the convoluted meaning ascribed to it in the impugned legislation – being prohibited in cyberspace, if played for any prize or stake whatsoever. The cause for bringing the amendments does not appear to have any nexus with the effect that has resulted thereby; and that, in essence, is the unreasonableness and grossly disproportionate feature of the impugned statute.
>
> (Junglee Games India Private Limited v. State of Tamil Nadu & Others, 2021)

The court ultimately ruled that offering online games of skill like rummy and poker for stakes is a fundamental right under Article 19(1)(g) of the constitution and a complete and overarching ban on the activity is arbitrary, capricious and disproportional. While leaving it open for the state to frame a law governing the field of gambling and betting which conforms to the constitutional sense of propriety, the court noted that states' legislative competence to frame laws on 'betting and gambling' under

Entry 34 of List II of the Seventh Schedule of the Constitution of India (**'Entry 34 of the State List'**) has to be construed as limited to betting on games where chance is involved, and the field of Entry 34 of the State List cannot be interpreted to give states' competence to legislate on games of skill.

However, it may be noted that Special Leave Petitions filed by the Tamil Nadu government against the decision are pending before the Supreme Court (*The State of Tamil Nadu v. Junglee Games India Private Limited & Others*, 2023). The Supreme Court by an order dated 22nd September, 2023, has granted leave in the petitions filed by the Tamil Nadu government and is expected to finally hear the Tamil Nadu government's appeals.

Following the decision of the Madras High Court, a single-judge bench of the Kerala High Court while approving of the decision in Junglee Games struck down an amendment to a notification issued by the state government under Section 14A of the Kerala Gaming Act, 1960, which excluded online rummy when played from stakes from the exemption granted to games of skill under the said legislation (*Head Digital Works Private Limited v. State of Kerala*, 2021).

The court held that the online version of rummy would also be a game of skill just as the physical version of the game and that the game of rummy would remain to be one involving skill even when played with stakes (*Head Digital Works Private Limited v. State of Kerala*, 2021). The court thus observed that the notification including online rummy played for stakes within the penal provisions of the Kerala Gaming Act is arbitrary, illegal and in violation of Articles 14 and 19(1)(g) of the Constitution (*Head Digital Works Private Limited v. State of Kerala*, 2021). An appeal against the order of the single judge of the Kerala High Court is however pending before the division bench of the same High Court (*State of Kerala v. Head Digital Works Private Limited*, 2022).

While citing with approval the decisions of both the Madras and Kerala High Courts, the Karnataka High Court also struck down various provisions of the Karnataka Police (Amendment) Act, 2021 that specifically included risking of money on any online game, including a game of skill within the definition of gaming, and making offering or playing such online games for money an offense (*All India Gaming Federation v. State of Karnataka*, 2022).

The Karnataka High Court in its judgment ruled that the provisions of the Karnataka Police (Amendment) Act, 2021 insofar as it sought to impose a complete prohibition on online games of skill played for stakes is *ultra vires* Articles 14 and 19(1)(g) of the Constitution (*All India Gaming Federation v. State of Karnataka*, 2022). However, the state government's appeal against the order of the Karnataka High Court is also pending final consideration in the Supreme Court, which is tagged and expected to be heard along with Tamil Nadu government's appeal (*The State of Karnataka v. All India Gaming Federation & Others*, 2023).

Another single-judge bench of the Karnataka High Court, in the context of quashing a Goods and Services Tax (GST) show cause notice issued to an online rummy company while referring to the *Junglee Games* (*Junglee Games India Private Limited v. State of Tamil Nadu & Others*, 2021), *Head Digital Works* (*Head Digital Works Private Limited v. State of Kerala*, 2021) and *All India Gaming Federation* (*All India Gaming Federation v. State of Karnataka*, 2022) judgments concluded that there is no difference between the physical and online version of rummy and both are substantially and preponderantly games of skill (*Gameskraft Technologies Private Limited v. Directorate General of Goods and Services Tax Intelligence (Headquarters)*, 2022). The court further stated that a game of skill played with or without stakes does not amount to gambling and concluded that the online/electronic/digital version of rummy are not taxable as 'betting' and 'gambling' as contended by the tax authorities (*Gameskraft Technologies Private Limited v. Directorate General of Goods and Services Tax Intelligence (Headquarters)*, 2022).

It may however be noted that the Supreme Court by an order dated 6th September, 2023 (*Directorate General of Goods and Services Tax Intelligence (HQS) v. Gameskraft Technologies Private Limited & Others*, 2023) has issued an ad interim stay on the judgment of the Karnataka High Court in *Gameskraft Technologies* (*Gameskraft Technologies Private Limited v. Directorate General of Goods and Services Tax Intelligence (Headquarters)*, 2022), and the issue is pending further determination before the apex court.

Recently, the Madras High Court struck down and read down certain provisions of a second legislation passed by the Tamil Nadu legislature, i.e., the Tamil Nadu Prohibition of Online Gambling and Regulation of Online Games Act, 2022 that sought to classify online games of rummy and poker as games of chance and prohibit them (*All India Gaming Federation v. State of Tamil Nadu*, 2023). The court noted that while the state is competent to legislate to the extent of prohibiting online gambling, i.e., games of chance, it has got the authority to regulate but not completely prohibit online games of skill (*All India Gaming Federation v. State of Tamil Nadu*, 2023). The court also observed that the state government miserably failed to demonstrate that online games of rummy and poker are different from their offline versions (*All India Gaming Federation v. State of Tamil Nadu*, 2023).

The state of Tamil Nadu has however preferred to file a Special Leave Petition (*The State of Tamil Nadu v. All India Gaming Federation*, 2023) against the order of the Madras High Court in the *All India Gaming Federation* case (*All India Gaming Federation v. State of Tamil Nadu*, 2023). The Supreme Court by an order dated 5th February, 2024, issued notice in the Tamil Nadu government's petition and tagged the matter along with other similar pending appeals filed by the Karnataka government and the Tamil Nadu government's pending appeal against striking down of its earlier online gaming legislation by the Madras High Court.

2.4 CONCLUSION: FINAL CLARITY ON ONLINE GAMES OF SKILL AWAITED

Several High Courts have been unequivocal in holding that online games of skill such as rummy, poker and fantasy sports, regardless of whether played for stakes or not, fall outside the ambit of gaming legislations and do not amount to either 'gambling' or 'betting'. The courts have also held that state legislatures cannot impose a total prohibition on such online games, while leaving open the issue of whether states could impose other less onerous restrictions on such games.

In such a situation of a regulatory vacuum, the central government has notified the Information Technology (Intermediary Guidelines and Digital Media Ethics

Code) Amendment Rules, 2023 (‘**IT Amendment Rules’**) with a view to create self-regulatory bodies to oversee online real money gaming intermediaries.

The IT Amendment Rules define a ‘online real money game’ as an online game where a user makes a deposit in cash or kind with the expectation of earning winnings on that deposit (Information Technology (Intermediary Guidelines and Digital Media Ethics Code Amendment Rules, 2023). The IT Amendment Rules also envisage creation of a new category of intermediaries, i.e., online gaming intermediaries which would be made responsible for following due diligence under the said rules to exercise due diligence while discharging its duties, including not hosting, transmitting, uploading, publishing or sharing an online game not in conformity with Indian law, including any law on betting or gambling.

Moreover, the IT Amendment Rules also mandate that online real money gaming intermediaries should display a registration mark on all online games registered by a self-regulatory body indicating that they are certified as a ‘permissible online real money game’ by such self-regulatory bodies. The online real money gaming intermediaries are also responsible for informing its users regarding its policy related to withdrawal or deposit, manner of determination and distribution of winnings, fees and other charges, adhering to Know Your Customer (KYC) procedure and responsible gaming policies, etc.

It may however be noted that the obligations pertaining to online gaming intermediaries under the IT Amendment Rules shall only be made applicable three months from the date on which at least three online gaming self-regulatory bodies have been designated or if the central government publishes a notification in the official gazette directing such obligations to be applicable from a certain date (Information Technology (Intermediary Guidelines and Digital Media Ethics Code Amendment Rules, 2023).

The central government has neither notified any self-regulatory bodies for online gaming nor provided any date for enforcing the obligations of online gaming intermediaries under the IT Amendment Rules. In fact, it has been indicated that the central government may put the proposal for forming self-regulatory bodies for online gaming on hold and revisit the regulatory framework for online gaming (Das, 2024; Business Standard, 2023).

Thus, despite several clear judicial rulings that online games of skill played with stakes do not amount to ‘gambling’ or ‘betting’, the online gaming industry still awaits final clarity on the proposed regulatory framework.

Further, several appeals from High Court rulings are pending adjudication in the Supreme Court on whether states have legislative competence to ban or regulate online gaming, and whether a complete online skill-based games is proportionate and reasonable under the constitutional framework (*The State of Tamil Nadu v. Junglee Games India Private Limited & Others*, 2023; *The State of Karnataka v. All India Gaming Federation & Others*, 2023; *The State of Tamil Nadu v. All India Gaming Federation*, 2023).

Based on the outcomes of such appeals as well as the central government releasing a regulatory framework in the form of either parliamentary or delegated legislation, there will be conclusive clarity on the status of real money online games played for stakes and whether skill-based games played online or virtually have the same character as the physical version.

REFERENCES

All India Gaming Federation v. State of Karnataka, 2022 SCC OnLine Kar 435.

All India Gaming Federation v. State of Tamil Nadu, WP No. 13203/2023.

Avinash Mehrotra v. Union of India & Others, Special Leave Petition (Civil) Diary No(s) 18478/2020.

Business Standard. (2023, September 29). *IT ministry puts plan to form self-regulatory body for gaming on hold*. www.business-standard.com. www.business-standard.com/industry/news/it-ministry-puts-plan-to-form-self-regulatory-body-for-gaming-on-hold-123092900169_1.html.

Chandresh Sankhla v. State of Rajasthan & Others, 2020 SCC OnLine Raj 264.

Das, S. (2024, January 1). Online gaming self-regulation hits roadblock, Meity weighs direct control I Mint. *Mint*. www.livemint.com/industry/online-gaming-self-regulation-hits-roadblock-meity-weighs-direct-control-11704104343456.html.

Directorate General of Goods and Services Tax Intelligence (HQS) v. Gameskraft Technologies Private Limited & Others, Special Leave Petitions (Civil) No(s). 19366-19369/2023.

Dr. KR Lakshmanan v. State of Tamil Nadu, AIR 1996 SC 1153.

DVR Recreation Club v. State of Karnataka, Review Petition No. 20029 of 2016 (Kalburgi Bench of Karnataka High Court).

Emperor v. Ahmad Khan, I.L.R. 34 All 96; Aziz Ismail v. Emperor, MANU/UP/0319/1928.

Executive Club, Formed by Lalitha Estates Pvt. Ltd., Vijayawada v. State of Andhra Pradesh, 1998(5) ALD 216.

Friends Cultural & Sports Society Club, Hyderabad v. Principal Secretary, Home Department, Hyderabad & Others, WP No. 30597 of 2014.

Gameskraft Technologies Private Limited v. Directorate General of Goods and Services Tax Intelligence (Headquarters), WP No. 19570 of 2022.

GS Ananthswamy Iyer & Ors v. State of Karnataka, 1982 CriLJ 2121.

Gugai Palam Makkal Narpani Mandram v. The Commissioner of Police, Salem, MANU/TN/0985/2002.

Gurdeep Singh Sachar v. Union of India & Others, 2019 SCC OnLine Bom 13509.

Hari Singh v. Emperor, (1907), 6 C.L.J 708.

Head Digital Works Private Limited v. State of Kerala, 2021 SCC OnLine Ker 3592.

Information Technology (Intermediary Guidelines and Digital Media Ethics Code) Amendment Rules, Rule 2(1)(qc), 2023.

Information Technology (Intermediary Guidelines and Digital Media Ethics Code) Amendment Rules, Rule 4B, 2023.

Junglee Games India Private Limited v. State of Tamil Nadu & Others, 2021 SCC OnLine Mad 2762.

Kirana S v. State of Karnataka, Criminal Petition No. 7648/2013.

MJ Sivani v. State of Karnataka & Others, AIR 1995 SC 1770.

'Online Gaming in India: Reaching a new pinnacle', A study by KPMG in India and Google (May 2017), available at https://assets.kpmg.com/content/dam/kpmg/in/pdf/2017/05/online-gaming.pdf (webpage last accessed on 29th December, 2023).

Patamata Cultural & Recreation Society v. Commissioner of Police & Others, 2005(1) ALD 243.

Periyampatti Friends Recreation Club v. Superintendent of Police, MANU/TN/3382/2010.

R.M.D. Chamarbaugwala v. Union of India, AIR 1957 SC 628.

Ravindra Singh Chaudhary v. Union of India & Others, 2020 SCC OnLine Raj 2688.

Saligram Khettry v.Emperor, AIR 1933 Cal 8.

State of Andhra Pradesh v. K. Satyanarayana, AIR 1968 SC 825.

State of Kerala v. Head Digital Works Private Limited, WA No. 725/2022.

The State of Karnataka v. All India Gaming Federation & Others, Civil Appeal Nos. 6132-6143/2023.

The State of Maharashtra v. Gurdeep Singh Sachar & Others, Special Leave Petition (Civil) Diary Nos. 42282/2019 (Order Dated 6th March, 2020).

The State of Tamil Nadu v. All India Gaming Federation, Special Leave Petition (Civil) No(s). 1588-1592/2024.

The State of Tamil Nadu v. Junglee Games India Private Limited & Others, Civil Appeal Nos 6124-6131/2023.

Varun Gumber v. Union of India & Others, Special Leave Petition (Civil) Diary No(s) 35191/2019 (Order Dated 4th October, 2019).

Varun Gumber v. Union Territory of Chandigarh & Others, Review Petition (Civil) Diary No(s) 5195/2022 (Order Dated 9th November, 2022).

Varun Gumber v. UT of Chandigarh & Others, 2017 Cri LJ 3827.

3 In Regulatory Purgatory

How Many Lives Left Before Mission Success for the Indian Gaming Industry?

Vidushpat Singhania and Pujaarchana Talukdar

3.1 INTRODUCTION

The online gaming industry in this modern era is one where experts expect to see exponential growth, and the industry's continued dynamism makes it special in diverse ways. However, with the advent of recent developments in the legal structure governing online games in India, such as the removal of the bifurcation between taxation applicable on game of chance and games of chance and the levy of the same at 28% (The Central Goods and Services Tax (Third Amendment Rules, 2023)), there have arisen more questions and conjecture than answers, leading to considerable confusion in the Indian gaming landscape.

With the appointment of the Ministry of Electronics and Information Technology (**MEITY**) as the nodal ministry for the regulation of online gaming in India ('MeitY Appointed as Nodal Ministry for Online Gaming Matters', 2022), and the subsequent introduction of the Information Technology (Intermediary Guidelines and Digital Media Ethics Code) Amendment Rules, 2023 (IT Rules, 2023a), games that are online based are to be governed by the Self-Regulatory Bodies (SRBs) (IT Rules, 2023b), which would be under the supervision of the MEITY. The MEITY introduced said IT Rules on 06.04.2023, paving the way for a new framework in order to facilitate the regulation of online games and in the process declared online gaming involving 'betting' and 'wagering' to be prohibited activities. This is evident from a perusal of the amended IT Rules which defines the term *'permissible online game'* to mean *'a permissible online real money game or any other online game that is not an online real money game' with an 'online real money game'* (IT Rules, 2023c).

Up until this juncture, online gaming had been treated as a state subject owing to 'Betting and Gambling', terms often interchangeably used in an Indian context, featuring under Entry 34 of the State List of the Seventh Schedule of the Constitution of India (The Constitution of India, 1950). As a result, online gaming has seemingly been governed as per relevant state laws and the respective state gambling acts. The existing position of gaming in most States of India stems from the Public Gambling Act (1867) which grants an exception for the offering of games of skills for stakes while prohibiting the offering of games of chance. With there being no objection

DOI: 10.1201/9781032624204-4

or observation by legislations or courts of law with respect to extending the applicability of the Public Gambling Act to deal with and exclude games of skill, it was widely accepted that the exception granted also extended the applicability, thereby cementing the power of states to legislate games of skill as well as games of chance.

The regime that has been proposed, with the MEITY being appointed as the nodal ministry to oversee all online games provided within the country, shall now supersede the understanding stated above. The IT Rules shall now be the applicable law to be adhered to by all Online Gaming Intermediaries ("OGIs"), and the legally appointed SRBs alone shall be in charge of approving any online game(s) that the OGIs want to offer. Subject to the game's review and fulfillment of specific requirements, the SRBs shall issue their approval. Following this, the OGIs shall be obliged to perform the due diligence requirements imposed on them by the IT Rules. It is to be noted, however, that the obligations placed on OGIs shall only be applicable from a date three months subsequent to the official designation of three identified SRBs as stated in Rule 4B of the aforementioned IT Rules.

The IT Rules include the term 'permissible online game' (definition reproduced above) with an 'online real money game' further being defined (IT Rules, 2023d) therein to mean 'an online game where a user makes a deposit in cash or kind with the expectation of earning winnings on that deposit' and a 'permissible online real money game' being defined (IT Rules, 2023e) as 'an online real money game verified by an online gaming self-regulatory body under rule 4A'.

However, the IT Rules remain silent with respect to drawing a proper distinction between games of chance and games of skill and have rather provided the requisites to be met by the OGIs, in order for the games (offered by the OGIs) to qualify as a 'permissible online real money game'. The reason behind the same was later clarified by the Hon'ble Minister of State for Electronics and Information Technology, Mr. Rajeev Chandrashekhar, who stated that "there is no need in this framework to get into nuances of chance or skill, because the harm of wagering is directly being prohibited – regardless of nature of game" vide a communication from his official handle on the social media platform, X ('Wagering Barred in All Forms, Be It Game of Skill or Chance: MoS IT Rajeev Chandrasekhar', 2023).

While there is an argument to be made that the 'Online Gaming' is to be treated as an activity that is inherently distinct in comparison to 'Betting and Gambling' as accounted for in the Public Gambling Act and its various iterations, the fact remains that to date, the dominant legislation in the country pertaining to the gaming industry remains the principles of the Public Gambling Act with its state amendments. This is particularly relevant with the current scenario being such that no SRBs have been formally inducted to their prescribed role as per the amended IT Rules despite months passing since the amendment was passed ('Govt Defers Plan for Gaming Self-regulator; Internet Firms Introduce Per-order Charges', 2023). It is also to be noted that 'Gaming', 'Betting', and 'Gambling' have been used interchangeably over the years in the Indian jurisprudential context and without there being distinctions laid down under the laws governing the activity, merely distinguishing them on face value for the purpose of governance, only adds to the confusion. The existing issues pertaining to the legal status assigned to the various constituents of 'gaming, gambling, and betting' needs to be resolved, and the way ahead needs to be created.

3.2 POSITION OF WAGERING AND GAMBLING IN INDIA AND LEGAL CONCERNS ASSOCIATED WITH RECENT REGULATION

Wagering and gambling are two activities that have been deemed prohibited unless licensed, for offering in the territory of India. This includes various activities such as 'Sports Betting' for instance. However, despite the fact that 'sports betting' has not been licensed, in most of India, the number of operators providing the service from 'gray markets' has seen a significant increase in recent years. This is so because operators while operating offshore, in an attempt to avoid legal consequences, are found to utilize servers that are not situated in India and work to create an apparent absence from the country. They then provide a variety of games of chance, under the disguise of being legitimate businesses. Similarly, transactions made are often made *vide* individual accounts and not accounts associated with any related entities or their own business enterprise, and this makes such transactions tougher to track and monitor too. Such a development is concerning not only because it has created a means of evading the law by using offshore servers, but it also represents a lost chance to generate significant foreign exchange and taxes. Various instances have been reported in this regard with respect to the noncompliance of laws broken by such foreign operators.

Lately, the presence of these entities in the gray market has become a significant issue. As has been reported, by April 2023, 38 betting and gambling websites had received notifications from the Directorate General of GST Intelligence regarding accusations of money laundering and diverting taxes (Shukla, 2023).

Offshore betting operators have challenged the government through their efforts to advertise and promote their illegal services to the Indian population. It is not uncommon to find news relating to arrests of individuals for engaging in betting on sports events/games by using illegal betting apps. These incidents highlight the societal threat posed by the uncontrolled betting market.

It is to be noted that while keeping in mind the aforementioned, that operators majorly resort to operating from the gray market since no legal and accepted method becomes available to them, due to lack of a regulation that specifically addresses online gaming and wagering in sports. Regulation, therefore, can attract operators willing to operate their businesses legitimately and responsibly.

Moreover, with certain states adopting different positions in comparison to others, the issue of territorial applicability also arises with respect to the legislation of gaming in India. The regulation of Permissible Online Real Money Games by the MEITY on a central level threatens at leading to a dysfunctional mechanism owing to the geographical restrictions, e.g., the Sikkim Online Gaming Act contemplated that the licenses would allow the licensee to offer the games within the State of Sikkim. Such a license may be deemed irrelevant in the event a game is deemed non-permissible for offering by SRBs in contrast to the status it may enjoy in Sikkim per the licensing regime. Same would be the case in Nagaland, where a similar legislation exists.

Lacunae such as the same, and pertaining to the blanket prohibition on 'betting, wagering and gambling', needs redressal. To this extent, The Law Commission of India (LCI) in its 'Report No. 276, Legal Framework: Gambling and Sports Betting including in Cricket in India' (July 5, 2018) while examining the legality of betting in India recommended for the classification of 'Gambling' into two categories for the purposes of regulation – *'proper gambling'* and *'small gambling'*. *'Proper gambling'* pertains to gambling characterized by higher stakes and should only be permitted for 'indulgence' by individuals belonging to the higher-income group of society while *'small gambling'* is classified as a means wherein individuals may not stake higher amounts. The legislative intent of the LCI was clearly focused toward identifying the vices associated with the activity while identifying avenues through which it may be utilized by various sections of the society.

The LCI also stressed that amendments be made to the Indian Contract Act to exempt transactions in a regulated environment pertaining to 'wagering agreements' by stating in its report that

> those who argue in favour of betting and gambling being regulated contend that under Section 30 of the Indian Contract Act, 1872 a wager is void and unenforceable, but at the same time it is not forbidden by law and hence, cannot be termed illegal.

The LCI furthermore discussed the equation of morality and betting and stated that illegal activities can be divided into two categories: (A) activities which definitely cause damage to the society viz. trade in contraband substances, and (B) activities like gambling and betting which cause damage to the individuals but whose social impact varies. The LCI thereafter, while evaluating the argument of the rise in revenue generation through taxation on the proceeds derived from regulating betting and gambling, stated that

> …'Immorality', per se, cannot be a ground to challenge the Constitutional validity of an enactment as morality is a subjective concept… ..Morality is a ground for imposing reasonable restrictions on individual's freedom. It is said that the law remains in a state of flux while defining morality, for it is required that the law must continuingly evolve to accommodate the needs of changing time.

From a perusal of the aforementioned observations of the LCI, it becomes apparent that it is essential to recognize the complexity with respect to the assessment of activities such as gambling and betting or games of chance involving stakes, and their potential impact on individuals, the society at large. However, it is also important to establish morality in relation to the same through regulation and control. Morality as a concept is subjective in nature and may evolve over time while being within the protection of legal frameworks, and an integration of morality into law, particularly for such a conflicting topic, is a complex task indeed.

3.2.1 Games of Chance and Games of Skill and Regulation Thereof

While addressing the topic of drawing distinctions between games of skill and games of chance, it is essential to mention that the IT Rules has categorically left the online games of chance industry to fend for itself, by not differentiating between games of skill and games of chance, with respect to their legality. This is also a cause of concern since wagering on games of skill for instance is deemed permissible while wagering on games of chance isn't, and activities such as wagering on horse racing which demand an exception on account of the same being recognized by the Hon'ble Supreme Court as a game of skill (*Dr. KR Lakshmanan v. State of Tamil Nadu*, 1996) as per the pre-IT Rules regime shall be left in limbo without such a distinction being incorporated in the law.

The necessity for regulating online games involving stakes, whether of chance or skill, has amplified with the implementation of new GST regulations. These regulations impose a uniform 28% tax on the total value of bets placed in online games, irrespective of whether the game predominantly relies on skill or chance. Such an application may be perceived as inherently problematic as one activity among the two was treated as a permissible activity in the erstwhile regime and recognized as a legitimate business activity ('Online Gaming: 28% GST Applicable on Entry-Level Value, Irrespective of "Skill" or "Chance"', 2023). Pooling the same and imposing prohibitive taxation is bound to hinder the industry. This accentuates the significance of establishing a scrutinized and comprehensive regulatory framework that treats both types of games fairly, under a tax structure and a structured position for the various types of online games in toto.

While the IT Rules touch upon the compliance involved in mechanisms to evaluate and approve games offered by operators and the ways through which the SRBs shall identify a game as a 'permissible online real money game', it has failed to provide any scope of regulation for those games they categorize as impermissible. When considering game of chance involving stakes, it is essential to note the favorable impact the same may have upon being regulated instead of being subjected to a blanket ban. The government treasury is likely to see economic growth due to generation of revenue since tax benefits and fees are to arise from such games of chance. Moreover, regulation is known to ensure fair treatment of players due to the legal framework that shall have to be in place, to provide safeguards against fraudulent activities and addictive tendencies backed by proactive responsible gaming guidelines. This is likely to mitigate the negative social impacts associated with gambling, such as addiction, by instituting measures for responsible gaming and providing resources for those affected by it within a regulatory frame.

In addition to this, regulation aims at providing a framework for monitoring and controlling the operations of gaming entities, ensuring compliance with laws and ethical standards. Legalizing and regulating games of chance involving stakes is likely to also result in increased employment options, creating jobs for positions relating to game development to customer services. It is also to be noted that many games of chance have cultural or recreational significance, and regulating the same shall allow for the preservation of these activities while mitigating potential harms attached to them.

A blanket ban on game of chance involving stakes may eliminate these benefits and act as a catalyst to all such activities operated underground, making it even harder to regulate and potentially exacerbating associated issues like illegal gambling and lack of consumer protections. Finding an equilibrium between permitting these activities and safeguarding public welfare is crucial. Implementing stricter regulations becomes essential to prevent exploitation, particularly among vulnerable groups within society. These regulations serve as a protective measure, ensuring fair and responsible engagement while mitigating potential risks associated with these activities.

It is proposed that the liability associated with games involving high monetary stakes should be regulated with higher compliance requirements. The degree of risk associated with games of chance involving stakes shall be estimated by the SRBs in correlation with the stakes at play. Similar to the assessment outlined for games of skill to qualify as Permissible Online Real Money Games, those reliant on chance should also undergo regulation. The framework yet to be created with respect to determining what a Permissible Online Real Money Game is should also propel the creation of a suitable framework for games of chance. This shall ensure a standardized oversight for all games and provide for a regulated environment which permits different types of gaming experiences.

While the appointment of these SRBs is still in the works, it is to be noted that as per news reports, the All India Gaming Federation (**AIGF**), Federation of Indian Fantasy Sports (**FIFS**), and E-gaming Federation (**EGF**) had jointly submitted two distinct applications seeking recognition as an SRB following MEITY guidelines. It had further been reported that a total of 120 gaming startups, who are majorly members of AIGF and the FIFS and EGF, had filed two separate applications while working toward the formation of SRBs. One of these applications was submitted and worked on by approximately 100 startups, associated with the AIGF, and the second application was the collective work done by members of the EGF and FIFS (Sarkar, 2023). Additionally, the All India Gaming Regulator (AIGR) Foundation has been reported to be currently in the process of forming an SRB while the MEITY is taking its time to evaluate the applications and assess factors in relation to the formation of SRBs. A look into the existing structure and functioning of these entities sheds light into what one might expect of an SRB once they are formally in place.

The 'Charter for Online Fantasy Sports Platforms' (OFSP) by FIFS provides for the minimum standards and expectations entities offering an OFSP should carry out. In an OFSP contest, the skill component of it is predominantly determined by the manual selection of team by users. Therefore, the opportunity or option to auto-select or auto-fill any part or portion of the fantasy sports teams is not something that is offered to the users of OFSP. Moreover, all contests on an OFSP are to lock prior to the commencement of the underlying real-world competition to which the contest relates, and users are not to be permitted to make any changes to their fantasy team during the course of a match or afterwards, which affects the tabulation of points with respect to such match.

'The Online Games of Skill Charter' by the AIGF also provides for the essential ingredients of pre-approved games, i.e., Online Fantasy Sports Games. In the said charter, it has been stated that

> a winning outcome in a fantasy sports game shall always reflect the relative knowledge and skill of the user. A winning outcome and every aspect of a fantasy sport game shall always be determined predominantly by the incontrovertible statistical results and elements of players'/athletes' performances.

Moreover, it states that the fantasy game format shall define the substitution conditions and the predetermined deadline post which all users will be restricted from drafting or editing their fantasy sports team or responses, for a particular round.

While taking into consideration the existing regulatory roles that entities such as AIGF and FIFS conduct, to consider the same to evaluate all online games would be unjustified. To consider AIGF, FIFS, and EGF, for undertaking the role of an SRB as per the IT Rules, it is imperative to note that all three entities have been primarily set up to regulate the game of skill industry. Therefore, if the same entities are to be appointed as SRBs to regulate online games, the likelihood of games beyond traditionally accepted games of skill being approved for public offering is slim, and this could also result in tension within the industry.

3.2.2 Adoption of a Regulatory Framework

Adoption of a suitable model for such regulation of games of chance/wagering on games may be done through the existing models in several foreign jurisdictions. With the introduction of an Interstate Treaty on Gambling in 2021 (Glücksspielstaatsvertrag, 2021), Germany brought forth a licensing regime for operation of sports betting activity in the country without which penalties may be imposed under the German Criminal Code. Betting or wagering on horse racing (as is the practice in India presently) does not require a license as per the current legislation; however, any other form of betting or wagering in sport requires a license which shall be granted by the newly formed Joint Gambling Authority in Saxony-Aanholt. It is to be noted that only 'fixed odds betting' is licensable for sports in Germany. Bets on spreads are prohibited.

Similarly, in Denmark, in Chapter 2 of the Gambling Act (2020), betting is defined as activities where a participant has a chance to win a prize and where bets are placed on the outcome of a future event or the occurrence of a future event. Therefore, no distinction is provided between any mode in which a 'bet' or 'wager' may be placed or what event such a bet is placed on. The relevant legislation states that "*Betting are games where the participants try to predict the result of an event. Not only betting on sporting events are covered by the term. A wager on who becomes the next prime minister is also considered betting*". Betting under the Gambling Act is covered only upon the participants paying a stake or if the payment provides the participant with a chance to win any prize. Betting with stakes and prizes must only be provided with a license issued by the Danish Gambling Authority.

Fantasy Betting as per Danish Law pertains to events which involve payment to back a 'league' or 'portfolio' selection in relation to sports or shares. Fantasy Sports are therefore understood to be classified as a 'Betting' activity and therefore permissible for operation under a license issued by the Danish Gambling Authority. Denmark recognizes the fact that Fantasy Sports, in a manner comparable to that of games that involve sports betting, relies on future outcomes whereas the two activities are treated as almost polar opposites in Indian law.

In Ireland, players are enabled to gamble on sports, casino games, poker, bingo, lotteries and more on licensed and legal gambling websites. So as long as gambling is conducted on websites holding a valid gambling Irish license or a valid remote gambling license from a reputed authority such as the UKGC, i.e., UK Gambling Commission, online gambling is considered legal in Ireland. Betting on sports such as football as well as betting on horse racing through the internet is legal pursuant to the implementation of the Betting (Amendment) Act in 2015.

Section 1 of the Betting Act of 1931 provides that the word '*bet*' includes a wager, and that cognate words must be construed accordingly. The scope of this definition has been established by a relatively small body of case law. The Betting Act 1931 has been amended by the Betting (Amendment) Act 2015.Gaming is defined as "*playing a game (whether of skill or chance or partly of skill and partly of chance) for stakes hazarded by the players*" and is governed by the Gaming and Lotteries Acts 1956 which prohibits gaming unless a gaming license or permit is obtained. A '*stake*' is defined as any payment for the right to take part in a game or any other form of payment required to be made as a condition of taking part in the game but does not include a payment made solely for facilities provided for the playing of the game (Section 2, Gaming and Lotteries Act).The Betting Act does not define the act of 'betting', except to say that it includes activities such as wagering. Therefore, under Irish law, sports betting is treated in the same way as non-sports betting.

A comprehensive governance and licensing scheme has been in place in the United Kingdom (UK) allowing gaming, betting, and lotteries to be regulated by the Gambling Commission of Great Britain through the Gambling Act (2005). GA defines these three forms of regulated gambling, 'Betting' as is understood to be the staking of money or other value on the outcome of a doubtful issue. 'Gaming' is considered as the playing of a game for a prize regardless of being a game of chance or a game that combines skill and chance. 'Sport' is specifically excluded from the definition of gaming (Rohsler, n.d.). With respect to the issue of skill or chance, the amount of chance required to fulfill the test is not defined leaving the determination or identification of any game to be skill based or chance based, upto the discretion of the courts.

With the legalization of betting in the UK a long time ago, land-based and online sports betting were enabled to be considered legal activity. 'As to the issue of skill or chance, the amount of chance required to fulfill the test is not defined and hence is determinable by the court'.

In Switzerland, the Federal Law on Money Games (The Gaming Act) enacted in January 2019 provides under Article 3 (d) for the definition of 'Skill Games' as – "*Money games in which the winnings of the game depend entirely or predominantly on the skill of the player*".

'*Gambling Games*' have been categorized as – "*Games in which a monetary gain or other monetary advantage is promised in return for a monetary stake or the conclusion of a legal transaction*"; *and 'Sports Betting' as* – "*Money games in which winnings depend on the correct prediction of the course or outcome of a sports event*"; under Articles 3(a) and 3(c), respectively.

Therefore, it is worthy to note that the above-mentioned legislations aim to draw distinction between the different forms of gaming (wherever applicable) and approve the offering of such forms of gaming with a license regime in place.

A perusal of the aforementioned jurisdictions and the status associated with online games thereof hints at the needs for a well-laid out legislation which is capable of assessing pure games of chance. This shall pave the way for users to indulge in activities which can reward them for their knowledge in one of the most invigorating aspects of the modern society that is online gaming.

3.3 CONCLUSION

The introduction of the IT Rules hasn't entirely clarified how states with their individual legislation governing 'betting and gambling' will regulate games of skill and games of chance. The recent amendments fail to distinguish between wagering on games of skill and those of chance. This lack of differentiation has raised due concerns among current operators of online skill-based games for stakes. The ambiguity poses challenges, especially in states with existing gambling laws, potentially impacting how these games are categorized and regulated, causing uncertainty for operators within the online gaming sphere.

Furthermore, the IT Rules have not provided any exception for Horce Racing, i.e., wagering on horse, which has been recognized by the Hon'ble Supreme Court as a game of skill. The new GST regime effective from 01.10.2023 also fails to draw any distinction between games of skill and that of chance, thereby imposing a 28% tax on online gaming, casinos, and horse racing on the full-face value. On account of the same, online gaming platforms are expected to face their profit margins immensely squeezed and operators are likely to run their gaming platforms offshore to avoid these regulatory hurdles. If a framework is indeed in the works with respect to the regulation of online games of chance, the same needs to be spelled out for public review and consideration.

One of the primary objectives of such centrally appointed authority should be to separately define 'Gaming', 'Gambling', and 'Betting' so that the confusion pertaining to their interchangeable use across legislations and judicial orders be addressed. In addition to the same, recognition and clear definition of various types of games and 'Games of Mixed Skill and Chance' may be done so that any operator intending to enter the market and existing operators are well aware of the scope of gaming under which their offerings may be brought under. Definitions as adopted by Switzerland and listed herein above and the adaptation of the concept of 'Mixed Skill and Chance' as laid down hereinabove in the cases of Australia for instance may be relied on as the basis of the same.

As worded currently, the IT Rules prevents any activity that may involve 'wagering on future outcomes' from being offered in India. The contents of this report highlight the fact that Fantasy Sports also come under such a definition along with games involving prediction in sports. Considering how various legislations listed herein such as Denmark, UK, etc. treat both Fantasy Sports and games involving sports betting similarly, a similar approach may be adopted by India.

A comprehensive overhaul of how the gaming industry is governed is certainly a necessity from an Indian context. Keeping a more open-minded approach rather than adopting a paternalistic approach is what the authors propose with respect to how gaming should be governed in India. Implementation of the above-listed means could prove to be crucial in setting the gaming industry forward at a time where the scope for investment and growth in the industry is at an all-time high.

While the introduction of SRBs and a self-regulated industry was touted by the introduction of the IT Rules as explained hereinabove, presently, it appears that implementation of the policy may be hindered atleast temporarily. Recent reports from government sources suggest that no SRBs have been identified or designated in the manner proposed by the provisions of the IT Rules. Until such regulatory clarity is obtained as to how the principles sought to be introduced by the IT Rules may be implemented, the existing legislative framework is expected to govern the gaming industry.

REFERENCES

Department of Justice, Ireland, Betting (Amendment Act) 2015.

Dr. KR Lakshmanan v. State of Tamil Nadu, AIR 1996 SC 1153

Glücksspielstaatsvertrag, July 1, 2021, https://mi-sachsen--anhalt-de.translate.goog/fileadmin/Bibliothek/Politik_und_Verwaltung/MI/MI/3._Themen/Gluecksspiel/201029_Gluecksspielstaatsvertrag_2021_-_Druckfassung.pdf?_x_tr_sl=de&_x_tr_tl=en&_x_tr_hl=en&_x_tr_pto=sc

Govt Defers Plan for Gaming Self-regulator; Internet Firms Introduce Per-order Charges. (2023, September 29). *The Economic Times*. https://economictimes.indiatimes.com/tech/newsletters/morning-dispatch/govt-defers-plans-for-gaming-self-regulator-consumer-net-cos-opt-for-per-order-fees/articleshow/104029904.cms?from=mdr

Information Technology (Intermediary Guidelines and Digital Media Ethics Code) Rules, 2023a.

Information Technology (Intermediary Guidelines and Digital Media Ethics Code) Amendment Rules, Rule 4A, 2023b.

Information Technology (Intermediary Guidelines and Digital Media Ethics Code) Amendment Rules, Rule 2(1)(qd), 2023c.

Information Technology (Intermediary Guidelines and Digital Media Ethics Code) Amendment Rules, Rule 2(1)(qe), 2023d.

Information Technology (Intermediary Guidelines and Digital Media Ethics Code) Amendment Rules, Rule 2(1)(qf), 2023e.

Legal Framework: Gambling and Sports Betting Including in Cricket in India. (2018, July). In *Law Commission of India*. Government of India. https://images.assettype.com/barandbench/import/2018/07/Report276.pdf.

MeitY Appointed as Nodal Ministry for Online Gaming Matters. (2022, December 27). *The Economic Times*. https://economictimes.indiatimes.com/tech/technology/meity-appointed-as-nodal-ministry-for-online-gaming-matters/articleshow/96541726.cms?from=mdr.

Online Gaming: 28% GST Applicable on Entry-Level Value, Irrespective of "Skill" or "Chance." (2023, September 8). *Outlook Business*. https://business.outlookindia.com/economy-and-policy/online-gaming-28-gst-applicable-on-entry-level-value-irrespective-of-skill-or-chance.

Rohsler. (n.d.). Gambling Law: United Kingdom. *Lexology*. www.lexology.com/indepth/the-gambling-law-review/united-kingdom#footnote-069.

Sarkar. (2023, July 9). Online Gaming Rules: MeitY Likely to Take 3 Months to Finalise Self-Regulatory Bodies. *Inc42*. https://inc42.com/buzz/online-gaming-rules-meity-likely-to-take-3-months-to-finalise-self-regulatory-bodies/.

Shukla. (2023, September 29). Tax Heat on Offshore Gaming Companies. *The Economic Times*. https://economictimes.indiatimes.com/industry/banking/finance/tax-heat-on-offshore-online-gaming-companies/articleshow/99392249.cms.

The Central Goods and Services Tax (Third Amendment) Rules, 2023.
The Constitution of India, Schedule 7, List II, Entry 34, 1950.
The Gambling Act, 2020.
The Public Gambling Act, 1867.
Wagering Barred in All Forms, Be It Game of Skill Or Chance: MoS IT Rajeev Chandrasekhar. (2023, April 13). *The Economic Times*. https://economictimes.indiatimes.com/tech/technology/wagering-barred-in-all-forms-be-it-game-of-skill-or-chance-mos-it-rajeev-chandrasekhar/articleshow/99467329.cms.

4 Pathways to Stakeholder-Led Regulation in Online Gaming

Abhinav Shrivastava, Eshwar Ramachandran, Ananya S. Menon, and Sanjay Ravi

4.1 INTRODUCTION

The online gaming industry in India has grown rapidly but cautiously in light of the principle-based differentiation of pay-to-play games of skill (permissible) from games of chance (illegal). The pressing demand for a space to innovate on game formats and for greater clarity and consistency in policy imperatives to fuel the next stage of growth for the industry while balancing various stakeholder interests (specifically consumers) has led to calls for better oversight and regulation. Self-regulation is a potential solution for the unique challenges posed by the online gaming sector in India. This chapter examines the case for self-regulation in India's online gaming regulation landscape.

Firstly, this chapter will look at the need for regulation in the online gaming space and then proceed to outline the self-regulation framework proposed by the Ministry of Electronics and Information Technology ("**MEITY**") under the Information Technology (Intermediary Guidelines and Digital Media Ethics Code) Rules, 2021 ("**Rules**") and its expectations from self-regulatory bodies (SRBs). Against the backdrop of the framework proposed by MEITY, the chapter will then proceed to consider the pros and cons of proceeding with a self-regulatory framework. It will highlight key takeaways and challenges in the context of the framework envisaged under the Rules. The chapter will conclude by outlining the way forward for self-regulation in Indian online gaming.

4.2 THE NEED TO REGULATE ONLINE GAMING IN INDIA

The online gaming industry in India has experienced an unprecedented surge in growth and adoption, resulting in a reported overall revenue generation of USD 2.6 billion in Financial Year 2022 – a thirty (30) percent increase from the reported revenue of the previous Financial Year, with skill-based real money gaming contributing more than half of the industry's revenue (Ajaykumar, 2023). According to one forecast, the industry will continue to grow rapidly and generate up to USD 5 billion by 2025 (CNBCTV, 2023).

 DOI: 10.1201/9781032624204-5

The industry's rapid growth has fuelled increased concerns about risks associated with participation in online games, including fair and transparent advertising, format definition and responsible gaming. As a first step to introduce to ensure informational transparency and fairness in advertising practices, in 2020, the Advertising Standards Council of India ("**ASCI**") issued guidelines relating to online gaming advertisements, stipulating that such advertisements shall not in any manner suggest that individuals under the age of 18 can play a game of Online Game for Real Money Winnings. The ASCI guidelines also require these advertisements to carry a clear disclaimer that such games involve elements of financial risks and may be addictive and that they must not be considered as an income opportunity or alternative source of employment (Ministry of Information and Broadcasting, 2020).

The next area of concern is the nature of the game and the need for guardrails to preserve the character of permissible real money games as games of skill, i.e., games in which aspects of skill predominate over the element of chance in the determination of winning outcomes and not wagering on outcomes (*State of Andhra Pradesh v. K Satyanarayana*, 1996). In the absence of a regulatory mechanism to differentiate between games of skill and chance and arrive at a determination, the responsibility for the determination of the character of each game format shifts to courts, who have to make their determinations in a reactive manner, i.e., post-facto examinations that involve looking at the rules and structures of games and format-specific evaluations of whether skill or chance is the dominant factor. While these pronouncements have provided insights and broad principles for evaluation, the determination itself is limited to the specific game format evaluated by the court – this is an inhibiting factor for innovation as it leaves the operator with an inordinate amount of risk for deviating from the format evaluated and determined to be a game of skill. Proactive and upfront regulation of the online gaming industry can enable it to draw on the dominant factor test to define principles and criteria for evaluation and allow industry experts to make upfront determinations in a scientific and statistically supported manner.

Regulation is also a means to apply principles of responsible gaming and hard-coding it into operator practice. Alongside safeguarding consumers, responsible gaming practices also engender trust between the industry and its consumers while ensuring transparent communication, awareness of risks, and clear pathways for dispute resolution.

Regulation is imperative to establish a fair playing field for operators of real money online games, safeguard consumers from exploitative practices, and to set a framework for responsible gaming. A well-regulated industry can support innovation and growth, build consumer trust, attract investment and partnerships, and drive economic and technological progress. Absent a robust regulatory environment and industry-wide policy framework, operators are likely to safeguard their own interests without consideration of the broader industry, exacerbating risks to users and industry operators. There thus exists a need for comprehensive regulation that ensures consistency and coherence and creates a level playing field within the industry.

4.3 THE MEITY RULES: A CLOSER LOOK

MEITY introduced a draft amendment on January 2, 2023, to supplement the existing Rules. While the Rules originally set out norms for the governance of online intermediaries and content platforms, the proposed draft amendment aimed to expand their scope by adding specific provisions for regulating the online gaming industry and its associated intermediaries in India. MEITY invited public comments on this draft amendment.

Subsequently, on April 6, 2023, MEITY notified the 'Information Technology (Intermediary Guidelines and Digital Media Ethics Code) Amendment Rules, 2023' ("**2023 Amendment**"). The 2023 Amendment to the Rules introduces principle-based norms for online gaming, focusing on safeguarding users from harm and format verification. The 2023 Amendment proposes to involve self-regulatory bodies ("**SRBs**") in discharging core-regulatory functions within the principle-based framework established by the Rules. Thus, it intends to adopt a hybrid cooperative model of regulation involving State and non-state bodies across different touchpoints in the regulatory framework. This model intends to rely on MEITY-recognised SRBs for game format verification and operational supervision of gaming intermediaries through SRB-facilitated policy frameworks and dispute resolution.

The 2023 Amendment defines an 'online game' as a game accessible through the internet via a computer resource or intermediary, with 'online gaming intermediaries' referring to intermediaries that enable access to online games through their computer resources.

'Online real money games' pertain to games where users deposit money or goods with the expectation of winning, and 'permissible online real money games' are real money games verified by an SRB as permissible based on such game's compliance with the criteria set out in the Rules (detailed in the next section) and the framework adopted by the SRB.

As the 2023 Amendment is a part of the Rules, which prescribe due-diligence norms for intermediaries to operate within India with the safety of the safe harbour from liability for third-party content (Information Technology Act, 2000, § 79), online intermediaries, such as play-stores, web platforms, and similar enterprises, are responsible for ensuring that any online games offered on their services remain 'permissible online games', i.e., either permissible online real money games or other online games (not involving payment for winnings) (IT Rules, 2023, Rule 3(1)(b)(ix)). With intermediaries forming the backbone of the digital market, the effect of such rendering is that the Rules play to the self-interest of online intermediaries to make access to the Indian digital market by an online game provider subject to its game (if it is a real money game) being verified through an SRB as a permissible real money online game.

Without such verification, the online game operator will not be able to offer its online game as an online real money game and would have to rely on other means of commercialisation (advertising, sponsorship, premium features, or subscription fees) to sustain itself.

4.4 WHAT DO THE PROPOSED REGULATIONS EXPECT FROM SRBS?

The crux of the 2023 Amendment is the recognition and involvement of SRBs within the regulatory framework. Under the 2023 Amendment, SRBs have been tasked with devising and implementing frameworks for the offer of permissible online real money games and are responsible for verifying online real money games for permissibility to offer in the Indian digital market.

To be recognised as an SRB under the 2023 Amendment, applicants are required to meet prescribed norms set out in the 2023 Amendment, which includes: (i) registration as a Section 8 company under the Companies Act, 2013; (ii) a board of directors with no conflicts of interest and with expertise in areas such as online gaming, education, mental health, and child rights protection, (iii) industry representative membership with the practice of responsible offer and promotion of games, and (iv) charter documents with clear specification of arms-length functioning and dispute resolution, accountability to members, and membership criteria (IT Rules, 2023 Rule 4A(2)).

Under the 2023 Amendment's scheme, SRBs play a pivotal role in verifying the legitimacy of online real money games. They can declare a game to be permissible after verifying its compliance with the qualifying criteria as follows:

(i) Wagering on Outcomes: SRBs must ascertain that the online real money game does not involve wagering on any outcome. The jurisprudence of the term 'wagering' arises primarily under Indian contract law, with a degree of application in the context of gaming when considering contracts for participation. Under Indian contract law, contracts in the nature of a 'wager' are void and unenforceable (ICA, 1872, § 30). A 'wager' in this context refers to a contract that is determined by an uncertain event, over which the parties have no control (*Gherulal Parakh v. Mahadeodas Maiya*, 1959). In the context of gaming, this reading of the term 'wager' has been employed to differentiate 'gaming' from 'betting or wagering', where gaming has been determined to involve staking by players on contests whose result depends on participation and exercise of skill by the players while 'betting or wagering' involves winning or losing of the stake solely upon the occurrence of an uncertain event (*Public Prosecutor v. Verajilal Sheth*, 1945). The element of participation and influence of the game outcome through the exercise of skill is a key differentiator and so if a party to an online game has "the event in his own hands", the online game will lack an essential ingredient of a wager (*Dayabhai Tribhovandas v. Lakshmichand*, 1885). In setting out a bar against games involving wagering on outcomes as a core principle, the Rules seek to ground the norms for permissible online real money games on the principle of player determination and skill predominance in game outcomes.

(ii) Compliance with Regulations: SRBs must verify that the associated online gaming intermediary and the online real money game are in compliance with the provisions of Rules 3 and 4, which set out user terms and disclosures and seek to ensure that only permissible online games are offered and promoted.

This compliance ensures adherence to essential regulatory norms and user protection.

(iii) Age Requirements: SRBs are also responsible for verifying compliance with any laws related to the age at which individuals are competent to enter into contracts in the online real money game. This ensures that minors are protected from risks associated with online gaming activities.

(iv) Framework Compliance: SRBs must confirm that the online real money game is in due compliance with the framework established by the SRB as per Rule 4A (8) of the Rules (detailed below). This framework includes critical measures for responsible gaming and user protection.

Under Rule 4A(8) of the Rules, SRBs are mandated to create and prominently publish a framework for verifying an online real money game. While SRBs have the freedom to design their verification frameworks and render them appropriate for verification of newer formats and versions of online real money games on offer, the 2023 Amendment lays down certain mandatory inclusions in the framework: measures to protect national sovereignty and integrity, safeguarding users against harm, classifying games by age rating, and measures to prevent addiction, financial loss, and fraud (IT Rules, 2023, Rule 4A (8), Rule 4A (6), Rule 4A (12) and Rule 4C). The framework is intended to provide granular principles and practice norms for implementation across members and ensure that SRBs engage in the operational supervision of the industry. Additionally, SRBs have the authority to suspend or revoke verification of an online real money game. This adds to the heft of the regulatory powers of the SRBs.

As a measure to ensure accountability of SRBs, the Rules provide for a multi-tier check on the functioning of SRBs. SRBs are required to publish grievance redressal mechanisms for redressal of grievances pertaining to the functioning of the SRB. Additionally, MEITY can require SRBs to explain the rationale behind its verification of a game as a permissible online real money game. If dissatisfied, MEITY may instruct the SRB to take corrective measures. MEITY also holds the power to suspend or revoke the online gaming SRB status after providing a fair hearing. Separately, MEITY may also direct an SRB to disclose specified information on its platform.

Additionally, the 2023 Amendment also imposes strict due-diligence requirements on online gaming intermediaries and entities that enable users to access online games. These intermediaries are responsible for publishing their rules, regulations, privacy policies, and user agreements. They must also ensure that users do not host, display, or share any unlawful or harmful information. Other obligations include appointing Chief Compliance Officers, Nodal Contact Persons, and Resident Grievance Officers and regularly publishing compliance reports.

The 2023 Amendment allows a grace period for intermediaries to comply with new due-diligence requirements concerning online games – a conclusion of three months from the date on which at least three SRBs are designated by the government. However, MEITY reserves the right to notify the applicability of these obligations at any time within this three-month period.

Under the Rules, MEITY holds the authority, for reasons related to national sovereignty, security, public order, friendly relations with foreign states, or preventing user harm, to direct an intermediary in respect of a non-online real money game to observe similar obligations as those for permissible online real money games.

Overall, MEITY's 2023 Amendment introduces a structured regulatory framework for online gaming, with specific provisions empowering authorities to oversee and regulate the industry while prioritising user safety and regulatory compliance. The Regulations also nudge the government toward considering information published by the SRBs before issuing directions regarding the blocking of access to permissible online real money games. This is indicative of the key position envisaged for SRBs under the framework of the Rules.

4.5 UNDERSTANDING THE RATIONALE FOR SELF-REGULATION AND ITS PROS AND CONS IN THE ONLINE GAMING INDUSTRY

Industry self-regulation entails an industry organisation (e.g., a trade association or professional society), rather than a government or firm-level entity, being responsible for enforcing regulations and standards that govern firm conduct within the industry. Although this regulatory model emphasises industry-led oversight, it does not exclude government intervention entirely. Some form of governmental oversight and the potential for direct regulation must coexist effectively with industry self-regulation. The primary responsibility to formulate and enforce regulatory standards to be followed by firms lies with the industry organisations, as opposed to government agencies (Gupta and Lad, 1980). Self-regulation involves the targets of regulation imposing commands and consequences upon themselves (Coglianese and Mendelson, 2010).

Self-regulation empowers the target of regulation to play an active role in determining how their industry must be regulated, partially shifting discretion in applying regulatory principles from a government regulator. Scholars contend that this regulatory approach benefits the industry, as those being regulated typically possess a deeper understanding of their operations and the industry at large. This knowledge informs the formulation of industry rules to give effect to government-postulated regulatory principles. Moreover, when targets have a hand in shaping regulations, they are more likely to perceive them as reasonable, thereby enhancing compliance. Self-regulation should be employed when it is in the best interest of firms within an industry to adjust their behaviour for the long-term benefit of the industry.

Self-regulation would place the onus of differentiating between games of skill and chance on SRBs comprising representation from online gaming companies, who possess greater industry knowledge and understanding of game mechanics, which places them in a better position to make this determination. Allowing online gaming companies to be involved in the process of segregating games which allows wagering on outcomes from those that do not may instil in them greater confidence in the determination mechanism.

While it may be in the best interest of firms to regulate themselves, and they are more equipped informationally to find solutions to problems faced by consumers, do they really have the incentive to do so?

It has been argued that the possible divergence between the private interests of a firm and the interests of the public and the industry at large makes the prospect of firms policing their own behaviour an uncomfortable thought (Gunningham and Rees, 1997). A firm is a competitor in an industry, and its interests as a competitor are materially divergent from its interests in ensuring the public good. It is economically rational for firms to prioritise individual interest over collective interests within the industry, as a firm can never be sure that it is not placing itself at a disadvantage by interpreting regulations which apply to them more strictly than a competitor does. A counter-argument to this holds that firms can often be incentivised to view actions in service of public good as a mechanism to prevent onerous obligations being placed on them in the future. For instance, JUUL, a manufacturer of nicotine vaping devices, restricted the sale of sweet and fruity flavours which are attractive for children, to reduce support for stricter regulation among key stakeholders in the future (Malhotra, 2019).

While SRBs may be qualified to create an effective regulatory landscape of online gaming in India, is it really in their best interests to consider the interests of all stakeholders, especially consumers? If consumer welfare is considered an integral part of the rationale for the regulation of online gaming, it is important to consider whether firms in the industry are incentivised to prioritise such interests.

Experiences suggest that SRBs could indeed lend appropriate importance to consumer interests. Courts have highlighted the role of the Federation of Indian Fantasy Sports ("**FIFS**"), specifically the FIFS Charter, as a self-regulatory mechanism to regulate online fantasy sports. The mentioned Charter establishes rules and regulations for FIFS to ensure that the games conducted by its members are categorised as "games of skill" rather than gambling or betting activities. Additionally, the FIFS has created Ombudsman Rules, requiring the Ombudsman to be a retired Judge from the Supreme Court or a High Court. The role of the Ombudsman is to effectively address any disputes or grievances which a participating player in online games may have, in a fair and transparent manner (*Ravindra Singh Chaudhary v Union of India*, 2019).

The primary weakness of self-regulatory mechanisms is the potential absence of infrastructure to align the incentives of the targets of regulation and the interests of consumers (Cusumano, 2021). Any code of conduct or regulation which is collectively created by firms in an industry often faces problems with respect to implementation and enforcement. Firms can easily defect from the results of regulation arising from collective action (Olson, 1971). Therefore, self-regulation can often lead to 'under-regulation' due to a lack of enthusiasm on the part of firms in the industry to impose regulations (Cusumano, 1998). It is also a mechanism employed by members of an industry to avoid the prospect of more stringent regulation, as explained earlier. Self-regulation works best when the targets of regulation realise that it is in their best interest to not defect from collective action regulations (Cusumano, 1998). If compliance with industry regulations is against the interests of firms in the industry, firms will require an external source of pressure to provide an incentive to voluntarily comply with these regulations.

Should the government act as a source of external pressure in the regulatory process to ensure that firms comply with regulatory requirements? Who are the other stakeholders involved in the process? These questions will be answered by discussing the models of self-regulation and scrutinising the proposed Rules for online gaming.

4.6 MODELS OF SELF-REGULATION AND HOW THEY APPLY TO ONLINE GAMING IN INDIA

Self-regulation can adopt a variety of modes.

The first model is a self-regulatory regime which is established by firms within an industry through a voluntary code of conduct. A number of industries have developed codes of conduct without any government interference, often to avoid government regulation. This form of regulation is based on agreements made by firms within an industry to adhere to regulations which are collectively agreed upon. These agreements may provide for sanctions when the regulations are breached and may also provide for dispute mechanisms such as mediation. The source of power to initiate and enforce regulation lies within the industry itself. In this model of regulation, consumer interests and fear of governmental regulation encourage compliance among firms. Firms are accountable to each other with respect to compliance with regulations. Adherence to these regulations is primarily enforced through peer pressure and driven by the ethical promise of consumer-focused behaviour.

Self-regulation may also involve firm-defined regulation, where firms within the industry take the responsibility of developing and enforcing regulations, and this responsibility may or may not be enforced by a government statute. In this model of regulation, there is no SRB, and the government retains the power to certify these regulations and determine how they apply to firms. Firms are accountable to the government, and the government can impose sanctions with respect to non-compliance of such regulations. In essence, this model of regulation involves firms creating rules and regulations which apply to them owing to their resources and expertise, but the power to enforce these regulations rests with the government. This form of enforced self-regulation requires more accountability from firms and makes the process of enforcement of regulations more stringent. This model effectively combines the advantages of self-regulation with stricter enforcement mechanisms. However, smaller firms may find it difficult to function within this regulatory framework.

Another model of self-regulation is supervised self-regulation (Cusumano, 1998). In this model, an SRB is given the power to make regulations, and this body comprises of industry professionals. The SRB is accompanied by oversight from a specialised government body. Regulations can be made by both bodies, and the firms who are members of these industry bodies must maintain adequate compliance systems. Key responsibilities such as monitoring and oversight are shared between the two bodies, with the specialised government body usually performing appellate functions. It is essential for SRBs to have the necessary expertise and incentive to effectively introduce and apply regulatory measures and also demonstrate the commitment to enforce them.

In India, the online gaming operators endeavoured to regulate the space through industry bodies such as FIFS and the All-India Gaming Federation (AIGF). These bodies adopted charters, which, among others, addressed issues such as the nature of games that may be offered, transparency standards to be followed, and governance standards to be adhered to. By rendering membership of the bodies and concomitant benefits, conditional on compliance with the charters, industry buy-in was sought to be obtained by these bodies.

4.7 WHAT ARE THE PROSPECTS OF SELF-REGULATION FOR THE INDUSTRY

This section endeavours to investigate the prospects of self-regulation in the online gaming industry, encompassing a comprehensive analysis of the potential influence it could have on regulating the online gaming industry.

Central to the implementation of self-regulation within the online gaming sector, MEITY's directives delineate a roadmap for SRBs to verify the authenticity of online real money games and ensure strict adherence to predefined criteria. By promulgating technical guidelines, this framework not only advocates responsible innovation but also bolsters user protection measures, aligning harmoniously with global best practices. MEITY's proactive involvement signifies its commitment to nurturing a competitive yet secure online gaming ecosystem.

4.7.1 Addressing Regulatory Ambiguities

Historically, the absence of a unified national regulatory framework for online skill gaming in India has impeded industry growth and investor confidence. Ambiguities surrounding the classification of games as skill-based or chance-based have burdened the judiciary and hindered dispute resolution. MEITY's endorsement of industry-driven self-regulatory endeavours seek to alleviate this burden by establishing clearer regulatory pathways. This emphasis on self-regulation fosters not only consumer protection but also an environment conducive to industry growth and innovation.

4.7.2 Structured Grievance Redressal Mechanisms

MEITY's proactive approach to implementing a three-tier grievance redressal mechanism within the gaming sector illustrates its commitment to enhancing transparency and bolstering consumer confidence. By mandating the appointment of grievance officers and an ombudsman within gaming platforms, this structured approach aligns with the text's emphasis on fostering trust and providing effective dispute-resolution avenues. These mechanisms are designed not just to ensure transparency but also to reinforce consumer trust, fortifying the foundation of the envisioned self-regulatory framework.

4.7.3 Enforcement and Oversight

MEITY's pivotal role transcends mere guidance, encompassing active enforcement and oversight to ensure the efficacy of self-regulatory measures within the gaming industry. The 2023 Amendment empowers MEITY to monitor and enforce compliance with established norms and standards, lending robustness to the self-regulatory framework. Through this proactive enforcement role, MEITY augments industry accountability and market stability, potentially fostering an environment conducive to responsible gaming practices and fair competition.

The 2023 Amendment grants MEITY the discretion to revoke or suspend SRB status in cases where non-compliance or divergence from regulatory norms is identified. MEITY's prerogative to intervene, following due hearings and with reasons recorded in writing, highlights the proactive role for the government in enforcing compliance standards. This power to revoke SRB status serves as a deterrent against deviations from prescribed guidelines and reinforces industry accountability and safeguarding user interests.

MEITY's strategic emphasis on fostering responsible innovation, fortifying consumer protection, and resolving regulatory ambiguities through industry-led self-regulatory measures is a welcome measure to support an emerging industry and establish a stakeholder-led regulatory framework. This symbiotic relationship between self-regulation and state oversight has the potential to steer the online gaming sphere towards sustainable growth and ethical practices, paving the way for a well-regulated and competitive industry landscape.

4.8 CONCLUSION

There is a pressing need for a robust regulatory framework pertaining to online gaming in India. The emergence of self-regulation in other industries has provided a promising avenue to address this need. While the Rules have espoused a promising framework, no SRB is yet to be designated. Accordingly, no data exists to determine the efficacy of SRBs.

Nonetheless, it is clear that the path forward for the regulation of the online gaming industry in India must be geared towards a balanced regulatory framework, which commands concerted efforts from the industry and government stakeholders and active engagement from consumers to safeguard stakeholder interests. The efficacy of self-regulation in online gaming is dependent on a regulatory framework that successfully achieves a combination of self-regulatory models to promote industry expertise, consumer confidence, and robust enforcement.

REFERENCES

Ajaykumar, S. (2023, May 29). Regulating online gaming: Economic pursuit over civic responsibility. https://20.244.136.131/expert-speak/regulating-online-gaming.

CNBCTV (2023, February 28). Here's how India's online gaming market fared in 2022. www.cnbctv18.com/technology/indias-online-gaming-market-dream11-my11circle-rummycircle-games-24-7-ipl-mpl-16062901.htm.

Coglianese, C. & Mendelson, E. (2010). Meta-Regulation and Self-Regulation (Publication No. 12-11) [Research Paper No. 12-11, University of Pennsylvania Law School]. https://deliverypdf.ssrn.com/delivery.php?ID=175031100004093102078120115091100002127084029081049078120117108110125026069030065071102061063097020028117124091124094067124122024026024023001031096095069116066011050021009021116008123088007120086124086087091003095069125096031111005076010092029031013&EXT=pdf&INDEX=TRUE.

Cusumano, M. (1998). The Privatization of Regulation: Five Models of Self-Regulation. *Ottawa Law Review*, 29(2). https://doi.org/https://papers.ssrn.com/sol3/papers.cfm?abstract_id=2723562.

Cusumano, M. (2021). Can Self-Regulation Save Digital Platforms? *SSRN*. https://doi.org/10.2139/ssrn.3900137.

Dayabhai Tribhovandas v. Lakshmichand, (1885) ILR 9 Bom 358.

Gherulal Parakh v. Mahadeodas Maiya (AIR 1959 SC 781).

Gunningham, N. & Rees, J. (1997). Industry Self-Regulation: An Institutional Perspective. *Law & Policy*, 19(4), 363–414. https://doi.org/10.1111/1467-9930.t01-1-00033.

Gupta, A. K. & Lad, L. J. (1980). Industry Self-Regulation: An Economic, Organizational, and Political Analysis. *Academy of Management Review*, 416–425. https://doi.org/10.5465/AMR.1983.4284383.

Indian Contract Act, 1872, §30.

Information Technology (Intermediary Guidelines and Digital Media Ethics Code) Rules, 2023, Rule 3(1)(b)(ix).

Information Technology (Intermediary Guidelines and Digital Media Ethics Code) Rules, 2023, Rule 4A(2).

Information Technology (Intermediary Guidelines and Digital Media Ethics Code) Rules, 2023, Rule 4A (6).

Information Technology (Intermediary Guidelines and Digital Media Ethics Code) Rules, 2023, Rule 4A (8).

Information Technology (Intermediary Guidelines and Digital Media Ethics Code) Rules, 2023, Rule 4A (12).

Information Technology (Intermediary Guidelines and Digital Media Ethics Code) Rules, 2023, Rule 4C.

Information Technology (Intermediary Guidelines and Digital Media Ethics Code) Rules, 2023.

Information Technology Act, 2000, § 79.

Information Technology Act, 2000.

Malhotra, N. (2019, May 4). Why Self-Regulation Can Pay Off. www.forbes.com/sites/neilmalhotra/2019/03/04/why-self-regulation-can-pay-off/?sh=67741f1b765e

Ministry of Information and Broadcasting (2020, December 15). Guidelines on Online Gaming Issued by Advertising Standards Council of India. https://mib.gov.in/sites/default/files/Advisory.pdf

Olson, M. (1971). *The Logic of Collective Action: Public Goods and the Theory of Groups, Second Printing with a New Preface and Appendix*. Harvard University Press. https://doi.org/10.2307/j.ctvjsf3ts.

Public Prosecutor v. Verajilal Sheth, AIR 1945 Mad 15.

Ravindra Singh Chaudhary v Union of India, Civil Writ Petition No. 20779/2019, Rajasthan High Court.

State of Andhra Pradesh v. K Satyanarayana, AIR 1968 SC 825.

5 Regulatory Progress and Challenges in India's Booming Online Gaming Market

Niyati Pandey and S. Tarun

5.1 INTRODUCTION

The online gaming industry in India is a 79-billion-dollar business that is predicted to rise to 182 billion dollars by 2025 (Murthy, 2022). The Ministry of Electronics and Information Technology ('MeitY') on April 6, 2023, introduced the Information Technology (Intermediary Guidelines and Digital Media Ethics Code) Amendment Rules, 2023 ('IT Rules') to regulate this booming industry. This follows the Finance Act, 2023, which imposed a 30% tax on winnings from online gaming (Rana, 2023).

This amendment classifies games as 'online games' [Rule 2(1)(qa), IT Rules, 2021)] and 'online real money games'. The former is available to the users online through various intermediaries, whereas in the latter, the "*user makes a deposit in cash or kind with the expectation of earning winnings on that deposit*" [Rule 2(1)(qd), IT Rules, 2021]. As per the new rules, Online Game Intermediaries ('OGIs') would be able to offer only those games that have been verified by self-regulating bodies ('SRBs').

Under the IT Rules, SRBs are mandated to publish the report containing the list of verified online real money games ('ORMGs'), the basis for their approval, their validity period, and details of the applicants [Rule 4A(4), IT Rules, 2021]. This amendment to the rule provides a streamlined and efficient approach to the verification compared to the complicated process suggested by the draft rules. Another benefit of recognition through this amendment is that now the OGIs have obligations similar to those of social media intermediaries (Rule 3 & 4, IT Rules, 2021). However, the obligations become even more stringent when it comes to ORMGs. This rule includes demonstrable and visible marks [Rule 4C(1)(a), IT Rules, 2021], prohibition of third-party financing, and verification of the users before accepting the deposit [Rule 4(7), IT Rules, 2021].

It also provides a framework for grievance redressal mechanism, such as OGIs are mandated to form a grievance redress mechanism as per Rule 3(2) of the IT Rules. The grievance should be acknowledged within twenty-four hours, and resolution should be given in fifteen days. The details regarding the grievance officer must be

DOI: 10.1201/9781032624204-6

published on the website or mobile app [Rule 4C(11), IT Rules, 2021]. Providing a platform to address the user grievances and an adequate timeframe for resolution safeguards user interest and provides better regulation regarding OGIs.

The major criticism against online games has been their potential to perpetuate financial, psychological, and even physical harm. It is addressed by Rule 3(1) of the IT Rules, which establishes that the onus is on OGIs to make reasonable effort and ensure that any content concerning user harm is not being hosted. User harm is defined as "*any effect which is detrimental to a user or child, as the case may be*".

With all its welcoming changes, the new amendment is not without its flaws. The major drawback is the ambiguity and vagueness of certain phrases. For instance, the term 'deposit' in the definition of ORMGs can also be interpreted as including in-game purchases, which can bring free esports games under the ambit of online real money. Similarly, the term 'user harm' is defined as "*any effect which is detrimental to a user or child, as the case may be*". The objective behind the deliberate use of the term might be bona fide, but it has the potential to cause adverse repercussions. However, other legislations, like the Digital Personal Data Protection Act, 2023, can aid us with a more precise definition of harm.

Interestingly, the amendment was also challenged in the High Court of Delhi on the ground of an administrative challenge wherein the power of the State was delegated to the SRBs (Bazaz, 2023). These bodies, in turn, were funded by the lobbying of various online gaming corporations. The government countered that it was proxy litigation and the purpose behind the guidelines was to regulate online gaming and protect the interests of various stakeholders.

This amendment is a step forward by acknowledging the online games are under the ambit of IT Rules and provides a regulatory framework. The clear classification of online gaming and real money games, the establishment of SRBs, and the streamlined process for report publication are desired and much needed outcomes. A few aspects of this amendment, like vague definitions and ambiguous terms, raise concerns among OGIs. Even with its shortcomings, it is a considerable effort to balance the diverse online gaming landscape, establish the regulatory framework, and safeguard user interest.

5.2 LEGAL CERTAINTY FOR THE ONLINE GAMING INDUSTRY

The amended rules focus on self-regulation and due diligence in the online gaming market. The rules pertaining to online gaming delineate a framework for the industry, encompassing the definition of online games and intermediaries. ORMGs, involving deposits with an expectation of winnings, must be verified by SRBs to be deemed permissible. MeitY is empowered to appoint these bodies, subject to specific criteria, including Section 8 company status and industry representation. Notably, the IT Rules explicitly prohibit real money games that allow wagering on outcomes. The regulatory framework emphasises the responsibility of SRBs in implementing safeguards against addiction and harm, advocating for parental controls, and endorsing an online game classification system based on type and content. In essence, the amendment aims to ensure the legality and responsible conduct of online gaming through stringent criteria and oversight mechanisms.

5.3 GREY AREAS

1. Online Game Categorisations and Regulatory Challenges
   The online gaming industry in India faces challenges in categorising games as either skill-based or chance-based, impacting their legality under the Public Gambling Act (Makam, 2023). The introduction of MeitY's regulations provides certified online games with a secure safe harbour, but difficulties in enforcing regulations, especially in states that do not allow games of chance, persist. This highlights the need for a more uniform and clarified legal framework to address ambiguities and ensure consistent compliance.
2. Legal and Regulatory Intricacies in the Digital Frontier
   The rapid growth of India's gaming market has led to increased legal and regulatory complexities. The IT Rules introduced significant changes, requiring further clarity to navigate and implement these amendments effectively. The co-regulatory framework between the MeitY and SRBs necessitates clear and consistent regulatory guidelines to govern the diverse aspects of the evolving online gaming landscape.
3. Distinguishing Online Gaming from Online Gambling
   Despite the regulatory framework provided by the IT Rules, there is a crucial need for comprehensive governance measures to clearly distinguish between online gaming and online gambling. This distinction is essential for crafting effective regulatory strategies that address the unique characteristics of each activity, ensuring appropriate oversight and compliance within the industry.
4. Enhancing Player Protection and Responsible Gaming Practices:
   While the IT Rules and the role of SRBs aim to provide regulatory assurance and supervision, there is a requirement for further clarity and comprehensive governance measures. Strengthening player protection and promoting responsible gaming practices within the online gaming industry is essential. This involves addressing potential risks associated with online gaming and implementing measures to ensure the adequate safeguarding of players, enhancing the overall integrity of the gaming ecosystem.

5.4 SELF-REGULATION MODEL

As stated earlier, the IT Rules advocate for the self-regulation of OGIs and the creation of SRBs; let's take an overview of this self-regulation model. To begin with, these bodies are primarily responsible for verifying online real money games to declare them as permissible. SRBs are expected to have a structured board composition, including experts in various fields, and must maintain sufficient capacity, both operationally and financially, to perform their functions effectively. They also have the task of ensuring that the games they verify do not involve wagering of any outcome. A framework for multiple SROs has been released (*Economic Times*, 2023) to determine whether a real money game is permitted or not (IANS, 2023).

These SROs, forming the core of the regulatory framework, are tasked with certifying permissible online games. The rules mandate due diligence by OGIs and prohibit hosting or sharing of any unverified online game. This move is seen as a significant step towards a more regulated and responsible online gaming environment in India. These SROs consist of industry representatives, educationists, and other experts such as child experts, psychology experts, etc. The SROs are responsible for declaring online games permissible based on whether games offer wagering and will consist of industry representatives, educationists, and other experts such as child experts, psychology experts, etc.

MeitY has received proposals for the formation of SROs from different entities like the All India Gaming Federation (AIGF), Esports Players Welfare Association (EPWA), All India Gaming Regulator (AIGR), Federation of Indian Fantasy Sports (FIFS), and combined proposal from the E-Gaming Federation (EGF) (Rajeev Chandrasekhar, 2023). This regulatory framework aims to safeguard player interests, foster responsible gaming practices, and support the growth of the online gaming industry in India. It also seeks to protect Indian gamers and their funds against online scams and frauds, encourage responsible gaming, and protect young and vulnerable users against online abuse and indecency (Hirani, 2023).

SROs in India, such as the AIGF and EGF, are relatively new entities. They are tasked with certifying permissible online games, promoting ethical practices, and ensuring a stable regulatory environment and aim to enhance stakeholder confidence, boost user confidence through grievance redressal, and encourage competitiveness through research and development. The success of SROs in India is still under evaluation, given their recent introduction. However, there is optimism that they will mirror the success seen in other sectors and contribute significantly to the industry's growth and regulation. Concerns remain about impartiality and the ability to enforce regulations effectively, given the diversity and scale of the Indian online gaming market.

India's approach to regulating its fast-growing online gaming industry through SROs is crucial. Compared to countries like the United Kingdom, where a strong regulatory environment helps SROs function effectively, India's system is still developing. For SROs to work well in India, they need to operate independently from the gaming industry, have the ability to adapt quickly to new technologies, and possess real power to enforce rules. By setting up clear, strict guidelines and ensuring SROs have the resources they need, India can create a safer, more responsible gaming environment. The success of this approach will depend on how well India can learn from other countries and tailor its SROs to local needs.

5.5 IMPLICATION OF DISALLOWING WAGERING GAMES: INTEGRITY AS OPPOSED TO AVOIDANCE

Banning sports betting might initially seem like a viable solution, yet in today's tech-driven era, such a prohibition could inadvertently lead individuals towards unregulated, illegal betting avenues, especially given the lack of awareness and clarity. Rule 4A of the IT Rules is the provision which specifies the conditions of when an online gaming SRBs can declare an applicant as a permissible online real game. The Rule categorically states that such a body should be satisfied that the online real money game does not involve wagering on any outcome. The definition or its lack of clarity thereof causes great confusion since there have been multiple judgements of High Courts and the Supreme Court (*State v. Chamarbaugwala*, 1957) which have held that "The difference between the two classes of competitions (game of skill and game of chance) is as clear-cut as that between commercial and wagering contracts", thus holding that games like rummy would be categorised as games of skill and not come under the ambit of gambling.

India's surge in illegal online sports betting stems from both economic growth and the technological boom witnessed across South-East Asian nations in recent years (UNODC, 2021). Reports suggest that the pandemic played a crucial role in the increase of users of online wagering sites. Although the monetisation in 2021 was considerably lesser than other South-East Asian counterparts, the number of Indian online game users were about 360 million in 2020 and the market revenue of the industry was $1.80 billion (Vijayaraghavan, 2021).

With the advent of technologies such as Monero Transactions, the market is bound to see growth where wagering is perceived as a recreational way of making a quick buck. Verified online sites governed by rules is far better than banning such sites. The black market of online wagering sites is not a novel concept, and with the development in technologies such as virtual private network ('VPN's'), the access to harmful online wagering sites poses risks to users and the economy, making regulated platforms a necessary safeguard. Although the bans have been brought into force on paper, online wagering sites continue to advertise on various social media platforms (Rekhi, 2023). The lack of comprehensive implementation brings into doubt the efficacy of these bans. This begs the question: How feasible is it to enforce such bans in light of technological advancements?

The United States ('US') is a prime example of what the regulation of a resourceful industry would look like. Post the ruling of the US Supreme Court (*Murphy v. Governor of New Jersey*, 2018), and the introduction of the Sports Wagering Market Integrity Act (SWMIA), the online sports wagering market of the United States has seen significant growth. The American Gaming Association reported sportsbook revenue at $7.5 billion. Betting companies projecting the US market estimate a $40 billion revenue by the decade's end (Yakowicz, 2022). The SWMIA's implementation of exclusive data provision incentivises league collaboration. A similar regulation in India would promote user integrity, safeguard data privacy, and significantly diminish the risk of fraud. In 2020, the Gambling Commission of the United Kingdom reported the gambling risk scores of regulated casinos to various illicit activities such as terrorist financing and money laundering as low (Gambling Commission, 2023). This can be attributed to the legal and regulated online sports wagering sector.

Prohibiting online wagering in India raises concerns about safeguarding sensitive data. In today's digital realm, reliance on electronic devices for storing personal information and conducting financial transactions amplifies the risk of unregulated sites compromising user data for illicit trade. Regulating the online sports wagering market can enforce stringent cybersecurity protocols on service-hosting sites, ensuring robust protection for customer information (Gorsline, n.d.). Enforcing regulations would compel operators to thoroughly review their hosting domains, mitigating potential vulnerabilities that jeopardise user data. This measure encourages hosting sites to adhere to rules, imposing stricter protocols to combat financial fraud and safeguard their reputation. Maintaining transaction records ensures proper revenue accounting, substantially reducing the risk of funds flowing into the black market.

5.6 UNDERSTANDING THE DEFINITION OF ADDICTION VIS-A-VIS PSYCHOLOGICAL AND SOCIAL IMPACT OF ONLINE GAMING

The definition of 'addiction' as provided under the IT Rules restricts the scope of addiction to gambling or the monetary consequences of it, thus disregarding the social and psychological impact of addiction. Addiction has been narrowed down to its financial consequences and therefore the safeguards too are limited to monetary spending limits and defined time limits (Ministry of Electronics & IT, 2023). The online gaming industry is ever increasing and is cited as the leading cause of declining social interactions, causing strained relationships, social isolation, and a myriad of psychological disorders such as depression, esteem issues, and anxiety (Fleming, 2004).

Gaming addiction leads to escapism and ensues detrimental effects on personal, professional, and academic responsibilities. Studies indicate that escapism leads to low perceived social support leading to higher depression levels as seen by 53% variance scores (A Fleming, 2004). Pathological gaming also disturbs cognitive functions such as attention span and retention abilities. In safeguarding the financial detriments of gaming addiction, the social and psychological impact cannot be disregarded since they are of primary importance in shaping the future and also adversely impact the physical health of citizens.

The definition must be comprehensive and include the social and mental effects of addiction not only to recognise and gain awareness but to ensure active efforts to reduce the ill effects of addictions. Inclusive understanding of addiction leads to improved diagnosis and awareness, aides research, reduces stigma, and enables regulatory amendments and nuanced legal framework. A nuanced legal framework allows healthier and sustainable gaming in the country. Safeguards against psychological and social effects of gaming addiction are essential to promote healthy online gaming habits.

Education programs are the need of the hour to promote awareness regarding this issue not only in the public but also lead to self-awareness regarding the same. Community-wide efforts of ensuring physical activity and in-person interactions are essential to reduce the impact of social isolation caused by gaming. Moreover, support groups and treatment and therapy centres are necessary to aide those suffering.

These safeguards shall be effective when the stigma surrounding the plurality of online gaming consequences is tackled; this is possible only through inclusive practices which need to be propagated by the regulators and lawmakers. It is thus of paramount importance that the legislators incorporate a comprehensive approach in dealing with sensitive issues related to addiction and enact legislation that not only addresses traditional facets such as gambling but also recognises the evolving needs of addictive behaviours.

5.7 CROSS-JURISDICTIONAL ANALYSIS OF THE REGULATORY FRAMEWORK

5.7.1 United Kingdom (UK)

With the paradigm shift into the digital age, the UK government envisages regulatory changes in the gaming industry and come up with policies to avoid risks against user integrity due to newly available data and technology. To this end, the Gambling Commission ('Commission') established under the Gambling Act of 2005 ('Gambling Act') released a white paper for the UK government to review the existing laws and explore gambling reforms for the digital age ('High Stakes: Gambling Reform for the Digital Age', 2023).

5.7.1.1 Account-Level Protections

The Commission proposes more prescriptive rules on when online operators must conduct checks to understand if a customer's gambling is likely to be harmful in the context of their financial circumstances. The proposal will help monitor three crucial risks: excessive gambling, substantial and unsustainable losses over time, and customers facing financial vulnerability. These start with subtle evaluations at moderate spending levels and escalate to more detailed assessments for the highest spenders.

On the other hand, the IT Rules require the Self-Regulatory Bodies ('SRBs') to lay down a framework for verification ('verification framework') of online real money games ('ORMGs'). The verification framework will incorporate measures to protect users from the dangers of gaming addiction, financial loss, and financial fraud. It will include issuing warning messages more frequently than usual during a gaming session that exceeds a reasonable duration.

Users can limit the time or money they spend and exclude themselves from further participation once these limits are reached. In contrast to the proposed account-level protections by the Commission, the harm standard is kept broad and adopting a suitable measure to avoid financial risks remains the prerogative of the SRBs. However, both highlight the importance of monitoring and preventing harm, emphasising financial safeguards and user-centric tools.

5.7.1.2 Safety by Design

The Commission suggests rules to enhance the intrinsic safety of games for all participants, emphasising product design. It allows operators room for innovation and game development based on customer preferences. The Commission will persistently monitor post-implementation changes and may make additional updates if necessary. First, removing specific features or eliminating non-compliant games may incur development costs. Second, statutory limits will be imposed on the stakes allowed in online products.

The Amendment does not explicitly address safety by design for online games. This implies no interference at the product design stage, and no safety features have been mapped out, rendering any such product unfit for the users. However, the OGIs must comply with due diligence provisions to ensure reasonable levels of user safety, transparency, and privacy. Moreover, the OGIs have been permitted to offer only those ORMGs verified by an online gaming SRB.

5.7.1.3 Collaborative Data Sharing and Privacy

The Commission contemplates implementing compulsory harm prevention system involvement through operator data sharing. The approach includes soliciting guidance from the Information Commission, conducting a public consultation led by the Commission, and subjecting credit reference agencies and operators to rigorous testing. Sharing of live data with gambling enterprises will only occur if the required licence conditions and data safeguards have been established.

The measures implemented by the Commission will ensure that these checks are conducted when deemed essential and for valid purposes such as preventing harm, considering the significant ramifications for collecting and handling sensitive consumer data. They should not be employed for promotional purposes or to harm prosperous clients. The Commission will also safeguard clients' credit ratings and prevent the adverse consequences of reciprocal data sharing.

Operators might exchange customer data to mitigate harm while complying with data privacy regulations. Account verification is necessary due to the inherent dangers of gambling, particularly for minors, and the vulnerability of online gaming account information. In contrast, the IT Rules do not provide any measures involving handling sensitive user data to prevent financial risks for users.

The OGIs and operators shall be subject to the Digital Personal Data Protection Act, 2023, for processing and sharing such personal data of the users. Further, user verification must be done through the know-your-customer ('KYC') procedure based on the Reserve Bank of India's Master Direction on KYC Directions 2016 ('KYC Master Directions'). The advantage of following the KYC Master Directions is the ease of access with government agencies to identify high-risk users. Thus, a similar harm prevention system using data sharing can be adopted soon.

5.7.1.4 Age-Gating

The Gambling Act restricts many licensed gambling activities and products from being offered to minors (below eighteen years) and penalises any such act. The operators of online gambling must verify the identity of account holders to meet the minimum threshold of eighteen years before accepting any monetary deposit and gambling online or permitting access to free-to-play games. The Commission also plans to bring reforms for age-gating by strengthening the verification process through changes in policies such as consulting to lower the criteria for conducting risk assessments in online financial transactions.

On the other hand, the IT Rules lay down the Code of Ethics ('Code') to be adhered to by a publisher of online curated content. The Code prescribes access control mechanisms based on the rating, including a technical measure through which access to online curated content may be restricted based on verification of the identity or age of a user. If such a publisher produces content classified as U/A 13+ or higher, they must ensure that access control mechanisms, including parental locks, are provided for such content.

For content or programs classified as 'A', the publisher must establish a dependable age verification mechanism for viewership. Every publisher offering access to online curated content with an 'A' rating must make diligent efforts to limit a child's access to such content by implementing suitable access control measures. While both jurisdictions prioritise safeguarding minors, the UK's approach centres on financial transactions, and India focuses on regulating content based on age-appropriate classifications.

5.7.1.5 Marketing and Advertisement

The Commission adopts a proactive stance in regulating marketing and promotional offers within the gambling sector. The primary objective is to limit promotions for clients who exhibit indications of harm while also guaranteeing the appropriate design of incentives, such as free bets and bonuses. The focus of efforts to enhance consent for direct marketing lies in offering clients a more comprehensive range of options and mandating consent to promote new items.

The cooperative method employed by the Advertising Standards Authority focuses on addressing content marketing that may potentially inappropriately target minors. The examination of the function of online platforms in ensuring advertising safety is a component of a more extensive endeavour, wherein platforms provide the option for individuals to refrain from receiving gambling advertisements. Licensees are responsible for the actions of their marketing associates.

In India, the IT Rules stipulate that intermediaries are prohibited from hosting, displaying, or promoting any information about advertisements or surrogate advertisements of online games that are not authorised. The recommendation from the Ministry of Information and Broadcasting extends this prohibition to media platforms, advising them to abstain from broadcasting advertisements on betting platforms.

The UK focuses on accountable advertising methods, user decision-making, and cooperation. In contrast, India focuses on regulating directly to limit the marketing of non-permissible online games and betting platforms across different media channels. In India, the emphasis is on limiting the advertising of prohibited online games and betting platforms on several digital and traditional media platforms.

5.7.2 South Korea

The Game Industry Act is the primary legislation for real money games in South Korea supplemented with other supporting legislations (Hyun et al., 2023). The Ministry of Culture, Sports, and Tourism in South Korea and the Game Rating and Administration Committee ('GRAC') are the key regulatory bodies. South Korea has stringent regulations against games involving speculative activities (EY, 2023). The IT Rules, however, do not specifically mention prohibitions related to speculative activities in games.

5.7.2.1 Loot Boxes

Loot boxes, frequently encountered in video games and frequently acquired by a substantial number of players, are deemed appropriate for acquisition by children

(Macey & Hamari, 2018). The unpredictable nature of loot boxes has sparked worries regarding their similarity to gambling behaviours ('Immersive and Addictive Technologies: Fifteenth Report of Session 2017–19', 2019). The South Korean government seeks to regulate loot boxes, utilising a legal and self-regulatory strategy to improve user protection.

The Game Industry Act Promotion Act, an amendment to the Game Industry Act, was enacted by the National Assembly of the Republic of Korea in March 2023. This amendment proposes the inclusion of a fresh interpretation for the term 'loot boxes' and requires game developers, distributors, and service providers to divulge details regarding the nature of loot boxes as well as the likelihood or possibility of acquiring specific things.

Although the IT Rules do not provide a specific definition for 'loot boxes', these items can be considered as part of online real money games (ORMGs). ORMGs are online games in which users deposit money with the anticipation of winning prizes based on their performance and in compliance with the game's rules. 'Winnings' encompasses any reward, whether monetary or non-monetary, that is given or intended to be given to users based on their performance in the online game.

5.7.2.2 User Verification and Preventive Measures

As per the provisions of the Game Industry Act, operators of gaming businesses are required to implement measures aimed at preventing game addiction, with only a limited number of exceptions. The measures include verifying the authenticity of names and ages when creating an account, obtaining consent from legal guardians, imposing restrictions on product usage and time limits as requested by minors or their guardians, providing notifications about game features and payment policies, issuing warnings about excessive usage, and displaying the duration of a user's gameplay on the screen. Operators are required to set responsible gaming limitations, such as monthly payment limits, and comply with age-rating regulations. This is like the IT Rules, which require SRBs to show warning messages regularly after a reasonable amount of time spent gaming. Users can also choose to exclude themselves when they reach predetermined limits for time or money spent. These measures are in line with the preventive actions described in the Game Industry Act.

5.7.2.3 Age-Rating

Although South Korea and India have similar goals regarding age-rating and user protection regulation, their precise specifics, techniques, and considerations differ greatly. South Korea prioritises and emphasises the regulation of speculative activities, particularly play-to-earn (P2E) games, through the implementation of specific guidelines (Hyun et al., 2023). India, on the other hand, employs a more extensive categorisation system that includes a wide range of content descriptors. The South Korean government adopts a definitive position on P2E games, encompassing those that incorporate blockchain or cryptocurrency. Consequently, GRAC refrains from assigning ratings to these games due to their perceived elevated dangers.

India's IT Rules lack explicit provisions regarding P2E gaming, and there is no apparent opposition towards blockchain or cryptocurrency-based games. The IT Rules mandate the monthly filing of compliance reports, whereas the GRAC stipulates that game developers must disclose content revisions within twenty-four hours, allowing for timely adjustments to age ratings. In addition, the South Korean government enforces legal penalties, including as imprisonment or fines, for the distribution of games that lack age ratings. Conversely, the IT Rules do not include explicit legal ramifications for the dissemination of online curated content without adequate age classifications.

5.8 CONCLUSION AND WAY FORWARD

The recent change introduced by the MeitY in India's online gaming business is a noteworthy milestone in its constantly changing landscape. As we explore the intricacies of this legal change, it becomes clear that the regulatory process involves carefully managing the expansion of the industry while also protecting the interests of users. The distinction between 'online games' and 'online real money games' demonstrates a profound understanding of the various aspects inside the sector. The strict regulations placed on the latter exemplify a dedication to ethical gaming protocols. The implementation of SRBs to authenticate online gambling platforms is a notable achievement, highlighting a shared obligation for the industry's welfare.

Nevertheless, like to any system of regulations, the amendment is susceptible to criticism. The presence of ambiguity in specific terminology, such as the concept of 'deposit' in online real money games, gives rise to issues regarding multiple interpretations and unexpected implications. The legal dispute in the Delhi High Court highlights the intricate nature of transferring governmental authority to SRBs that receive funding from online gambling businesses. As we consider the future, it is crucial to tackle these deficiencies and define ambiguous clauses. Effective navigation of the online gambling ecosystem relies heavily on the cooperation of regulatory agencies and industry players. The future of the industry will be influenced by well-defined guidelines, reliable supervision, and a dedication to promoting responsible gaming.

In addition to the immediate concerns addressed by the amendment, there are larger issues that are emerging and need to be considered. The classification of internet games, legal complexities in the digital realm, and the nuanced equilibrium between gaming and gambling necessitate ongoing scrutiny. Regulatory modifications need to be flexible and able to change as the industry grows. It is essential for the government and industry stakeholders to work together in a harmonic relationship. Simultaneously, the domain of online sports betting necessitates a subtle and sophisticated approach. The necessity of user integrity, data privacy, and financial accountability is emphasised by successful regulatory regimes, such as the one applied in the United States. Achieving this delicate equilibrium will be crucial in establishing a sustainable and accountable online betting industry.

An in-depth understanding of addiction, which includes both financial and wider social and psychological consequences, is essential for implementing effective measures of protection. To effectively combat the stigma associated with gaming addiction, it is necessary to adopt a legislative approach that acknowledges and tackles the ever-changing characteristics of addictive behaviours. The transfer of regulatory power to self-regulatory entities presents a novel framework, giving rise to valid apprehensions regarding transparency and oversight mechanisms. It is crucial to maintain a harmonious relationship between industry self-regulation and government oversight to cultivate a competitive, inventive, and responsible online gaming ecosystem in India.

A detailed examination of regulatory strategies in the UK and South Korea demonstrates common difficulties in adjusting inclusive frameworks to the changing dynamics of online gaming. Regulators worldwide adhere to the guiding principle of integrating financial safeguards, user-centric technologies, and preventive steps to counter speculative activity. Ultimately, the regulatory process in India's online gaming industry exemplifies the intricate relationship between the expansion of the sector and the safeguarding of user interests. As we transition to a new phase, it is imperative for the key players in the business to collaborate to improve, adjust, and successfully manage the intricate challenges that await. The development of India's online gambling legislation is ongoing, and the responsibility for determining its future lies with those who influence it.

REFERENCES

Bazaz, S. (2023, November 18). Centre has the right to regulate Online Gaming: MeitY tells Delhi High Court. CNBCTV18. www.cnbctv18.com/business/meity-responds-to-pil-filed-in-delhi-hc-by-ngo-soch-against-online-gaming-rules-18357611.htm

ETtech. (2023, April 7). Govt Notifies Rules for Online Gaming, to Appoint Multiple SROs, *The Economic Times*. https://economictimes.indiatimes.com/tech/technology/it-ministry-notifies-final-rules-for-online-gaming/articleshow/99297771.cms

Fleming Seay, A. (2004). The Social and Psychological Impact of Online Gaming [Thesis]. https://www.cs.cmu.edu/~afseay/files/seay_proposal.pdf

Gaming Law 2023 – South Korea | Global Practice Guides | Chambers and Partners. (n.d.). https://practiceguides.chambers.com/practice-guides/gaming-law-2023/south-korea

Gorsline. (n.d.). *The Importance of Cybersecurity in the Online Sports Betting Industry*. J.S. Held. Retrieved December 22, 2023, from www.jsheld.com/insights/articles/the-importance-of-cybersecurity-in-the-online-sports-betting-industry

High Stakes: Gambling Reform for the Digital Age. (2023, April). In GOV.UK (CP 835). Department for Culture, Media & Sport. Retrieved December 22, 2023, from https://assets.publishing.service.gov.uk/media/644923b5814c6600128d0723/1286-HH-E02769112-Gambling_White_Paper_Book_Accessible1.pdf

Hirani, A. (2023, April 28). *New Regulations for Online Gaming in India – An Early Milestone In A Long Journey*. Mondaq. www.mondaq.com/india/gaming/1310046/new-regulations-for-online-gaming-in-india--an-early-milestone-in-a-long-journey-

Hyun et al. (2023, November 28). Gaming Law 2023 - South Korea. *Chambers and Partners*. https://practiceguides.chambers.com/practice-guides/gaming-law-2023/south-korea

IANS. (2023, June 25). Understanding the Perils of Online Gaming and a Call for Regulation. *Indo-Asian News Service*. https://ians.in/english-wire-detail/understanding-the-perils-of-online-gaming-and-a-call-for-regulation1918198

Immersive and addictive technologies (Fifteenth Report of Session 2017–19). (2019, September 9). In *UK Parliament* (HC 1846). House of Commons Digital, Culture, Media and Sport Committee. Retrieved December 22, 2023, from https://publications.parliament.uk/pa/cm201719/cmselect/cmcumeds/1846/1846.pdf

IT Ministry unveils key amendments to online gaming rules, industry elated. (n.d.). Moneylife NEWS & VIEWS. www.moneylife.in/article/it-ministry-unveils-key-amendments-to-online-gaming-rules-industry-elated/70385.html

Macey, J., & Hamari, J. (2018, July 16). eSports, skins and loot boxes: Participants, practices and problematic behaviour associated with emergent forms of gambling. *New Media & Society*, 21(1), 20–41. https://doi.org/10.1177/1461444818786216

Makam, G. (2023, June 19). Regulatory Landscape of Online Gaming in India: Challenges and Prospects. *SSRN*. https://ssrn.com/abstract=4484558 or http://dx.doi.org/10.2139/ssrn.4484558

Mayank. (2023, September 15). *SROs for online gaming sector to be notified by September end: Rajeev Chandrasekhar*. G2G News. https://g2g.news/online-gaming-laws/sros-for-online-gaming-sector-to-be-notified-by-september-end-rajeev-chandrasekhar/

Ministry of Electronics & IT. (2023, April 20). Government ushers in new era of responsible online gaming through strict guidelines for ensuring safety of Digital Nagriks and accountability of online gaming industry. *Press Information Bureau*. Retrieved December 23, 2023, from www.pib.gov.in/PressReleasePage.aspx?PRID=1918383

Murthy, R. N. (2022, June 9). Gamers nation. India – a nation of gamers. *The Hindu Business Line*. www.thehindubusinessline.com/data-stories/data-focus/india-proves-to-be-a-nation-of-gamers-as-numbers-spike/article65482841.ece

New frontiers Navigating the evolving landscape for online gaming in India. (2023, December). In *ey.com*. EY. Retrieved December 23, 2023, from https://assets.ey.com/content/dam/ey-sites/ey-com/en_in/news/2023/12/ey-new-frontier-online-gaming-report.pdf

Philip D. Murphy, Governor of New Jersey, et al. v. National Collegiate Athletic Association, et al., 584US_(2018). https://supreme.justia.com/cases/federal/us/584/16-476/

Rana, S. S. (2023, February 14). New TDS Norms on E-Gaming Bounty-Budget. *S.S. Rana & Co. Advocates*. https://ssrana.in/articles/budget-new-tds-norms-e-gaming/

Rekhi, D. (2023, April, 27). Ads of Betting, Gambling Sites Still in Play on Social Media, *The Economic Times*. https://economictimes.indiatimes.com/tech/technology/ads-of-betting-gambling-sites-continue-on-social-media/articleshow/99795304.cms

The Information Technology (Intermediary Guidelines and Digital Media Ethics Code) Rules, 20211 [updated as on 6.4.2023]. www.meity.gov.in/writereaddata/files/Information%20Technology%20%28Intermediary%20Guidelines%20and%20Digital%20Media%20Ethics%20Code%29%20Rules%2C%202021%20%28updated%2006.04.2023%29-.pdf

The State of Bombay v. R.M.D Chamarbaugwala, AIR 1957 SC 699.

UNODC Global Report on Corruption in Sport. (2021). *Illegal Betting and Sport*. www.unodc.org/res/safeguardingsport/grcs/section-9_html/SPORTS_CORRUPTION_2021_S9.pdf.

Vijayaraghavan, A. (2021, October 21). One Country's Online Gaming Business Turns into Serious Opportunity, *Forbes*. www.forbes.com/sites/zengernews/2021/10/20/one-countrys-online-gaming-business-turns-into-serious-opportunity/?sh=7a8f426941f4

Yakowicz, W. (2022, January, 19). New Yorkers Wagered $150 Million During First Weekend of Legal Mobile Sports Betting, *Forbes*. www.forbes.com/sites/willyakowicz/2022/01/19/new-yorkers-wagered-150-million-during-first-weekend-of-legal-mobile-sports-betting/?sh=55274d1a388b

6 Of Monopolistic Attitude, Power Mongering and Trust Deficit

Soumitra Bose

The Indian online gaming business has ebbed and flowed over the last four years or so. Ever since catching the imagination of the sport-loving common man during COVID times, the online gaming business has traversed a tumultuous path in spite of a burgeoning user base and its enormous potential to generate revenue. Yet, the business is shrouded in uncertainties and in an atmosphere where even the government has failed to rein in the operators and bind them by a uniform code of conduct; the industry runs the risk of either falling apart or getting restricted to among a clutch of operators who have the power and money to negotiate turbulent times.

Ever since the Indian government recognised the potential of the online gaming business and constituted the Animation, Visual Effects, Gaming and Comics (AVGC) taskforce in April 2022 to enable *the sector reach its full potential* (Anand, 2022), operators and developers saw a fabulous opportunity to express their creativity primarily through technological innovations. The emergence of more than 500 platforms, regardless of their business sizes, reflected the tremendous enthusiasm particularly in the online gaming business. This euphoria also saw its downside as bigger and established players became wary of competition and started adopting unethical means to control the business and thwart creative developers to exploit the gaming and entertainment space with attractive products. Over a period of time, this monopolistic attitude by the 'big' boys hurt the collective consciousness of the gaming business in India.

Not everything was doom and gloom when COVID-19 struck. The online gaming business was perhaps the biggest beneficiary as the common man took to playing social and casual games to escape boredom and long periods of isolation during quarantine times. The access to low-cost internet and access to cheaper varieties of smart phones only fuelled the affinity towards online games. Playing games like ludo not only provided family entertainment but also mental relaxation.

The popularity of ludo can be gauged from the fact that the app Ludo King was among the five top-most installed mobile games worldwide in 2020. According to a report in *Sensor Tower* (Chappell, 2020), Ludo King, developed in India, saw a

 DOI: 10.1201/9781032624204-7

huge surge in downloads and installation amid the COVID-19 pandemic and global lockdowns. According to available statistics, the app saw 26.8 million downloads in April, up 45.5 percent from March and 142 percent from February. India, in particular, saw a massive surge in downloads since the government ordered a *nation-wide lockdown* (PIB, 2020) in March 2020 to contain the deadly virus.

The rising legion of casual gamers tasted a new genre of gaming once live sporting action resumed after COVID-19 halted sports competitions around the world. From an Indian point of view, the *resumption of the Indian Premier League in September 2021* (Reuters, 2021) in the United Arab Emirates triggered new interest in fantasy sport where gamers could win cash prizes after paying an entry fee. While it fetched pots of money to platform owners, how many people actually won cash rewards was a mystery due to the surreptitious nature of the business. Dream11, a fantasy platform owned by Sporta Technologies Private Limited, grabbed millions of eyeballs with its smart and populistic marketing strategies. The platform used almost the entire Indian cricket team to showcase its pay-to-play platform and easily attracted millions of customers.

Cricket is religion in India and the IPL, *a multi-billion-dollar property* (Brand Finance, 2023), provided the perfect opportunity for online gaming platforms to advertise fantasy sports to the world. Backed by financers with deep pockets, some of the strongest ones from China, gaming companies ruled the roost. Joining Dream11 were brands like My11Circle (owned by Play Games 24x7 Pvt Limited), MPL and Winzo, who jumped onto the IPL bandwagon to win over customers with a high propensity to wager. Despite *court notices* (Bose, 2021) served on some of them, celebrities like Virat Kohli, MS Dhoni, Sourav Ganguly, Bharat Ratna Sachin Tendulkar and cine stars like Tamannaah Bhatia endorsed RMG products and easily caught the attention of vulnerable gamers. Be it fantasy or prediction-based games that required dollops of chance and virtually no skills, all these operators had one single agenda – make money by exploiting a gullible public afflicted by the cricket virus.

With virtually no regulations in place, operators *exploited the limitations* (Dubey, 2022) in an outdated law enacted way back in 1867 and rode their celebrity brand ambassadors to reach out to millions as the subscriber base (and earnings) grew at an exponential rate. Online and offline advertisements *had no disclaimers* (*Telangana Today*, 2020) as celebrities endorsed product that led to gamers to mindlessly indulge in pay-to-play games. Several cases were lodged in High Courts after cases of *suicides* (Reuters, 2022) left many south Indian states worried. But the law was weak and with administrators *clearly divided* (Nath, 2023) to arrest the social issues, a powerful platform like Dream11 threw *caution to the wind* (Kalra, 2021) and continued to make hay.

Better late than never, in December 2020, the Information and Broadcasting Ministry rose to the occasion, but only just. It advised online gaming operators to follow *Advertising Standards Council of India (ASCI) guidelines* (MIB, 2020) on responsible gaming but the ones with the right connections were defiant. The government advisory asked platforms to carry a *disclaimer* (Statesman News Service, 2020) clearly stating that real money game "involved an element of financial risk and may be addictive." Concerned with several misleading advertisements that were not in accordance to the strict rules and regulations of the Cable Television Act of 1995 and Consumer Protection Act of 2019, the government stated that "disclaimers should occupy no less than 20 per cent of the space in the advertisement and should be in normal speaking pace and in the same language as the advertisement is made in audio-visual media."

The efficacy of the advisory was *randomly flouted* (Khosla, 2022) by all forms of media – broadcast, print and digital. Major newspaper houses freely showcased RMG apps/games in premium positions like the front page, top news magazines like the *Outlook*, battling for survival due to financial reasons, freely carried ads of companies involved in betting and accorded space to games like casinos, while TV companies like STAR and SONY, with popular OTT (live streaming) apps, aired ads in return for high revenue. In this free-for-all and unregulated climate, the offshore betting and gambling companies made heavy inroads in Indian territory. It remains a massive threat since reports suggest that many such betting apps and websites, operating from places like Dubai, have the blessings of *heavyweight politicians* (Verma, 2023), sports and *Bollywood celebrities* (Livemint, 2023).

Tournaments like the IPL, a cash-rich domestic Twenty20 tournament conducted by the Board of Control for Cricket in India, provided fantasy platforms the *best opportunity* (Sood, 2019) to fill their coffers as two of the biggest players in this genre, Dream11s and My11Circle, continued their big-time association with cricket despite *legal questions* (Singh, 2021) being asked on whether fantasy was akin to betting and with a preponderance of chance. Interestingly, the Board of Control for Cricket in India allowed only fantasy sports among RMG games to be a partner, largely because fantasy owners claimed that they had won significant decisions in courts certifying that "fantasy was a game of skill."

The *Bombay High Court judgement* (Outlook, 2019) in July 2019 was significant for Dream11 and fantasy platforms in general. On a criminal Public Interest Litigation (PIL) filed by an advocate Gurdeep Singh Sachar, a division bench comprising judges Justice Ranjit More and Justice Bharat Dangre, said,

> The petitioner has lost sight of the fact that the result of the fantasy game contest on the platform of Dream11 Fantasy Pvt Ltd is not at all dependent on winning or losing of any particular team in the real-world game. Thus, no betting or gambling is involved in their fantasy games.

It meant outcome in fantasy games depended on the user's skills and knowledge of the game and the results are dependent on the participant's judgement and knowledge: thereby, it doesn't consist of luck or chance. In April 2017, the Punjab High Court had given a similar order after advocate Varun Gumber filed a writ petition. The dismissal of Special Leave Petitions in the Supreme Court only emboldened platforms like Dream11.

Industry insiders alleged in hush-hush tones that court proceedings were either rigged or heard without due diligence. Different High Court orders were apparently "cut and pasted" to give favourable decisions. If the judiciary was 'kind' to fantasy, the central government also provided some tacit support. During the 10th Global Sports Summit: FICCI 'TURF' 2020 in December 2020, the then *Union sports minister Kiren Rijiju* (FICCI, 2020) gave fantasy sports a massive thumbs-up by saying, "I see how fantasy sports is fuelling sports consumption. It is very important. Online fantasy sports is instrumental in revolutionising the manner in which sports enthusiasts engage with their respective favourite sports." Harsh Jain, the CEO and co-founder of Dream11 and Dream Sports, could not have asked for a better endorsement.

Jain's position as an industry leader only strengthened much to the chagrin of other top platform owners. This led to a lot of bad blood and ugly exchanges in private emails and WhatsApp chat groups. Industry bodies like FICCI and CII have remained silent spectators. In acrimonious and complex situations, these industry bodies often lose their relevance (and fairness) since composition of their committees are seen to be too top heavy and dominated by market leaders.

Then, there was more central support for fantasy. In December 2020, the Niti Aayog (Planning Commission) took the *first government initiative* (PTI, 2020) to regulate the online gaming business. It proposed a self-regulatory body (SRB) for the fantasy sports industry. In a draft report titled, 'Guiding Principles for the Uniform National-Level Regulation of Online Fantasy Sports Platforms in India', Niti Aayog suggested that the fantasy sports industry needed government recognition and should have its own identity. This palpable leaning on fantasy left several real money games operators bitter as Niti Aayog's call for recommendations and suggestions evoked sharp criticism from experts. To propose guidelines for the RMG sector as a whole would have been a better approach, considering Niti Aayog was seen as a judicious central body run by wise men.

Pertinently, since online gaming is a *state subject* (Nair, 2022), execution of any regulations was seen as a major roadblock. Regardless of that, among several *key observations made on the Niti Aayog draft* (*Response to Niti Aayog's Draft Guiding Principle for the Uniform National-Level Regulation of Online Fantasy Sports Platforms in India Background*, n.d.), it was pointed out by Consumer United and Trust Society (CUTS) that

> while intention of Niti Aayog of having a central regulatory framework for Online Fantasy Sports Platforms (OFSPs) is laudable, the spirit of cooperative federalism must be upheld, and extensive consultations with all states must be undertaken before finalising these principles. This is especially important, given that many states banned OFSPs from operating in their jurisdictions, in the interest of public good. It therefore becomes necessary to have inclusive state level consultations, while proposing a uniform national-level regulation for OFSPs.

At a time when a fledgling and promising industry needed consolidation and mature heads, the differences started to increase and it was clear that select custodians of the fantasy sports business were adopting unethical means to wrest control of the business. The Niti Aayog endeavour expectedly was a non-starter but that did not stop powerful platform owners to target states that allowed Real Money Gaming. In May 2022, a draft version of the *Rajasthan Virtual Online Sports (Regulation) Bill 2022* (Bose, 2022b) created more animosity among gaming platforms. In an effort to regulate online skill games, the Rajasthan Bill was skewed towards fantasy and completely ignored casual pay-to-play games like ludo, rummy or poker. A proposed licensing system with a hefty entry fee was also seen as a major roadblock.

The chapters in the Bill seemed tailor-made for fantasy sports and the provision for a "private self-regulatory body to work under a commission consisting of a retired High Court/Supreme Court judge, a retired government servant not below the rank of secretary and a person having vast experience in the field of sports and sports federations" set the cat among the pigeons. It was argued that if a private self-regulatory body enjoyed sweeping powers like "to issue directions or orders for compliance with the code of ethics and governance" and "to evaluate, certify and approve a format," it could lead to confusion and conflict of interest. That Bill never saw the light of the day!

That platforms were becoming increasingly suspicious of each other was clear when the Federation of Indian Fantasy Sports, founded by Dream11 owners in 2017, *lost three of its top members* (Bose, 2022a) – My11Circle, MPL and My Team 11 (endorsed by Virender Sehwag) – in April 2022. Established to protect consumer rights and create best practices, the Federation, once a powerful private self-regulatory body, lost its credibility apparently because its monopolistic attitude and dealings hurt fellow members. Coming as it did after the great FIFS fallout, industry insiders alleged that a leading fantasy platform had a hand in unilaterally drafting the Rajasthan Bill, which also invited the *wrath of the Esports Federation of India* (Bose, 2022c) which conducts skill-based electronic games in the country. Esports was a medal sport at the 2023 Hangzhou Asian Games.

The lack of solidarity among operators was now an open secret. Even as offshore betting companies made heavy inroads by taking advantage of the ineffective regulations and lack of enforcement of advisories by media houses, the government struggled to bring a semblance of order. The trust deficit would often rear its ugly head now and then and all that platform owners could do was whine and fight in private conversations.

The All India Gaming Federation, the oldest private self-regulatory body established in 2016, seemed to be a toothless tiger. The AIGF, comprising of judges and influential persons, represents almost 60 members in the online gaming fraternity. After the likes of MPL, Games 24x7 and My Team 11 deserted FIFS, the AIGF looked the strongest organisation on paper but were unsuccessful to convince the authorities that they had the backing of the industry at large and must play a leading role in policy making. AIGF were kind of neutralised because there were stronger forces at play at the corridors of power.

Even if the likes of Dream11 were proclaiming their holier-than-thou image, major rummy and poker operators were contesting expensive cases in High Courts. Tamil Nadu, for example, has been hell bent on banning real money games but its Tamil Nadu Gaming and Police Laws of 2021 was *struck down by the Madras High Court* (Nath, 2021) in a landmark judgement in August 2021. A Bench of Chief Justice Sanjib Banerjee and Justice Senthilkumar Ramamoorthy said that a blanket ban on games of skill falls foul of Article 19(1)(g) of the Indian Constitution that talks about the right to practice any profession, or to carry on any occupation, trade or business. The bench declared as unconstitutional, Part II of the TN Gaming & Police Laws (Amendment) Act, 2021, which banned betting or wagering in cyberspace and also games of skill if played for a wager, bet, money or other stakes. The court asked the state to regulate the business but not ban it. Despite this momentous court order, Tamil Nadu continues its battle against games played with stakes. The state *approached the Supreme Court* (TeamG2G, 2021) in September 2021. The matter is yet to be adjudicated.

The favourable decision of the Madras High Court came as a boost to the online gaming industry. The AIGF, the E-Gaming Federation (founded by Games 24x7 that runs the fantasy brand My11Circle and rummy brand Rummy Circle), and FIFS welcomed the move. The central government also renewed its attempt to regulate a promising but rather fractured business. In May 2022, the government, in keeping with Prime Minister Narendra Modi's vision of making India's digital gaming sector global, formed a *seven-member inter-ministerial taskforce (IMTF)* (PTI, 2022) comprising secretaries of Home affairs, revenue, industries and internal trade, electronics and IT, information and broadcasting, sports and the Niti Aayog.

The IMTF was tasked with identifying a nodal ministry to promote online gaming business, frame regulatory mechanism and protect gamers, among others. In its report submitted to the Prime Minister's Office (PMO), the IMTF recommended that Central governance is required to regulate online gaming businesses and that the Public Gaming Act of 1867, which is currently in force, is "*incapable of covering/defending/dealing*" (Bhardwaj, 2022) with digital-based activities and the emerging technologies associated with it. Identifying the Ministry of Electronics and Information Technology (MeitY) as the nodal body to form Central regulations, the IMTF observed that many states have adopted the pre-internet era Public Gaming Act and created an uncertain environment for online gaming companies. It also pointed out that "the PGA recognizes the distinction between games of skill and games of chance. Games of skill are specifically exempted from the scope of the PGA...PGA does not apply to games of skill."

With so much interest from all stakeholders, including the PMO's office, all roads led to the MeitY, which suddenly became a hub of activity. After meetings with private regulatory bodies like AIGF, EGF, FIFS, private conversations with select industry stalwarts and hours of legal introspection since January 2023, MeitY finally proposed a slew of *online gaming rules* (PIB, 2023) aimed at regulating the buoyant sector in April 2023. As a first step towards forming a Central lar, MeitY proposed *multiple self-regulatory organisations* (Vikas & Choudhury, 2023) or SRBs that will determine whether a Real Money Game is permitted in India or not, among many things. As per the rules, the SROs will comprise industry representatives, educationists and other experts from child, psychology domains, etc.

"These rules don't deal with all the sophistication into what is game of chance or game of skill," Union Minister of State for Electronics and IT Rajeev Chandrasekhar said in a press briefing on April 6. "We are bypassing that and laying out a basic principle that the moment an online game trespasses into involving betting and wagering, regardless of its core content, then it falls afoul of these rules. You don't have to go to SRO if you are only a gaming company, but only when there is money involved in the game," he added.

Even if private self-regulatory organisations like FIFS and AIGF felt the MeitY rules are comprehensive, support innovation, propel technology and boost the 'Make in India' mantra, the reactions were more to please the government and nothing else. When dissected, the rules had major shortcomings. Among *major flaws* (Sayta, 2023), the rules, among others, have contradictory provisions and do not distinguish between games of skill and chance; do not have penal provisions, and more importantly, outsource regulatory functions of the state to private organisations. In short, the rules raised more questions than answers and, if enforced, would only widen existing fault lines among platform owners.

In January 2024, the inevitable happened. The MeitY could not form a single SRO in nine months and its minister Rajeev Chandrasekhar admitted that the rules *have failed* (Das, 2024) to produce the desired results. The government has now considered taking direct control of the regulations and devise a mechanism of approval for games and companies. "There has been no progress on the appointment of self-regulatory bodies. We have received only one application so far and we did not like it," Chandrasekhar was quoted as saying. Perhaps, aware of the vicious relationship that exists among the top operators, it was amply clear that the government was keen to put a stop to influential platform owners from 'doctoring' the efficacy of SROs and swing things blatantly in their favour.

Starting from December 2020 to January 2024, the government actually wasted precious time, energy and money in trying to formulate regulatory structure and impartial SROs that would run the online gaming sector with no strings attached. Given this uncertain times, the online gaming business confronted one more serious challenge – 28% GST on face value of money staked by users on gaming platforms and therefore, *retrospective taxation* (Vikas, 2023). It emerged that the top companies like Dream11 were the *biggest defaulters* (Chanchani, 2023). The matter, which first went to the High Court in September 2023 and then to the Supreme Court, largely stems from the debate if fantasy should be classified as a game of skill or involved betting, gambling or wagering. Research has shown that fantasy is addictive in nature. It has been quoted in *Psychatrist.com* (Madhu et al., 2023) that since

> the majority of players engage in fantasy games for recreational purposes, there is a subset that may develop addictive behaviours. Addiction arises when the pursuit of gaming becomes excessive and interferes with an individual's daily life, leading to negative consequences.

Case studies have indicated that "when players are addicted, they can be excessively preoccupied with their fantasy team, spend significant amounts of time and money on the activity, neglect important aspects of life, and experience distress when unable to engage in the game." Platform owners are aware of this phenomenon. Data in possession of platforms have shown that gamers who are successful in betting are also the best fantasy players. Naturally, platform owners do not want to admit this in public.

The dynamic and largely uncertain times for the online industry is certainly not good news. While there is a need to form Central laws to regulate the gaming business, their enforcement on states will remain a serious challenge. But first, from a purely business point of view, the government needs to decide whether it will claim in full or a portion of the *1.5 lakh crore GST* (Express News Service, 2023) it has levied on gaming companies as retrospective dues for the period 2017–2022 based on computation of face value of a bet. The matter now *rests with the Supreme Court* (Yadav & Das, 2024).

The value of the online gaming industry is worth 135 billion Indian Rupees and is expected to worth over 231 billion INR by 2025. In 2023, the online gaming business rose to become the *fourth largest segment* (Sharma, 2023) in the Indian media and entertainment industry. The increasing propensity towards digital modes of sports and entertainment consumption have propelled online game producers to develop a plethora of games to attract a wide range of customers. Innovation remains key to the success of the gaming business, but it is exactly here where unbiased and justified regulations are required to provide a level playing field and clearly categorise games of chances and those that need an overwhelming level of skill.

Multiple issues plague the industry. There are tell-tale signs of immaturity, and the high-handed nature of certain industry leaders has only added to the trust deficit. Although there is no approved data, industry bodies estimate that at any given time, 200 operators, big and small, have engaged in online real money gaming in India. That number has already significantly reduced, and industry watchers estimate finally only 20 operators may be able to *sustain their business* (Yadav & Das, 2023) in the long run and make profits.

Interestingly, at least three major lobby groups are keen to form a *three-tier regulatory mechanism* (Mukul, 2023) where SRBs are brought under an oversight committee formed by the government. Since three-tier systems are already in place in the financial (SEBI) and OTT (live streaming) domain, this sounds like a plan but there are apprehensions. Reportedly, the lobby groups have signed a *voluntary code* (Express News Bureau, 2023a, 2023b) and seek to govern the business themselves. Since the code is not legally binding, its execution is a grey area. The three lobby groups are Internet and Mobile Association of India (IAMAI), EGF and AIGF. It is worth noting that IAMAI is headed by Jain, the co-founder of *Dream11* (TeamG2G, 2024) and EGF is blessed by Sports 24 x 7 that runs the fantasy brand My11Circle. Pertinently, AIGF has always been at odds with other private regulators like FIFS and EGF. Given its notorious past and the way lobby groups have clawed each other, the future is tense!

REFERENCES

Anand, D. (2022, December 26). AVGC task force recommends national mission to boost content creation in India. *CNBCTV18*. www.cnbctv18.com/technology/avgc-task-force-bullish-on-future-in-india-can-create-20-lakh-jobs-15513361.htm

Bhardwaj, D. (2022, November 14). Interministerial panel proposes central law to govern online gaming. *Hindustan Times*. www.hindustantimes.com/india-news/interministerial-panel-proposes-central-law-to-govern-online-gaming-101668399356965.html

Bose, S. (2021, January 28). *Online Gaming: Sourav Ganguly, Virat Kohli's Role Irks Madras High Court after Spate of Suicides*. Outlookindia.com. www.outlookindia.com/website/story/sports-news-online-gambling-virat-kohli-sourav-ganguly-get-high-court-notices-for-endorsing-fantasy-cricket-apps/363551

Bose, S. (2022a, April 23). *As IPL 2022 Peaks, Fantasy Cricket Body Loses Punch as Big Online Gaming Companies Quit*. www.outlookindia.com/sports/as-ipl-2022-peaks-top-online-gaming-companies-quit-federation-of-indian-fantasy-sports-news-192800

Bose, S. (2022b, May 21). *Draft of Rajasthan Virtual Online Sports (Regulation) Bill 2022: Non-Fantasy Sports Operators See Red*. www.outlookindia.com/Sports/Draft-of-Rajasthan-Virtual-Online-Sports-Regulation-Bill-2022-Non-Fantasy-Sports-Operators-See-Red-News-197727.

Bose, S. (2022c, June 5). *Why Esports Clubbed with Fantasy in Draft of Rajasthan Virtual Online Sports (Regulation) Bill 2022? Asks Angry ESFI*. www.outlookindia.com/sports/as-ipl-2022-peaks-top-online-gaming-companies-quit-federation-of-indian-fantasy-sports-news-192800

Brand Finance. (2023). *IPL 2022 | The Annual Brand Value Ranking | Brandirectory*. Brandirectory.com. https://brandirectory.com/rankings/indian-premier-league/

Chanchani, M. (2023, September 29). *$3-bn notice spells tax nightmare for Dream11 – The Arc Web*. The Arc. https://thearcweb.com/article/dream11-gst-evasion-notice-harsh-jain-fantasy-gaming-gameskraft-4LhnDXXSODwgxKoO

Chappell, C. (2020, May). *Top Mobile Games Worldwide for April 2020 by Downloads*. Sensortower.com. https://sensortower.com/blog/top-mobile-games-worldwide-april-2020-by-downloads

Das, S. (2024, January 1). It's over to govt now in gaming regulation. *Mint*. www.livemint.com/industry/online-gaming-self-regulation-hits-roadblock-meity-weighs-direct-control-11704104343456.html

Dubey, B. (2022, December 2). *Online gaming and gambling — a debt-and-death trap for rural youth*. www.gaonconnection.com. www.gaonconnection.com/lead-stories/online-gambling-gaming-debt-children-suicides-mental-health-psychology-mobile-phones-cyber-laws-deaths-money-51454

Express News Bureau. (2023a, December 6). Online gaming lobby groups sign voluntary code of ethics. *The Indian Express*. https://indianexpress.com/article/business/economy/online-gaming-lobby-groups-sign-voluntary-code-of-ethics-9056104/

Express News Service. (2023b, December 6). GST evasion of Rs 1.51 lakh-crore detected till October; 71 notices to online gaming companies. *The Indian Express*. https://indianexpress.com/article/business/economy/gst-evasion-of-rs-1-51-lakh-crore-detected-till-october-71-notices-to-online-gaming-companies-9056122/

FICCI. (2020, December 9). *Online fantasy sports is instrumental in revolutionising sports, says Rijiju, Fact News, Dec 9, 2020*. Ficci.in. https://beta.ficci.in/ficci-in-news-page.asp?nid=27893

Kalra, A. (2021, October 9). India's Dream11 app faces police case after introduction of gaming ban. *Reuters.com*. www.reuters.com/world/india/indias-dream11-app-faces-police-case-after-introduction-gaming-ban-2021-10-09/

Khosla, V. (2022, April 13). Fantasy sports firms violating advertising guidelines: ASCI. *Mint*. www.livemint.com/industry/advertising/fantasy-sports-firms-violating-advertising-guidelines-asci-11649789997100.html

Livemint. (2023, October 6). Why B-town celebs are under scanner in Mahadev betting app scam. *Mint*. www.livemint.com/news/india/why-b-town-celebs-are-under-scanner-in-mahadev-betting-app-scam-11696565747234.html

Madhu, A. C., Rahman, A. M. A. U., & Uvais, N. A. (2023, December 21). Exploring the Addictive Nature of Fantasy Games Beyond Skill Mastery. *The Primary Care Companion for CNS Disorders*, 25(6). https://doi.org/10.4088/pcc.23cr03586.

MIB. (2020, December 4). *Advisory on Advertisements on Online Gaming, Fantasy Sports etc*. https://mib.gov.in/sites/default/files/Advisory.pdf

Mukul, P. (2023, December 5). Online gaming firms seek new regulatory model; suggest three-tier oversight mechanism. *The Economic Times*. https://economictimes.indiatimes.com/tech/technology/online-gaming-firms-seek-new-regulatory-model-suggest-three-tier-oversight-mechanism/articleshow/105759824.cms

Nair, R. (2022, August 25). Why are as many as five states against e-gaming? *TimesNow*. www.timesnownews.com/business-economy/industry/why-are-as-many-as-five-states-against-e-gaming-article-93782569

Nath, A. (2021, August 4). Madras HC strikes down Tamil Nadu law banning online gaming of rummy, poker with stakes. *India Today*. www.indiatoday.in/law/story/madras-hc-tamil-nadu-gaming-act-online-gaming-rummy-poker-1836430-2021-08-03

Nath, A. (2023, March 17). '40 suicides in 3 yrs': As DMK & governor clash over ban, online gambling takes deadly toll in TN. *ThePrint*. https://theprint.in/india/40-suicides-in-3-yrs-as-dmk-governor-clash-over-ban-online-gambling-takes-deadly-toll-in-tn/1449074/

Outlook. (2019, July 18). www.outlookindia.com/website/story/sports-news-fantasy-cricket-platform-dream11-not-a-betting-site-says-bombay-high-court/334433. Outlookindia.com. www.outlookindia.com/website/story/sports-news-fantasy-cricket-platform-dream11-not-a-betting-site-says-bombay-high-court/334433

PIB. (2020, March 24). *Government of India Issues Orders Prescribing Lockdown for Containment of COVID-19 Epidemic in the Country*. Pib.gov.in. https://pib.gov.in/newsite/PrintRelease.aspx?relid=200655

PIB. (2023, April 6). *Government Notifies Amendments to the Information Technology (Intermediary Guidelines and Digital Media Ethics Code) Rules, 2021 for an Open, Safe & Trusted and Accountable Internet*. Pib.gov.in. https://pib.gov.in/PressReleaseIframePage.aspx?PRID=1914358

PTI. (2020, December 6). *Niti Aayog proposes self-regulatory body for online fantasy sports industry*. @Bsindia; Business Standard. www.business-standard.com/article/economy-policy/niti-aayog-proposes-self-regulatory-body-for-online-fantasy-sports-industry-120120600307_1.html

PTI. (2022, May 27). Govt forms inter-ministerial panel to regulate online gaming. *The Times of India*. https://timesofindia.indiatimes.com/business/india-business/govt-forms-inter-ministerial-panel-to-regulate-online-gaming/articleshow/91821159.cms?from=mdr

Response to Niti Aayog's Draft Guiding Principle for the Uniform National-Level Regulation of Online Fantasy Sports Platforms in India Background. (n.d.). Retrieved January 14, 2024, from https://cuts-ccier.org/pdf/comments-on-priciples-for-online-fantasy-sports-platforms.pdf

Reuters. (2021, September 18). IPL resumes in UAE after COVID-19 disruption. *Reuters*. www.reuters.com/lifestyle/sports/ipl-resumes-uae-after-covid-19-disruption-2021-09-18/

Reuters. (2022, December 8). *Debt to suicides, as Indians take up online games, gambling fears grow*. HT Tech. https://tech.hindustantimes.com/gaming/news/debt-to-suicides-as-indians-take-up-online-games-gambling-fears-grow-71670483175689.html

Sayta, J. (2023, January 4). Gaming lawyer Jay Sayta's 5 concerns with India's online gaming rules. *MediaNama*. www.medianama.com/2023/01/223-jay-sayta-5-concerns-indias-online-gaming-rules/

Sharma, D. (2023, December 8). *Gaming Culture in India: A Rising Phenomenon*. www.investindia.gov.in. www.investindia.gov.in/team-india-blogs/gaming-culture-india-rising-phenomenon

Singh, S. (2021, February 7). How legal are India's online fantasy games? *TheQuint*. www.thequint.com/sports/cricket/fantasy-gaming-the-legality-the-grey-area-and-the-imminent-future#read-more

Sood, J. (2019, May 10). *Gambling Act Is "Weak", Dream11 Helicopters Online Cricket Gaming to a World of Fantasy*. Outlookindia.com. www.outlookindia.com/magazine/story/sports-news-gambling-act-is-weak-dream11-helicopters-online-cricket-gaming-to-a-world-of-fantasy/301583

Statesman News Service. (2020, December 5). I&B ministry issues advisory on online gaming, fantasy sport ads. *The Statesman.* www.thestatesman.com/sports/ib-ministry-issues-advisory-online-gaming-fantasy-sport-ads-1502939142.html

TeamG2G. (2021, September 16). Tamil Nadu moves Supreme Court against Madras HC order that quashed online rummy ban law. *G2G News.* https://g2g.news/gaming/tamil-nadu-moves-supreme-court-against-madras-hc-that-quashed-online-rummy-ban-law/

TeamG2G. (2024, January 13). Dream11 onboards 55 million users in 2023 amidst tax challenges. *G2G News.* https://g2g.news/gaming/dream11-attracts-55-million-users-in-2023-amidst-tax-challenges/

Telangana Today. (2020, December 5). Disclaimer must for online gaming ads. *Telangana Today.* https://telanganatoday.com/disclaimer-must-for-online-gaming-ads

Verma, G. (2023, November 16). Chhattisgarh: how has The Mahadev App "scam" affected the Congress' and BJP's prospects? *The Wire.* https://thewire.in/politics/chhattisgarh-has-the-mahadev-app-scam-paradoxically-bolstered-congresss-electoral-prospects

Vikas, S. (2023, August 11). *Explained: GST Council's 28% tax on India's real-money gaming sector.* Moneycontrol. www.moneycontrol.com/news/business/explained-gst-councils-28-tax-on-indias-real-money-gaming-sector-11159151.html

Vikas, S. N., & Choudhury, D. (2023, April 6). *Online gaming rules: MeitY to allow multiple SROs to determine whether a real-money game is permitted or not.* Moneycontrol. www.moneycontrol.com/news/business/online-gaming-rules-meity-to-allow-multiple-sros-determine-whether-a-real-money-game-is-permitted-or-not-10374481.html

Yadav, K., & Das, S. (2023, December 15). Gaming cos get no relief in SC on tax claims exceeding Rs1 trillion. *Mint.* www.livemint.com/industry/gaming-cos-get-no-relief-in-sc-on-tax-claims-exceeding-rs1-trillion-11702646741089.html

Yadav, K., & Das, S. (2024, January 8). SC to hear landmark online gaming tax case within two months. *Mint.* www.livemint.com/industry/sc-to-hear-landmark-online-gaming-tax-case-within-two-months-11704706078078.html (EOM)

7 Regulating Online Gaming

Centre Versus State Competence

Ananya Giri Upadhya and Gyan Tripathi

7.1 LEGISLATIVE COMPETENCE OVER ONLINE GAMING

Scholars argue that competence in online gaming would depend upon whether the particular game is one of skill or chance, with the former falling under the Centre (under Entry 42 of List I of the Seventh Schedule) and the latter under the States (under Entry 34 of List II) (see Bhardwaj, 2023). However, we show that the States have legislative competence over both skill and chance games, and thus, the skill/chance distinction is irrelevant for these purposes.

Before adverting to questions of jurisdiction, a brief description of the skill/chance divide may be made, although this chapter's scope does not permit a deeper jurisprudential inquiry. The divide stems from Entry 34 ('betting and gambling'), which means that the Centre cannot legislate on games involving betting or gambling, which have since been accommodated under the umbrella term 'games of chance.' Much judicial ink, therefore, has been spilt assessing whether particular games are of skill or chance. The Supreme Court has assessed games on whether skill or chance is predominant since no game would depend purely on skill or on chance (*Chamarbaugwalla v. Union of India*, 1957). The Court has decided that rummy (involving the dextrous memorising of cards), horse-race betting (requiring considerable knowledge about the horses), and fantasy sports are skill games (see *Andhra Pradesh v. Satyanarayana*, 1968; *Lakshmanan v. Tamil Nadu*, 1996; *Mehrotra v. Rajasthan*, 2020).

What adds to the confusion is the manipulation of machines/software by the game developers to make the games 'more addictive' with lesser payouts than the normal probability of the game would afford. The Supreme Court (*Sivani v. Karnataka*, 1995) and the 2022 Justice Chandru Committee Report have relied on this to state that certain video games or online games could not be considered skill games even if skill predominates. As any match-fixing scandal reveals, deceit can occur in any sport and cannot negate the skill required of bona fide players.

DOI: 10.1201/9781032624204-8

7.2 LEGISLATIVE COMPETENCE OVER CHANCE GAMES

Chance games are largely settled as falling under Entry 34 of List II ('betting and gambling'). As we find later in this chapter, Entry 34 is motivated by a federal intent to allow States the freedom to regulate chance games.

The federal division has also been maintained to concerning two Central laws. Firstly, after the Government of India Act of 1935 (which first made 'betting and gambling' a State subject) was enacted, the Public Gambling Act of 1867 ceased to have national application and came to apply only to States that expressly adopted it, like Haryana and Madhya Pradesh. Secondly, the Prize Competitions Act 1955, regulating inter-state gambling and betting, binds only States whose legislatures passed resolutions to be bound by it under Article 252(1) of the Constitution.

7.3 LEGISLATIVE COMPETENCE OVER SKILL GAMES

Skill games present more difficulties in terms of legislative competence since there is no Entry expressly dealing with them (this is not surprising since both terms 'games of skill' and 'games of chance' are judicial inventions). We proceed on two parallel paths. Firstly, we explain that skill games are found in Entry 33 of List II ('sports, entertainment and amusements') and thus fall within the States' competence. Secondly, we rebut the placing of skill games under certain Entries of List I dealing with communications and inter-state and foreign commerce.

7.3.1 State Competence: Sports, Entertainment and Amusements

Entry 33 of List II provides for States' legislative competence over 'sports, entertainment and amusements.' Arguably, card and board games like chess and bridge which the Sports Authority of India recognises can fall within 'sports' even in their online versions since there is no distinction between the skills involved (see *Junglee Games v. Tamil Nadu*, 2021). Even in sports like football, where the skill involved varies between the offline and online modes, skills like modulating force and aim on the device can qualify the online versions as 'sports.' However, many e-sports involve virtual acts that would not be permissible as a sport or game offline, like 'PUBG' and 'Call of Duty.' Can these be classified as 'amusements' or 'entertainment' instead?

Partial answers can be found in High Court verdicts. The Bombay High Court observed in 1955 that "the subjective entertainment or amusement which a person may receive" through a game cannot fall within Entry 33 (*Bombay v. Chamarbaugwalla*, 1955). This was interpreted by the Madhya Pradesh High Court to mean that if a person had to 'perform something' (such as exert skill), to derive entertainment, such entertainment could not be considered as being 'provided' by the videogame parlour and thus fall outside of Entry 33 (*Wilson v. Madhya Pradesh*, 1982).

Notably, these cases were based on taxation (whether or not the provider, parlour or platform, could be taxed), leaving it unsuitably narrow for the present discussion on regulation. In any case, later judgements have taken the opposite view. The Allahabad High Court held that there is no need for a distinct 'entertainer,' but a person playing a video game could be both the entertainer and the entertained (*Agarwal v. Uttar*

Pradesh, 1982; *Darbari v. Uttar Pradesh*, 1983). The Karnataka High Court also clarified that video games can constitute a source of entertainment or amusement for the purposes of Entry 33 (*Radhakrishnan v. Karnataka*, 1990).

7.4 EXTENDING CENTRAL COMPETENCE TO SKILL GAMES?

Those seeking to bring online gaming within Central competence refer to List I Entries such as 31 ('posts and telegraphs; telephones, wireless, broadcasting and other like forms of communication'), 41 ('trade and commerce with foreign countries'), and 42 ('inter-state trade and commerce'). This section examines the flaws in this approach.

7.4.1 The Scope of Central Competence over 'Intermediaries'

Bringing anything 'happening over the Internet' under Central competence via Entry 31 merely because it happens over the Internet is dangerous. It may render several necessary Entries in the State List meaningless, such as the sale of liquor, public health, and betting and gambling (Bhardwaj, 2023). As the Supreme Court has identified, every attempt should be made to harmonise conflicting Entries and reject those constructions which would empty any Entry of its content (*Calcutta Gas v. West Bengal*, 1962). Along with the principle of *generalia specialibus non-derogant*, that a general entry must be construed as excluding the content of any specific entry (*Waverly Mills v. Raymon & Co.*, 1963), this would mean that the scope of Entry 31 of List I would exclude the specific content of Entries 33 and 34 of List II.

The counterpoint is whether this approach will render Entry 31 of List I itself nugatory by reducing its content to a nullity (since activities conducted over the Internet probably have offline forms under other Entries). Where can the line of balance be drawn? We respond that while the regulatory procedure, registration, and other obligations on intermediaries can be under the Centre, the permissibility of games based on their content and nature, as well as obligations on game developers and consumers, must fall under the States' competence (for example, the minimum age of players and maximum money which can be invested).

Is the recent Amendment to the IT Rules aligned with this approach? Insofar as the Amendment is directed towards intermediaries and not the developers or the consumers of those games, it is not an overreach. It is akin to how the IT Act, 2000, and Rules allow the Centre to issue content-blocking orders or due diligence requirements to intermediaries. However, the Amendment requires platforms to verify their games with an industry self-regulatory body (SRB) and states that the SRB shall not permit games that involve wagering. This is an overreach over State powers in Entries 33 and 34. Goa and Sikkim, for instance, would no longer be able to permit games of chance as they currently do by way of the Goa, Daman, and Diu Public Gambling Act, 1976, and the Sikkim Regulation of Gambling (Amendment) Act, 2005.

The Ministry of Electronics and Information Technology (MeitY) must, therefore, clarify that the SRB's decision on permissibility would not affect States that already have a law expressly permitting, prohibiting, or regulating a particular game. An alternative might be to require this Amendment – and therefore the SRB's decisions – to be adopted by a State's legislature before being applied to it, as was done with the Public Gambling Act and Prize Competitions Act.

7.4.2 Central Competence over Foreign and Inter-State Trade and Commerce

Other attempts to place skill games within Central competence – while ignoring Entry 33 of List II – look towards Entries 41 and 42 of List I, dealing with foreign and inter-state trade and commerce, respectively, as well as Article 245 of the Constitution.

Article 245 restricts States to making laws 'for the whole or any part' of their respective territories. Additionally, courts have held that States cannot exercise their jurisdiction on sports extra-territorially (*Zee v. Union of India*, 2005; *Narinder Batra v. Union of India*, 2005). How can this position be reconciled with a field like online gaming, wherein a regulation by one State where the intermediary is located will necessarily impact the consumers of said game though residing in another State?

One solution is for the State legislations to themselves account for present and future legislations by other states. An example of this is the Nagaland Prohibition of Gambling and Promotion and Regulation of Online Gaming Act, 2015, which seeks to 'prohibit gambling' and 'promote online games of skill.' Although the Act provides a broad-ranging list of games of skill, including virtual versions of physical sports and fantasy sports, it still stipulates that a game holding such licence shall only be valid in other States if they have permitted games of skill. Moreover, the Act entitles games which have been "determined to be games of skill by Indian or international courts or other statutes" and non-chance games which have "domestic and international competitions or tournaments" to a licence. Another example is the Sikkim Online Gaming (Regulation) Amendment Act, 2015, which allows both skill and chance games but only within its territory through intranet and not online gaming terminals.

Meanwhile, Article 245(2) provides that only the Centre, and not the States, can make laws with extra-territorial operation (that is, which can be enforced by courts in India although the cause of action is abroad). The Parliament has invoked this extra-territorial operation in the IT Act, thus allowing Indian courts to prosecute an offence committed outside of India if it involves a "computer, computer system or computer network located in India." However, such jurisdiction arises due to the need for powers of enforcement and does not extend to powers over content. Since the Centre can make a law similar to the Nagaland Act, requiring platforms to not provide a game which is banned elsewhere to those users, the foreign jurisdiction argument cannot be invoked to accord the Centre competence on the content of games in the first place.

7.4.3 Public Interest

We now turn to the last way in which the federal balance may be tipped by the Centre attempting to acquire the States' competence. Entry 52 of List I allows the Parliament to invoke 'public interest' to assume control of a particular industry (while industries in general are under Entry 24 of List II). Such invocations have been made through the Food Safety and Standards Act, 2006, Coffee Act, 1942, and Tobacco Boards Act, 1975. Notably, this is despite the fact that 'public order' and 'public health' are both within the State List (Entries 1 and 6).

The alleged risks from online gaming, including effects on mental health (addiction, attention disorders, and self-harm), content-related concerns (such as violent and inappropriate content being accessible to minors), and consequential financial loss and money-laundering concerns (MeitY, 2023), if supported by sufficient evidence, can stand to constitute 'public interest' for the purpose of bringing the online gaming industry within Central competence. On a related note, 'national interest' can also be invoked to vest the Centre with legislative competence over a State subject under Article 249.

However, moving an industry under the Centre does not amount to its complete removal from List II. Instead, matters contained within Entry 27 of List II ('production, supply, and distribution of goods') as well as pricing would still stay with the State (*Shriram v. Union of India*, 1996). This once again indicates that while regulatory bodies can be set up at the national level (like the SRBs) to oversee online gaming, the final decision on whether to allow real money gaming and chance games rests with the States.

7.5 SCOPE OF COMPETENCE: FUNDAMENTAL RIGHTS

Where the skill/chance divide actually matters, however, is in deciding the scope of regulation that the State legislature can impose on a game vis-a-vis the players' and providers' fundamental rights to profession (*Lakshmanan v. Tamil Nadu*, 1996), equality (more specifically, non-arbitrariness) (*Head Digital Works v. Kerala*, 2021), and free expression and personal liberty (*AIGF v. Karnataka*, 2021). The underlying logic, noted by the Supreme Court decades prior, is that chance games are *res extra commercium* or outside commerce and could thus not be regarded as a trade unlike skill games (*Chamarbaugwalla v. Union of India*, 1957). As recently as November 2023, courts have used this distinction to allow complete bans to continue on chance games but set them aside with respect to skill games (*AIGF v. Tamil Nadu*, 2023).

Thus, restrictions on skill games must not only pass the Article 14 test of non-arbitrariness but also Article 19(6). As the 2022 Justice Chandru Committee Report recommends, if States wish to restrict games harmful to players' mental health or finances, they must do so on grounds of public order and not by general exercise of their legislative competence. In the abovementioned cases, the States had failed to provide 'sufficient scientific or empirical evidence' justifying a complete ban. The Supreme Court has held that restrictions on skill games would not be subject to the usual 'reasonableness' standard but a higher one involving the purpose, the extent and urgency of the evil, and proportionality (*Sivani v. Karnataka*, 1995).

Instead, the States in these cases referred to the public perception of gambling as 'evil.' As noted by the Law Commission in its 2018 Report on gambling, constitutional morality and not public morality ought to be the touchstone for restricting fundamental rights. Thus, while only regulation and not prohibition will be constitutionally valid for skill games (barring exceptional circumstances), chance games may be wholly banned without meeting similarly lofty criteria.

7.6 FEDERALISTIC MOTIVATIONS

We now examine the federalistic motivations underlying the vesting of competence over gaming to the States. In general, arguments for federalism, that is, for greater devolution of powers from the Centre to the State, have included economic and non-economic arguments. Economic arguments have included the idea that the Centre cannot possess enough information to make tailored policies for different States and that a common policy across States is not optimal for non-national, non-public goods (Hayek, 1948). Further, the development of different policies in different States facilitates 'experiments' and the sharing of lessons (Rose-Ackerman, 1980). There are also, of course, several arguments for fiscal federalism or decentralisation, but we have not ventured into these since it requires a chapter by itself.

The non-economic arguments include the protection of minority groups and the preservation of their interests and culture (Carla, 2018) and contributing to stability and trust so as to alleviate conflicts. Notably, the Supreme Court in *SR Bommai v. Union of India* (1994) also highlighted the importance of federalism based on the bearings it has on democracy (Singh, 2015, pp. 495–496).

The Constituent Assembly was notably ahead of its time in assessing these motivations in deciding where to place gaming in the Seventh Schedule. Although several members called for a prohibition on gambling due to its 'immoral' nature, Dr BR Ambedkar opined that States must be allowed to decide according to their unique socioeconomic requirements and notions of morality (*Law Commission of India Report*, 2018, pp. 28–29).

Accordingly, States have enacted their laws to deal with betting and gambling, with varying stances on gambling, licensing, and punitive measures. Notably, Goa (with a sizeable Christian population of 25%) and States in Northeast India have among the most lenient gaming regulations in the country. While no empirical study has been conducted in this area, the unique historical and cultural legacy of Goa has been cited by legislatures of other States to distinguish it as having different "socio-cultural mores, values and traditions" and thus allow for a difference in the legality of gaming (see *Law Commission of India Report*, 2018, p. 34).

It is noteworthy that mainland India has a strong societal prejudice against gambling, which the Law Commission traces back to texts like the *Mahabharata*, *Rig Veda*, and *Manusmriti (Law Commission Report*, 2018, pp. 7–12). Therefore, societies and communities that do not adhere to mainstream Hinduism are possibly more welcoming towards gaming. However, as shown by the Meghalaya experience where a bill to open government casinos was repealed after local backlash, this cannot be generalised (Scroll, 2022).

The position of allowing States regulatory freedom based on socio-cultural aspects can also be related to the aforementioned economic benefits of tailored policy-making and experimentation, not to mention the economic benefits from online gaming itself, which is estimated to reach USD 3.5 billion by 2025 (KPMG, 2021). It was with the same motives that the United States supported gaming for the "economic development and self-sufficiency" of Native Americans, which has since played a significant role in their upliftment (see Indian Gaming Regulatory Act, 1988; Taylor & Kalt, 2004).

In closing, we refer to the Public Gambling (Haryana Amendment) Bill, 2002, since it highlights the interplay of moral and economic considerations behind online gaming. While the Bill, which sought to allow casinos to generate infrastructural growth, foreign investment, and tourism, was passed by the Haryana Assembly, the Governor reserved it on grounds that it received 'strident criticism' from society and that Haryana's 'socio-cultural mores' differed from Goa. Later, while the Ministry of Home Affairs expressed a 'national policy of discouraging gaming,' the Department of Tourism supported the Bill.

7.7 CONCLUSION

Competence over both games of chance and skill vests with the State under Entry 34 (betting and gambling) and Entry 33 (sports, entertainment, and amusement) of List II. While States can prohibit games of chance, as many have done, the question of whether States can completely prohibit games of skill is answered in the negative, not for lack of jurisdiction but because games of skill have been accorded a higher standard of protection under Article 19 of the Constitution.

While the Centre can still regulate gaming 'intermediaries' under Entry 31, this is limited to only some aspects, such as regulatory procedures, and the States can still regulate the content, nature, and permissibility of online games. The approach taken by Nagaland in balancing the games it permits with the legality of the same games in other jurisdictions can be applied to avoid regulatory overlap or conflict. What the Centre ought not to do, however, is to use its extraordinary power under Entry 52 of List I and declare 'online gaming' as an industry over which it has powers since this can be damaging to the federal structure, which has been crucial to the question of online gaming jurisdiction since the Constitution was framed.

As for the way ahead, the Justice Chandru Report makes an interesting argument that the offline binary of 'games of skill' and 'games of chance' is itself outmoded in the online world since a game of skill may still be manipulated by the developer to create 'pseudo-randomness' and make it more addictive. This creates two sub-categories within skill games based on whether there is scope for manipulation or not. Regulation, such as by an SRB, would, therefore, have to account for the intricacies of each game and software on a case-by-case basis.

REFERENCES

All India Gaming Federation v. State of Karnataka, WP 18703/2021 (Kar HC).

All India Gaming Federation v. State of Tamil Nadu, SCC OnLine Mad 6973.

Avinash Mehrotra vs The State of Rajasthan, SLP (C) No. 18478/2020 (SC).

Bhardwaj, S. (2023). Regulating the Online Gaming Industry: Legislative and Executive Competence. *NLUD Journal for Legal Studies*. https://doi.org/https://ssrn.com/abstract=4504253.

Calcutta Gas Company (Proprietary) Ltd v. State of West Bengal, AIR 1962 SC 1044.

Carla, A. (2018). Peace in South Tyrol and the Limits of Consociationalism. *Nationalism and Ethnic Politics*, 24(3), 251–275. https://doi.org/10.1080/13537113.2018.1489486.

Dr KR Lakshmanan v. State of Tamil Nadu, AIR 1996 SC 1153.

Gopal Krishna Agarwal v. State of Uttar Pradesh, 1982 ACJ 262.
Harris Wilson v. State of Madhya Pradesh, AIR 1982 MP 171.
Hayek, F. A. (1948). *The Economic Conditions of Interstate Federalism* (pp. 268–269). Individualism and Economic Order.
Head Digital Works Pvt. Ltd. v. State of Kerala, WP (C) No. 7785/2021 (Ker HC).
Junglee Games India Pvt Ltd v. State of Tamil Nadu, 2021 SCC OnLine Mad 2762.
KPMG. (2021). Beyond the Tipping Point: A Primer on Online Casual Gaming in India. KPMG Assurance and Consulting Services LLP. https://assets.kpmg.com/content/dam/kpmg/in/pdf/2021/06/digital-mobile-casual-gaming-in-india.pdf.
Law Commission of India. (2018). Legal Framework: Gambling and Sports Betting Including Cricket in India. Law Commission of India. https://cdnbbsr.s3waas.gov.in/s3ca0daec69b5adc880fb464895726dbdf/uploads/2022/08/2022081655-1.pdf (2022, October 13). Meghalaya repeals gambling law after backlash from local groups. Scroll. https://scroll.in/latest/1034964/meghalaya-repeals-gambling-law-after-backlash-from-local-groups.
M Radhakrishnan v. State of Karnataka, ILR 1990 Kar 1542.
MJ Sivani v. State of Karnataka, AIR 1995 SC 1770.
Narinder Batra v. Union of India, AIR 2005 Del 1234.
RMD Chamarbaugwalla v. Union of India, AIR 1957 SC 628.
Rose-Ackerman, S. (1980). Risk Taking and Reelection: Does Federalism Promote Innovation? *The Journal of Legal Studies*, 9(3), 593–616.
Shalabh Darbari v. State of Uttar Pradesh, 1983 SCC OnLine All 105.
Shriram Industrial v. Union of India, AIR 1996 All 135.
Singh, M. P. (2015). *The Oxford Handbook of the Indian Constitution*. Oxford Publication.
State of Andhra Pradesh v K Satyanarayana, AIR 1968 SC 825.
State of Bombay v. RMD Chamarbaugwalla, 1955 SCC OnLine Bom 2.
Taylor, J. B., & Kalt, J. P. (2004). Cabazon, The Indian Gaming Regulatory Act and the Socioeconomic Consequences of American Indian Governmental Gaming. American Indians on Reservations: A Databook of Socioeconomic Change Between the 1990 and 2000 Censuses. The Harvard Project on American Indian Economic Development. https://hwpi.harvard.edu/files/hpaied/files/americanindiansonreservationsadatabookofsocioeconomicchange.pdf?m=1639579024.
Waverly Jute Mills Co. Ltd. v. Raymon and Co. (India) Pvt. Ltd., AIR 1963 SC 90.
Zee Telefilms v. Union of India, AIR 2005 SC 2677.

8 Walking on Eggshells

Prospects of Self-Regulating Online Gaming in India

Shirin Suri and Kuldeep Kaur

8.1 INTRODUCTION

In recent years, the gaming landscape in India has undergone a remarkable transformation. The proliferation of high-speed Internet, affordable smartphones, and a burgeoning youth population has fuelled the exponential growth of online gaming. As this industry continues to gain momentum, questions surrounding its regulation and the potential for self-regulation have come to the forefront. India has witnessed an unprecedented surge in online gaming, driven by factors such as increased digital connectivity, a young demographic eager for entertainment, and the popularity of esports (Gupta, 2022). Games ranging from skill-based card games like poker and rummy to fast-paced battle royales and fantasy sports have captured the imagination of millions. The Indian gaming market is projected to reach new heights, presenting both opportunities and challenges for stakeholders. The Ministry of Electronics and Information Technology (the "Ministry") established an inter-ministerial task force in May 2022 to address the pressing need for online gaming regulation. The task force's report recommended the creation of a self-regulatory body (or "SRO") for the online gaming industry, which would have the power to certify different gaming formats, decide what qualifies as a game of skill or chance, and oversee compliance and enforcement (Chaturvedi, 2023). A draft amendment to the Information Technology (Intermediary Guidelines and Digital Media Ethics Code) Rules, 2021 (the "Rules") about online gaming was made available for public consultation by the Ministry on January 2, 2023 (Ministry of Electronics & IT, 2023). The Rules specify the methodology to be followed by the SRO in charge of game registration and approval, as well as the prerequisites for customers evaluating complaints and putting in place a structured procedure for handling them.

Self-regulation can mean different things to different people; it can apply to industry-wide goals or an individual firm. In contrast to co-regulation, which calls for increased state participation, self-regulation limits the state's involvement despite its crucial role. The notion of self-regulation denotes a type of digital platform governance whereby industry platforms collectively oversee their own activities (Gawer, 2021). This is in contrast to the fact that these platforms are governed by laws. To achieve this, operators of digital platforms must create and implement sector-specific agreements or shared codes of behaviour while adhering to certain legal

DOI: 10.1201/9781032624204-9

requirements and state security, as outlined in draft Rules 5(b) and 5(c). Given that the self-regulation targets are the ones who understand their operations the best, such a system is appealing, since the targets of self-regulation are the ones who know their operations the best. Self-regulation can be advantageous in that it can save expenses and enhance flexibility, but as a regulatory tool, it needs to be carefully considered (United States Department of Commerce, 2023).

The current chapter provides an outline of some of the challenges related to how the SROs are expected to operate under the Rules, given its narrow scope. The chapter's **Part II** begins with a brief description of some of the rule's shortcomings, which the government should address before finalising the regulations. These include unclear definitions of online games, the categorisation of gaming platforms as intermediaries, and explicit worries about the self-regulatory body. In **Part III**, leading theories of self-regulation are used to analyse the expected function of SROs and how they might be able to solve the challenges that have been found. As is customary, its goal is to ascertain whether the self-control methods are feasible. **Part IV** concludes the dialogue and discusses the necessity of filling the gap that currently persists.

8.2 IDENTIFYING FALLACIES IN THE RULES

Uncertainty in the definition, the involvement of the government, and the inherent complexity of the self-regulatory systems are some of the negatives mentioned in the discourse surrounding the Rules. In the section that follows, the shortcomings noted in this section will be looked at in greater detail from a regulatory perspective.

8.2.1 Vagueness in the Definition of "Online Gaming"

Rule 2(1) (qa) defines an "online game" as one that is available on the Internet and can be accessed by a user via a computer resource, provided that the user deposits money with the hope of winning prizes (IT Rules, 2021). Notably, both monetary and non-monetary forms are included in the definitions of "deposit" and "winnings" found in Rule 2(1) (qa)(ii) and (iii) (Waghre, 2023). Although the latter may have been added to address non-monetary items like "tokens" or "online game currencies," its inclusion could cause games that don't require any financial investment or give users any financial rewards to be classified as "online games" and subject to regulations. Moreover, it is unclear if the scope of this legislation includes non- gambling online games (Fang ching, 2023).

8.2.2 Engagement in Various Self-Regulatory Organisations

Although online gaming intermediaries may approach or join various SROs, the Rules may lead to a fractured gaming market. This could lead to disparities in standards across SROs and substantial differences in how rules are applied. Online gaming intermediaries can selectively select an SRO that construes these terms in a way that suits their interests, or they may even create a new SRO with less stringent requirements due to the already expansive and possibly confusing criteria. A comparable risk of dangerously splitting uniform rules controlling the gaming sector could result from the growth of varied regulatory organisations, ultimately jeopardising end-user interests.

8.2.3 Uncertainty Regarding State Laws

The existing regulations concerning online gaming need to be more precise in the interpretation and application of state legislation within a centralised authority framework. Rule 3(1)(ii) and (ix) stipulate that a self-regulatory organisation (SRO) is responsible for ensuring compliance of online games with Indian laws, inclusive of state regulations governing betting and gambling. However, a notable ambiguity arises when determining the applicability of these regulations in states like Tamil Nadu, where activities such as playing cards, including rummy and poker, are deemed illegal. Compounding this issue is the absence of a clearly defined mechanism to address situations where a game, previously endorsed by an SRO, is subsequently declared illegal by state law. This regulatory gap raises concerns about the clarity and potential legal ramifications for stakeholders involved in the online gaming industry.

Recognising these deficiencies, there is a pressing need to revise and augment the existing guidelines. An updated set of regulations should incorporate a comprehensive and explicit list of activities deemed illegal in online gaming. This should encompass offshore gambling and betting activities, providing a more robust legal framework to govern such practices. Furthermore, it is imperative to establish a distinct inventory of game formats acknowledged for their reliance on skill (Mondaq, 2023). This step would contribute to a more nuanced understanding of the diverse nature of online games, allowing for more precise distinctions between games of skill and those predominantly based on chance. In essence, a comprehensive overhaul of the regulatory framework is essential to address the imprecisions and gaps in the current guidelines. This involves incorporating explicit definitions of illegal gaming activities, refining the recognition of skill-based games, and establishing a coherent mechanism to address conflicts between central regulations and state laws, thereby fostering a more transparent and legally secure environment for the online gaming industry in India (Dua & Dua, 2023).

8.2.4 The Government's Role

The proposed amendments to the regulatory framework bestow considerable authority upon the Ministry, thereby affording the government a substantial role in influencing the self-regulatory mechanism. Rule 4B (10) delineates a sweeping mandate wherein the Ministry, at its discretion and with the issuance of a written justification, possesses the prerogative to suspend or revoke the registration of a self-regulatory entity. The language employed in this rule introduces an element of arbitrariness to this authority, employing phrases such as "as it may deem necessary" and "if it is satisfied that it is necessary so to do." This, coupled with the power to issue instructions or interim directions, amplifies the discretionary nature of the Ministry's involvement. While Rule 4B(10) incorporates safeguards for the self-regulatory entity by allowing an online gaming intermediary to present its case before the Ministry issues an order, the expansive powers vested in the Ministry remain a potential source of concern. The criteria and considerations guiding such decisions are elucidated in Rules 4B (2) to 4B (9) (Draft Notification, 2023).

Furthermore, Rule 4B (9) delineates that if the Ministry determines that a self-regulatory body has deviated from the prescribed rules, it retains the authority to notify the body in writing, directing it to rectify its actions. Although self-regulatory bodies are entrusted with the registration of online gaming intermediaries, the broad powers conferred upon the Ministry introduce a significant level of discretion in selecting and exercising these powers, thereby augmenting government involvement in the regulatory process (Kripalani & Mathur, 2023).

Rule 6A further empowers the Ministry to identify and classify specific games as "online games" under the purview of these rules. This authority is exercised through a notification published in the Official Gazette, contingent upon the satisfaction of certain conditions, including the absence of a deposit requirement and the Ministry's belief that such games may pose a risk to the sovereignty, integrity, or security of the State, or impact friendly relations with foreign States or the public. Nevertheless, the absence of clarity in Rule 6A regarding the interpretation of the phrase "harm among children" necessitates establishing the government's understanding of such concepts to forestall inconsistent rule application and potential misuse of this formidable power. The provision of the "risk of harm to sovereignty" further widens the scope for potential misuse, prompting a critical examination of the parameters delineating the exercise of this discretionary authority (Xiao, 2023).

8.2.5 Absurd Requirements for Advertisements

The guidelines crafted to curb illicit advertisements on social and digital media platforms in India strategically target the pervasive challenge posed by unlawful promotions of betting and gambling services by offshore entities. A central tenet of these guidelines places the onus on platforms to scrutinise the registration status of online games with the relevant self-regulatory organisations (SROs) before facilitating any advertising endeavours. However, the practical implementation of such a mandate is called into question, given the exorbitant multitude of gaming applications available on platforms such as the Google Play Store and Apple's App Store. The sheer volume of these applications renders the meticulous verification of each game's registration status an ostensibly impractical and onerous task.

Amidst this regulatory landscape, the proposed Rules for Online Gaming in India encounter noteworthy challenges that merit in-depth exploration. Chief among these challenges is the ambiguity inherent in the definition of "online gaming," a critical facet that necessitates elucidation for a more nuanced comprehension of the regulatory framework. Additionally, the potential consequence of fostering a fragmented gaming market emerges as a salient concern, driven by the allowance of membership in multiple self-regulatory organisations, thereby necessitating a discerning evaluation of the implications on market dynamics.

Compounding these complexities is the lacuna in clarity regarding the alignment of these proposed rules with state laws, particularly in jurisdictions where the legality of playing cards such as rummy and poker remains a subject of contention. This regulatory ambiguity engenders a climate of uncertainty, requiring meticulous examination for a holistic understanding of the regulatory terrain.

Foremost among the identified issues is the overarching concern regarding the government's role and the wielded power to intercede in the self-regulatory mechanism. The proposed Rule 4B(10) endows the Ministry with considerable discretion to suspend or revoke the registration of self-regulatory entities, introducing an element of arbitrariness through phrases such as "as it may deem necessary" and "if it is satisfied that it is necessary so to do" (Vyas, 2023). While Rule 4B(10) offers a semblance of safeguarding by allowing online gaming intermediaries to present their case, the broad powers vested in the Ministry accentuate government intervention in the regulatory process. In the subsequent section, a meticulous regulatory analysis will be undertaken to delve into these multifaceted issues, unravelling the intricacies of the proposed Rules for Online Gaming in India and offering a comprehensive perspective on their potential implications.

8.3 PRACTICAL EVALUATION USING THEORIES AND PRACTICES OF SELF-REGULATION

In delving into this chapter's expansive segment, the scope transcends the mere rectification of previously identified issues. Rather, it undertakes a meticulous and thorough analysis of the pertinent gaming rules, seeking to illuminate their salient features with precision and nuance. This analytical endeavour extends beyond the periphery of mere problem-solving, venturing into the realm of a comprehensive examination of the regulatory framework governing the gaming landscape. The overarching assessment reveals a multifaceted landscape of gaming regulations, showcasing a myriad of intricacies and nuances inherent to the industry. At first glance, the positive attributes are apparent – a commendable inclusion of robust fraud prevention mechanisms and vigilant enforcement systems. These elements, undoubtedly, represent significant strides towards fostering integrity within the gaming ecosystem, signalling an earnest commitment to curbing malpractices and ensuring a fair and secure environment for participants.

Yet, beyond the surface of these positive attributes, there is a subtle disclosure that seriously jeopardises the regulatory system's overall sustainability. The examination reveals intricate relationships and interdependencies that raise doubts about the effectiveness of the regulatory structure despite the admirable efforts made to prevent and enforce fraud. The problems at hand are not limited to lone instances or shortcomings; rather, they are a complex web of systemic worries that jeopardise the regulatory structure itself.

A crucial element that surfaces from the examination is the complex equilibrium that must be struck between encouraging innovation and guaranteeing legal compliance. Regulators face a constant struggle due to the dynamic nature of the gaming sector, which is characterised by rapid technical improvements and increasing user preferences. Maintaining regulatory standards while welcoming innovation can be a difficult balance that calls for ongoing attention to detail and flexibility. Moreover, the examination reveals the possible unforeseen outcomes of strict regulatory actions. Although implementing strong fraud protection measures is commendable, overly strict regulations could unintentionally hinder the expansion and vitality of the gaming industry. The delicate dance between security measures and industry vibrancy becomes a tightrope walk, necessitating a nuanced approach to avoid hampering the very vitality that makes the gaming landscape thrive (Király, 2018).

This section of the chapter, then, goes beyond being just a problem-solving exercise and becomes a thoughtful and perceptive examination of the complexities entailed in gaming legislation. A comprehensive reassessment of the regulatory framework is necessary due to the interplay of positive attributes and systemic challenges uncovered by this analysis. Stakeholders are urged to take a collective approach towards developing a governance structure that is more resilient, adaptable, and ultimately viable for the dynamic gaming industry.

8.3.1 The Legal Certainty and Outcome-Based Regulatory Approach

One of the fundamental principles of the rule of law, the need for legal certainty, is a well-known fulcrum that is often mentioned in the fast-paced fintech sector. Its essential function is shown not just as a rule of thumb but also as an outcome-focused strategic framework. Within the complex terrain of self-regulatory organisations (SROs) facing several obstacles and the imprecise boundaries of the concept of "online gaming," legal certainty surfaces as a guiding light, providing a logical route to settlement. The imperative requirement to negotiate the complexities and ambiguities that abound in the contemporary regulatory environment forms the basis of this regulatory strategy (Garrido, 2022). Legal certainty, when deftly wielded in conjunction with extant rules, serves as a potent instrument to address the inherent problems afflicting diverse SROs and the unsettling vagueness enveloping the sphere of online gaming. The linchpin of this strategy lies in its capacity to meticulously delineate and establish regulatory boundaries with utmost precision and clarity.

In addition, platforms could find it difficult to understand expectations in the absence of clear guidelines, which could make them reluctant to invest in new services or technology. This might result in a less dynamic industry and a slower rate of innovation. Regulations that are ambiguous or open to different interpretations make it challenging for businesses to budget for and make new product and service investments. This might hinder innovation by making it more difficult for investors and entrepreneurs to evaluate the legal risks involved in new business endeavours. Therefore, the absence of clarity around the classification of intermediaries in the online gaming industry foreshadows detrimental outcomes for both the innovation and growth of the sector (Bansal, 2023).

8.3.2 The Duck Type

The "duck type" regulatory practice, which is also related to fintech, is significant since it calls for regulating the "same risk with the same rule." Mandating that organisations that expose similar risks and engage in similar activities be exposed to the same degrees of regulatory scrutiny promotes regulatory fairness by preventing any domain from being unfairly given preference over another. As previously mentioned, the Draft Regulations might allow for various online gaming intermediaries to be included in SROs with various requirements. This would make it possible for businesses to choose organisations with less stringent compliance standards, circumventing the goals of the regulations. Furthermore, businesses would select SROs whose criterion of decision fits their games to circumvent rules about "betting" or games of chance.

Thus, one of the main goals of regulation would be violated – the idea of regulatory fairness. Therefore, the author suggests that gaming platforms should be limited to joining a single SRO (Bedi, 2023).

8.3.3 Minimal Governmental Intervention

The widely acknowledged advantages of self-regulation, wherein entities within an industry proactively establish and adhere to their own standards, notably include the alleviation of governmental burdens and the provision of greater autonomy to companies. This dynamic equilibrium, where regulatory responsibilities are shouldered by industry players, affords them a measure of flexibility and adaptability that may be constrained within the rigid confines of government-imposed regulations. However, this advantageous arrangement is not without its intricacies, and a nuanced examination reveals a complex interplay between industry autonomy and government involvement, particularly through appointed nominees.

Undoubtedly, the infusion of government nominees into the governance structures of self-regulatory organisations (SROs) serves as a moderating force, ostensibly ensuring that industry self-regulation remains within the bounds of broader societal interests and legal frameworks (Edwards, 2017). These nominees wield a certain influence, acting as conduits through which governmental perspectives and concerns can be channelled into the self-regulatory arena. While their participation may ostensibly be a check and balance mechanism, it introduces an element of external oversight that partially offsets the autonomy granted to industry players.

8.3.4 Enforcement

The issue of enforcement and the possible lack of such enforcement tools is a relevant concern with industry-specific rules. Interestingly, self-regulation often has lax enforcement mechanisms and is prone to producing conflicts of interest that need to be carefully examined. This lack of self-control is not unique to India. Globally, industries have generally failed to reach sufficient degrees of self-regulation; this failure has been heavily blamed for the 2008 financial crisis. But despite these obstacles, the number and acceptance of self-regulatory organisations have steadily increased over time, which is seen as a sign of the maturing business ecosystems. The issue of enforcement and the possible lack of such enforcement tools is a relevant concern with industry-specific rules. Interestingly, self-regulation often has lax enforcement mechanisms and is prone to producing conflicts of interest that need to be carefully examined. This lack of self-control is not unique to India (Gray, 2014). Globally, industries have generally failed to reach sufficient degrees of self-regulation; this failure has been heavily blamed for the 2008 financial crisis. But despite these obstacles, the number and acceptance of self-regulatory organisations have steadily increased over time, which is seen as a sign of the maturing business ecosystems.

8.4 WAY FORWARD

In the complex world of gambling, the creation of a strong foundation for significant self-regulation is of utmost importance. Industry executives are faced with a dilemma: maintaining the unflinching faith of their customers requires them to carefully balance the need for government action against independent self-regulation (Sitdikova & Shilovskaya, 2016). The Rules represent the government's commitment to promoting self-regulation in the digital sphere and are evidence of the changing nature of the regulatory landscape. Nonetheless, the practical accomplishment of the regulations' goals is still dependent on resolving the gaps in the present draft law. This chapter's analysis, hinging on the "draft" nature of the legislative framework delineating the intended functions of self-regulatory organisations (SROs) for online gaming, inherently restricts the depth of its insights. The embryonic nature of the self-regulatory structure, tethered to a preliminary legislative draft, imposes limitations on the comprehensive understanding of its efficacy and practical implementation. The nascent stage of this regulatory evolution underscores the imperative of addressing inherent gaps to fortify the foundation upon which the regulatory edifice stands.

At first, distinct SROs ought to be precisely categorised according to various game genres. It is not reasonable to expect SROs to evaluate games according to vague criteria and comprehend the intricacies of every game type. It is a known truth that the prerequisites and needs for various online games vary greatly. As a result, not every type of game developer's needs can be met by a single SRO. Moreover, one representative of the online gaming community should be on the SROs. Not every kind of game can have its interests advanced by a single individual. As a result, it is necessary to change the makeup of the Board in order to include more than one of these individuals to represent the participants in various games. The majority of categories would have their demands met by the new Board, which would also make sure that the experts in each category handled the games in which they are qualified. Lastly, in developing markets, preventing potential SRO disputes is crucial. Initiatives aimed at increasing transparency can help with this. It should be mandatory for SROs to periodically release a report that includes a list of online games they evaluated for registration, those they rejected, and the reasons behind those decisions. It would provide an open record of activity and notify other SROs if a game they were considering was already rejected. This change will lessen the appeal of forum shopping and encourage the development of more consistent standards across different SROs. This cooperative and adaptable strategy, which promotes synergies between industry autonomy and governmental monitoring, can strengthen the relationship between the two organisations. As a necessary evolutionary step, co-regulation helps to maintain important public interests, including consumer protection, safety, and justice. In addition, it offers the online gaming industry a crucible for fostering both innovation and operational efficiency (Roy, 2018).

In conclusion, the complex field of online gaming requires a deliberate self-regulation strategy that involves a careful balance between sector activities and regulatory frameworks. The Rules represent official support for self-regulation, but to properly achieve their goals, a careful revision of the existing form is required. Following the introduction of SROs, an ongoing commitment to evaluation becomes essential, opening the door to the investigation of co-regulatory models that have the potential to reconcile conflicting interests and strengthen the mutually beneficial relationship between the government and business.

REFERENCES

Bansal, A. (2023, February 10). Online gaming industry braces for Information Technology Rules Amendments. *Acumen Juris*. www.acumenjuris.com/article-single.php?id=44

Bedi, M. (2023, August 19). Unveiling the online gaming commission: Examining its role and impact on state jurisdiction. *IRCCL*. www.irccl.in/post/unveiling-the-online-gaming-commission-examining-its-role-and-impact-on-state-jurisdiction.

Chaturvedi. (2023, April 8). Self-regulation: The only way ahead for online gaming sector. *Economic Times*. https://government.economictimes.indiatimes.com/blog/self-regulation-the-only-way-ahead-for-online-gaming-sector/99329631#:~:text=MeitY%20will%20designate%20three%20SRBs,the%20notified%20rules%20and%20regulations..

Draft Notification. (2023). Government of India Ministryofelectronics and Informationtechnology. www.meity.gov.in/writereaddata/files/Draft%20notification%20for%20amendment%20to%20IT%20Rules%202021%20for%20Online%20Gaming.p

Dua, T., & Dua, P. (2023, September 15). *Evolving legal framework of online skill-based and chance-based games*. Lexology. www.lexology.com/library/detail.aspx?g=b0db6475-d09a-4830-8b1e-cdff3b0dbb0b.

Edwards, B. P. (2017). "The Dark Side of Self-Regulation". *Scholarly Works*, 1117. https://scholars.law.unlv.edu/facpub/1117.

Fang ching, P. (2023, June 9). *RPC law X Web3: Gambling regulations – Don't play games of chance with the law – Fin tech – Singapore*. Mondaq. www.mondaq.com/fin-tech/1312766/rpc-law-x-web3-gambling-regulations--dont-play-games-of-chance-with-the-law.

Gawer, A. (2021, January 15). *Social media companies should self-regulate. Now*. Harvard Business Review. https://hbr.org/2021/01/social-media-companies-should-self-regulate-now.

Gray, C. H. (2014). Who pays the price?: Regulation of data tracking & online behavioural advertising. *SSRN Electronic Journal*. https://doi.org/10.2139/ssrn.2556525.

Gupta. (2022). *Impact of Regulatory Uncertainty on Ease of Doing Digital Business in India*. CUTS International. https://cuts-ccier.org/pdf/dp-impact_of_regulatory_uncertainty_on_ease_of_doing_digital_business.pdf.

Király, O. (2018, August 5). *Policy Responses to Problematic Video Game Use: A Systematic Review of Current Measures and Future Possibilities*. National Library of Medicine. www.ncbi.nlm.nih.gov/pmc/articles/PMC6426392/.

Kripalani, V., & Mathur, A. (2023, May 21). *Gaming code pushes for self-regulation*. The Hindu Business Line. www.lexology.com/library/detail.aspx?g=b0db6475-d09a-4830-8b1e-cdff3b0dbb0b.

Ministry of Electronics & IT (2023). Government notifies amendments to the information technology (Intermediary guidelines and digital media ethics code) rules, 2021 for an open, safe & trusted and accountable internet. Press Information Bureau. https://pib.gov.in/PressReleaseIframePage.aspx?PRID=1914358 ('MeitY').

Mondaq. (2023). *Chapter 6 – Simulated gambling and gambling-like activities*. Parliament of Australia. www.mondaq.com/fin-tech/1312766/rpc-law-x-web3-gambling-regulations--dont-play-games-of-chance-with-the-law

Roy, A. (2018). *National Strategy for Artificial Intelligence*. Niti Aayog. www.niti.gov.in/sites/default/files/2023-03/National-Strategy-for-Artificial-Intelligence.pdf.

Sitdikova, L., & Shilovskaya, A. (2016). The role of self-regulatory organizations (SRO) in civil legal relations. *Contemporary Problems of Social Work, 2*(1), 150–156. https://doi.org/10.2139/ssrn.2556525.

The Information Technology (Intermediary Guidelines and Digital Media Ethics Code) Rules, 2021.

United States Department of Commerce (2023). *Chapter 3: Models for self-regulation | National telecommunications and information administration.* National Telecommunication and Information Administration. https://hbr.org/2021/01/social-media-companies-should-self-regulate-now.

Vyas. (2023, September 8). Why the RBI has proposed setting-up a self regulatory organisation for fintechs. *The Indian Express*. https://indianexpress.com/article/explained/explained-economics/rbi-self-regulatory-organisation-fintechs-8929936/

Waghre, P. (2023, January 12). *First read: Draft amendments proposed to the IT rules, 2021 in relation to online gaming*. Internet Freedom Foundation. https://internetfreedom.in/draft-amendments-to-it-rules-online-gaming/.

Xiao, L. Y. (2023). Breaking ban: Belgium's ineffective gambling law regulation of video game loot boxes. *Collabra: Psychology, 9*(1). https://doi.org/10.1525/collabra.57641.

9 Challenges and Prospects

An Analysis of Fantasy Sports Regulation in India

Animesh Anand Bordoloi and Sachin Kumar

9.1 INTRODUCTION

The Fantasy Sports (hereinafter referred to as, 'FS') industry in India has witnessed significant growth over the last decade, making it a lucrative market for investors and users alike. India's remarkable expansion in the realm of FS can be directly attributed to the growth of digital infrastructure in the country, which has made it possible for anyone and everyone to participate in fantasy sports contests. According to a report, online FS in India has grown at a compound annual growth rate (CAGR) of 212%, from 2 million users in 2016 to 90 million users in December 2019 (Federation of Indian Fantasy Sports, 2020). Furthermore, the report highlights that the fantasy sports business in India has the capacity to attract foreign direct investment exceeding INR 10,000 crore in the coming years and to produce 1.5 billion online transactions by 2023 (Federation of Indian Fantasy Sports, 2020). While economic growth has set sail, it is the regulatory problem that might hinder the growth of this business. This can be attributed to the lack of a uniform regulatory framework for the operation of this industry.

While FS in India was first introduced around 2001 through the launch of ESPN Star Sports' 'Super Selector fantasy game', it was around 2015 that the sector started to witness stupendous growth (TeamG2G, 2022). Such growth, among many others, can be attributed to three major factors: growth in India's digital infrastructure, which made the internet accessible and cheap; the mushrooming of several sports leagues in India, where the Indian Premier League (IPL) played a very significant role; and the increasing penetration of online payment gateways (KPMG India, 2019).

FS can be referred to as an online game where the users create a 'fantasy team' based on a selection of players from real-life sports judged on their abilities and past performances within that sport. These fantasy teams are then pitted against each other, with the users earning points based on the performance of their selected team of players. The user with the most cumulative points is declared the winner (Das, 2018; Hazarika, 2023).

DOI: 10.1201/9781032624204-10

The participants engage in the formation of virtual teams consisting of real-life athletes, with the performance of these athletes in real sports having a direct influence on the success of the fantasy team. Points are allocated or subtracted in accordance with the actual performance of players in the real world, including various metrics like goals scored, assists, runs, wickets taken, or touchdowns thrown. The exhilaration associated with the process of forming an ideal group of individuals, engaging in tactical decision-making, and engaging in competition with acquaintances or like-minded enthusiasts has captivated the interest and fascination of a vast number of individuals (Vinfotech, 2021). While in a broader sense, this could be referred to as FS, paradoxically to such growth, there has been no clear legal definition of FS in India.

This growth story, especially that of pay-to-play styled or real-money FS, has also faced significant irk owing to its often-questioned proximity to betting and gambling. Additional instances of individuals losing money and overtly depending on such games as a window to income have led to public call out of the industry, leading to even bans in certain states (Vinfotech, 2021). The legal uncertainty and regulatory vacuum only further add to this criticism. In the following sections, we will briefly look into the history of FS in India and its existing legal framework before delving deep into the underlying sociology and societal issues that the sector produces before the regulators. This chapter will also comparatively look into whether it is prudent to use soft regulation through the centre and state for better control over the concern.

9.2 EVOLUTION OF FANTASY SPORTS IN INDIA

In the early 1950s, baseball was brought in as the first game in the realm of FS in the United States (U.S.). It was introduced as a board game named 'American Professional Baseball Association'. Later, in 1962, United States saw the introduction of FS in the realm of football through the emergence of the 'Greater Oakland Professional Pigskin Prognosticators League' (Zegura & Augustyn, 2023). Over time, the notion has broadened to encompass a range of sporting activities and has garnered significant attention with the emergence of the internet, resulting in the proliferation of Daily Fantasy Sports (hereinafter referred to as, 'DFS') platforms.

The advent of FS in India happened during the early 2000s, with cricket having the centre spot because of its popularity (TeamG2G, 2022). The FS platforms have played a pioneering role in the development and popularisation of this kind of sports engagement. Notably, these platforms have extended their offerings beyond cricket to encompass a wider range of sports, with a particular emphasis on the Indian Premier League (IPL) (Federation of Indian Fantasy Sports & Deloitte, 2022). The explosive growth of FS in India can be attributed to several factors, including its judicial clarity as a game of skill, partnerships with sports leagues, and effective marketing strategies. These factors have collectively propelled fantasy sports into the mainstream, transforming them into a popular form of entertainment and engagement for sports enthusiasts. Furthermore, the future of FS appears promising, with ongoing innovation and expansion expected to further enhance its appeal and reach.

The Indian FS industry has around 20 crore users and more than 300 platforms (Federation of Indian Fantasy Sports, 2020). It is the fastest-growing market in the world. This can be ascertained from the growth in numbers. While in 2016, the country only had ten operators, such numbers have now touched the three-digit figure (Federation of Indian Fantasy Sports, 2020). While all of this can be considered important in the context of economic growth, the fantasy sports industry has a lot of potential to grow with time, considering that it has grown substantially in the last 5 years. But herein comes the problem of the legality and regulatory vacuum for the FS industry in India.

The legal or regulatory status of FS in India varies across the states and union territories of India. There are states like Odisha, Telangana, Andhra Pradesh, and Karnataka that have banned FS and online gaming (International Comparative Legal Guides, 2023). On the other hand, states like Maharashtra, Rajasthan, Punjab, and Haryana have considered fantasy sports to be legal through the various judgements passed by the High Courts of these states (International Comparative Legal Guides, 2023).

The legal status of FS in India as of now has been regulated through the Public Gambling Act (1967), in addition to the separate regulation by different states. As per the statute, a game is conferred the status of being legal only in cases wherein the game constitutes an element of 'skill'. But the act fails to define or provide a description of what can come within the ambit of 'game of skill'. Thus, when it comes to providing clarity on this issue to the industry, it has often been the judiciary that has played a significant role rather than the legislature.

The Supreme Court has categorised FS as a 'game of skill' and 'not chance', thereby distinguishing them from gambling or betting, which are banned (Varun Gumber, 2019; Mathur & Gupta, 2020). Several judgements from multiple high courts and the Supreme Court have agreed to the idea that FS predominantly involve greater aspects of 'skill' than 'chance'. In *State of Andhra Pradesh v. K. Satyanarayana* (1968), the court laid down a two-part test to determine whether a game has a preponderance of skill or chance and if the organiser makes any profit or gain from the activity. The same standards have been used to analyse the validity of FS and their legality in India. While there is no direct judgement from the Supreme Court, a series of judgements from various High Courts and its indirect recognition of the same by the Supreme Court in *Avinash Mehrotra v. State of Rajasthan* (2022), *Gurdeep Singh Sachar v. Union of India and Ors.* (2019), and *Varun Gumber v. UT Chandigarh & Ors.* (2017) have established FS as a game of skill, taking it away from the idea of gambling.

However, more significantly, the judgements do not serve as a blanket exemption for all sorts of FS operators or DFS operators. In *Varun Gumber* (2017), legality was granted to a company called Dream 11, but the legality of other fantasy games that might differ from this operator in their structure may have been looked into on a case-by-case basis. It is difficult for the courts to move away from such an approach by creating a blanket exemption for all types of FS companies, as it would risk transgressing the thin line between interpreting and creating law. A better approach by the Supreme Court could perhaps have been to formulate guidelines as criteria within the judgements to differentiate between 'skill' and 'chance' in FS. Another corollary of this argument that has impacted FS or most new-age developments in sports is that sports, betting, and gambling in India are state subjects, while for a uniform regulation, it is the centre that has been traditionally expected for regulation. As a consequence of this, different states have treated this issue differently.

At the state level, the regulatory framework exhibits a heterogeneous assortment of diverse approaches. The measures taken by states to regulate have also been inconsistent with their classification of games that fall within the ambit of 'games of skill'. Considering the recent draft of the Rajasthan Virtual Online Sports Regulation Bill (2022), as a case study, while the draft regulatory bill is a positive measure, it does not provide definition for 'game of skill' and 'game of chance', which has been time and again provided by the various courts in their judgements. It raises significant concerns by excluding sports such as rummy and poker from the scope of regulation, which have been held to be games of skill and not chance by a judgement of the Madras High Court in the case of *All India Gaming Federation v. State of Tamil Nadu* (2023). Furthermore, the bill conspicuously lacks a proper appeal mechanism for the users in a situation wherein proper redressal is not afforded (Anand et al., 2022). Such concerns regarding inconsistencies are not specific to this bill alone. Regulatory efforts from almost all states face these issues.

The presence of this variance gives rise to apprehensions regarding the expansion of the industry in the absence of standardised regulatory supervision. The necessity for a comprehensive and standardised regulatory framework at both the federal and state levels is emphasised by the financial significance of the business, the considerable number of participants involved, and India's position as the largest market for FS. The need to strike a balance between effective regulation and the prevention of industry migration to unregulated platforms or the formation of illicit marketplaces becomes of utmost importance in influencing the future course of fantasy gaming in India.

The Union Government, in its bid to control the operators from using the lack of regulations as an opportunity to depict online gaming as a means of generating income or a viable work prospect, has also engaged strategies of soft regulation through the Advertising Standards Council of India (ASCI), a self-regulatory organisation in the Indian advertising sector, to address the issue of deceptive advertising practices adopted by fantasy gaming platforms (Advertising Standards Council of India, 2020). Moreover, NITI Aayog, a prominent policy think tank in India, in its 'Discussion Paper' titled "*Guiding Principle for Uniform National-Level Regulation of Fantasy Sports of Online Fantasy Sports Platforms in India*", not only highlighted the problems but also presented a prospective framework for regulating through the establishment of a self-regulatory entity with an autonomous supervisory board (NITI Aayog, 2021). Such initiatives are also a reflection that both the Union and the States are aware of the issues and needs surrounding the fantasy industry for its regulated growth and user protection.

9.3 IN THE BALANCE: NAVIGATING BETWEEN BAN AND REGULATION

In the global context, the jurisprudential understanding of the U.S. regulation gives a significant outlay into how India must approach these problems with FS. In addition to being the largest FS market in the world before being overtaken by India, there is considerable similarity to India vis-a-vis the federal structure of the United States that has led to diverse regulations in different states. Much like in India, the federal setup in the United States allows both the state and centre to have jurisdiction over FS (Das, 2018; Edelman, 2017). The history of the development of regulations in the United States highlights two interesting similarities with India. First, much like in India, the regulatory framework in the United States has been demand-driven, often also meaning that the regulations or laws have been reactive to situations. Second, the different stances taken by individual states, similar to India, have led to confusion in legislating FS. However, over the years, there has been extensive development in the area in the United States with an understanding of the economic benefits and potential of the sector. This led to the subsumption of the definition of FS within that of DFS, which was developed to "appeal to aggressive fantasy sports players looking for more instant gratification than traditional fantasy leagues can offer (Edelman, 2016)". To this end, the court in *Murphy v. National Collegiate Athletic Ass'n* (2018), by holding the Professional and Amateur Sports Protection Act (PAPSA), which prohibited states from authorising sports gambling, unconstitutional, paved the way for the States to legalise and regulate sports gambling (Legal Information Institute, 2006).

DFS, even today, under U.S. law, is governed as an exception to FS under the Unlawful Internet Gambling Enforcement Act of 2006 (UIGEA). Despite these developments spearheaded by the judiciary, the States have been cautious in their approach, even when they are lifting their bans and regulating this area. While post the Murphy case, around 26 states have enacted laws to regulate DFS (Shefrin, 2019), what is interesting is that they have done so by enacting their sports gambling laws, which raise questions on whether DFS is gambling or whether such games should continue to be governed by the exception under UIGEA (Edelman, 2017). These grey areas create significant issues for how DFS and its industry would cope with the consequent challenges.

The reason for the United States' regulatory history and its response to the scenarios becomes significant in trying to understand the country's response to the problems dealing with fantasy gaming, which inevitably leaves a lot for India to understand, introspect, and learn from. While the Indian courts, through a series of judgements and the use of several judicial tests, including the predominant purpose, chance test, and material element test, have identified FS as a game of skill, the larger question still remains on who and how FS should be regulated.

On the regulatory jurisdiction, after some initial uncertainty, the central government in 2022 identified the state government's mandate to regulate FS under Entry 34 (betting and gambling) of the Constitution (The Constitution of India, 1950).

While both of these positions have led to significant clarity on the issue, it is the approach after these developments that needs attention. Most states have so far taken three approaches to dealing with the issue of fantasy sports (Federation of Indian Fantasy Sports & Deloitte, 2022):

A. A complete ban on FS has been adopted by states like Odisha, Assam, and Telangana (Chandra, 2021; Sharma, 2020).

B. Developing a regulatory framework, which has been enacted by states such as Sikkim, Meghalaya, Rajasthan, and Nagaland (Sharma, 2020).
C. No clarity or regulatory framework – almost 21 out of 28 states have no regulatory framework (Hazarika, 2023). Although they allow the OFSPs to operate, the lack of structure leads to regulatory problems and scepticism among investors.

While the debate around bans or regulations has taken much attention, it is the uncertainty with states that has given the OFSPs freedom to play the game with no rules. Moreover, while the court has identified FS as a game of skill, the legal difficulties highlighted with DFS, considering its specific nature in the United States, also reflect that legal questions regarding its validity might be an issue in India as well. This also calls for clarity on the regulatory jurisdiction for all such matters so that rules and guidelines on the same can be established to benefit all relevant stakeholders. In between the questions of who should govern the area of FS or how it is to be governed, we think that perhaps it is first essential to establish the importance of this requirement.

9.4 THE NECESSITY TO REGULATE

There have been studies in India that have looked into aspects like age, income groups, and geographical locations of users in various FS, including DFS (Hazarika, 2023). They have shown that in the age category, it is the group between 25 and 34 years that forms the largest consumers of FS, accounting around 40% of the consumer base, followed by those aged between 18 and 24 years, who form around 35% of the consumers, and people above 35 years fill in the remaining 25% of the consumer share. The same study also highlighted that Tier 2 and Tier 3 cities have a larger user base than Tier 1 cities, edging the latter by 20% (Federation of Indian Fantasy Sports & Deloitte, 2022). When it comes to questions of gender, while it has traditionally been a male-dominated area, women's participation is now growing, with them forming around 30% of the present user base (Federation of Indian Fantasy Sports & Deloitte, 2022). Another exploratory research-based study (Sondhi, n.d.), that focused specifically on Indian consumers who play FS based solely on cricket, looked into the same age groups but from the perspective of understanding their motivation for participation. They divided the user base into three categories (Hazarika, 2023):

(a) **Entertainment-centric:** those who play FS for fun and entertainment.
(b) **Game-centric:** those who play FS in the game they love or watch and do it to keep their connection to the sport.
(c) **Control-centric:** those who get the illusion of control over their team and enjoy the process of structuring a team with strategic ideas to tackle the odds of winning.

The entertainment-centric groups are aged between 26 and 35 years, while control seekers and game-centric players are primarily students aged between 18 and

25 years. It also interestingly looked into the income levels of the users to find that almost 90% of the users in its research had an annual income less than Rupees 5 lakh (Hazarika, 2023). The income levels most attached to the game's users call for attention to better understand if the prize money involved is a significant driver for the user. A KPMG report highlights that the lowest income groups, which in these studies were the ones below 5 lakhs, spend the most amount of time, invest the most amount of money, and see fantasy sports as a medium for earning significant amounts of money, which is a cause for concern (KPMG India, 2019). If we consider the different studies, it is interesting to also note that the highest user base, which is aged between 18 and 25 years, would mostly be students or youths from Tier 2 or Tier 3 cities who may also see FS as an opportunity to earn money, thereby becoming financially vulnerable (KPMG India, 2019). Circumstantially, it is significant to analyse the reason behind user participation to understand the underlying issues and consequently address them in the regulations. The need to regulate is necessitated not only for uniformity in regulating the game for better growth and revenue but also because of the vulnerability users find themselves in owing to the lack of a formal structure. Some of these concerns will be discussed in an attempt to understand how any subsequent regulation or intervention can be beneficial in resolving them.

9.4.1 Financial Risk and Addiction

Various reports and news in India have already pointed out the problems that exist because of FS, especially DFS. Many lower-income individuals or households have been forced into significant and often unpayable debts due to losses in such games, often invested in the hope of earning a large lump sum at once (Evans, 2023). This is also aggravated by the lure of significant prize money that such FS companies promise in their advertisements. While the ASCI has more recently become active in calling out and adding guidelines by operators for the inclusion of financial risk and addiction, the reality remains that such warnings have had little to no influence on user patterns. To further this point, the ASCI also mandates that companies or operators should not depict individuals under the age of 18 engaged in playing this game as protection against their use; however, many of the cases of addiction have involved individuals under 18 years (Tiwari, 2023).

Another very crucial part of the guidelines that must be strictly adhered to by the companies is that they point out the 'element of financial risk and the risk of addiction'. This reflects the government's recognition of the negative side of such games. While studies and operators themselves have tried to distinguish FS from direct allegations of addiction, the Indian government has recognised the adverse effects of online gaming (Hazarika, 2023). Addiction and financial risks, much like gambling, can be seen as a combined issue rather than looking at them as individually. States like Tamil Nadu have also used issues like addiction and financial risks, often leading to social problems like suicide, as reasons to ban FS (Nagaraj & Chandran, 2022). While many studies, often backed by judgements in support of FS, have argued against such concerns being related to games of skill, it is essential to recognise the sociological and societal impact of such instances (Federation of Indian Fantasy Sports & Deloitte, 2022). This becomes even more essential while considering DFS, which is more often linked to concerns relating to financial risk and the instant monetary lure.

DFS, unlike traditional FS, which take place over a sporting season, takes place daily, where a player would pay to participate in the game and have a chance at winning a significant prize for the match on a particular day (Lindholm, 2021). DFS provides operators with the opportunity to bring in more cash into the FS with a higher frequency of games. But this also increases the factors of chance and luck, bringing it closer to gambling (Das, 2018, 2021). In India, the growth of DFS shifted around the same time the industry saw its growth in the United States (Chanchani, 2019). However, both jurisdictions have followed a different regulatory course. While in India neither the regulators nor the judiciary have distinguished between match-long, day-long, or season-long FS as factors relevant for determining legality (Kamath et al., 2021), in the United States, the New York (NY) Appellate Court in *White v. Cuomo* (2020) ruled that DFS was akin to gambling. Although other courts in the United States have also had judgements to the contrary, the position in NY is a significant one that highlights the need to distinguish the different types of FS in India for legal clarity and to avoid sociological catastrophe.

9.4.2 Consumer Issues

In addition to the aspects of financial risks associated with FS, there have been significant concerns relating to the resolution of user complaints against the operators. Traditional gambling has a history of being operated by fly-by-night operators, which is also sometimes seen in the case of DFS (Hazarika, 2023). While the boom in the Indian market has ensured that operators have not yet faced issues with payment of prize money because of liquidity in cash, such concerns have been present in more mature markets like the United States. Many FS startups and DFS operators have had claims of default in payments in the United States which has called for scrutiny and regulations to protect the users (Edelman, 2017).

In this regard, the NITI Aayog's suggestion to register all such operators may be the first of the many reforms necessary for consumer protection, as these would ensure better compliance (NITI Aayog, 2021). Future regulations can also focus on learning from the financial markets to ensure that all such companies have a minimum liquidity obligation in a separate bank account. Such obligations can ensure that users are paid, thereby reducing instances of defaults on prize money by the operators.

Another issue with such consumer issues would be that the varying state regulations for FS may lead to varying degrees of fairness and transparency for the consumer. This in turn leads to varying degrees of rights and remedies for the consumer, something that is not only complex but also unheard of within the judicial setup. In this situation, while NITI Aayog's suggestion of creating a self-regulatory body to ensure adherence to uniform guidelines, principles, and best practices seems like the right course of action, the implementation is the challenging part (NITI Aayog, 2021).

Such registration with the requirements of strict documentation and compliance will potentially prevent fly-by-night operators from reducing the risks of consumers losing out on money and transparency (Hazarika, 2023). One potential solution for relevant stakeholders would be to ensure compliance by following the already existing consumer laws in India. A government-supported self-regulatory body can have the power and be obligated to function within the realm of consumer laws, leaving the adjudicatory powers in cases of dispute to the courts.

9.4.3 Contracts with Users

An issue also highlighted by NITI Aayog in its suggestions was the protection and prevention of users under 18 years from contesting in pay-to-play formats of FS (NITI Aayog, 2021). This issue of player participation below the age of 18 is perhaps more complex than one would imagine. Contracts with users are essential for all remedies, rights, and claims to prizes that the operators offer. Combining this with the legal age for contracts under Indian laws raises issues about whether individuals under the age of 18 would be given any rights at all. This may be the easier question to answer, with the answer being no. However, from a practical aspect, it is difficult to ascertain the age of the user as they can use different identification proofs to open an account. While many studies have suggested the use of government ID cards or driver's licences as requisite requirements for opening an account (Edelman, 2017), we would suggest the use of technology to make this process more stringent. Today, many mobile applications use face recognition or other such technologies to ascertain that the person whose ID is upheld is the same as the one using it. This can be a positive deterrent to prevent the misuse of FS applications. Furthermore, such an additional layer will also ascertain that if anyone aged below 18 years uses somebody older to open an account, the liability in case of any unforeseen event would lie on the users who try to bypass the regulations or law. These steps can be made mandatory through either regulations or through soft regulations, as has been the trend so far in India.

9.4.4 Data Protection and Privacy Concerns

Another correlated issue with consumers and their protection is that of data protection and cyber security. OFSPs have significant data available to them, beginning with bank account details, PAN card details (My11Circle, n.d.) demographic data (MPL, n.d.), and even the gender of the users. With already increasing cases of scams, sharing such information with operators who are not directly regulated under any uniform legislation also creates triggers for hostile party compromises through fraudulent engagements (Sinha, 2023). While many companies have guidelines for 'do's and don'ts' for their users, the burden of keeping the accounts secure from phishing or third-party interventions almost entirely lies with the user (Edelman, 2017). Concerns relating to a lack of regulations can perhaps also be connected to other underlying long-term concerns about fantasy sports being used as a tool for money laundering (Risacher & Valenti, 2015). Fortunately, such issues have not gone unnoticed. The Ministry of Electronics and Information Technology (MeitY) has come up with rules requiring OFSPs to mandatorily affiliate with self-regulatory bodies and comply with mandatory KYC (know your customer) measures to tackle the incidence of fraud. The rules are also intended to provide grievance redressal mechanisms, policies for withdrawals, refunds of deposits, and the determination and distribution of winnings. However, the implementation of such rules is still under way, with the ministry now working on proposals for identifying and appointing self-regulatory bodies that can take on the mantle of implementing these steps (Ministry of Electronics and Information Technology, 2023).

Another additional issue relating to data that has received less attention is access to player statistics and match events, which can be crucial in determining the behaviour of users (Gautam & Eshani, 2021). Such availability of data is crucial in developing the games in ways that lead to more user participation through more registration and increased time spent. This issue of data privacy and protection is significantly related to addiction issues, and the OFSPs target users will also be the ones who are most vulnerable to playing and paying more (Gautam & Eshani, 2021). In this regard, the lack of a central privacy law also harms Indian users.

In countries like the United States, there have also been concerns about the use of such data by people with access to benefit from it. In the United States, such instances have been found with employees of the OFSPs who are also users of the platforms and have access to all the data necessary for them to have an advantage, as seen as being akin to 'Insider Trading' (Edelman et al., 2022). A scandal of this nature happened in 2015 with the U.S. company DraftKings, where an employee used company data to place bets on rival companies and won a $350,000 prize (Drape & Williams, 2015). This led to many states passing legislation preventing such company employees from engaging in fantasy sports (Edelman et al., 2022). Notably, not much attention has been put into this in India, thereby leading to the absence of any such regulation or guideline for future protection against such instances.

9.5 STRATEGIES FOR THE FUTURE AHEAD

The FS industry has already contributed a cumulative GST of INR 2800 crore between 2018 and 2022. Till 2027, this cumulative figure is expected to rise to 17,500 crores (Federation of Indian Fantasy Sports & Deloitte, 2022). With such numbers expected to rise every year, it is reasonable to expect the government to regulate the industry to formalise benefits and eliminate potential bottlenecks. While bodies such as the Federation of Indian Fantasy Sports (FIFS), the E-Gaming Federation (EGF), and the All India Gaming Federation (AIGF) have currently taken the mantle to self-regulate by ensuring compliance and addressing consumer issues, the measures of such protection mostly vary. Uniformity in such cases will not only benefit the industry through certainty and investment but will also ensure greater protection for the users. These first steps would be important as fundamental blocks for addressing sensitive issues with the users (Federation of Indian Fantasy Sports & Deloitte, 2022).

Such uniform regulations establish a single industry regulatory body that can oversee all issues. Many, including the NITI Aayog, have suggested a self-regulatory body that can be governed by an independent oversight board consisting of persons with considerable experience in governance, law, and administrative issues (NITI Aayog, 2021). While scholars have been cautious to directly support a single regulatory administration, suspecting large players undermining the role of other players in the board and infighting (Hazarika, 2023), we would argue that with adequate government intervention through checks and balance, such issues could be subsided. Any such regulatory body will be dependent on the memberships of OFSPs, many of whom will inevitably have varying influence over the body. But as has been the case with other sports too, where the member states have varying voting power and influence, it is not far-fetched to expect a self-regulatory organisation backed by the government to navigate such bottlenecks through innovative approaches.

While the question of who regulates is a significant one, the addressing of concerns relating to governance must start from two other significant axes. The first concern that must be addressed is to have a clear and predictable definition of FS. Such definitions of FS must also clearly distinguish them from any other online games, with significant weight given to the distinction between free-to-play and pay-to-play games. By considering the preexisting judicial precedents, any such legislation, rule, or regulation must be suggested with clearly defined criteria of elements that could help determine the minimum amount of skill necessary to meet the burden of a legal game of skill. In addition to such precedents, there must also be standardised areas as guidelines that the regulators should necessarily focus on to decrease the element of chance in the outcome of the game. This can be done by using more real-life scenarios, player performance, statistics, and data from past matches. Such regulations must also ensure that clarity is brought to the definition and legal position of DFS in India.

The second concern, that of jurisdiction and control, has been the primary bottleneck for creating a uniform framework for states and/or centre. As discussed earlier, while both gambling and sports are state subjects, the central government has been taking active steps through the Ministry of Electronics and Information Technology ('MeitY'), where it released 'matters related to online gaming' and the draft amendments to the Information Technology (Intermediary Guidelines and Digital Media Ethics Code) Rules, 2021 ('**Intermediary Rules**') to regulate this sector (Ministry of Electronics and Information Technology, 2023). Any future attempt to directly regulate by the centre must legally be done with the consultations of the states, as the onus of implementation would ultimately lie with them. In this case, NITI Aayog's suggestion to register the organisations/platforms as members can be crucial (Hazarika, 2023), as this will allow them to be centrally regulated while the states would have the power to determine the eligibility of whether to allow a particular sport or platform or not. In such a two-tier structure, the self-regulatory organisation ('SRO') will play the role of addressing issues relating to grievance redressal, transparency, and verification of users and platforms, while the states will have the licensing power. The SROs can also be crucial in increasing public awareness about responsible gaming and financial risks through promotional educational campaigns. Such authorities can also simultaneously work with other associations like the ASCI, which have already been working on these areas to regulate advertising.

An unregulated or poorly self-regulated sector gives too much power to the operators to work with. In such a scenario, it is the user who loses out. Considering the large-scale impact of participation in the pay-to-play section of these games, including potential deaths, addiction, and bankruptcy, the threat must be looked at more seriously than the present approach. Necessary steps are essential to establishing a framework for potential and present users.

There are many other advanced issues that would need addressing once the fundamental problems with the regulation of FS are addressed in India. In many jurisdictions, there have been concerns relating to ownership stakes in fantasy league companies by professional sports owners owing to their proximity to the players and their fear of influence on them. However, these arc discussions that can only be held once the fundamentals are clarified.

Indian legislators must realise that the continued success of FS sectors has traditionally been dependent on the integrity of the game and the accountability of operators. The key to having such a transparent and successful structure would heavily depend on the state's appreciation for soft or light touch regulations and their actions in creating governing laws, including for the grant of licences. With access to easy money, any future law must be drafted keeping in mind the lure for money that the users would be attached to. Another correlated issue that the drafters must be conscious of is that the same attachment to money will keep driving illegal operators to scam users. Only when issues like these are taken into consideration can the regulatory ecosystem provide enough confidence to potential users and grow the industry.

REFERENCES

Advertising Standards Council of India. (2020, November 24). Game's Up for Misleading Gaming Ads-Says ASCI [Press Release]. www.ascionline.in/wp-content/uploads/2022/09/press-release-gaming-guidelines.pdf

All India Gaming Federation v. State of Tamil Nadu, W.P. No. 13203 of 2023. www.verdictum.in/pdf_upload/all-india-gaming-federation-1559550.pdf

Anand, R., Jain, C., & Agrawal, S. (2022, June 8). An Insight into Proposed Regulatory Regime on Virtual Online Sports in Rajasthan. *BarandBench.* www.barandbench.com/law-firms/view-point/an-insight-into-proposed-regulatory-regime-on-virtual-online-sports-in-rajasthan

Avinash Mehrotra v. State of Rajasthan SLP (C) 18478/2022 (SC).

Chanchani, M. (2019, March 24). The rise & rise of Dream11 and fantasy sports gaming in India. *The Times of India.* http://timesofindia.indiatimes.com/articleshow/68543816.cms?utm_source=contentofnterest&utm_medium=text&utm_campaign=cppst

Chandra, S. (2021, November 13). The Legality of Online Fantasy Sports in India. *Bn'W.* https://bnwjournal.com/2021/11/13/the-legality-of-online-fantasy-sports-in-india/#:~:text=While%20some%20states%20like%20Andhra%20Pradesh%2C%20Assam%2C%20Sikkim%2C,is%20currently%20no%20central%20legislation%20on%20the%20same

Das, M. (2018). International Regulation of Fantasy Sports: Comparative Legal Analysis of US, Australian and Asian Laws. *UNLV Gaming Law Journal*, 8(2), 93–120. https://scholars.law.unlv.edu/cgi/viewcontent.cgi?article=1133&context=glj

Das, M. (2021). Fantasy Sports and Gambling Regulation in the Asia-Pacific. *The International Sports Law Journal*, 21(3), 166–179. https://doi.org/10.1007/s40318-021-00198-8

Draft of Rajasthan Virtual Online Sports Regulation Bill, 2022. https://finance.rajasthan.gov.in/PDFDOCS/REVENUE/10746.pdf

Drape, J., & Williams, J. (2015, October 5). Scandals erupts in unregulated world of fantasy sports. *The New York Times.* www.nytimes.com/2015/10/06/sports/fanduel-draftkings-fantasy-employees-bet-rivals.html?ref=sports

Edelman, M. (2016). Navigating the Legal Risks of Daily Fantasy Sports: A Detailed Primer in Federal and State Gambling Law, 2016. *University of Illinois Law Review*, 117, 127–29. http://illinoislawreview.org/wp-content/ilr-content/articles/2016/1/Edelman.pdf

Edelman, M. (2017). Regulating Fantasy Sports: A Practical Guide to State Gambling Laws, and a Proposed Framework for Future State Legislation. *Indiana Law Journal*, 92(2), Article 6. www.repository.law.indiana.edu/ilj/vol92/iss2/6

Edelman, M., Holden, J.T., & Wandt, A.S. (2022). U.S. Fantasy Sports Law: Fifteen Years after UIGEA. *OHIO State Law Journal*, 83(1). https://moritzlaw.osu.edu/sites/default/files/2022-06/14.EdelmanHoldenWandt_v83-1_pp117-156.pdf

Evans, R. (2023, July 24). The Sinister Side to India's Fantasy Gaming Craze. *The Week*. https://theweek.com/news/world-news/961733/the-sinister-side-to-indias-fantasy-gaming-craze

Fantasy Sports. (2021, June). Six ways fantasy sports make users more intelligent. *Vinfotech*. https://blog.vinfotech.com/six-ways-fantasy-sports-make-users-more-intelligent

Federation of Indian Fantasy Sports. (2020, July). *The Business of Fantasy Sports*. https://fifs.in/wp-content/uploads/2020/07/Business-of-fantasy-sports_Final.pdf

Federation of Indian Fantasy Sports & Deloitte. (2022, February). *Fantasy Sports: Creating a Virtuous Cycle of Sports Development*. www2.deloitte.com/content/dam/Deloitte/in/Documents/technology-media-telecommunications/in-tmt-fantasy-sports-industry-report-noexp.pdf

Gautam, K., & Eshani, V. (2021, August). Regulation of Fantasy Sports Platforms in India. *The Dialogue*. https://thedialogue.co/wp-content/uploads/2021/08/Report_Fantasy-Sports-Final.pdf

Gurdeep Singh Sachar v. Union of India, (2019) 75 GST 258 Bombay.

Hazarika, A. (2023). Regulating a Fantasy for a Billion: Playing on a Smartphone in India. *UNLV Gaming Research & Review Journal*, 27, Paper 1. https://digitalscholarship.unlv.edu/cgi/viewcontent.cgi?article=1475&context=grrj

International Comparative Legal Guides. (2023, November). *Gambling Laws and Regulations Report 2024 India*. https://iclg.com/practice-areas/gambling-laws-and-regulations/india

Kamath, N., Shrivastava, A., & Shekar, R.S. (2021). Emerging from the Shadows: The Evolving Legal Treatment of Fantasy Sports in India. *International Sports Law Journal*, 21, 188–202. https://doi.org/10.1007/s40318-021-00190-2

KPMG India. (2019, March). *The Evolving Landscape of Sports Gaming in India*. https://assets.kpmg.com/content/dam/kpmg/in/pdf/2019/03/online-gaming-india-fantasy-sports.pdf

Legal Information Institute. (2006, October 13). 31 U.S. Code Subchapter IV – PROHIBITION ON FUNDING OF UNLAWFUL INTERNET GAMBLING. *US Code*. www.law.cornell.edu/uscode/text/31/5361

Lindholm, J. (2021). A Global Take on Legal Aspects of Fantasy Sports. *The International Sports Law Journal*, 21, 119–120. https://link.springer.com/article/10.1007/s40318-021-00199-7

Mathur, U., & Gupta, U. (2020). Game of Skill vs. Game of Chance: The Legal Dimensions of Online Games with special reference to Dream11, *Shimla Law Review*, 3, 115. www.hpnlu.ac.in/PDF/06c2d85d-f45b-45df-9461-63e2643e2f4f.pdf

Ministry of Electronics and Information Technology. (2023, April 6). *Draft Notification for Amendment to IT Rules 2021 for Online Gaming*. www.meity.gov.in/writereaddata/files/Draft%20notification%20for%20amendment%20to%20IT%20Rules%202021%20for%20Online%20Gaming.pdf

MPL. (n.d.). *Privacy Policy*. https://about.mpl.live/privacy/

Murphy v. NCAA, 138 S.Ct. 1461 (2018).

My11Circle. (n.d.). *Privacy Policy*. www.my11circle.com/privacy-policy.html

Nagaraj, A., & Chandran, R. (2022, December 13). While Centre drafts a law, Tamil Nadu has banned real-money online games to curb gambling addiction. *Scroll.in*. https://scroll.in/article/1039362/while-centre-drafts-a-law-tamil-nadu-has-banned-real-money-online-games-to-curb-gambling-addiction

NITI Aayog. (2021). *Guiding Principle for the Uniform National-Level Regulation of Online Fantasy Sports Platforms in India-Draft for Discussion*. www.niti.gov.in/sites/default/files/2020-12/FantasySports_DraftForCOmments.pdf

Risacher, B.J., & Valenti, J.A. (2015, October 29). Is Money Being Laundered Through Your Financial Institution Using Daily Fantasy Sports Sites?. *K&L Gates Hube*. www.klgates.com/Is-Money-Being-Laundered-Through-Your-Financial-Institution-Using-Daily-Fantasy-Sports-Sites-10-29-2015

Sharma, S. (2020, December 03). The Legality of Fantasy Sports in India. *BarandBench*. www.barandbench.com/apprentice-lawyer/the-legality-of-fantasy-sports#:~:text=The%20states%20of%20Sikkim%2C%20West%20Bengal%2C%20Goa%20and,excluded%20the%20games%20of%20skill%20from%20any%20regulations

Shefrin, S. (2019, May 17). Is Playing on DraftKings Legal? *LINEUPS*. www.lineups.com/betting/is-draftkings-legal/

Sinha, J. (2023, August 28). 200% spike in cyber fraud cases this year, recovery, arrest low: Data. *The Indian EXPRESS*. https://indianexpress.com/article/cities/delhi/rise-in-cyber-fraud-cases-data-on-cyber-frads-online-frauds-cyber-scams-2023-types-of-cyber-fraud-8912336/

Sondhi, N. (n.d.). *Understanding the Fantasy Cricket player: An Emerging Market Perspective*. https://archives.marketing-trends-congress.com/2019/pages/PDF/34.pdf

State of Andhra Pradesh v. K. Satyanarayana, Supreme Court of India, 1968 AIR 825.

TeamG2G. (2022, July 20). Evolution of fantasy sports in India – a short timeline. *G2G News*. https://g2g.news/fantasy-sports/evolution-of-fantasy-sports-in-india-a-short-timeline/

The Constitution of India, 1950, Entry 34.

Tiwari, A.K. (2023, July 20). In India, fantasy gaming is causing addiction and financial ruin. *ALJAZEERA*. www.aljazeera.com/economy/2023/7/20/in-india-fantasy-gaming-is-causing-addiction-and-financial-ruin#:~:text=Lack%20of%20regulation%20and%20massive,apps%20have%20raised%20addiction%20concerns.&text=Within%20a%20month%20of%20using,sent%20him%20for%20his%20tuition

Varun Gumber v. Union of India, SLP (Crl.) No. 009295 of 2019.

Varun Gumber v. UT, Chandigarh, 2017 SCC OnLine P&H 5372.

White v. Cuomo, 181 A.D.3d 76 (N.Y. App. Div. 2020).

Zegura, N., & Augustyn, A. (2023, August 2). Fantasy sport. *Encyclopedia Britannica*. www.britannica.com/sports/fantasy-sport

10 Online Gambling through an Anti-Money Laundering Perspective

A Cross-Jurisdictional Analysis

Anuj Berry, Sourabh Rath, Megha Janakiraman, and Agniva Chakrabarti

10.1 INTRODUCTION

The COVID-19 pandemic brought in unprecedented and multifaceted challenges, encompassing adverse impacts on public health, social well-being (Rasul & Nepal, 2021), and global economies (Mckinsey & Co., 2022). The repercussions of the pandemic have not been uniform across all industries. At the onset of the crisis, financial markets experienced a significant downturn. However, noteworthy is the resilience and relative stability of the gaming (including online gambling) and eSports sector, which emerged as one of the sectors least affected by the initial market decline (López-Cabarcos, Ribeiro-Soriano & Pineiro-Chousa, 2020).

The sector's evolution has resulted in a complex environment in which it operates. This has led to an increasing difficulty in regulating the sector as well as exposing it to the possibility of criminal exploitation. This regulatory void in online gambling has several consequences: the most concerning being the increased risk of money laundering (Financial Action Task Force, 2009). Online gambling platforms often handle digital currencies and electronic payment methods, which can provide a level of anonymity not easily achievable in brick-and-mortar casinos. Additionally, the absence of robust anti-money laundering ("**AML**") and know-your-customer ("**KYC**") procedures on many online gambling platforms makes it easier for individuals with illicit funds to participate without raising suspicion (Financial Action Task Force, 2009).

Laws have traditionally favoured betting on activities that rely on skill while prohibiting wagering on games of chance (*R.M.D Chamarbaugwalla v. Union of India*, 1957). Betting, involving the exchange of money or property, can occur either in person or through virtual channels (Wardle, 2021). The advent of the internet has ushered in a new era of gambling, creating a worldwide market for activities on which individuals can legally place bets within their respective jurisdictions. The ease of

DOI: 10.1201/9781032624204-11

access to gambling platforms with a global presence has made gaming industry regulation a significant concern. Gaming hosts have become interconnected networks, thanks to advances in technology and worldwide finance systems.

The distinction between "skill" and "chance" remains a pivotal factor in determining the legality of gaming enterprises in India. The differential treatment accorded to games of skill and games of chance, with the former permitted and the latter prohibited, has been a historic feature of Indian law (*K R Lakshmanan v. State of Tamil Nadu*, 1996). Drawing upon numerous judicial rulings (*State of A.P. v. K. Satyanarayana*, 1968) and the enactment of state laws across a substantial portion of Indian states, it is discernible that the category of skill gaming in India, particularly real money games, encompasses card games, fantasy sports, horse racing, and eSports. This classification serves as a foundational understanding within the Indian gaming regulatory landscape, recognizing these specific activities as falling within the purview of skill-based gaming.

The determination of the legality of gaming enterprises in India hinges significantly on the distinction between "skill" and "chance." This differential treatment, where games of skill are permitted while games of chance are prohibited, has deep historical roots in Indian law (*K R Lakshmanan v. State of Tamil Nadu*, 1996). Examining various judicial decisions, such as the one in *State of A.P. v. K. Satyanarayana* (1968), and the enactment of state laws across a considerable number of Indian states, it becomes evident that skill gaming in India, particularly in the realm of real money games, encompasses activities like card games, fantasy sports, horse racing, and eSports. This categorization forms a fundamental basis within the regulatory framework of Indian gaming, acknowledging these specific activities as falling under the domain of skill-based gaming.

10.2 THE NON-UNIFORMITY OF GAMBLING LEGISLATIONS ACROSS THE NATION

The Public Gambling Act, 1867 has been adopted by several states, including Uttar Pradesh, Madhya Pradesh, and Punjab & Haryana, with some states making their territory-specific amendments to it, too. Other states have enacted their own legislation to regulate gaming/gambling activities within their territories. Most of these are broadly modelled on the Public Gambling Act, albeit with suitable modifications. States with modern gambling legislations and an online gaming licence regime include Sikkim (Sikkim Online Gaming Regulation Act, 2008), Nagaland (Nagaland Prohibition of Gambling and Promotion and Regulation of Online Games of Skill Act, 2015), and Meghalaya (The Meghalaya Regulation of Gaming Act, 2021). In Sikkim and Meghalaya, online gaming (including online gambling) and sports games suffer the limitation that they can only be accessed in those states. In addition, Nagaland has a licence system for solely internet-based skill games, as well as a stringent gambling ban.

All real money online gaming operations, including skill gaming, are illegal in the states of Telangana and Andhra Pradesh (Minhaz, 2023). Legal challenges to these prohibitions have arisen in Karnataka and Tamil Nadu, leading to High Court rulings deeming them unlawful (Plumber, 2022). Meanwhile, certain states are in the process of formulating their gambling regulations, with particular focus on aspects related to fantasy sports and eSports (Vashisht, 2022). Additionally, variations in the interpretation of "game of skill" and "game of chance" among different states have introduced further disparities in the regulatory landscape. Therefore, due to the absence of explicit laws prohibiting online gambling in India, except for Telangana and Andhra Pradesh, and the allowance for games of skill, numerous gambling websites have been operating within the bounds of the law in India.

Online gaming institutions can be used to siphon money across the borders, even after appropriate checks and balances in place. Such institutions collect vast sums from the general public (the users/players). A common modus operandi used for siphoning money abroad is to route these funds through multiple bank accounts and finally remit it out of India by mis-declaring the purpose of remittances against import of services/goods (Thathoo, 2023). In fact, seizures made during searches include incriminating documents and electronic devices establishing foreign outward remittances of thousands of crores collected from public through gaming websites (Hindu BusinessLine, 2023). As such, there is a significant risk of money laundering in the operation of these gaming institutions.

10.3 THE LEGAL LANDSCAPE IN INDIA

Gaming websites hosted in India are subject to reporting obligations under the Prevention of Money Laundering Act, 2002 ("**PMLA**") and the Prevention of Money Laundering (Maintenance of Records) Rules, 2005 ("**PMLA Rules**"). Section 2 (wa) read with Section 2 (sa) of the PMLA stipulates that an entity carrying out "*activities associated with casino*" would be a "reporting entity" for the purpose of the statute. Section 12 of the PMLA places an obligation on reporting entities to maintain comprehensive records encompassing all transactions and documents pertinent to client identities. These records must be furnished within stipulated timeframes to the Director of the Financial Intelligence Unit. In tandem with this, the PMLA Rules impose substantial responsibilities on reporting entities. These responsibilities encompass the rigorous execution of customer due diligence during client onboarding and the maintenance of transaction records that meet specific criteria, including those considered "suspicious" or exceeding predetermined monetary thresholds.

Interestingly, the PMLA does not classify an operator offering games of skill as a "*reporting entity*" and hence obligations under the PMLA currently do not apply to a game of skill operator, unless the operators allow for transactions involving digital assets or instruments (as per Ministry of Finance Notification F. No. P-12011/12/2022-ES Cell-DOR dated 7 March 2023, "**Ministry of Finance Notification**").

Laws governing online gaming are undergoing a transformation. The Ministry of Electronics and Information Technology ("**MeitY**") notified the Information Technology (Intermediary Guidelines and Digital Media Ethics Code) Amendment Rules, 2023 ("**2023 Amendment**") to amend the Information Technology (Intermediary Guidelines and Digital Media Ethics Code) Rules, 2021 ("**Intermediary Guidelines Rules, 2021**"). The amendment defines Online Gaming Intermediary ("**OGI**") under Rule 2 (1) (qb) as "*any intermediary that enables the users of its computer resource to access one or more online games.*"

In addition to the existing compliance obligations applicable to intermediaries as stipulated in Rule 3, the 2023 Amendment introduces supplementary compliance requirements, particularly targeting OGIs who facilitate access to Permissible Online Real Money games. The term "Permissible Online Real Money games" is defined in Rule 2 (1) (qf) as "*online real money games that have undergone verification by a self-regulatory body*" ("**SRB**") (Information Technology (Intermediary Guidelines and Digital Media Ethics Code) Amendment Rules, 2023), as designated by the MeitY. It is a prerequisite that any online real money game must receive verification from the SRB before it can be offered to the public. To maintain the credibility of these SRBs, the rules stipulate that the board of these bodies must include experts from various fields, including online gaming, psychology, information technology, education, and policymakers. Additionally, beyond just enhancing credibility, these requirements empower the members of these SRBs to make independent decisions. This measure is put in place to prevent companies and intermediaries in the online gaming industry from exerting undue influence or control over these regulatory bodies.

Therefore, it becomes essential for online gaming intermediaries to have a clear understanding of what falls within the scope of the term "wagering." This understanding is crucial to ensure that the online games they offer do not fall under this category. Furthermore, online gaming intermediaries are obligated to approach these SRBs only if their games involve the deposit of money.

Furthermore, it is imperative for the OGI to meet the KYC requirement as per the norms set by the Reserve Bank of India. This requirement mandates that the user's identity be verified before accepting deposits from them, in accordance with Rule 4 (12). The KYC procedures play a crucial role in ensuring transparency and accountability within the online gaming industry. By acting as a safeguard against potentially fraudulent activities and money laundering attempts (Ministry of Electronics & IT Government of India, 2023), these procedures help maintain the integrity of financial transactions conducted on OGI platforms. By diligently verifying the identity of users and collecting pertinent information, OGIs can effectively mitigate risks and protect the interests of all stakeholders involved.

10.4 THE CHALLENGES IN THE APPARATUS DEALING WITH MONEY LAUNDERING THROUGH ONLINE GAMBLING INTERMEDIARIES

Gambling presents itself as an ideal instrument for facilitating money laundering, primarily for three compelling reasons:

1. **Significant Transaction Volume and Cash Flows:** Gambling activities involve a substantial volume of financial transactions and cash exchanges, which serve as essential components for concealing illicit money laundering operations (Quirk, 1996).
2. **Absence of Physical Infrastructure:** Unlike industries dealing with physical goods, the realm of gambling lacks tangible products, thereby significantly complicating the tracking and differentiation between actual and virtual monetary turnover.

3. **Tax-Free Gambling Winnings in Many Jurisdictions:** In many jurisdictions such as Canada and Germany, gambling winnings are exempt from taxation. This aspect enhances the appeal of gambling as a vehicle for money laundering, as it not only reduces the risk of detection but also offers the flexibility to manipulate revenue streams upward (for money laundering purposes) or downward (for tax evasion) (Hock, Button, Shepherd, & Gilmour, 2023).

Illustratively, the modus operandi of an online gambling platform used to launder money is as follows: Consider a drug dealer earning 10,000 INR in cash from his customers and converting it into 100 vouchers (of 100 INR each). The vouchers are then channelized through an online gambling account. The launderer then gambles/plays a round in the game and loses 500 INR. However, the rest of the 9,500 INR in his online gambling account he transfers to the bank account, thus completes the laundering operation (Fiedler, 2013).

Furthermore, since the gambling operators are incorporated offshore and unregulated, the operator is not bound to disclose information with regulatory authorities. Additionally, these gambling websites and payment processors exist for a limited period, thus making them virtually untraceable (Fiedler, 2013).

Illustratively, in the case of Beijing T Power, Chinese nationals operating in India took advantage of the loopholes in online casinos regulations. They floated multiple gambling websites. Most of them hosted through content delivery network (CDN) Cloudflare in the United States, which are private in its nature. These supposedly e-commerce websites attracted gullible people to become members and place bets in online games of chance. Agents were attracting new customers and members to develop a well-knit network. These agents created closed Telegram and WhatsApp-based groups and attracted countless Indian customers. New members joined these groups using the referral codes only. This also earned the sponsoring member a commission. Again, payment processors were providing services of collecting money and paying commission to all agent members; these online wallets had a lack of diligent mechanisms and their non-reporting of suspicious transactions to the regulatory authorities helped the company to launch pan-India operations (Times of India, 2020).

Furthermore, in the Mahadev online betting case, following the arrests made by law enforcement agencies, it has been alleged that M/s Mahadev Book maintained a network of closed group on messaging apps and used them to conduct benami transactions. There have been incidents where over 2,000 bank accounts (Naidu, 2023) have been opened on bogus KYCs to hold the money amounting to allegedly INR 5,000 crores. These accounts are operated only for a few months and are then closed, following which new ones are opened using identities of different people. MeitY following the arrests made in the Mahadev online betting case was also constrained to pass a blocking order against 22 illegal gambling apps and websites. The banning order came considering these websites collecting UPI payments through proxy bank accounts and then channelling it through hawala and virtual currency routes (*Times of India*, 2023).

Therefore, the use of online gambling platforms to launder money has gained prominence aided by the proliferation of gambling websites and small payment processors specializing in internet payments. The challenges in regulating the sector *inter alia* include the absence of regulation of the cash flow in the online gambling websites due to their offshore incorporation and lack of adequate diligence norms for the operators of gambling websites and the payment aggregators facilitating the transactions.

As demonstrated in the later section, there are a few jurisdictions which have been partly successful in tackling the complexities of the operations through tailored legislations, heightened KYC norms, and customer due diligence ("**CDD**"), which can serve as a roadmap for India to adopt.

10.5 LEGAL POSITION OF ONLINE GAMBLING CHECKS GLOBALLY

10.5.1 United Kingdom

The United Kingdom ("**UK**") was among the pioneers in opening its online gambling industry, initiating the process in 2005. Currently, it houses an extensive gambling sector with over 2,600 registered operators, encompassing both online and offline casinos as per a study of the UK Gambling Commission (Gambling Commission, 2020).

The online gambling AML regime aligns itself to the wider AML regime in the UK. It is pertinent to note that the Money Laundering Regulations of 2017 primarily apply to casinos, operating offline or online, leaving a significant portion of this sector outside their scope.

However, despite not falling directly under the MLRs, online betting operators are obligated by the Proceeds of Crime Act of 2002 ("**POCA**") and the Gambling Act of 2005 (Gambling Commission, 2020) to actively prevent criminal activities, including money laundering, within their industry. Consequently, they are required to establish robust AML policies and controls and report any suspicious activities to the National Crime Agency ("**NCA**"). Failure to comply with these regulations would result in a breach of POCA. The Gambling Act of 2005 has also led to the creation of the Gambling Commission. The commission is a public body under the aegis of the UK government, meant to regulate gambling supervise the enforcement of the Gambling Act of 2005.

In accordance with their AML obligations, gambling operators are tasked with several key priorities. Firstly, they must establish robust mechanisms for the early verification of customer profiles, a process commonly referred to as CDD.

Secondly, gambling operators are under a legal obligation to promptly submit suspicious activity reports ("**SARs**") to the NCA in accordance with guidelines provided by the regulatory authority, legislative mandates, and internationally recognized reporting standards. SARs serve as the primary instrument within the realm of AML, facilitating the notification of law enforcement agencies regarding potential instances of money laundering. This notification empowers law enforcement to initiate investigations and pursue legal actions against such cases.

Furthermore, gambling operators are mandated to conduct CDD when establishing a business relationship with a customer, when they have reason to suspect money laundering activities, or when there are doubts regarding the authenticity of identification documents provided by a customer.

Upon the completion of CDD procedures, a designated officer within the gambling operator's organization is required to promptly report to the NCA, via a SAR, any customer for whom they possess knowledge or suspicion of their involvement in money laundering activities. Failure to report such knowledge or suspicion renders the responsible official liable to criminal prosecution. In essence, the primary focus of both the NCA and the Gambling Commission has been to encourage gambling operators to establish reporting procedures that effectively identify and address suspicious cases while efficiently filtering out those of lesser relevance.

From its inception, the commission has embraced a risk-based approach, which aligns with the recommendations of the Report on Reducing administrative burdens: effective inspection and enforcement sanctioned by the UK government. This report called for a system-wide adoption of risk-based regulation in the UK, emphasizing its cost-effectiveness and minimal burden on regulated industries. The essence of the risk-based approach is to concentrate regulatory efforts on operators and activities that pose the highest risks to achieving regulatory objectives.

10.5.2 United States

The United States has undergone significant changes in online gambling/betting legislation and enforcement. These developments have led to a highly regulated gaming industry (Hing & Smith, 2022). It is important to note that under United States federal law, interstate online gambling is prohibited, as well as any marketing, promotion, or advertising related to it. States have begun legalizing intrastate gambling, but wagers can only be made with licensed operators by individuals physically located within the state (Tidwell & Welte, 2015).

Several states have legalized various forms of intrastate online gambling and sports betting, with some requiring partnerships with licensed casinos, and others allowing decoupled online gambling. It's worth mentioning that federal statutes specifically prohibit certain forms of online gambling, such as interstate sports betting (Walters Law Group, 2020).

Numerous states have authorized diverse types of intrastate online gambling and sports betting, with specific regulations mandating collaborations with licensed casinos in certain instances, while others permit independent online gambling operations. It is noteworthy that certain types of online gambling, such as interstate sports betting, are explicitly restricted by federal statutes (Walters Law Group, 2020).

Across the years, the US authorities have relied upon the Interstate Wire Act of 1961 ("**Wire Act**") to establish the illegality of interstate online gambling. This law prohibits interstate betting on sporting events or other contests using "wire" systems, which include telephones or the internet (Interstate Wire Act, 1961). However, court decisions have narrowed the scope of this law to cover only wagering on sporting events, excluding casino gambling. Various other federal laws, such as the Illegal Gambling Business Act, 1955, the Wagering Paraphernalia Act, 1953, and the Travel Act, 1952, may apply to certain online gambling activities, depending on the type of gaming activity and the state laws in effect where the activity occurs.

In 2006, the U.S. Congress passed the Unlawful Internet Gambling Enforcement Act ("**UIGEA**"), which prohibits the acceptance of funds for illegal online gambling and places obligations on banks and financial service providers (payment gateways like PayPal) to detect and block such transactions. The U.S. Treasury Department's administrative regulations offer a way for certain online gaming businesses to continue using U.S. financial institutions for their transactions if they can provide a "reasoned legal opinion" supporting their activities. According to the UIGEA's plain language, it only prohibits financial transactions related to wagers that are illegal in the jurisdiction where they are initiated. Therefore, some financial transactions related to gambling may be prohibited by the UIGEA, while others may not.

Following the passage of the UIGEA, many online gambling sites catering to the U.S. market began to block U.S. players and deposits (Conon, 2009). These indictments effectively led the online poker industry to exit the U.S. player market. Apart from federal law, individual states have enacted their own legislation regarding online gambling, sweepstakes, fantasy sports, and skill gaming (Edelman, 2017).

Most of these laws focus on prohibiting the operation of online gambling businesses, while a few also criminalize placing bets online. With an increasing number of states passing laws related to online gaming, the situation has become increasingly complex. Certain forms of internet gambling may be legal in certain states but completely prohibited or subject to criminal penalties in others.

Efforts to pass uniform federal online gambling legislation have repeatedly failed. Therefore, the United States has adopted a state-by-state approach to internet gaming policy development. Many states have legalized some form of online gambling for individuals within their borders. For example, online casinos operate in Delaware, Michigan, New Jersey, Pennsylvania, and West Virginia, and online poker is available in Delaware, Michigan, Nevada, New Jersey, and Pennsylvania. It is expected that other states will follow suit, although some states will continue statutory bans or simply not address the issue.

Attempts to establish consistent federal regulations for online gambling in the United States have faced repeated setbacks. As a result, the country (the United States) has opted for a decentralized strategy, addressing internet gaming policy on a state-by-state basis. Numerous states have authorized various types of online gambling for residents within their jurisdictions. For instance, Delaware, Michigan, New Jersey, Pennsylvania, and West Virginia permit online casinos, while Delaware, Michigan, Nevada, New Jersey, and Pennsylvania offer online poker services. Anticipated is the replication of such initiatives in additional states, although certain states may persist in upholding legal prohibitions or choose not to address the matter altogether.

With the US Supreme Court's 2018 (*Murphy v. National Collegiate Athletic Association*, 2018) decision striking down the federal statute known as Professional and Amateur Sports Protection Act, sports betting can now be legalized within any state. Colorado, Illinois, Indiana, Iowa, New Jersey, Pennsylvania, Rhode Island, and West Virginia have issued licences for multiple online sports books, and many others are exploring these opportunities. However, the Wire Act may create hurdles for any online sports betting that involves the interstate wire system.

Following the 2018 ruling by the Supreme Court in Murphy v. National Collegiate Athletic Association, the federal statute named Professional and Amateur Sports Protection Act was invalidated, opening the possibility of legalizing sports betting in any state. Currently, various states, including Colorado, Illinois, Indiana, Iowa, New Jersey, Pennsylvania, Rhode Island, and West Virginia, have granted licences for numerous online sportsbooks, and other states are actively considering similar prospects. Nevertheless, challenges may arise for online sports betting utilizing the interstate wire system due to potential implications of the Wire Act.

10.5.3 European Union

Applying the subsidiarity principle and given social and cultural factors specific to each member state of the EU, the EU decided that the supply of online gambling services is not subject to a specific regulation at the EU level There is no sector-specific EU legislation in the field of gambling services. EU countries are autonomous in the way they organize their gambling services, if they comply with the fundamental freedoms established under the Treaty on the Functioning of the European Union, as interpreted by the Court of Justice of the EU.

In fact, online gambling as a service industry is subject to several EU secondary legislative acts such as the data protection directive, the directive on privacy and electronic communication, the unfair commercial practices and unfair contract term directives, the distance selling directive as well as the directive on consumers' rights. It is also subject to the rules and provisions to guard against money laundering (Casabona, 2014).

10.6 PROPOSED CHANGES TO THE REGULATORY FRAMEWORK GOVERNING ONLINE GAMBLING IN INDIA

The COVID-19 pandemic has had far-reaching impacts on various industries and has highlighted the evolving nature of the gaming and eSports sector, which has demonstrated resilience in the face of economic challenges. However, this sector's growth and evolution have exposed potential issues related to money laundering and regulatory ambiguities. To address these concerns, the following changes to the Indian legal framework should be considered:

1. The Indian government should enact comprehensive regulations specifically tailored to the online gaming industry, addressing issues such as money laundering, licensing, taxation, and player protection. These regulations should distinguish between games of skill and games of chance, providing clarity for operators and players (Refer to Section II, The Non-Uniformity of Gambling Legislations Across the Nation.). Furthermore, the government must establish a dedicated regulatory authority for online gaming, similar to the approach taken by other countries. This authority should be responsible for overseeing the industry, issuing licences, setting standards, and enforcing compliance with AML and KYC requirements (Refer to Section IV, The Missing Link in Indian Regulatory Apparatus in Dealing with Money Laundering through Online Gambling Intermediaries).

2. All online gaming operators should be required to implement robust AML and KYC procedures. This includes reporting suspicious transactions, verifying player identities, and ensuring transparent financial transactions. Non-compliance should result in stringent penalties (Refer to Section IV, The Missing Link in Indian Regulatory Apparatus in Dealing with Money Laundering through Online Gambling Intermediaries).
3. In this context, the Indian government may also consider adopting legal provisions used in other countries (Refer to Section V, Legal Position of Online Gambling Checks Globally). In the United Kingdom, a pioneer in the online gambling industry, robust regulations and enforcement measures have been established under the Gambling Act of 2005. The shift towards more proactive enforcement in recent years demonstrates the ongoing need for vigilance in regulating this industry. Similarly, the United States has adopted a state-by-state approach, with variations in laws and regulations regarding online gambling. While some states have legalized various forms of online gambling, federal laws like the Wire Act and the UIGEA continue to influence the landscape. Therefore, India too can adopt a risk-based approach to AML measures. Operators should employ stricter controls based on perceived risks. This approach considers the type of game, location, transactions, and customer profiles.

The gaming and eSports sector has experienced remarkable growth and change, presenting both opportunities and challenges. By implementing comprehensive regulations, strengthening AML and KYC compliance, legalizing and regulating online gambling, and fostering international cooperation, India can create a more secure and responsible online gaming environment. These measures will help protect consumers, combat money laundering, and ensure the industry's long-term sustainability and ensure a level playing field in terms of the regulatory framework.

10.7 CONCLUSION

The COVID-19 pandemic had a profound impact on various sectors, including the gaming and eSports industry, which demonstrated remarkable resilience during the initial market downturn. As governments worldwide implemented lockdowns and stringent restrictions to curb the spread of the virus, millions of individuals were compelled to spend prolonged periods within the confines of their homes. In this context, the gaming and eSports industry experienced a surge in popularity and engagement throughout the first half of 2020. With an increasing number of people seeking solace and entertainment online, the industry witnessed an acceleration in its growth (Refer to Section V, Legal Position of Online Gambling Checks Globally).

However, the rapid growth of online gaming, particularly in India, has raised concerns relating to money laundering, regulatory frameworks, and the need for updated laws. The sector's dynamic nature and regulatory void create an environment susceptible to criminal exploitation, with significant potential for money laundering. The non-uniformity of gambling legislations across different states in

India complicates the regulatory landscape further. Some states have adopted the Public Gambling Act, while others have created their gaming laws, introducing disparities in the interpretation of "game of skill" and "game of chance." This lack of uniformity has led to confusion and variations in the regulatory treatment of online gaming.

The missing link in the Indian regulatory apparatus is the need for enhanced AML programs and improved KYC procedures within the gaming industry. These programs should be risk-based and adaptable to the unique aspects of the industry, while industry professionals should be trained to recognize common money laundering warning signs. Recent changes *vide* the Ministry of Finance Notification have brought the online gaming industry under the purview of the PMLA and the PMLA Rules, in case the operators allow for transactions involving digital assets. In addition, the 2023 Amendment introduced compliance requirements for OGIs who offer permissible online real money games. They must undergo verification by a self-regulatory body designated by the MeitY.

In this context, it is also pertinent to note that countries around the world have taken distinct approaches towards the online gaming industry to strike a balance between harnessing the economic benefits of this industry while ensuring the protection of their citizens.

In conclusion, the gaming and eSports industry has demonstrated remarkable resilience and growth, driven by technical advancements and the shift in consumer behaviour during the pandemic. While the growth is promising, it has also revealed the potential for money laundering and financial crimes within the industry. India stands at a crossroads, where it must balance the growth and economic potential of the gaming sector with the need for comprehensive and uniform regulation. Such regulation should address AML measures, KYC procedures.

REFERENCES

Casabona, S. (2014, January 19). The EU's online gambling regulatory approach and the crisis of legal modernity. EUC Working Paper No.19. https://aei.pitt.edu/47671/1/WP19-Online-Gambling-Regulations.pdf

Conon, J. (2009). Aces and Eights: Why the Unlawful Internet Gambling Enforcement Act Resides in Dead Man's Land in Attempting to Further Curb Online Gambling and Why Expanded Criminalization if Preferable to Legalization. *Journal of Criminal Law and Criminology*, 99(4), 1157–1193. https://scholarlycommons.law.northwestern.edu/cgi/viewcontent.cgi?article=7340&context=jclc

Dinker. V. (2022, June 17). Rajasthan draft law could put online skill gaming industry in disarray. *The Hindu Business Line*. www.thehindubusinessline.com/opinion/rajasthan-draft-law-could-put-online-skill-gaming-industry-in-disarray/article65537332.ece

Fiedler, I. (2013). *Online Gambling as a Game Changer to Money Laundering*. SSRN. https://doi.org/10.2139/ssrn.2261266

Gambling Commission (2020, November 1). Duties and responsibilities under the Proceeds of Crime Act 2002. https://assets.ctfassets.net/j16ev64qyf6l/6QuVw2XGPlXepcm3h5UyHC/eee37f7f2d0967798a165be9643b63cb/Duties_and_responsibilities_under_POCA_4th_Ed_Rev_1__Clean_version_.pd

Hindu BusinessLine. (2023, May 24). ED cracks down on offshore registered online gaming companies. *Hindu BusinessLine*. www.thehindubusinessline.com/news/ed-crackdown-against-offshore-registered-online-gaming-companies-sniffs-laundering-of-4000-crore/article66889596.ece

Hing, N., & Smith, M. (2022). How Structural Changes in Online Gambling Are Shaping the Contemporary Experiences and Behaviours of Online Gamblers: An Interview Study. *BMC Public Health*, 22, 1620.

Hock, B., Button, M., Shepherd, D., & Gilmour, P. M. (2023). What Works in Policing Money Laundering? *Journal of Money Laundering Control*. https://doi.org/10.1108/JMLC-07-2023-0109

Information Technology (Intermediary Guidelines and Digital Media Ethics Code) Amendment Rules, 2023, Rule 4-A.

Interstate Wire Act, 1961 18 US § 1084.

K R Lakshmanan v. State of Tamil Nadu, (1996) 2 SCC 226.

López-Cabarcos, M. Á., Ribeiro-Soriano, D., & Pineiro-Chousa, J. (2020). All That Glitters Is Not Gold. The Rise of Gaming in the COVID-19 Pandemic. *Journal of Innovation & Knowledge*, 5(4), 289–296. https://doi.org/10.1016/j.jik.2020.10.004

Marc Edelman (2017). Regulating Fantasy Sports: A Practical Guide to State Gambling Laws, and a Proposed Framework for Future State Legislation. *Indiana Law Journal*, 92(2), 653–691.

Mckinsey & Co. (2022, April 13). COVID-19: Implications for business. *Mckinsey & Co.* www.mckinsey.com/capabilities/risk-and-resilience/our-insights/covid-19-implications-for-business

Minhaz, A. (2023, April 20). New amendments to IT Rules lack clarity, fall short in defining key aspects. The Hindu. https://frontline.thehindu.com/society/new-amendments-to-it-rules-lack-clarity-fall-short-in-defining-key-aspects/article66740489.ece

Ministry of Electronics & IT Government of India (2023, April 20). Government ushers in new era of responsible online gaming through strict guidelines for ensuring safety of Digital Nagriks and accountability of online gaming industry. Press Information Bureau. www.pib.gov.in/PressReleasePage.aspx?PRID=1918383

Murphy v. National Collegiate Athletic Association, No. 16-476, 584 U.S. (2018).

Nagaland Prohibition of Gambling and Promotion and Regulation of Online Games of Skill Act, 2015.

Naidu, J. (2023, August 25). Mahadev online betting racket: How two Chhattisgarh men amassed Rs 5,000 Cr. *Indian Express*. https://indianexpress.com/article/explained/mahadev-online-betting-racket-how-two-chhattisgarh-men-amassed-rs-5000-cr-8909166

Plumber, M. (2022, February 14). Karnataka High Court Strikes Down Law Banning Online Gaming with Stakes. Live Law. www.livelaw.in/top-stories/karnataka-high-court-strikes-down-law-banning-online-gaming-karnataka-police-amendment-act-2021-191889

Quirk, P. J. (1996, June 1). Macroeconomic Implications of Money Laundering. *International Monetary Fund*. www.elibrary.imf.org/view/journals/001/1996/066/article-A001-en.xml?ArticleTabs=related%20documents

Rasul, G. & Nepal, A. K. (2021, February 24). Socio-economic implications of COVID-19 pandemic in South Asia: Emerging risks and growing challenges. *Frontiers*. www.frontiersin.org/articles/10.3389/fsoc.2021.629693/full.

R.M.D Chamarbaugwalla v. Union of India, AIR 1957 SC 628.

Sikkim On-line Gaming (Regulation) Act, 2008.

State of A.P. v. K. Satyanarayana AIR 1968 SC 825.

Thathoo, C. (2023, August 17). How a Gaming Co Allegedly Syphoned Off INR 700 Cr to Tax Havens Via a Nexus of 400 Entities in India. INC42. https://inc42.com/buzz/how-a-gaming-co-allegedly-syphoned-off-inr-700-cr-to-tax-havens-via-a-nexus-of-400-entities-in-india/4

The Meghalaya Regulation of Gaming Act, 2021.

Tidwell, M., & Welte, J. W. (2015). Gambling Modes and State Gambling Laws: Changes from 1999 to 2011 and Beyond. *Gaming Law Review and Economics*, 19(1), 13–26.

Times of India. (2020, August 14). Chinese national among 4 held for Rs 1,100cr online gambling racket. *Times of India*. https://timesofindia.indiatimes.com/india/chinese-national-among-4-held-for-rs-1100cr-online-gambling-racket/articleshow/77535499.cms

Vashisht, D. (2022, February 23). Regulation, not Prohibition. *The Hindu*. www.thehindu.com/opinion/op-ed/regulate-online-gaming-dont-prohibit-it/article65074606.ece

Vulnerabilities of Casinos and Gaming Sector. (2009, March 1). Financial Action Task Force. www.fatf-gafi.org/en/publications/Methodsandtrends/Vulnerabilitiesofcasinosandgamingsector.html

Walters Law Group. (2020). Online Gaming Overview: Basic Information Regarding Online Gaming Law. *Walters Law Group*. www.firstamendment.com/online-gambling-information/#:~:text=This%20law%20prohibits%20interstate%20betting,events%2C%20not%20including%20casino%20gambling.

Wardle, H. (2021). When Games and Gambling Collide: Modern Examples and Controversies. In: *Games Without Frontiers? Leisure Studies in a Global Era*. Palgrave Macmillan, Cham. https://doi.org/10.1007/978-3-030-74910-1_3

11 Cyber-Security and Data Privacy Challenges in Online Gaming

Analyzing the Cyber-Security Risks and Challenges Faced by Online Gaming Platforms in India

Saloni Tyagi Shrivastava

11.1 INTRODUCTION

The rapid proliferation of online gaming platforms in India has ushered in a new era of entertainment and engagement. The dynamic landscape of digital gaming has transformed the way individuals across the country interact with technology, socialize, and seek recreational activities. As more players immerse themselves in virtual worlds, the cyber-security and data privacy aspects of these platforms have taken center stage.

11.1.1 Background and Significance

Online gaming has emerged as a multi-billion-dollar industry globally, and India is no exception to this trend. The nation has seen an increase in the amount of people engaging in online gaming due to the widespread use of cellphones, reasonably priced internet access, and a growing youth population. Millions of people have been drawn in by the appeal of online gaming, whether they are participating in e-sports competitions, exploring rich virtual worlds, or fighting opponents in multiplayer settings. However, a number of difficulties are brought about by the enormous popularity of online gaming, especially in the areas of data privacy and cyber-security. Technology, personal data, and virtual ecosystems all interact to create a setting where privacy breaches and cyberthreats are a constant concern. It is imperative that these issues be resolved in order to protect players' interests as well as the integrity and long-term viability of the online gaming sector.

DOI: 10.1201/9781032624204-12

11.1.2 Objectives of the Chapter

This chapter aims to provide a comprehensive analysis of the cyber-security and data privacy challenges faced by online gaming platforms in India. By exploring the evolving landscape of online gaming and its associated risks, this chapter seeks to achieve the following objectives:

1. **Identification of Cyber-Security Risks:** To highlight the various cyber-security risks and threats that online gaming platforms encounter, ranging from account hijacking to cheating and hacking.
2. **Examination of Data Privacy Challenges:** To delve into the privacy concerns arising from the collection, sharing, and potential mishandling of player data within the online gaming context.
3. **Regulatory Context:** To provide insights into the existing legal and regulatory frameworks in India pertaining to cyber-security and data privacy in the online gaming sector.
4. **Strategies for Mitigation:** To propose practical strategies and best practices those online gaming platforms can adopt to enhance their cyber-security measures and protect the data privacy of their users.

11.1.3 Structure of the Chapter

The subsequent sections of this chapter will delve into the core themes outlined in the objectives. "Cyber-Security Risks in Online Gaming" will dissect the various threats faced by gaming platforms, while "Data Privacy Challenges" will navigate the intricacies of player data collection and its potential misuse. The regulatory landscape in India will be explored in "Regulatory Landscape," followed by actionable insights in "Strategies for Enhancing Cyber-Security and Data Privacy."

In a digital era where technology continues to evolve and connectivity becomes ever more pervasive, understanding the intersection of online gaming, cyber-security, and data privacy is paramount. By shedding light on the challenges and providing guidance for mitigation, this chapter endeavors to contribute to a safer and more secure online gaming ecosystem in India.

11.2 CYBER-SECURITY RISKS IN ONLINE GAMING

The landscape of online gaming is rife with dynamic challenges, particularly in the realm of cyber-security. As players immerse themselves in virtual worlds, a plethora of cyber threats and risks loom over gaming platforms. Understanding these risks is crucial for both players and platform operators to fortify their defenses. This section delves into key cyber-security risks encountered in the context of online gaming platforms in India.

11.2.1 Account Hijacking

Account hijacking is a prevalent threat where malicious actors gain unauthorized access to player accounts, often leading to identity theft, financial loss, and disruption of gameplay. The compromise of user credentials through various means, such as phishing attacks or weak passwords, poses a significant risk.

Risk Mitigation

- **Multi-Factor Authentication (MFA)**: Implementation of MFA adds an extra layer of security, requiring users to provide multiple forms of identification for account access.
- **Educational Initiatives:** Player education on recognizing phishing attempts and employing strong, unique passwords helps mitigate the risk of account hijacking.

11.2.2 Distributed Denial-of-Service (DDoS) Attacks

DDoS attacks involve overwhelming a gaming platform's servers with traffic, causing disruption and rendering the service inaccessible to legitimate players. These attacks can be motivated by competition, vengeance, or ransom.

Risk Mitigation

- **Traffic Filtering and Redundancy:** Implementing traffic filtering mechanisms and redundant server setups helps absorb and mitigate the impact of DDoS attacks.
- **Collaboration with ISPs:** Cooperation with Internet service providers (ISPs) can enhance the ability to identify and thwart DDoS attacks.

11.2.3 Cheating and Hacking

Cheating and hacking pose a dual threat, undermining the integrity of the gaming experience and potentially compromising the security of the platform. Players using unauthorized third-party tools or manipulating game files can gain unfair advantages and disrupt fair play.

Risk Mitigation

- **Anti-Cheat Systems:** Deployment of robust anti-cheat systems that continuously monitor player behavior and game files.
- **Regular Software Updates:** Timely updates and patches help address vulnerabilities that could be exploited by hackers and cheat developers.

11.2.4 Phishing and Social Engineering

Phishing attacks targeting players often involve deceptive tactics to trick individuals into revealing sensitive information, such as login credentials or personal details. Social engineering exploits human psychology to manipulate players into unintended actions.

Risk Mitigation

- **Player Education**: Comprehensive awareness programs to educate players about recognizing and avoiding phishing attempts.
- **Email Verification**: Implementation of email verification processes during account creation and recovery.

11.2.5 Malware Distribution

Malicious actors may distribute malware through fake gaming platforms, infected game files, or deceptive advertisements. Players unknowingly downloading compromised files can lead to a range of cyber-security issues.

Risk Mitigation

- **Secure Download Channels**: Ensuring that game downloads are exclusively from secure and verified channels.
- **Regular Security Audits**: Periodic security audits to identify and eliminate potential vulnerabilities in game files and platforms.

In navigating the complex terrain of online gaming cyber-security, a multi-faceted approach is essential. Platforms must continuously adapt and fortify their defenses against these risks, prioritizing the creation of a secure and trustworthy gaming environment for players. Player education and collaborative efforts within the gaming industry are pivotal in mitigating the evolving threats that accompany the ever-expanding world of online gaming in India.

11.3 DATA PRIVACY CHALLENGES IN ONLINE GAMING

The thriving online gaming industry in India, while providing immersive experiences, also raises significant data privacy concerns. As players engage with virtual worlds, the collection, processing, and potential misuse of their personal data become critical issues.

11.3.1 Collection of Personal Data

Online gaming platforms routinely collect a myriad of personal data from players, including but not limited to usernames, email addresses, age, location data, and in some cases, even biometric information. The sheer volume and sensitivity of this data present inherent privacy challenges.

Challenges

- **Informed Consent**: Ensuring that players provide informed and explicit consent for the collection of their personal data.
- **Age Verification**: Addressing challenges related to age verification, especially considering the diverse age groups participating in online gaming.

11.3.2 Third-Party Sharing

The sharing of player data with third-party entities, such as advertisers or analytics firms, for targeted marketing or other purposes, raises concerns about transparency and control over personal information.

Challenges

- **Transparency**: Ensuring transparency in data-sharing practices, including providing clear information to players about third-party engagements.
- **User Control**: Empowering players with the ability to control the extent to which their data is shared with third parties.

11.3.3 User Tracking

Online gaming platforms often employ tracking mechanisms to monitor player behavior, preferences, and interactions within the virtual environment. While this data is valuable for improving user experience, it poses challenges related to user privacy.

Challenges

- **Granular Consent**: Offering granular options for players to consent to specific types of data tracking.
- **Data Anonymization:** Implementing measures to anonymize tracking data to protect individual privacy.

11.3.4 Geolocation Data

The use of geolocation data in online gaming, especially in mobile applications, raises privacy concerns, particularly regarding the tracking of players' physical locations.

Challenges

- **Explicit Consent**: Ensuring that players explicitly consent to the collection and use of their geolocation data.

- **Protection of Minors**: Implementing additional safeguards for the collection of geolocation data from underage players.

11.3.5 Data Breaches

Data breaches pose a severe threat to player privacy, as unauthorized access to personal information can result in identity theft, financial loss, and other forms of exploitation.

Challenges

- **Security Measures**: Implementing robust security measures, including encryption and secure storage, to protect against data breaches.
- **Incident Response**: Establishing effective incident response plans to mitigate the impact of potential data breaches.

In navigating the intricate landscape of data privacy, online gaming platforms must strike a delicate balance between providing an engaging user experience and safeguarding the privacy rights of players. This involves transparent data practices, robust security measures, and a commitment to empowering players with control over their personal information. As the regulatory landscape evolves, platforms need to stay proactive in adapting their practices to align with emerging privacy standards and expectations.

11.3.5.1 Regulatory Framework

Cyber-security and data privacy policies in the online gaming industry are significantly shaped by the legislative framework that governs the sector in India. It's becoming more and more important to comprehend the current legal and regulatory frameworks as the online gaming industry grows quickly.

The Indian online gaming market has grown at an exponential rate because of rising user interaction and bold investment. Government regulation of the online gaming industry is therefore long overdue, especially in cases where the games are paid for with real money and present a significant risk of cyberbullying, security breaches, offensive content, moral dilemmas, cheating and hacking, social isolation, and other health and physical problems for players.

The Central Government finally notified the Information Technology (Intermediary Guidelines and Digital Media Ethics Code) Amendment Rules, 2023 issued by the Ministry of Electronics and Information Technology via Gazette notification dated April 6, 2023 to amend the Information Technology Rules, 2021. This was due to the recent unprecedented surge in the number of people participating in online gaming, particularly during the pandemic.

To counteract damaging content on social media, the Content Technology (Intermediary Guidelines and Digital Media Ethics Code) Rules, 2021 were released in February 2021. Given the growing popularity of online gaming, the Information Technology (Intermediary Guidelines and Digital Media Ethics Code) Amendment Rules, 2023 were released. The amendment defined the words "online game," "online gaming intermediary," "online real money game," "permissible online game," and "permissible online real money game" and established an online gaming self-regulatory organization to oversee online gaming.

The amendment defines an "online game" as a game available on the internet that users can access via a computer resource or an intermediary. An "online gaming intermediary" is someone who allows users of its computer resources to access online games. The online gaming self-regulatory body is an agency intended to verify online gaming real money games as acceptable real money games under revised rule 2(1)(qc) read with rule 4A. The government may inform as many online gaming self-regulatory organizations as it deems appropriate.

"Online real money games" are those in which a user deposits cash or in kind with the prospect of winning money on that deposit. A permissible online game is any online game that is not an online real money game, whereas "permissible online real money games" are those online real money games that have been validated by an online gaming self-regulatory authority under rule 4A.

11.3.5.2 Online Gaming Self-Regulatory Body

An online gaming self-regulatory body is an institution with the authority to certify an online real money game as a legal online real money game. According to regulation 4A, the Central Government may appoint as many online gaming self-regulatory organizations as it deems appropriate. An entity that meets the conditions outlined in regulation 4A(2) may apply to the Ministry for recognition as an online gaming self-regulatory body:

- The entity must be a firm registered under Section 8 of the Companies Act, 2013;
- Its membership must be representative of the gaming industry;
- Its members must have responsibly offered and promoted online games.
- Its Board of Directors consists of individuals of repute who have no conflict of interest and have special knowledge or practical experience suitable for the performance of the functions of such a self-regulatory body; and
- The entity must have sufficient capacity, including financial capacity, to perform its functions as an online gaming self-regulatory body in accordance with the rules, and so on.

According to regulation 4A(3), the online gaming self-regulatory body has the authority to declare an online real money game as a permitted online real money game if an application is submitted to it. Before issuing such a declaration, the authority may conduct all required investigations to ensure that:

- The online real money game does not involve wagering on any outcome;
- The online gaming intermediary and the online game are in full compliance with the provisions of rules 3 and 4 as well as any law relating to the age at which an individual is competent to enter into a contract; and
- The online gaming intermediary and the online game are in full compliance with the framework established by the online gaming self-regulatory body under sub-rule(8).

Sub-rule 8 requires such a self-regulatory organization to publicly publicize a methodology for validating an online real money game. However, as a temporary solution, the regulatory body has been permitted to rely on the information provided by the applicant for verification of the online real money game and to declare such game lawful for a period not exceeding three months and during said three months. The regulatory organizations are required to conduct an investigation and then either approve the online real money game or notify the applicant that such online game does not meet the criteria of the regulations.

11.3.5.3 Grievance Redressal Mechanism

Clause (c) of sub-rule (1) of rule 4 states that an online gaming intermediary must appoint an Indian resident Grievance Officer to receive complaints from users or victims of violations of this rule. When an officer receives one of these complaints, they have to acknowledge it within 24 hours and resolve it within 15 days. The name, contact details, and mode of complaint submission for victims must be prominently displayed by the intermediary on both its website and mobile application.

The intermediary is required to take reasonable measures to either remove or restrict access to any content that appears to violate an individual's privacy upon receiving a complaint. It is also necessary to establish a robust complaint handling process that will enable the complainant to track the progress of these complaints by giving each one a distinct ticket number.

11.4 CONCLUSION

The Central Government has made an encouraging move toward regulating uncontrolled internet gambling firms. Though the laws are still being tested on the ground, the regulatory standards will provide a safer environment for online gaming customers, particularly owing to the necessity to undertake appropriate verification of online games using real money, cash, or kind contributions. The government has enacted severe rules to secure the safety and protection of users, as well as to enable it to fulfill its goal and purpose of regulating previously uncontrolled online gambling firms.

The Central Government's recognition of online gaming would allow this sector to expand further and compete on a worldwide scale, while also assisting India in becoming one of the top countries in the gaming business.

REFERENCES

Information Technology (Intermediary Guidelines and Digital Media Ethics Code) Rules (2021).

Information Technology (Intermediary Guidelines and Digital Media Ethics Code) Amendment Rules (2023).

12 Blockchain in Online Gaming
Navigating the Legal Landscape for India and the World

Subhrajit Chanda and Ashiv Choudhary

12.1 INTRODUCTION

The intersection of entertainment and technology has resulted in several innovations and advancements in the gaming sector. One such advancement and innovation is the incorporation of blockchain tech into gaming platforms, which possesses extensive probability for transforming the entire gaming experience. Blockchain technology gives augmented security and transparency in gaming. By adopting decentralized networks, a game developer could confirm that every transaction within a game is logged on an immutable ledger, forming it nearly not possible for cheating or fraud to arise. Besides, a player has greater control over his/her in-game assets as rights of ownership are stored steadily on the blockchain. It allows a player to sell or trade his/her virtual or electronic items with confidence, forming a new economy within online games. Furthermore, the intersection of online gaming and blockchain presents critical challenges and opportunities for a developer in the gaming sector. By leveraging the technology of blockchain, game development could form a more rewarding, immersive, and player-centric experience of gaming. Nevertheless, integrating blockchain technology into online games also shows numerous issues such as user adoption, scalability, and regulatory hurdles.

The legal implications of blockchain are emerging and multifaceted. As blockchain technology in online gaming remains to transform the gaming sector, it is significant to recognize the regulatory and legal concerns that can occur. Like any other online game, blockchain technology in online gaming is subject to intellectual property and copyright laws. These laws safeguard the creations of game developers and confirm that they get appropriate compensation for their work. Furthermore, game players could be dejected by the technical intricacy needed to adopt blockchain and crypto technology like placing a crypto wallet and obtaining NFTs (non-fungible tokens)

DOI: 10.1201/9781032624204-13

prior to being able to participate. The regulatory and legal landscape for blockchain technology is emerging and complex. As the sector remains to emerge, it is significant to navigate these concerns to confirm compliance with regulations.

Since blockchain technology undeniably results in legal complexities, the chapter will discuss the unique legal issues arising from decentralization and addressing security, privacy, and consumer rights. The chapter then discusses the Indian legal landscape and global perspective on regulating blockchain-enabled gaming. Finally, it will provide practical recommendations for policymakers and stakeholders so that the use of blockchain technology in gaming can be effectively implemented without legal complications.

12.2 NAVIGATING THE LEGAL COMPLEXITIES OF BLOCKCHAIN INTEGRATION

Blockchain refers to a distributed database that manages a regular emerging ordered records list, called blocks. It is a communal, incontrovertible ledger that eases the procedure of tracking assets and recording transactions in a business network. Blockchain assists in the traceability and verification of multistep transactions requiring traceability and verification. It could speed up data transfer processing, decrease compliance costs, and secure transactions (Belotti et al., 2019). There are several characteristics of blockchain such as immutable indicates the blockchain is an unalterable and permanent network, every network participant has a copy of the ledger for ample transparency, every record is individually encrypted, it adds another security layer to the complete procedure on the blockchain network, and blockchain technology does not have central authority controlling the network. Other characteristics are every network participant agrees to the records' validity prior to they could be added to the network and all blockchains have a consensus to assist the network to make unbiased and quick decisions (Sharma & Jain, 2019).

12.2.1 A Brief History – Blockchain Gaming

CryptoKitties was the first known gaming of blockchain which was launched in 2017 (Jiang & Liu, 2021). Although it did not obtain extensive attention from the gaming section until 2021, during 2017–2021, gaming firms, developers, and users criticized the blockchain in virtual gaming for being environmentally not sustainable and unessential. There had not been a breakout success in virtual games adopting blockchain by the early 2020s. In 2021, blockchain gaming started to vary the rules in the gaming glove, making users, instead of developers, the emphasis. By the end of 2021, numerous major publishers, such as Square Enix, Take-Two Interactive, Electronics Arts, and Ubisoft, described that NFTs and blockchain-based games were under severe consideration for their firms in the future (Tavares et al., 2023). After 2021, the trend of blockchain-based online gaming is continuously increasing in India and around the world.

12.2.2 NFTs: A Revolutionary Concept for Virtual Asset Ownership and Trade

NFTs are identified as unique digital assets adopting blockchain technology to authenticate provenance and ownership. This has formed a novel market for collectibles, digital art, and other distinct items earlier impossible to trade or authenticate. They could probably change the gaming sector by making a novel market for digital assets (Fairfield, 2022). A player could now buy, trade, and sell digital items with ownership that is certifiable. This allows new forms of gameplay and new economic systems within games. Furthermore, NFTs exchange arises with cryptocurrencies like bitcoin of specialist sites.

Blockchain's chief aspect of immutability confirms that when the data is recorded, it could not be changed or tempered. In the context of the metaverse, this could be adopted to develop reliable and transparent record-keeping mechanisms for several transactions like online land, online assets, or even virtual identities. A player may rely on transparency to confirm the genuineness and asset history, decreasing the danger of counterfeit items or fraud. Furthermore, decentralization in blockchain-based gaming gives a sense of possession or control. A developer could leverage blockchain to form decentralized, community-driven games in which a user has a say in game development decisions. Blockchain technology also permits the formation and ownership of distinct in-game assets via NFTs (Siddique et al., 2023). Users may earn actual value by vending their in-game assets; therefore, turning games into a probable lucrative endeavour. Moreover, blockchain allows provable fairness in games by leveraging its intrinsic strengths. For instance, tournament rules could be developed on-chain, apart from information regarding the entrants, and smart contracts are executed to give rewards to the winners. It confirms that the gaming outcomes are recognized in an indiscriminate and transparent manner (Laser, 2023).

12.2.3 Unique Legal Challenges Arising from Decentralization

In blockchain, decentralization is the transfer of decision-making and control from the centralized entity (group, organization, or individual) to a distributed network. Although decentralization poses unique legal issues that institutions, regulators, and policymakers have to consider, being a decentralized ledger, the blockchain nodes could span several locations all around the globe. In other words, blockchain has the ability to cross jurisdictional boundaries because the nodes on the blockchain could be placed anywhere across the globe. It may pose multifaceted jurisdictional concerns which need thorough consideration in regard to the rational contractual relationships (Sharma & Jain, 2019). It also leads to an overwhelming number of legislation and rules that may apply to the blockchain network. It also makes it tough to identify a transaction's location if that specific transaction turns out to be erroneous or fraudulent (Lexology, 2022).

12.2.4 Comprehensive Analysis: Addressing Security, Privacy, and Consumer Rights

In the view of Heister & Yuthas, it has been said that "privacy is not a property of any blockchain". Instead, there are privacy layers that could be adopted to any blockchain (including gaming). Developers have to carefully or thoroughly recognize which parties are permitted to write and read transactions and how transactions are stored, validated, and broadcast. Additional concerns associated with how security and permissions measures are enforced and updated are also significant considerations. Decisions regarding who possesses the data or information and how information could be adopted by institutions and computer applications further complicate discussions related to privacy (Heister & Yuthas, 2021). In addition, distributed ledger technologies and blockchain could give new opportunities for safeguarding user data via decentralized identity and other methods. It is significant to identify issues and restrictions connected to implementing blockchain-based gaming.

Furthermore, blockchain gaming allows users to directly exchange digital assets without centralized or intermediate authorities, which may result in probable security breaches. Blockchain technology could be adapted to conform to transparent and secure environments for direct peer-to-peer exchanges (Chappelow, 2018). It is also significant to conduct comprehensive smart contract audits to recognize and mitigate vulnerabilities. Collaborating with prominent third-party auditing institutions also confirms reliability and transparency. Moreover, a smart contract, which supervises transactions and connections in blockchain gaming, could have security challenges. A thorough method is required to deal with these concerns, recognizing the several elements of a smart contract and blockchain security (De Giovanni, 2020).

Additionally, there is a need to develop transparent governance methods for the blockchain-based game and engage the communities in decision-making procedures to confirm fairness. The establishment of global legal frameworks for consumer rights safeguarding in blockchain-based games is necessary. These frameworks ought to deal with the distinct nature of crypto exchanges, crypto-assets, and the dangers connected to blockchain technology (Demertzis & Wolff, 2018). There is also a need to precisely describe and communicate the rights of users to possess and deliver in-game assets. Furthermore, customers or users ought to be educated regarding the risks and advantages of blockchain-based games to safeguard their rights and make informed decisions. Blockchain gaming developers and platforms could contribute to awareness and education of their rights by giving transparent data and resources to players.

12.3 THE INDIAN LEGAL LANDSCAPE AND GLOBAL PERSPECTIVE ON REGULATING BLOCKCHAIN-ENABLED GAMING

In India, it can be seen that the online gaming industry is one of the fastest growing industries and it is expected to consistently develop and emerge in the upcoming years. From playing "Snake" on Nokia phones to the amplified reality games present on every smartphone at the present time, the nation has come a long way. The mobile gaming sector presently stands at 1.5 billion dollars and is anticipated to reach nearly 5 billion dollars by 2025 (Yadav, 2023). There has been an extraordinary growth of approximately 40% between 2019 and 2020, surpassing the advancements seen in other media sectors such as social media, OTT platforms, and television (Patil & Bachani, 2022). The Indian online gaming market is anticipated to emerge from 2.8 billion dollars in 2022 to 5 billion dollars in 2025, emerging at a CAGR of 28%–30%.

The number of gamers is predicted to rise to 450 million by 2023 from 420 million in 2022, and it hit 500 million by 2025. India is the globe's largest fantasy market of sport with over 13 crore players in more than 200 platforms (Yadav, 2023).

India currently lacks specific laws or frameworks regulating virtual currencies, including bitcoin and other cryptocurrencies. These digital assets serve as payment mediums and operate without central authority oversight. The absence of regulations, rules, or established standards for resolving conflicts related to cryptocurrencies leaves investors exposed to potential risks, emphasizing that trading in bitcoin and other cryptocurrencies carries inherent uncertainties (Tambe, 2023).

In the Lok Sabha, the 2021 Cryptocurrency and Regulation of Official Currency Bill was introduced with an attempt to form a favourable framework for the digital currency creation that would be issued by the RBI (Reserve Bank of India). It is presently at the stage of consultation, and a consultation paper is anticipated from the government, which would be the initial measure to regulate cryptocurrency and bitcoin. The proposed bill produces virtual currency and dispenses it to the public. It regulates the risks connected to bitcoin and cryptocurrencies and provides numerous cautions concerning the probable risks of investing in them (Global Legal Insights, 2023b).

The RBI has introduced proposals that can significantly impact blockchain gaming in the country. The suggested 30% tax rate on income from the transfer of any virtual digital asset (VDA) and the 1% tax deduction at source (TDS) on transactions exceeding a monetary threshold bring forth financial considerations for participants in blockchain gaming (Chauhan, 2022).

Furthermore, with the absence of a specific legal framework, VDAs like bitcoin and other cryptocurrencies operate in a neither prohibited nor regulated space in India. While entities and individuals can engage in transactions, investments, and holdings of VDAs, compliance with existing laws is essential. This includes due diligence requirements for banks and other institutions regulated by the RBI, aligning with present regulations applicable to financial service providers under RBI's jurisdiction.

The uncertainty surrounding TDS on in-app purchases and rewards in crypto gaming apps poses a tangible challenge, potentially impacting gamers' income. To mitigate this challenge, there is a pressing need for a comprehensive clarification of tax laws governing in-app purchases of gaming assets in the crypto gaming sphere. Clear guidelines are crucial to delineate whether taxes apply per asset purchase or as a one-time charge, providing users with a transparent understanding of their financial obligations within the evolving landscape of crypto gaming in India (Joshi & Rachakonda, 2022).

12.3.1 Legal Hurdles and Prospects of Blockchain Integration

Blockchain technologies are unrestricted to one territory or area and the biggest issue is that it is not under one organization's hands. This made the obligation to comply with the laws of every jurisdiction and every data retention policy which is difficult to adopt. Furthermore, cryptocurrency transactions are determined as "pseudonymous" in nature, which shows that although the data points are not directly associated with a particular person, they could still be connected together on the basis of several appearances and distinct points of data of that individual (Rysin & Rysin, 2020). An individual's whole lifetime's worth of anonymous transactions can be formed public when the data is connected to them. Because of transaction history's persistence on the blockchain, this risk or challenge is certain to emerge over a period of time. When the corporation winds up, the data would also be deleted. However, the issue with blockchains is that the data stored could not be deleted (Srivastava et al., 2022).

In the view of Khan, the swift development of cryptocurrencies and blockchain technology has influenced the monetary sector by forming a novel crypto-economy (Khan et al., 2021). The subsequent generation of decentralized applications without engaging a third party have grown, thanks to the smart contracts, which are protocols framed to automatically enforce, verify and facilitate the agreement and negotiations among several untrustworthy parties. Regardless of the bright side of smart contracts, numerous legal issues consistently weaken their adoption such as (i) law conditions or clauses are unquantifiable; therefore, it remains intricate to model these conditions in a smart contract so that they are quantifiable and appropriate for machines to execute them; (ii) all nations have their own regulations and law, thus, it is multifaceted to confirm compliance with every regulation; (iii) governments are interested in controlling and regulating the use of blockchain technologies in several applications, although it can be seen that the untrustworthy networks would regress to a trusted third party framework. (Khan et al., 2021).

Moreover, on the legal side, issues arise concerning peer-to-peer trading's impact on traditional revenue models, particularly the challenge of maintaining control over in-game economies. Developers may be wary of potential disruptions caused by player-driven markets and cross-platform trading. However, the prospect of implementing blockchain for peer-to-peer economies is seen as a potential solution to align incentives for both players and developers (Chappelow, 2018). This decentralized model could enhance player experiences and sustain profits over a game's lifecycle. Unlike the traditional model, where the players can trade items with other players only within the same game and within the same gaming platform, using the decentralization blockchain technology, the ability to trade assets even across multiple platforms and games offers a steady revenue stream for developers even in late stages by expanding the trading community and making in-game economies more dynamic (Qiao, 2019).

12.3.2 Global Comparative Analysis

The Indian mobile gaming sector is anticipated to reach USD 5 billion by 2025. On the other hand, between 2017 and 2020, the gaming industry in the nation enlarged at a Compound Annual Growth Rate (CAGAR) of 38%, compared to 10% in the United States and 8% in China (Yadav, 2023). Different countries have different regulatory approaches to regulating blockchain in gaming.

12.3.2.1 United Kingdom (UK)

The government in the United Kingdom recognizes blockchain-based cryptocurrencies as valid. Cryptocurrency regulation is not completely resolute at the moment. While the Bank of England, although sceptical of bitcoin, expresses confidence in the underlying blockchain technology. According to the Governor of the Bank of England, distributed ledgers hold great promise for central banks as they can enhance resilience by eliminating the single point of failure risk present in centralized systems (Demartino, 2016). In 2015, the UK Gambling Commission addressed bitcoin gambling sites, emphasizing the need for a licence to offer gambling opportunities to UK residents, even if conducted through digital currency (Hombrebueno, 2015). The Commission takes a neutral stance on bitcoin, focusing on proper regulation of gambling products.

Blockchain in gaming is valid and its regulatory frameworks come under the present legislations and rules for virtual currencies and virtual gambling. The UKGC (United Kingdom Gambling Commission) is liable for regulating every form of gambling operations, including virtual and also recognizes the virtual currencies used in gaming activities (Bland, 2022). In addition, the FCA (Financial Conduct Authority) is also a regulatory body that regulates crypto-assets to confirm compliance with counter-terrorist financing (CTF) and anti-money laundering (AML), which safeguards UK citizens from the web of blockchain in gaming.

12.3.2.2 United States (US)

The cryptocurrency industry in the USA still lacks comprehensive regulation. Presently, there is no particular regulatory framework for crypto gambling in the nation. All US states could introduce their own regulations respecting the usage of gambling services and cryptocurrencies. Blockchain is very frequently regulated, e.g., in Arizona, Ohio, etc. Nevertheless, the situation differs across states. While for instance states like Florida and Maryland issue warnings regarding investments in blockchains, the liberal regulatory regime of Wyoming makes it a very blockchain-friendly destination.

The classification of cryptocurrencies varies on a continuum, with ICOs and security tokens falling under SEC regulation, while payment tokens are overseen by the CFTC. Utility tokens and NFTs may or may not face regulation, depending on circumstances, sometimes leading to overlapping authority between the SEC and the CFTC (Verstein, 2019).

Concerning in-game asset tokenization, utility tokens, like XAwesome tokens in Game X, ideally remain unregulated when solely listed within the game's platform. If utility tokens are listed on a mainnet, the SEC's considerations hinge on restricted transferability to the platform's users. Distinguishing between private and public platforms is crucial. NFTs within games, being non-exchangeable, typically avoid regulatory scrutiny (Qiao, 2019).

Furthermore, the Uniform Law Commission passed the Uniform Regulation of Virtual Currency Businesses Act particularly created from state banking regulation, which values digital representation that is adopted merely within a game and sold by the alike game publisher or developer (Vondrova, 2023).

12.3.2.3 Malta

Malta, once hailed as "Blockchain Island," is witnessing a regulatory shift in its blockchain gaming sector following the resignation of Prime Minister Joseph Muscat, a key advocate for blockchain-friendly policies, which has triggered a reevaluation of Malta's regulatory landscape (Hamacher, 2020). The Malta Gaming Authority (MGA), a key regulator, is undergoing a thorough review of its approach, actively engaging in a comprehensive study and public consultation to enhance its stance on cryptocurrency use among licensees. The MGA's Sandbox Regulatory Framework, established in 2018, involves live/simulated testing of blockchain assets in a controlled environment, serving as a crucial tool to evaluate the feasibility of their introduction to the market. This framework plays a pivotal role by providing a controlled environment that safeguards against money laundering and terrorism funding, fostering experimentation and innovation. Additionally, it allows the MGA to assess potential risks and complications associated with distributed ledger technologies and smart contracts in the gaming industry (Malta Gaming Authority, 2019)

Despite aspirations to be a global blockchain hub, Malta faces challenges with stringent regulations and associated high licensing fees, resulting in a limited number of gaming licences issued. The ongoing Sandbox test gains significance in assessing the real-life impact of virtual assets in gaming, guiding regulatory decisions (Bastos, 2020). The departure of major cryptocurrency exchanges and banking challenges further contribute to uncertainties for blockchain gaming startups in Malta, emphasizing the need for adaptability in a changing regulatory landscape (Hamacher, 2020).

12.3.2.4 Japan

Japan is a major player in digital gaming, ranking third globally with a revenue of over $29 billion in 2021 (Globaldata, 2021). Additionally, 77% of Japanese gamers buy in-game items or virtual goods, highlighting a clear opportunity for blockchain (Bastos, 2020). The government in Japan also deals with blockchain-connected laws as cryptocurrencies are determined valid in this nation. There are no omnibus regulations supervising blockchain-based tokens. The government imposes heavy taxes on crypto-assets. Its precise and clear regulatory framework for blockchain gaming proposes an outline of what gaming firms could and could not do, imparting confidence in businesses to expand and embrace the dynamic space (Global Legal Insights, 2023a).

The cryptocurrency exchanges are regulated under the Payment Service Act, recognizing virtual currency as a method of payment. Cryptocurrency operators must register with the Japanese Finance Bureau, adhering to regulatory measures, with the Financial Services Agency overseeing compliance. These regulations strengthen the gaming industry's adoption of cryptocurrency payments (Ishida et al., 2017).

Japanese gaming trends reveal the impact of digital technology, with 26% of the population engaging in online gaming. Esports, however, faced limitations due to restrictive gambling laws, resolved through a licensing system by the Japanese Esports Union. Recent regulatory changes have spurred investment, with a Hong Kong casino operator planning an esports (Bastos, 2020).

12.3.2.5 China

The approach of the Chinese government towards blockchain goes outside the limit of cryptocurrencies, which is why the nation is one of the foremost nations regardless of their illegality. The cryptocurrencies' illegality is necessary because of the policy of the nation that "while blockchain technology is essentially decentralized, regulation in China has aimed to guarantee state control over its development and application". In 2019, the Blockchain Information Management Regulations was introduced by the Cyberspace Administration of China that give rules for entities proposing blockchain functionality as a service (Vondrova, 2023)

The global regulatory landscape for blockchain in gaming is intricate. The United Kingdom and United States navigate decentralized frameworks, while Malta adapts to regulatory challenges. Japan leads with a clear regulatory framework, contrasting with China's stringent control. Jurisdictional challenges persist globally, highlighted by cases like Tezos Securities Litigation. Successful models should balance decentralization and security, as seen in Japan and Malta. Policymakers are urged to adopt market-specific legislation, fostering responsible adoption through collaboration and standardized practices.

12.3.3 Jurisdictional Quandaries: Cross-Border Implications and Challenges

There are many challenges involved in decentralization of blockchain, and one of the main challenges is jurisdictional quandaries. The distributed nature of blockchain technology may thwart the purpose of courts' jurisdictions and governing legislations in lawful disputes. For instance, several challenges were faced in the Tezos Securities Litigation case in dealing with the jurisdictional concerns associated with blockchain-based securities (Yang, 2023). Furthermore, most nations have particular regulations respecting virtual assets and currencies which could affect the usage of blockchain-based gaming. A game developer has to navigate via these lawful frameworks while confirming the privacy and security issues of their users' data. Since blockchain transactions are transparent, this may instigate issues regarding player confidentiality and data safeguarding.

12.3.4 Chief Visions from Successful Regulatory Models Globally

In the context of the gaming sector, it is imperative to establish precise regulations that delineate the treatment of blockchain technology. These regulations must exhibit flexibility to adapt to the rapidly evolving technological landscape. Striking a delicate balance between decentralization, security, and scalability is pivotal for blockchain to achieve a significant milestone in online gaming. This equilibrium can be attained through continuous innovation and collaborative efforts involving regulatory bodies, users, and gaming developers.

Furthermore, it is crucial to acknowledge the significance of combatting illegal activities in blockchain-based gaming. Compliance with Combatting the Financing of Terrorism (CTF) and Anti-Money Laundering (AML) regulations is essential in mitigating the risks associated with illicit operations within the gaming sector (Rysin & Rysin, 2020).

To ensure accountability and adherence to regulations, the implementation of robust registration and licensing processes is warranted. Additionally, proper taxation mechanisms need to be established for this technology to ensure its integration aligns seamlessly with regulatory frameworks. In essence, a comprehensive approach that addresses technological nuances, regulatory compliance, and financial considerations is vital for the successful integration of blockchain within the gaming industry (Bonnici, 2017).

12.3.5 Instances of Nations with Progressive Approaches

The Japanese government has shown a practical stance in encouraging the adoption and development of blockchain gaming with progressive regulatory growth, abridged regulatory frameworks, and crypto-friendly tax. Furthermore, blockchain-friendly jurisdiction has been placed in Malta to encourage blockchain in gaming and other sectors (Bastos, 2020).

12.4 PRAGMATIC RECOMMENDATIONS FOR STAKEHOLDERS AND POLICYMAKERS

Industry Players' Blueprint: Developers, Publishers, and Platforms

12.4.1 Developers

For developers entering the realm of blockchain gaming, the key lies in utilizing smart contracts to systematize game logic and incorporating NFTs to add a unique layer representing in-game characters or items. The priority should be on creating games that go beyond being mere blockchain gimmicks, aiming for true engagement and enjoyment for users. Central to this strategy is the free-to-play model, leveraging its low entry barrier to attract a diverse player base. Careful management of microtransactions is essential to avoid impeding player progression. By targeting a select group of high-spending players ("whales"), developers can optimize profits. Integrating blockchain for peer-to-peer economies not only addresses transaction concerns but also facilitates seamless cross-platform trading, ultimately enhancing the player experience and ensuring sustained profits over time (Qiao, 2019).

Blockchain technology opens avenues for novel revenue streams through token sales, providing developers with the opportunity to raise funds for online gaming development. This mechanism also facilitates user involvement through token-based economies, as highlighted by Lee (2019). However, developers should prioritize user-friendliness, ensuring accessibility for a broad spectrum of users, including those unfamiliar with blockchain technology.

Additionally, adherence to legal guidelines is paramount. Platforms facilitating the trading of NFTs and other blockchain-based assets must align with the Information Technology Act 2000, specifically section 79. Compliance with this act includes implementing due diligence measures, having a grievance redressal mechanism, warning users against obscene/illegal content, and transparently displaying user policies (Mathus, 2022). By integrating these considerations, developers can navigate the blockchain gaming landscape responsibly and effectively.

12.4.2 Publishers

Publishers in the gaming industry should strategically invest in blockchain-based gaming projects that have the potential to attract a substantial player base and generate significant revenue. However, it is imperative that such investments are directed towards legally compliant ventures that prioritize the complete security and protection of players. Recognizing the importance of collaboration, publishers should seek partnerships with experienced developers proficient in the creation of effective blockchain gaming experiences. Providing resources and support to assist developers in seamlessly integrating blockchain technology into their online gaming offerings is essential for success in this innovative space.

One of the key advantages of blockchain technology is its potential to enhance interoperability, enabling users to transfer their in-game assets across various gaming platforms. The decentralized nature of blockchain not only fosters interoperability but also contributes to improved security, safeguarding intellectual property (IP) and mitigating piracy issues, as highlighted by Cai et al. (2024). Publishers, by aligning with reputable developers and leveraging the inherent strengths of blockchain, can navigate the evolving landscape of gaming while ensuring both innovation and security for players and their digital assets.

12.4.3 Platforms

Platforms facilitating blockchain gaming should prioritize the creation of user-friendly interfaces, ensuring that players can easily access and engage with the gaming experience. Moreover, the reliability and security of these platforms are paramount, necessitating robust measures to safeguard the confidential data and information of players or users. It is crucial for platforms to implement strong security protocols to instil trust among their user base. In line with fostering user engagement, platforms should consider offering incentives to players who choose their platform for blockchain gaming. This could include specific discounts, gifts, or rewards (Scekic et al., 2018).

Additionally, platforms have the opportunity to empower players by allowing them to truly own their in-game assets. This not only nurtures a sense of possession but also adds intrinsic value to the gaming experience. By implementing these recommendations, platforms can enhance user satisfaction, attract a larger player base, and contribute to the overall success and longevity of blockchain gaming within their ecosystem.

12.5 EMPOWERING POLICYMAKERS: NAVIGATING THE DYNAMICS LANDSCAPE OF REGULATION

Adoption of market-specific legislation: Relying on whether or not blockchain gaming is private or public, stakeholders have to be aware of the regulation that exists in their nation of operation. Acceptance of market-specific legislation could assist in fortifying the internal infrastructure of blockchain gaming while confirming the obeying of predominant legislation that could be distinct from nation to nation.

Thorough understanding of the regulatory framework, blockchain technologies, and gaming sector: Every policymaker ought to endeavour to establish a thorough awareness of the regulatory countryside, the primary technologies of blockchain, and the distinct issues and occasions of the gaming sector. This understanding would allow policymakers to form informed decisions and form a forecastable and steady regulatory environment that fortifies innovation (Tillemann et al., 2019).

Responsible and transparent adoption of blockchain technology: A policymaker ought to encourage a level playing area that encourages users' faith and accountability adoption of blockchain technology. It may be accomplished by needing every developer to be transparent with players regarding tokenized digital assets and working with them to form methods that support accountable adoption of blockchain technology (Gadekallu et al., 2022).

12.5.1 Collaboration Approach

In blockchain gaming, the value of gaming tokens is on the basis of physical assets and real-life cash. Since assets and real-life cash are privy to prevailing laws of asset based in a nation, the alike would also be adopted to these gaming tokens. Thus, it is significant for companies of blockchain gaming to collaborate with distinct municipalities and governments to be well-informed of the local legislations – confirming that their games could be played in any place with the best lawful acceptance (Chang, 2022).

In India and globally, collaborate and implement steps to safeguard consumers from confidentiality breaches and fraud and confirm transparent and fair exercises in the blockchain game. For instance, stakeholders should focus on creating smart contracts that could be audited for protection; a clear and decentralized system could decrease the danger of fraudulent operations (Hewa et al., 2021). In addition, educational programs for stakeholders and policymakers also increase awareness of blockchain technology and its adoption in games. For instance, educational attempts of Ethereum give resources to assist players aware of blockchain and its probable effects (breaching of privacy or confidentiality) (Gadekallu et al., 2022).

Ease collaboration between platforms related to blockchain games to allow unified asset transfer and e-gaming experiences for players. This could be accomplished via the implementation of general standards and guidelines, like ERC-1155 and ERC-721 token standards for NFT. India should also encourage the adoption of sustainable blockchain measures to decrease environmental or climate affect. For instance, the distinction in energy consumption between the proof of stake as well as the proof of work consensus method is profound. It is estimated that around 99% more energy is consumed by proof of work such as bitcoin in comparison to proof of stake networks like Solana, Polkadot, or Tezos (CCRI, 2022).

12.6 CONCLUSION

Exploring blockchain in online gaming unveils its transformative potential in legal intricacies. This chapter emphasizes the need for comprehensive discussions as blockchain reshapes virtual gaming monetization, ownership dynamics, and the overall gaming experience. While promising, the legal implications, encompassing consumer rights and privacy, are multifaceted, demanding careful stakeholder navigation for compliance. The global analysis underscores the collective necessity for nations to establish clear regulatory frameworks, demystifying blockchain integration into gaming and addressing associated challenges, thereby guiding the industry towards a harmonized and regulated future.

Given India's nascent stage in this domain, it is prudent for the nation to contemplate the establishment of a Sandbox Regulatory Framework, taking inspiration from the model implemented by the MGA. This framework would encompass live/simulated testing of blockchain assets, creating a controlled environment conducive to thorough evaluation and experimentation. This framework would serve as a crucial tool for India to systematically evaluate the feasibility of introducing blockchain assets to the market. India should also encourage the adoption of sustainable blockchain measures to decrease environmental or climate affect. For instance, it is estimated that around 99% more energy is consumed by proof of work such as bitcoin in comparison to proof of stake networks like Solana, Polkadot, or Tezos. Since blockchain gaming exploits the rights, security, and privacy of consumers, there is a need to adopt the range of frameworks and methods discussed above to mitigate these legal challenges. The challenges, ranging from TDS on in-app purchases to the uncertainties enveloping tax laws in India, necessitate joint efforts from stakeholders to adeptly navigate these intricate complexities. The facilitation of collaboration between platforms in the blockchain gaming sphere emerges as a crucial undertaking, not only enabling seamless unified asset transfers but also significantly elevating e-gaming experiences for players.

In light of these discussions, practical recommendations for policymakers and stakeholders are paramount. By fostering a transparent and collaborative regulatory environment, policymakers can pave the way for effective implementation of blockchain technology in gaming, mitigating legal complications. These recommendations aim to strike a balance, allowing for innovation and growth in the industry while ensuring the protection of consumer rights, privacy, and overall legal compliance. In doing so, the online gaming sector can harness the full potential of blockchain technology, ushering in a secure and compliant era of innovation and progress.

REFERENCES

Ahlawat & Associates (2022, March 30). *Top 15 legal issues to look out for your Blockchain start-up*. Lexology. www.lexology.com/library/detail.aspx?g=e2ccba98-930b-454d-8687-f402db0296f5.

Bastos, N. (2020). A Change on the Horizon for the Gaming Industry: Trends, Blockchain Technology, and Cryptocurrency. *UNLV Gaming Law Journal*, 10(1). https://scholars.law.unlv.edu/glj/vol10/iss1/7

Belotti, M., Bozic, N., Pujolle, G., & Secci, S. (2019). A Vademecum on Blockchain Technologies: When, Which, and How. *IEEE Communications Surveys & Tutorials*, 21(4), 3796–3838. https://doi.org/10.1109/COMST.2019.2928178

Bland, J. (2022). Gambling on Video Games: The Global Esports Betting Market and the Dawn of Legalized Esports Gambling in the United States. *University of Miami International and Comparative Law Review*, 29(2). https://repository.law.miami.edu/umiclr/vol29/iss2/3

Bonnici, E. P. (2017). The challenges and opportunities of blockchain technology and cryptocurrencies in the ambit of gaming law [Doctoral Thesis, University of Malta]. University of Malta Library – Electronic Thesis & Dissertations (ETD) Repository. www.um.edu.mt/library/oar/handle/123456789/29227

Cai, D., Qian, Y., & Nan, N. (2024). Blockchain for Timely Transfer of Intellectual Property (Working Paper 30913). *National Bureau of Economic Research.* https://doi.org/10.3386/w30913

Chang, H. (2022, June 2). Why blockchain gaming needs more rules and regulations. *Forkast.* https://forkast.news/why-blockchain-gaming-needs-more-rules-regulations/

Chappelow, J. (2018). *Peer-to-Peer (P2P) Economy.* Investopedia. www.investopedia.com/terms/p/peertopeer-p2p-economy.asp

Chauhan, E. (2022). Cryptocurrency Taxation in India. *Indian Journal of Integrated Research in Law*, 2(4), 575–587. https://ijirl.com/wp-content/uploads/2022/07/CRYPTOCURRENCY-TAXATION-IN-INDIA.pdf

De Giovanni, P. (2020). Blockchain and Smart Contracts in Supply Chain Management: A Game Theoretic Model. *International Journal of Production Economics*, 228. https://doi.org/10.1016/j.ijpe.2020.107855

DeMartino, I. (2016, June 18). Bank of England Explores Blockchain, Says Digital Currency Is Far Off. *CoinDesk.* www.coindesk.com/markets/2016/06/17/bank-of-england-explores-blockchain-says-digital-currency-is-far-off/

Demertzis, M., & Wolff, G. B. (2018). *The economic potential and risks of crypto assets: Is a regulatory framework needed? (Policy Contribution Issue No. 14).* Bruegel. www.bruegel.org/sites/default/files/wp-content/uploads/2018/09/PC-14_2018.pdf

Fairfield, J. A. T. (2022). Tokenized: The Law of Non-Fungible Tokens and Unique Digital Property. *Indiana Law Journal*, 97(4). www.repository.law.indiana.edu/ilj/vol97/iss4/4

Gadekallu, T. R., Huynh-The, T., Wang, W., Yenduri, G., Ranaweera, P., Pham, Q. V., Da Costa, D. B., & Liyanage, M. (2022). Blockchain for the Metaverse: A Review. *ArXiv Preprint (ArXiv:2203.09738).* https://doi.org/10.48550/arXiv.2203.09738

Global Legal Insights. (2023a). *Blockchain & Cryptocurrency Laws and Regulations 2023.* www.globallegalinsights.com/practice-areas/blockchain-laws-and-regulations/japan#:~:text=Regulatory%20framework%20and%20definition,-Back%20to%20top&text=In%20Japan%2C%20there%20is%20no,as%20BTC%2C%20ETH%2C%20etc

Global Legal Insights. (2023b). *Blockchain & Cryptocurrency Laws and Regulations 2023.* www.globallegalinsights.com/practice-areas/blockchain-laws-and-regulations/india

Globaldata. (2021). *Market Size of Video Gaming in Japan (2021, $ billion).* Globaldata. www.globaldata.com/data-insights/technology-media-and-telecom/market-size-of-video-gaming-in-japan/#:~:text=Many%20companies%20in%20the%20gaming,of%20the%20global%20market%20size.

Hamacher, A. (2020). Is this the end of Malta's reign as Blockchain Island? *Decrypt.* https://decrypt.co/17024/is-this-the-end-of-maltas-reign-as-blockchain-island

Heister, S., & Yuthas, K. (2021). How blockchain and AI enable personal data privacy and support cybersecurity. In Fernández-Caramés, T. M. & Fraga-Lamas, P. (Eds) *Advances in the Convergence of Blockchain and Artificial Intelligence.* IntechOpen. https://doi.org/10.5772/intechopen.96999

Hewa, T., Ylianttila, M., & Liyanage, M. (2021). Survey on Blockchain Based Smart Contracts: Applications, Opportunities and Challenges. *Journal of Network and Computer Applications*, 177, 102857.

Hombrebueno, C. (2015). UK Gambling Commission warns bitcoin gambling websites. *CalvinAyre.* https://calvinayre.com/2015/07/01/bitcoin/uk-gambling-commission-warns-bitcoin-gambling-websites/amp

Ishida, M., Mears, E., & Takeda, R. (2017). Japan Regulatory Update on Virtual Currency Business. *DLA Piper*. www.dlapiper.com/en/japan/insights/publications/2017/12/japan-regulatory-update-on-virtual-currency-business/

Jiang, X. J., & Liu, X. F. (2021). CryptoKitties Transaction Network Analysis: The Rise and Fall of the First Blockchain Game Mania. *Frontiers in Physics*, 9. https://doi.org/10.3389/fphy.2021.631665

Joshi, A., & Rachakonda, S. (2022). The legal considerations of blockchain gaming in India. *The Indian Express*. https://indianexpress.com/article/explained/explained-legal-considerations-blockchain-gaming-7817450/lite/

Khan, S. N., Loukil, F., Ghedira-Guegan, C., Benkhelifa, E., & Bani-Hani, A. (2021). Blockchain Smart Contracts: Applications, Challenges, and Future Trends. *Peer-to-Peer Networking and Applications*, 14, 2901–2925. https://doi.org/10.1007/s12083-021-01127-0

Laser, C. (2023) Legal Issues in Blockchain, Cryptocurrency, and Nfts. *Nebraska Law Review*, 102(4). https://ssrn.com/abstract=4591858

Lee, J. Y. (2019). A Decentralized Token Economy: How Blockchain and Cryptocurrency Can Revolutionize Business. *Business Horizons*, 62(6), 773–784. https://doi.org/10.1016/j.bushor.2019.08.003

Malta Gaming Authority. (2018). *The MGA Publishes Guidelines on its Sandbox Framework for the Acceptance of Virtual Financial Assets and the Use of Distributed Ledger Technology Within the Gaming Industry at the Delta Summit, Malta Gaming Authority*. www.mga.org.mt/the-mga-publishes-guidelines-on-its-sandbox-framework-for-the-acceptance-of-virtual-financial-assets-and-the-use-of-distributed-ledger-technology-within-the-oamino_industrv-at_the_delta-qummit_2018/

Patil, S., & Bachani, Y. (2022). Overview and Analysis of the Indian Gaming Industry. *International Journal of Recent Advances in Multidisciplinary Topics*, 3(5), 152–157.

Qiao, D. (2019). This Is Not a Game: Blockchain Regulation and Its Application to Video Games. *Northern Illinois University Law Review*, 40(2), 176. https://heinonline.org/HOL/Page?handle=hein.journals/niulr40&div=9&g_sent=1&casa_token=&collection=journals

Rysin, V., & Rysin, M. (2020). The money laundering risk and regulatory challenges for cryptocurrency markets. In Dziura, M., Jaki, A., & Rojek, T. (Eds) *Restructuring Management Models-Changes-Development*, pp. 187–201. Crackow University of Economics.

Scekic, O., Nastic, S., & Dustdar, S. (2018). Blockchain-Supported Smart City Platform for Social Value Co-Creation and Exchange. *IEEE Internet Computing*, 23(1), 19–28. https://doi.org/10.1109/MIC.2018.2881518

Sharma, K., & Jain, D. (2019). Consensus Algorithms in Blockchain Technology: A Survey. 2019 10th International Conference on Computing, Communication and Networking Technologies (ICCCNT), 1–7. https://doi.org/10.1109/ICCCNT45670.2019.8944509

Siddique, H. M. A., Yaqub, R. M. S., Akram, H. M. Z., & Khurshid, R. (2023). Determinants of AI Non-Fungible Tokens Gaming and Blockchain based Digital Marketing: A Revolution of Metaverse in Asia Pacific Region. *Pakistan Journal of Humanities and Social Sciences*, 11(2), 1909–1931. https://doi.org/10.52131/pjhss.2023.1102.0488

Srivastava, A., Bhat, S., & Sharma, B. (2022). A Critical Analysis of Potential Legal Challenges for Blockchain Technology in Competition Law. *Journal of Positive School Psychology*, 6(9), 4192–4196. https://journalppw.com/index.php/jpsp/article/view/13084

Tambe. (2023). All you need to know about India's Crypto bill. *Forbes Advisor*. www.forbes.com/advisor/in/investing/cryptocurrency/crypto-bill

Tavares, R., Sousa, J. P., Maganinho, B., & Gomes, J. P. (2023). Gamers' Reaction to the Use of NFT in AAA Video Games. *Procedia Computer Science*, 219, 606–613. https://doi.org/10.1016/j.procs.2023.01.329

Tillemann, T., Price, A., Tillemann-Dick, G., & Knight, A. (2019). The blueprint for blockchain and social innovation. *New America*. https://na-staging.s3.amazonaws.com/documents/The_Blueprint_for_Blockchain_and_Social_Innovation_2019-01-22_153559.pdf

Verstein, A. (2019). Crypto Assets and Insider Trading Law's Domain. *Iowa Law Review*, 105(1). https://ilr.law.uiowa.edu/print/volume-105-issue-1/crypto-assets-and-insider-trading-laws-domain

Vondrova, T. (2023). *A comparative study of Governments' practices in response to Blockchain technology* [Master's thesis, Masaryk University]. Information System of Masaryk University. https://is.muni.cz/th/cjxh9/Thesis_Vondrova_final.pdf

Yadav, P. (2023). Explained: How rapidly is the gaming industry growing in India. *India Times*. www.indiatimes.com/explainers/news/how-rapidly-is-the-gaming-industry-growing-in-india-589059.html

Yang, Y. P. A. (2023). When Jurisdiction Rules Meet Blockchain: Can the Old Bottle Contain the New Wine? *Stanford Journal of Blockchain Law & Policy*, 6(1). https://stanford-jblp.pubpub.org/pub/jurisdiction-rules-blockchain

13 A Study on the Legal Challenges in Online Gaming with Special Reference to Network, Accessibility, and Piracy

Angesh A. Panchal and Vidhi Shah

13.1 INTRODUCTION

In the rapidly evolving landscape of online gaming in India, a confluence of legal, technological, and social factors presents unique challenges and opportunities. This chapter delves into the intricate legal framework governing online gaming in India, highlighting recent legislative developments and their implications for the industry. We explore the constitutional basis, central and state legislative actions, and the pivotal role of the Information Technology (Intermediary Guidelines and Digital Media Ethics Code) Amendment Rules of 2023 in shaping the regulatory environment.

A significant portion of our study is devoted to the network challenges in India, analysing the impact of the country's network infrastructure on the online gaming industry. We examine how the digital divide, particularly between urban and rural areas, affects accessibility and user experience. Legal concerns stemming from network issues, such as consumer rights and data privacy, are scrutinized under the existing legal framework, including the Consumer Protection Act 2019 and the Information Technology (Reasonable Security Practices and Procedures and Sensitive Personal Data or Information) Rules 2011.

Furthermore, our chapter addresses the critical issues of accessibility and inclusivity in online gaming. We analyse economic barriers, social perceptions, linguistic diversity, and cultural relevance in the context of Indian gaming. Legal perspectives, such as the Rights of Persons with Disabilities Act 2016 and anti-discrimination laws, are explored for their potential application in promoting inclusivity in digital entertainment.

The menace of piracy in the Indian online gaming industry is another focal point. We discuss the scope, reasons, and legal challenges of piracy, including the enforcement of copyright laws and the industry's response to this pervasive issue.

DOI: 10.1201/9781032624204-14

In conclusion, we offer strategic recommendations for navigating these legal challenges, emphasizing the need for enhanced network infrastructure, legal compliance, promotion of accessibility and inclusivity, and holistic approaches to combat piracy. Our study underscores the necessity for a multifaceted and proactive approach, combining legal reforms, technological advancements, and socially responsible practices to ensure the sustainable growth of the Indian online gaming industry.

13.2 THE LEGAL FRAMEWORK GOVERNING ONLINE GAMING IN INDIA

13.2.1 Overview of the Indian Legal System and Online Gaming

The Indian legal framework has traditionally not been explicit about online gaming. The recent developments, particularly the Information Technology (Intermediary Guidelines and Digital Media Ethics Code) Amendment Rules of 2023, mark a significant shift in this approach. The Ministry of Electronics and Information Technology (MeitY) has played a pivotal role in these developments, aiming to create a regulatory environment that balances the needs of consumers, the industry, and the government.

The Constitution of India, while not specifically addressing online gaming, sets the groundwork for legislative and executive actions in this arena. The fundamental rights and directive principles provide a basis for regulating businesses and protecting consumer interests, which are crucial in the context of online gaming.

Central and state governments have varying jurisdictions over gambling and gaming, with the Public Gambling Act of 1867 being the central legislation. However, this Act does not explicitly cover online gaming, leading to legal ambiguities. Different states have adopted their own approaches to this issue, with some states enacting specific legislation to regulate or ban online gambling and gaming.

13.2.2 Current Legislation and Policies

The Information Technology (Intermediary Guidelines and Digital Media Ethics Code) Amendment Rules of 2023 represent a comprehensive effort to regulate online gaming. These rules define critical terms such as 'online game', 'online gaming intermediary', and 'online real money game'. This clarity is essential for legal and regulatory purposes, helping to distinguish between different types of games and platforms.

The Amendment Rules require intermediaries to appoint a Grievance Officer, responsible for addressing user complaints. This role is crucial for consumer protection, ensuring that grievances related to online gaming are heard and resolved in a timely manner.

The rules also mandate online gaming intermediaries to inform users about permissible online games and to assist government agencies in investigative or protective activities. This is a significant step towards ensuring that online gaming platforms operate within the legal framework and cooperate with law enforcement agencies.

Intermediaries are required to publish periodic compliance reports and maintain a physical contact address in India. These requirements increase the transparency and accountability of online gaming platforms, making them more responsive to the legal and regulatory environment in India.

13.3 NETWORK CHALLENGES AND LEGAL IMPLICATIONS

13.3.1 The State of Network Infrastructure in India

The growth trajectory of India's online gaming industry is closely tied to the development of its network infrastructure. In FY 2021, India had 433 million online gaming users, with revenues reaching Rs 136 billion ($1.6 billion), and these figures are expected to significantly increase by 2025. The expansion of high-speed internet, affordability, and increased smartphone penetration have been pivotal in this growth.

However, the digital divide remains a significant challenge. Urban areas enjoy better connectivity compared to rural regions, affecting the accessibility and quality of online gaming experiences. This disparity not only impacts user satisfaction but also poses a challenge for businesses that depend on widespread and reliable internet access.

13.3.2 Legal Concerns Arising from Network Issues

From a legal perspective, poor network quality can become a consumer rights issue under the Consumer Protection Act, 2019. The Act provides for the protection of the interests of consumers and ensures freedom from unfair trade practices. Consequently, gamers could potentially demand quality service as a right, given the increasing reliance on online platforms for entertainment.

Data privacy and security in online gaming networks are other critical concerns. With the Information Technology (Reasonable Security Practices and Procedures and Sensitive Personal Data or Information) Rules, 2011, there is an onus on companies to implement reasonable security practices to protect personal data. Online gaming platforms, involving significant data transfer, must comply with these standards to ensure user data protection and privacy.

13.4 ACCESSIBILITY AND INCLUSIVITY IN ONLINE GAMING

13.4.1 Economic and Social Accessibility

The economic barriers to online gaming in India are significant. The cost of gaming devices, like consoles and high-end PCs, coupled with the expense of high-speed internet, makes online gaming inaccessible to lower-income groups. This economic divide is exacerbated by the rural-urban divide, where rural areas often lack the necessary infrastructure.

Social factors also impede accessibility. Gaming is often perceived as a leisure activity predominantly for the youth, leading to a lack of focus on older demographics. Additionally, cultural norms can influence the types of games that gain popularity, with a preference for certain genres over others.

13.4.2 Language and Cultural Barriers

India's linguistic diversity presents unique challenges. Most high-profile games are released in English, alienating a large segment of the population who are more comfortable with regional languages. This not only affects gameplay experience but also understanding of critical information such as terms of service, privacy policies, and in-game instructions.

Culturally, the content of many games does not align with Indian traditions and narratives, which can affect their appeal and accessibility. The lack of representation in games can deter potential gamers who seek cultural resonance in the games they play.

13.4.3 Legal Perspectives

From a legal standpoint, the Rights of Persons with Disabilities Act, 2016, can be a tool for advocacy. While not directly addressing online gaming, the principles of inclusivity and accessibility in the Act could be extended to digital entertainment platforms. Game developers and publishers could be encouraged or mandated to create games that are accessible to persons with disabilities, such as including features for the visually or hearing-impaired.

Anti-discrimination laws, though not explicitly tailored for the digital realm, might be invoked in the future to address issues of inclusivity in online gaming. These laws can potentially be applied to ensure that game content does not discriminate on the basis of race, gender, or religion, promoting a more inclusive gaming environment.

13.4.4 The Role of Policymakers and Industry

Policymakers have a crucial role in bridging these gaps. Regulations that encourage or mandate the inclusion of multiple Indian languages and culturally relevant content can significantly enhance accessibility. Incentives for developers to create games that cater to a broader audience, including those with disabilities, can also be an effective approach.

The gaming industry itself needs to be cognizant of these barriers. Emphasizing the development of games that are not only linguistically diverse but also culturally representative can broaden their market reach. Engaging with local communities to understand their needs and preferences can lead to the creation of more inclusive gaming content.

Accessibility and inclusivity in online gaming in India are multifaceted issues, encompassing economic, social, linguistic, and cultural dimensions. The legal framework, while not explicitly addressing these challenges, provides avenues for advocacy and policy formulation. The collaboration between policymakers, the gaming industry, and communities is vital in making online gaming a more inclusive and accessible form of entertainment.

13.5 THE MENACE OF PIRACY IN ONLINE GAMING

13.5.1 Scope and Reasons for Piracy

Piracy in the Indian gaming industry is not merely a matter of illegal downloading; it encompasses a broader spectrum of activities, including the use of unauthorized copies and the sharing of game files. Cultural factors play a significant role in this. For many in India, particularly in older generations, gaming is not viewed as a serious pastime or a pursuit worthy of investment. Consequently, spending substantial amounts on original games is often not a priority, fuelling the demand for pirated versions.

Economic factors also contribute significantly to piracy. The direct conversion of game prices from Western currencies to Indian Rupees makes many games prohibitively expensive for the average consumer. This disparity in pricing, combined with limited disposable income, drives many towards pirated games, which are available at a fraction of the cost.

13.5.2 Legal and Industry Challenges

From a legal perspective, the enforcement of copyright laws in the realm of online gaming faces several hurdles. The digital nature of piracy, involving various internet protocols and file-sharing platforms, makes tracking and prosecuting these activities challenging. The Information Technology Act, 2000, addresses some aspects of digital piracy, but its application to the specific nuances of online gaming piracy is complex and often inadequate.

The gaming industry, both domestically and globally, suffers significant revenue losses due to piracy. The lack of funds not only affects the profitability of gaming companies but also limits their ability to invest in new projects and innovation. Furthermore, pirated games often do not offer the full experience, lacking official support, updates, and multiplayer functionality, which can degrade the overall perception of the gaming experience.

13.5.3 Consumer Awareness and Industry Response

Raising consumer awareness about the impacts of piracy is crucial. Many consumers may not fully understand the legal and ethical implications of using pirated games. Educating gamers about the benefits of using original content, such as continuous updates, customer support, and a more immersive gaming experience, could help reduce piracy.

The industry can also play a role in addressing piracy. Adopting region-specific pricing strategies, offering more localized content, and increasing accessibility can make original games more appealing and affordable. Additionally, game developers and publishers might consider stronger digital rights management (DRM) systems, although these must balance security with user convenience to avoid alienating legitimate customers.

Piracy remains a significant challenge in the Indian online gaming industry, influenced by cultural, economic, and legal factors. Tackling this issue requires a multifaceted approach, including effective law enforcement, consumer education, and industry strategies tailored to the unique needs of the Indian market. Collaborative efforts between the government, industry stakeholders, and the gaming community are essential to create a sustainable ecosystem that supports the growth of legitimate gaming practices in India.

13.6 CONCLUSION

In addressing the legal challenges faced by the Indian online gaming industry, a comprehensive and proactive strategy is essential for sustainable growth. This strategy encompasses several key areas:

- Strategic Recommendations for Navigating Legal Challenges:
  To enhance network infrastructure, particularly in rural and underserved areas, fostering collaborations between the government and private sector is recommended. This effort is in line with the Digital India initiative, which aims to improve connectivity and digital access. Alongside this, there is a significant need to increase awareness campaigns about consumer rights in relation to online services. Educating consumers about the quality of internet services and the importance of data privacy is crucial in this digital age. Furthermore, there is an urgent requirement to fast-track the implementation of comprehensive data protection laws. These laws, akin to the European Union's General Data Protection Regulation (GDPR), would bolster the legal framework for protecting user data, especially in the realm of online gaming.
- Promoting Accessibility and Inclusivity:
  Encouraging game developers to create content that is inclusive and culturally relevant is highly recommended, especially focusing on content that is available in multiple Indian languages. This approach aims to foster diversity in gaming content. In addition, developing and enforcing guidelines to ensure that online games are accessible to people with disabilities is another crucial step that should be taken. This move towards inclusivity ensures that gaming experiences are available to a broader audience. Additionally, it is advised that gaming companies engage with local communities. By doing so, they can better understand the cultural nuances, preferences, and needs of these communities, leading to more resonant and relevant gaming experiences. This community engagement is pivotal in creating a gaming ecosystem that is reflective of its diverse user base.
- Combating Piracy Through Holistic Approaches:
  Enhancing the enforcement of copyright laws, including the creation of specialized units to address digital piracy, is a vital step in strengthening legal enforcement. Alongside this, launching educational initiatives is essential to highlight the negative impacts of piracy and underscore the importance of

original content. This approach aims to raise awareness and change public perception regarding the value of intellectual property. Furthermore, adopting region-specific pricing strategies can make games more affordable, which in turn could reduce the incentive for piracy. This strategy considers the economic variances across different regions, making gaming more accessible while respecting copyright laws. Additionally, collaboration with internet service providers (ISPs) is a key strategy. Working together with ISPs to monitor and limit the distribution of pirated games can significantly aid in curtailing the spread of pirated content. This collaborative approach harnesses the capabilities of ISPs to support the protection of intellectual property in the digital realm.

- Long-term Vision for the Indian Online Gaming Industry:
  Developing flexible legal frameworks that can adapt to the rapid technological changes in online gaming is a necessity. These adaptive frameworks are crucial to ensure that the legal system remains effective and relevant in the dynamic world of gaming technology. In addition, supporting research and development in gaming technology, with a focus on innovations tailored to the Indian market, is highly recommended. This support will foster technological advancement and cater to the unique needs and preferences of the Indian audience. Engaging in international collaborations is also important, as it can help in adopting best practices and global standards in the Indian gaming ecosystem. Such collaborations can bring a wealth of knowledge and expertise, benefiting the local gaming industry.

Furthermore, encouraging sustainable business models that balance profitability with social responsibility and legal compliance is crucial. This approach ensures that the gaming industry not only thrives economically but also contributes positively to society and adheres to legal norms. Finally, continuous dialogue among all stakeholders, including government, industry, academia, and the gaming community, is essential. This engagement is key to ensuring that policies and practices reflect a comprehensive understanding of the industry's challenges and opportunities. Such a collaborative and inclusive approach can lead to more effective and well-rounded policies that support the growth and sustainability of the gaming industry.

In conclusion, the Indian online gaming industry's future success depends on its ability to navigate legal complexities while fostering an environment that supports innovation, inclusivity, and legal compliance. By integrating legal reforms, technological advancements, and socially responsible practices, the industry can achieve sustainable growth.

BIBLIOGRAPHY

Arora. (2018, April 5). Gaming Is Too Damn Expensive in India. *Gadgets 360*. Retrieved December 8, 2023, from www.gadgets360.com/games/opinion/gaming-is-too-damn-expensive-in-india-1833274

Fox Mandal. (2023, February 12). Online gaming: challenges in protection of intellectual property. *Lexology*. Retrieved December 8, 2023, from www.lexology.com/library/detail.aspx?g=f9e442a1-1a62-440b-88c8-fbed029cf737

Hanspal, & Bhalla. (2023, June 19). Regulation of Online Gaming in India: An Analysis of the Recent Legal Amendments Introduced by the Indian Government. *The Legal 500*. Retrieved December 8, 2023, from www.legal500.com/developments/thought-leadership/regulation-of-online-gaming-in-india-an-analysis-of-the-recent-legal-amendments-introduced-by-the-indian-government/

India Today. (2021, February 18). More than 50% of Indian students in rural and urban areas don't have access to internet: Survey. *India Today*. Retrieved December 8, 2023, from www.indiatoday.in/education-today/latest-studies/story/more-than-50-of-indian-students-in-rural-and-urban-areas-don-t-have-access-to-internet-survey-1770308-2021-02-17

IT Intermediary Amendment Rules 2023 notified for online gaming industry. (2023, April 12). Retrieved December 8, 2023, from www.lakshmisri.com/newsroom/news-briefings/it-intermediary-amendment-rules-2023-notified-for-online-gaming-industry/#

Ministry of Communications and Information Technology. (2011, April 11). Information Technology (Reasonable security practices and procedures and sensitive personal data or information) Rules, 2011. In *Ministry of Communications and Information Technology (Department of Information Technology)*. Ministry of Communications and Information Technology (Department of Information Technology). Retrieved December 8, 2023, from www.meity.gov.in/sites/upload_files/dit/files/GSR313E_10511(1).pdf

Ministry of Electronics and Information Technology. (2023, April 6). Information Technology (Intermediary Guidelines and Digital Media Ethics Code) Amendment Rules, 2023. In *Ministry of Electronics and Information Technology*. Ministry of Electronics and Information Technology. Retrieved December 8, 2023, from www.meity.gov.in/writereaddata/files/244980-Gazette%20Notification%20for%20IT%20Amendment%20Rules%2C%202023-%20relating%20to%20online%20gaming%20%26%20false%20information%20about%20Govt.%20business.pdf

Ministry of Electronics & Information Technology. (n.d.). Annual Report 2022–23. In *Ministry of Electronics & Information Technology*. Ministry of Electronics & Information Technology. Retrieved December 8, 2023, from www.meity.gov.in/writereaddata/files/AR_2022-23_English_24-04-23.pdf

Ministry of Home Affairs. (1867, January 25). The Public Gambling Act, 1867. In *Ministry of Home Affairs, Department of Internal Security*. Ministry of Home Affairs, Department of Internal Security. Retrieved December 8, 2023, from https://lddashboard.legislative.gov.in/sites/default/files/A1867-03.pdf

Ministry of Law and Justice. (2016, December 27). The Rights of Persons with Disabilities Act, 2016. In *Ministry of Law and Justice (Legislative Department)*. Ministry of Law and Justice (Legislative Department). Retrieved December 8, 2023, from www.ccdisabilities.nic.in/sites/default/files/2021-09/THE%20RIGHTS%20OF%20PERSONS%20WITH%20DISABILITIES%20ACT%2C%202016%20%28English%29.pdf

Ministry of Law and Justice. (2019, August 9). The Consumer Protection Act, 2019. In *Ministry of Law and Justice (Legislative Department)*. Ministry of Law and Justice (Legislative Department). Retrieved December 8, 2023, from https://consumeraffairs.nic.in/sites/default/files/CP%20Act%202019.pdf

Mitra. (2022, October 25). Online gaming in India: Experts explain financial, legal and social impacts of a booming industry. *ET Edge Insights*. Retrieved December 8, 2023, from https://etinsights.et-edge.com/online-gaming-in-india-experts-weigh-in-on-financial-and-social-impacts-as-government-begins-sector-regulation-discussions

Shukul. (2023, November 28). Challenges and opportunities in India's thriving gaming industry. *Financial Express*. Retrieved December 8, 2023, from www.financialexpress.com/business/brandwagon-challenges-and-opportunities-in-indias-thriving-gaming-industry-3318021/

14 Innovation and Policy

Balancing Technological Advancements with Regulatory Frameworks in Indian Online Gaming

Arup Poddar

14.1 INTRODUCTION

In this chapter, headed "Innovation and Policy: Balancing Technological Advances with Regulatory Frameworks in Indian Online Gaming," we examine the tension that emerges between the industry's rapid technological development and India's strict regulatory structure.

The massive population of India, the ever-increasing availability of the internet, and the explosive growth of the smartphone market have all led to the explosive expansion of the online gaming industry in the country. From e-sports to smartphone games to cutting-edge platforms that make use of artificial intelligence (AI), machine learning (ML), and blockchain, a wide variety of gaming genres have emerged in this ever-changing digital landscape.

This exponential growth, however, highlights the disconnect between the rate of innovation and the evolution of legal frameworks. The link between technology and politics is complex since regulation needs to protect consumer interests and maintain market integrity while creating an atmosphere favorable to innovation.

The goals of this chapter are twofold: first, to analyse the friction between technological progress and regulatory frameworks in India's online gaming industry; and second, to investigate possible means of achieving a harmonious equilibrium between these two factors. It will provide an understanding of the current regulatory landscape, highlight the key technological trends shaping the industry, discuss the challenges in balancing innovation and regulation, and recommend strategies for a balanced approach to policymaking.

14.2 TECHNOLOGICAL INNOVATIONS IN INDIAN ONLINE GAMING

Technological innovations have been instrumental in shaping the Indian online gaming landscape. The emergence of new gaming technologies has redefined the

DOI: 10.1201/9781032624204-15

dynamics of the gaming industry. Cutting-edge technologies like virtual reality (VR), augmented reality (AR), and cloud gaming are transforming gaming experiences, making them more immersive and engaging. VR and AR have enhanced the realism of games, while cloud gaming has allowed for high-end games to be played on low-end devices, democratizing the gaming landscape (Goette et al., 2019). However, the widespread adoption of these technologies is impeded by infrastructural limitations and high costs, raising questions about their immediate viability in the Indian context (Yuan, 2023).

The rise of mobile gaming has significantly impacted the Indian gaming industry, with smartphones becoming the preferred gaming device for many (Frith, 2023). Driven by increased smartphone penetration, affordable internet access, and a young demographic, mobile gaming has outpaced traditional PC and console gaming (Tarannum & Anand, 2023). However, the dominance of mobile gaming presents its own set of challenges, such as the lack of regulations for mobile-specific games and potential issues around digital well-being and addiction (Remmers & Weinert, 2018).

AI and ML are increasingly becoming significant contributors to the evolution of the Indian gaming industry (Columb et al., 2020). AI and ML can enhance game design, user personalization, cheat detection, and player behavior analysis (Stadelmann et al., 2021). The use of these technologies can elevate the gaming experience, but it also raises privacy concerns. The collection and analysis of user data for personalization may infringe on user privacy if not managed appropriately, necessitating robust data protection policies ("AlphaGO – an AI in Gaming," 2017).

Blockchain technology's application in online gaming, often referred to as "blockchain gaming," holds transformative potential. Blockchain games can offer true ownership of in-game assets, facilitate secure transactions, and introduce novel monetization models, such as play-to-earn mechanisms (Gainsbury & Blaszczynski, 2017). However, blockchain gaming also faces significant challenges, such as scalability issues, lack of regulatory clarity, and potential for misuse in fraudulent activities (Ron & Attias, 2017).

In conclusion, while these technological advancements have undeniably pushed the boundaries of online gaming in India, they also bring forth significant challenges that require thoughtful consideration. How these issues are resolved will have a major impact on the future of these technologies and how they shape the Indian online gaming sector.

14.3 REGULATORY LANDSCAPE FOR ONLINE GAMING IN INDIA

The legal framework for internet gambling in India is convoluted, with its combination of outdated directives, newly enacted laws, and state-by-state differences.

The Public Gambling Act of 1867 prohibited both the running of casinos and the patronage of such venues in India (Singh, 2023; Abbott, 2020). However, "games of skill" were excluded from the act's ambit, setting a precedent that continues to shape the legal environment for online gaming today (Heubeck, 2008). The Act had substantial loopholes and regulatory ambiguity because it did not foresee the development and proliferation of internet gaming.

Introduced in 2021 and updated in 2023, the Information Technology (Intermediary Guidelines and Digital Media Ethics Code) Rules represent a significant step toward regulating the digital space, including online gaming (Raghuwanshi, 2023; Lexology, n.d.). These guidelines impose due diligence requirements on intermediaries, necessitate a grievance redressal mechanism, and mandate adherence to a code of ethics (Rana et al., 2016). While the guidelines signify progress in digital regulation, they have been criticized for their broad wording and potential to infringe on the freedom of speech and privacy (Ostanina, 2020).

A unique facet of the Indian gaming regulatory framework is the legal distinction between games of skill and games of chance. Games of skill, where the outcome is predominantly determined by a player's skill, are typically exempt from gambling restrictions (Heubeck, 2008). However, defining what constitutes "skill" is subjective and has led to conflicting judgments. The landmark judgment by the Karnataka High Court, quashing a Rs. 21,000 crore GST notice on M/S Gameskraft Technologies, highlighted the need for clear jurisprudential distinction between these concepts (Economic Times, n.d.).

Despite the central regulations, gaming laws are primarily state subjects in India, leading to diverse state-wise regulations. Some states like Nagaland have progressive laws favoring online skill games, while others like Telangana and Tamil Nadu have restrictive laws barring most forms of online gaming (*Time for a Progressive Law on Online Gaming | Nagaland Post*, 2021). These inconsistencies have implications for the uniform growth of the gaming industry across the country and pose operational challenges for gaming companies (Morgan, 2009).

In conclusion, the regulatory landscape for online gaming in India is continually evolving, necessitating ongoing adaptation from industry stakeholders. Policymakers must strike a balance between nurturing the industry's growth and safeguarding players' interests in the face of rapid technological advancements.

14.4 CHALLENGES IN BALANCING INNOVATION AND REGULATION

Balancing innovation and regulation in the Indian online gaming industry presents numerous challenges, ranging from protecting consumer interests and encouraging industry growth to navigating legal ambiguities and addressing ethical concerns.

Protecting consumer interests is a crucial challenge. As online gaming evolves, players are exposed to new risks, including online fraud, privacy invasion, and addictive behaviors (Ellouze et al., 2022). The challenge lies in implementing robust regulatory mechanisms that safeguard consumer interests without stifling innovation (Simon et al., 2016). It requires meticulous planning to formulate regulations that ensure secure payment gateways, data privacy, and features that prevent gaming addiction, all while allowing room for technological advancements (Neily et al., 2022).

Encouraging industry growth and innovation while maintaining regulatory checks is a delicate balancing act. Policies must promote a conducive environment for startups and encourage technological advancements like AI and blockchain (Kim, 2020). Overly restrictive regulations could hinder these developments, slow growth, and deter potential investors (Columb et al., 2019). The challenge lies in creating an equilibrium that nurtures innovation while ensuring responsible gaming.

Navigating legal ambiguities, especially regarding the classification of games of skill and chance, presents another challenge (Edwards-Waller, 2020). Policymakers need to clearly define these terms to ensure fair and consistent application of the law, while technological innovations continue to blur this distinction (Esgalhado et al., 2021). Addressing this challenge demands ongoing collaboration between technologists, lawyers, and policymakers.

Finally, ethical concerns in online gaming pose significant challenges. These include issues related to minors' access to age-restricted games, the depiction of violence and other potentially harmful content, and the design of in-game transactions and loot boxes that can encourage problematic gambling-like behavior (Columb & O'Gara, 2017). Addressing these ethical issues requires proactive regulations and self-regulation by the industry. However, stringent rules might hamper creative freedom and innovation, necessitating a nuanced approach (Marimón Muñoz et al., 2022).

In conclusion, the task of balancing innovation and regulation in the Indian online gaming industry is intricate, necessitating a careful and holistic approach. Stakeholders must work in tandem to ensure consumer protection, promote industry growth, resolve legal ambiguities, and address ethical issues, all while fostering an environment conducive to innovation.

14.5 INTERNATIONAL PERSPECTIVES AND BEST PRACTICES

India can gain a lot of knowledge and best practices from the international online gaming business. India's approach to its online gaming ecosystem can be informed by a comparison of regulatory regimes, lessons from global best practices, and an appreciation of cross-border difficulties and potential.

When looking at how other countries handle online gaming regulation, it's clear that there are a variety of approaches. For example, the UK Gambling Commission, which regulates land-based and virtual casinos, has been in place since 2005 ("*UK Gambling Commission TGP Europe Limited and Fesuge Limited Public Statement*," 2017) in that country. It has rigorous licensing requirements and other safeguards for consumers. When it comes to gambling, however, Japan takes a much more stringent stance, strictly regulating everything from live casinos to many different kinds of internet games (Palansky et al., 2021). Meanwhile, nations like Malta and Gibraltar have positioned themselves as international hubs for online gambling enterprises due to their favorable tax laws and regulatory environments (Mangion, 2010) for the industry.

India may learn a lot from these international standards. For instance, India may adopt more stringent regulations to protect players from fraud and addiction after learning from the United Kingdom's approach (Nugzar, 2018). While Japan's stringent stance may not be relevant in India's setting, it does highlight the need for well-defined legal categories for games of skill and chance (Losak, 2021). Following the lead of Malta and Gibraltar, India may be able to lure foreign gaming enterprises by providing a conducive regulatory framework.

The necessity for a strong regulatory framework in India is bolstered by the fact that the country faces challenges and opportunities on a global scale. When trying to expand into new markets, online gaming companies worldwide frequently encounter difficulties on the legal and cultural fronts (Paulson & Weber, 2006). However, these challenges also present opportunities for collaboration and learning. The cross-border nature of the internet allows for the sharing of best practices and regulatory experiences that can be used to develop a more robust and innovative online gaming industry in India (Shrivastava, 2022).

In conclusion, international perspectives on online gaming regulation present a wealth of knowledge and best practices for India. Drawing lessons from these experiences can aid in the development of a robust, consumer-friendly, and innovation-promoting regulatory framework for online gaming in India.

14.6 CASE STUDIES

The interaction between innovation and regulation in the online gaming industry can be best understood through case studies that illustrate successes, challenges, and the impact of regulatory compliance on consumer trust.

One of the successful examples of innovation within regulatory bounds is that of Dream11, a fantasy sports platform in India. Dream11 offers games of skill that are not classified as gambling under Indian law, thus successfully circumventing stringent regulations against online gambling (Raza et al., 2021). The company has used ML to enhance the user experience, improve predictive accuracy, and offer a more immersive gaming experience (*Legitimacy of Dream11 In India*, 2020). By carefully understanding the regulatory landscape and innovating within its confines, Dream11 has become one of the largest online gaming platforms in India (*Wagering Agreements and Its Application on Fantasy Gaming – Legitimacy of Dream 11 in India*, 2021).

However, navigating the regulatory landscape is not always straightforward. One such example is of Gameskraft, an online gaming company that was slapped with a Rs. 21,000 crore GST notice (*The GST Conundrum of Online Gaming*, 2023). The Karnataka High Court eventually quashed the notice, clarifying the jurisprudential distinction between the concepts of "game of skill" and "game of chance" (French, 2017). The case underscores the ambiguity in the current regulatory environment and the potential financial and reputational risks gaming companies face (Harrell, 2021).

RummyCircle is a good example of the importance of following the rules when dealing with customers (*Technological Advancement of Gaming: Issues and Challenges*, 2022). The corporation has made significant investments in anti-fraud measures, age verification, and ethical gaming policies. RummyCircle has earned credibility among its users by strictly complying to the rules outlined in the Information Technology (Intermediary Guidelines and Digital Media Ethics Code) document. The platform's success with Indian gamers can be attributed in part to the company's efforts to remain compliant with relevant regulations (Supriyanto, 2012).

In conclusion, these studies show why it's crucial for the online gaming sector to strike a balance between innovation and regulation. To succeed, businesses need to be able to negotiate the ever-changing regulatory landscape, innovate to improve the customer experience, and gain consumer trust by adherence to the rules. In spite of obstacles, the Indian online gaming business has enormous potential, and with a comprehensive understanding of legal frameworks, the industry may flourish.

14.7 FUTURE PATHWAYS: RECOMMENDATIONS FOR A BALANCED APPROACH

Finding a happy medium between unbridled creativity and strict oversight is crucial to the success of India's online gaming sector. Collaboration among stakeholders, encouragement of responsible innovation, ongoing evaluation and adaptation of regulations, and promotion of a research and development ecosystem are all necessary to strike this balance.

For effective policymaking, stakeholder input is crucial. There are a wide variety of people involved in the gaming industry. To ensure rules are workable, enforceable, and growth-friendly for the industry as a whole, policymaking should be a collaborative effort including all relevant parties (Columb et al., 2020). For instance, public consultations and roundtable talks can shed light on the practical effects of proposed legislation.

We should promote technology innovation that is both safe and useful. When developing new products or services, businesses should keep in mind their potential ethical and societal impacts and not operate in a vacuum. There should be enough measures in place to protect user data and privacy while using AI and ML. Although revolutionary, blockchain technology must be used in a responsible manner to minimize abuse and keep players' faith in the online gaming community (Waldman, 2019).

Policies governing the use of the Internet to play games should be regularly evaluated and revised as necessary. Because of the speed with which technology develops, rules and laws can suddenly become irrelevant. As a result, it is important to conduct reviews on a consistent basis in order to spot problems, deal with emerging issues, and adjust to the ever-changing world of online gaming (Columb et al., 2020).

Finally, fostering an ecosystem for research and development can ensure that India stays at the forefront of online gaming innovation. Government and private sector investments can support research initiatives and incubate startups. Universities and research institutions should be encouraged to conduct studies on emerging gaming technologies, regulatory impacts, and societal issues related to online gaming (Esgalhado et al., 2021).

In conclusion, the future pathways for the online gaming industry in India will require a balanced approach. By embracing stakeholder collaboration, promoting responsible innovation, maintaining flexibility in policymaking, and supporting research and development, India can ensure a thriving and responsible online gaming industry.

14.8 CONCLUSION

The Indian online gaming industry finds itself at a crossroads, where unprecedented technological innovation intersects with an evolving regulatory landscape. As we have seen, both technology and policy have made strides, but often at a pace that challenges the other. Thc task of finding a harmonious balance is a complex but crucial endeavor for the future of the industry.

Going forward, the road ahead involves strategic collaboration between industry stakeholders, regulators, and technology experts. A regular review of policies to accommodate new technologies, coupled with responsible technological innovation keeping ethical considerations at the forefront, is essential. This balanced approach will not only foster a vibrant online gaming ecosystem but also protect the interests of all stakeholders.

As a final thought, the need for a proactive approach cannot be overstated. The industry, regulators, and policymakers must take collective responsibility to drive this harmonious balance. It is a call to action for everyone involved to ensure that India's online gaming landscape continues to thrive, innovate, and remain compliant in this rapidly evolving digital era.

REFERENCES

Abbott, M. (2020, July). The Changing Epidemiology of Gambling Disorder and Gambling-Related Harm: Public Health Implications. *Public Health, 184*, 41–45. https://doi.org/10.1016/j.puhe.2020.04.003

AlphaGO – An AI in gaming. (2017, June 7). *International Journal of Recent Trends in Engineering and Research, 3*(5), 566–568. https://doi.org/10.23883/ijrter.2017.3272.xwdqs

Code of Ethics on Responsible Communication in Gambling. (2018, May). *Gaming Law Review, 22*(4), 241–244. https://doi.org/10.1089/glr2.2018.2245

Columb, D., & O'Gara, C. (2017, November 16). A National Survey of Online Gambling Behaviours. *Irish Journal of Psychological Medicine, 35*(4), 311–319. https://doi.org/10.1017/ipm.2017.64

Columb, D., Griffiths, M. D., & O'Gara, C. (2019, August 1). Online Gaming and Gaming Disorder: More Than just a Trivial Pursuit. *Irish Journal of Psychological Medicine, 39*(1), 1–7. https://doi.org/10.1017/ipm.2019.31

Columb, D., Griffiths, M. D., & O'Gara, C. (2020, February 28). A Descriptive Survey of Online Gaming Characteristics and Gaming Disorder in Ireland. *Irish Journal of Psychological Medicine, 40*(2), 200–208. https://doi.org/10.1017/ipm.2020.5

Economic Times. (n.d.). *GST authorities issue notice to Gameskraft, seek Rs 21,000 crore*. The Economic Times. https://economictimes.indiatimes.com/industry/media/entertainment/bengaluru-gaming-company-gets-rs-21000-cr-gst-notice-reportedly-the-biggest-ever/articleshow/94439405.cms

Edwards-Waller, L. (2020, December). The Mysterious Affair at Squire: Using Code-Breaking Games to Deliver Law Library Skills. *Legal Information Management, 20*(4), 218–222. https://doi.org/10.1017/s1472669620000511

Ellouze, A., Ben Thabet, J., Maalej, M., Feki, R., Gassara, I., Smaoui, N., Omri, S., Zouari, L., Charfi, N., & Maalej, M. (2022, June). Gambling Disorder Risk Factors in a Population of Online Sports Betting Players in Sfax. *European Psychiatry*, *65*(S1), S822–S822. https://doi.org/10.1192/j.eurpsy.2022.2127

Esgalhado, G., Fernandes, A., & Pereira, H. (2021, April). Online Gaming Dependency, Attention Levels and Sleep Quality Among Online Gamers. *European Psychiatry*, *64*(S1), S573–S574. https://doi.org/10.1192/j.eurpsy.2021.1530

French, J. A. (2017, March). AED Switching: A Game of Skill or a Game of Chance? *Epilepsy Currents*, *17*(2), 103–104. https://doi.org/10.5698/1535-7511.17.2.103

Frith, J. (2023, February 23). Preserving the History of Mobile Gaming—A Review of The Retro Mobile Gaming Database. *Mobile Media & Communication*, 205015792311555. https://doi.org/10.1177/20501579231155533

Gainsbury, S. M., & Blaszczynski, A. (2017, September). How Blockchain and Cryptocurrency Technology Could Revolutionize Online Gambling. *Gaming Law Review*, *21*(7), 482–492. https://doi.org/10.1089/glr2.2017.2174

Goette, W., Delello, J. A., & McWhorter, R. R. (2019, July). Gendered Experiences of Mobile Gaming and Augmented Reality. *International Journal of Virtual and Augmented Reality*, *3*(2), 54–67. https://doi.org/10.4018/ijvar.2019070105

Harrell, E. (2021, March 24). *Online Sports Betting: The Opportunities and Risks for Banks*. "Online Sports Betting: The Opportunities and Risks for Banks" by Evan Harrell. https://scholarship.law.unc.edu/ncbi/vol25/iss1/17

Heubeck, S. (2008, June). Measuring Skill in Games: A Critical Review of Methodologies. *Gaming Law Review and Economics*, *12*(3), 231–238. https://doi.org/10.1089/glre.2008.12306

Kim, S. K. A. (2020, August 3). Strategic Alliance for Blockchain Governance Game. *Probability in the Engineering and Informational Sciences*, *36*(1), 184–200. https://doi.org/10.1017/s0269964820000406

Legitimacy of Dream11 In India. (2020, June 25). Indian Journal of Law and Public Policy. https://ijlpp.com/legitimacy-of-dream11-in-india/

Lexology. (n.d.). *Brief Overview of the Information Technology (Intermediary Guidelines and Digital Media Ethics Code) Amendment Rules, 2023*. Lexology. www.lexology.com/library/detail.aspx?g=1c7df7b7-c415-4baa-a868-d1aa01adf487

Losak, J. (2021, November). Player Pricing Mechanisms and the Daily Fantasy Sport Chance Versus Skill Debate. *International Journal of Sport Finance*, *16*(4). https://doi.org/10.32731/ijsf/164.112021.04

Mangion, G. (2010, June). Perspective from Malta: Money Laundering and Its Relation to Online Gambling. *Gaming Law Review and Economics*, *14*(5), 363–370. https://doi.org/10.1089/glre.2010.14507

Marimón Muñoz, E., Miranda Ruiz, E., & Stoppa Montserrat, A. (2022, June). Association between Mood Disorders, Problematic Internet Use and Online Gambling Addiction: A Systematic Review. *European Psychiatry*, *65*(S1), S834–S834. https://doi.org/10.1192/j.eurpsy.2022.2160

Morgan, G. (2009, July 24). Challenges of Online Game Development: A Review. *Simulation & Gaming*, *40*(5), 688–710. https://doi.org/10.1177/1046878109340295

Neily, C., Maalej, M., Gassara, I., Feki, R., Smaoui, N., Zouari, L., Zouari, A., Ben Thabet, J., Omri, S., Charfi, N., & Maalej, M. (2022, June). Factors Related to Gaming Addiction in Adults. *European Psychiatry*, *65*(S1), S367–S368. https://doi.org/10.1192/j.eurpsy.2022.934

Nugzar, G. A. (2018). How to Protect Young People from Social Drug Addiction. *Psychology & Psychological Research International Journal*, *3*(6). https://doi.org/10.23880/pprij-16000177

Ostanina, E. (2020, December 17). Internet Freedom of Speech and Privacy Protection: Is There a Contradiction? (A Study of Rating Sites). *Legal Issues in the Digital Age*, *3*(3), 125–139. https://doi.org/10.17323/2713-2749.2020.3.125.139

Palansky, S., Cox, L. M., Lanza, E., & Groumoutis, S. (2021, November 1). Responsible Gaming for Online Gaming. *Gaming Law Review*, *25*(9), 405–411. https://doi.org/10.1089/glr2.2021.29044.sle

Paulson, R. A., & Weber, J. E. (2006). Cyberextortion: An Overview of Distributed Denial of Service Attacks Against Online Gaming Companies. *Issues in Information Systems*. https://doi.org/10.48009/2_iis_2006_52-58

Raghuwanshi, A. (2023, June 1). Extending the Umbrella of Censorship in India to Encompass Online Games. *Gaming Law Review*, *27*(5), 234–239. https://doi.org/10.1089/glr2.2023.0006

Rana, N. P., Dwivedi, Y. K., Williams, M. D., & Weerakkody, V. (2016, June). Adoption of Online Public Grievance Redressal System in India: Toward Developing a Unified View. *Computers in Human Behavior*, *59*, 265–282. https://doi.org/10.1016/j.chb.2016.02.019

Raza, M. R., Shekhar, R., & Singh, U. (2021, September 10). *Gaming and Gambling: The Era of Dream11 and Crashing Dreams*. Gaming and Gambling: The Era of Dream11 and Crashing Dreams by Mohd Rameez Raza, Raj Shekhar, Ujjwal Singh:: SSRN. https://ssrn.com/abstract=3918189

Remmers, P., & Weinert, J. (2018, July). Sports Betting Presents Unique Challenges for Responsible Gaming Practices; Proactive Operators are Key. *Gaming Law Review*, *22*(6), 315–316. https://doi.org/10.1089/glr2.2018.22610

Ron, T. I., & Attias, S. (2017, July). Case Analysis for the Effect of Blockchain Technology in the Gaming Regulatory Environment. *Gaming Law Review*, *21*(6), 459–460. https://doi.org/10.1089/glr2.2017.21613

Shrivastava, A. (2022, November 1). Developing a Responsible Gaming Model for the Online Gaming Industry of India. *Gaming Law Review*, *26*(9), 450–462. https://doi.org/10.1089/glr2.2022.0033

Simon, O., Chebbi, R., Godall, A. O., Eicher, J., Zumwald, C., & Dickson, C. (2016, March). Clinical and Demographic Characteristics of Treatment Seeking Online Video Game Players. *European Psychiatry*, *33*(S1), S318–S318. https://doi.org/10.1016/j.eurpsy.2016.01.1086

Singh, A. (2023). Laws on Online Gaming and Online Gambling in India: Future Market of India. *SSRN Electronic Journal*. https://doi.org/10.2139/ssrn.4480470

Stadelmann, T., Keuzenkamp, J., Grabner, H., & Würsch, C. (2021, June 25). The AI-Atlas: Didactics for Teaching AI and Machine Learning On-Site, Online, and Hybrid. *Education Sciences*, *11*(7), 318. https://doi.org/10.3390/educsci11070318

Supriyanto, S. (2012, June 1). Using Rummy Game Method to Improve Students' Learning Activities and English Dialog. *Register Journal*, *5*(1), 101. https://doi.org/10.18326/rgt.v5i1.253

Tarannum, H., & Anand, M. (2023, March 1). Effects of Smart Phone Gaming on Hand Strength and Dexterity. *CARDIOMETRY*, *26*, 437–442. https://doi.org/10.18137/cardiometry.2023.26.437442

Technological Advancement of Gaming: Issues and Challenges. (2022, August 7). IJLLR. www.ijllr.com/post/technological-advancement-of-gaming-issues-and-challenges

The GST Conundrum of Online Gaming. (2023, April 9). IJLLR. www.ijllr.com/post/the-gst-conundrum-of-online-gaming

Time for a Progressive Law on Online Gaming | Nagaland Post. (2021, August 26). Time for a Progressive Law on Online Gaming | Nagaland Post. https://nagalandpost.com/index.php/time-for-a-progressive-law-on-online-gaming/

UK Gambling Commission TGP Europe Limited and Fesuge Limited Public Statement. (2017, June). *Gaming Law Review*, *21*(5), 390–392. https://doi.org/10.1089/glr2.2017.2159

Wagering Agreements and its Application on Fantasy Gaming – Legitimacy of Dream 11 in India. (2021, September 18). IJLLR. www.ijllr.com/post/wagering-agreements-and-its-application-on-fantasy-gaming-legitimacy-of-dream-11-in-india

Waldman, A. E. (2019, April 10). Law, Privacy, and Online Dating: "Revenge Porn" in Gay Online Communities. *Law & Social Inquiry*, *44*(04), 987–1018. https://doi.org/10.1017/lsi.2018.29

Yuan, V. (2023, June 14). Networking Technologies in Online Gaming: Current Status and Future Development. *Applied and Computational Engineering*, *6*(1), 938–946. https://doi.org/10.54254/2755-2721/6/20230962

15 Dark Patterns in the Gaming Industry

Legal Implications and Safeguarding User Rights

V.S. Gigimon and Narayana Sharma

15.1 INTRODUCTION

In the dynamic landscape of online gaming in India, where technological innovation and user engagement intersect, a concerning trend has emerged, "dark patterns." These deceptive design techniques, subtly embedded in-game interfaces and mechanics, manipulate player's choices, often leading to unintended consequences detrimental to their interests and rights. This chapter aims to unravel the complex web of dark patterns in the Indian gaming industry, examining their legal implications and exploring strategies to protect user rights.

The proliferation of online gaming in India has been meteoric, fuelled by widespread internet access and the affordability of smart devices. As per Deloitte's 2022 Global TMT (Technology, Media and Entertainment, Telecom) predictions, India will have a 1 Billion Smartphone user base by the year 2026 ("India to Have 1 Billion Smartphone Users by 2026: Deloitte Report," 2022) and as per the Annual Mobile Broadband Index (MBiT) report by Nokia, mobile data traffic in India has risen over 3.2 times in 2023. An individual's average monthly data consumption will increase to 46 Gigabytes in 2027 from 20 Gigabytes per month (Khan, 2023). All these trends showcase the immense growth and adaptability of electronic devices and the internet in India. While beneficial in economic growth and entertainment value, this boom has also opened avenues for exploitative practices. Dark patterns in gaming, ranging from inconspicuous in-app purchases to manipulative reward systems, pose significant challenges. They not only affect individual players, particularly vulnerable groups like children but also raise broader concerns about consumer rights and data privacy.

A major impact of dark patterns is on user rights, including financial exploitation, addiction, and privacy breaches. It sheds light on the ethical dilemmas and moral responsibilities of game developers and publishers, highlighting the fine line between engaging game design and manipulative practices.

DOI: 10.1201/9781032624204-16

15.2 WHAT ARE DARK PATTERNS?

Dark patterns, a term first coined by User Experience (UX) specialist Harry Brignull, refer to design tactics employed in websites and apps, including games, that nudge users into making decisions that may not be in their best interests (Goodstein, 2021). Dark patterns are not always an intentional design choice. Rather, they can also be created out of convenience by the designer, but in some way, making it difficult for the end user to achieve what he wants by manipulatively deceiving the user to either doing another task to achieve what the user wants or by forcing the user from not doing the intended task by making the user interface so complex. These tactics often exploit human psychology and can lead to unintended, usually negative, consequences for users. Let us explore various forms of dark patterns, specifically contextualised within online gaming interfaces (Maier & Harr, 2020).

Zagal et al. (2013) researched the utilisation of Dark Patterns in Games, which they refer to as "Dark Game Design Patterns." They provide a precise definition for these patterns:

> A dark game design pattern is a pattern used intentionally by a game creator to cause negative experiences for players which are against their best interests and likely happen without their consent.
>
> (Zagal et al., 2013)

These patterns are categorised into specific types based on how they exploit player psychology and expectations, as per Zagal et al.

1. **Temporal Dark Patterns**:
   - **Grinding**: Defined as performing repetitive and tedious tasks to progress in a game. The author emphasises that grinding places emphasis on time invested over skill. It can become a dark pattern when it coerces players into spending excessive time on monotonous activities, extending the game's duration beyond reasonable or enjoyable. This pattern often exploits players' competitive nature and disproportionately affects new or young players who may not accurately gauge the time commitment required.
   - **Playing by Appointment**: This involves requiring players to engage with the game at specific times set by the game, not the player. The author uses the example of crops in Farmville that wither if not harvested in time, forcing players to align their real-world activities to the game's schedule. This pattern becomes problematic when it imposes rigid time constraints, creating an obligation rather than a choice and can negatively impact players' real-life schedules. This pattern can be widely seen in games that ask the player to complete specified tasks; every task will have a stipulated time.
2. **Monetary Dark Patterns**:
   - **Pay to Skip**: This pattern involves monetising the solution to challenges within a game. Players can pay to bypass difficult levels or tasks, as seen in games like Angry Birds with the "Mighty Eagle" feature. This pattern exploits the player's desire for progress by creating intentionally

challenging or frustrating scenarios and offering a paid shortcut. This is also observed in scenarios where certain games require specific in-game purchases, such as a faster car for completing a level in a racing game; therefore, the players will be forced to make such a purchase to advance.
  - Pre-delivered content occurs when content is included in a game but locked behind a paywall. The author describes this as giving the impression of an incomplete game, compelling players to pay extra for content they presumed was already included in their initial purchase.
  - **Monetised Rivalries**: Also known as "Pay to Win," this pattern capitalises on player competitiveness, encouraging them to spend money to gain an in-game advantage or status. It often results in an uneven playing field, where the amount spent can influence success more than skill or effort.
3. **Social Capital-Based Dark Patterns**:
  - **Social Pyramid Schemes**: This pattern involves incentivising players to recruit others into the game for tangible in-game benefits, creating a cycle of obligation and recruitment.
  - **Impersonation**: The game impersonates players or their friends for actions they did not perform, misleading them about their in-game activities and potentially harming real-life social relations.

In summary, these dark patterns are exploitative techniques that manipulate players' time, money, and social relationships, often leading them to commit more resources to the game than initially intended or desired. These patterns raise significant ethical concerns, as they can profoundly impact the gaming experience and blur the lines between fair play and manipulation.

15.3 LEGAL LANDSCAPE OF DARK PATTERNS IN THE GAMING SECTOR IN THE USA

The United States has been at the forefront of addressing the challenges of dark patterns in the gaming sector. This section examines the legal landscape, including relevant laws, regulatory actions, and landmark cases, that shape how dark patterns are governed in the US gaming industry.

15.4 RELEVANT LAWS AND REGULATIONS

1. Children's Online Privacy Protection Act (COPPA):
  - COPPA plays a crucial role in protecting children under 13 from the unauthorised collection of their personal information by online services, including games. As seen in major cases like FTC vs. Epic Games, violations of COPPA have led to significant penalties for companies that fail to obtain parental consent before collecting data from children (Children's Online Privacy Protection Rule, n.d.).
2. Federal Trade Commission Act:
  - The FTC Act, particularly Section 5, which prohibits "unfair or deceptive acts or practices," has been instrumental in combatting dark patterns.

The FTC uses this Act to address deceptive practices, including misleading in-game purchases and manipulative interface designs (*Federal Trade Commission Act, Incorporating U.S. SAFE WEB Act Amendments of 2006*, n.d.).

3. State Consumer Protection Laws:
    - Various states have enacted consumer protection laws that may impact the gaming sector. For instance, California's Consumer Privacy Act (2020) and the forthcoming California Privacy Rights Act (CPRA) include provisions that could be used to challenge certain dark patterns that compromise consumer privacy.
4. The Deceptive Experiences to Online Users Reduction (DETOUR) Act (Nebraska, n.d.):
    - Proposed but not voted on, it aimed to outlaw dark patterns for large online platforms broadly. This legislative direction in the United States reflects efforts to balance user rights and compliance, focusing on the impact of practices on consumer autonomy.

15.5 CASE STUDY: *FTC VS. EPIC GAMES*

In December, a landmark legal development unfolded in the gaming world. Epic Games, the developer behind the wildly popular game "Fortnite," reached a staggering $520 million settlement with the US Federal Trade Commission (FTC). This case encapsulates critical consumer protection issues, online privacy, and digital ethics, particularly concerning minors (Thiess & Dimov, 2023).

The FTC accused Epic Games of violating the Children's Online Privacy Protection Act (COPPA) and employing dark patterns that led to unintended player purchases. The settlement, comprising a $275 million penalty and a $245 million refund to affected players, represents a significant moment in digital consumer rights history. Epic Games faced two major allegations under COPPA:

1. **Data Collection without Consent**: Despite knowing that children were playing Fortnite, Epic collected personal data from these minors without parental consent. This was evidenced through user surveys, marketing strategies, and internal communications (Feuer, 2022).
2. **Unsafe Default Settings**: By default, Fortnite enabled text and voice communication, exposing minors to potential bullying, harassment, and other psychological harms. Internal requests for safer opt-in options for voice chat were ignored.

Epic Games was also accused of using dark patterns to induce players into making accidental purchases. These included:

1. **Counterintuitive Interface Design**: Confusing button placements and single-click purchases without confirmation led to inadvertent purchases.
2. **Purchases During Inactivity**: Unintended purchases could occur when the game was awoken from sleep mode or during loading screens.

3. **Unauthorised Purchases by Minors**: Children could buy in-game currency without parental consent.
4. **Punitive Account Lockouts**: Disputing unauthorised purchases resulted in account lockouts, causing players to lose access to all previously purchased content.

The *FTC vs Epic* Games case marks a pivotal moment in recognising and addressing the challenges of dark online gaming patterns. It highlights the need for stringent consumer protection measures, especially for minors, and signals a potential legislative evolution to curb unethical digital practices. This case could catalyse more comprehensive legal frameworks governing digital consumer interactions, particularly in the gaming sector.

15.6 LEGAL LANDSCAPE OF DARK PATTERNS IN THE GAMING SECTOR IN THE EUROPEAN UNION

In the European Union, dark patterns are regulated through a multifaceted legal framework, primarily under the General Data Protection Regulation (GDPR), the Digital Services Act (DSA), the Digital Markets Act (DMA), and the Unfair Commercial Practices Directive (UCPD). While not explicitly defining dark patterns, these regulations address manipulative practices that affect consumer autonomy and privacy. For instance, the GDPR and ePrivacy Directive focus on informed consent in data processing. The DSA explicitly prohibits deceptive techniques that impair user choice, and the DMA addresses free user choice and consent. So, we could rely on the European Union primarily regulating dark patterns using existing data protection regulations, therefore showcasing a plurality of legislative objectives (Cooper et al., 2023).

15.7 LEGAL LANDSCAPE OF DARK PATTERNS IN THE GAMING SECTOR IN INDIA

The legal framework governing online gaming in India amalgamates traditional statutes, recent policies, and emerging guidelines. The primary legislative instruments relevant to consumer protection in online gaming include the Indian Contract Act of 1872, the Information Technology Act of 2000 (IT Act), and the Consumer Protection Act of 2019.

The Indian Contract Act governs the agreements between game providers and players, ensuring that the terms of service and user agreements meet the basic requirements of a valid contract. The IT Act, particularly through its rules concerning Reasonable Security Practices and Procedures, pertains to protecting personal data in the digital space. The Consumer Protection Act is pivotal for gamers, offering a legal recourse for unfair trade practices, which could include deceptive design elements and misleading advertising. The Department of Consumer Affairs (DoCA) implemented Guidelines for the Prevention and Regulation of Dark Patterns per Section 18 of the Consumer Protection Act of 2019. Their main goal is to suppress fraudulent activities and foster openness in the digital economy. This is a notable and praiseworthy advancement, given that the Indian legal system has not addressed dark patterns. (Kumar & Panwar, 2023) The rules define dark patterns as follows:

> any practices or deceptive design patterns using UI/UX (user interface/user experience) interactions on any platform; designed to mislead or trick users into doing something they originally did not intend or want to do; by subverting or impairing the consumer autonomy, decision making or choice; amounting to a misleading advertisement or unfair trade practice or violation of consumer rights.

Despite these regulations, the Indian legal system does not yet have specific provisions addressing the nuances of dark patterns in online gaming. The term "dark patterns" is not legally defined, and the current laws do not directly tackle the complex strategies used by online games to manipulate user behaviour.

15.8 CHALLENGES IN REGULATING DARK PATTERNS IN THE GAMING SECTOR IN INDIA

One of the most significant challenges is explicitly recognising dark patterns as a distinct legal issue. Existing laws like the Consumer Protection Act address unfair trade practices and deceptive advertisements but fall short of covering the subtleties of user interface designs and the psychological tactics employed in games.

Also, the consumer protection regulations present in India cannot bring in its ambit dark patterns found within games because they cannot be restricted only as a violation of consumer rights. Rather, such violations, if any, are only one facet of the larger problem. These regulations will only be fruitful if they are specifically drafted based on the needs of the gaming industry.

There is also a gap in enforcement. Even where laws could potentially apply, the mechanisms for monitoring and enforcing compliance in the fast-paced digital gaming environment must be developed. The rapid evolution of gaming technologies often outpaces the slower legislative processes, leading to a lag in the law catching up with industry practices.

Data privacy is another area of concern. The IT Act provides for data protection, but its application to the intricacies of data collection and consent within games, especially concerning dark patterns, could be more robust. The current Personal Digital Data Protection Act 2023 is a valid opportunity that is before the Indian government to be utilised as a proactive measure to regulate data sharing in the gaming sector which can limit the effect of some dark patterns even though it might not be a complete solution.

Moreover, the cross-border nature of many online gaming companies complicates jurisdictional enforcement. With many games developed and operated outside India, the applicability of Indian laws and the enforcement of user rights have become challenging.

Lastly, there is an educational gap. Users often need to be aware of their rights under the current legal framework and may not recognise dark patterns as potentially illegal or unethical. Even if they do, the pathways to seek redress have yet to be widely known or utilised.

15.9 RECOMMENDATIONS

India needs targeted legislation that explicitly defines and addresses dark patterns to bridge these gaps. Legal definitions must encompass the various forms of dark patterns and provide clear guidelines on permissible and impermissible practices in user interface design and consent mechanisms in online games.

Enforcement mechanisms must be strengthened, including establishing a regulatory body with the authority to oversee online gaming practices. Such a body could also create awareness campaigns to educate users about dark patterns and their rights.

Data protection laws must be updated to cover the gaming industry's practices, with clear consent and data usage rules. The enactment of the Personal Data Protection Bill could be a step in the right direction, providing a more modern framework for digital privacy.

Furthermore, cross-border cooperation is essential. International treaties and agreements could be leveraged to ensure that foreign companies comply with Indian laws when they target Indian consumers.

In summary, while India has a framework that could be interpreted to protect consumers against some aspects of dark patterns in online gaming, significant gaps need to be addressed through specific legislation, stronger enforcement, international cooperation, and enhanced user education.

15.10 CONCLUSION

By examining the deceptive tactics used in the gaming business, specifically in the Indian market, we have gained a detailed knowledge of how technology progress, user involvement, and ethical dilemmas intersect. This chapter has thoroughly examined dark patterns' complex and varied nature, closely analysing how they appear in online gaming interfaces and exploring the legal and ethical dilemmas they create.

Dark patterns, which include manipulative techniques like trick questions, bait-and-switch tactics, privacy violations, and forced actions, pose significant challenges in protecting consumer rights and maintaining fairness in the digital realm. Although the legal framework in India includes basic laws that can handle some aspects of these fraudulent schemes, it has noticeable gaps, creating a situation where consumers are vulnerable to abuse.

As we conclude this discussion, it becomes clear that protecting user rights from deceptive design techniques requires a focused and diverse effort. This includes not just strengthening legislative frameworks but also enforcing them rigorously, supported by industry self-regulation and an increase in public awareness. Education programs play a crucial role by providing users with the knowledge and skills to recognise and combat deceptive tactics.

The future of the online gaming industry in India depends heavily on striking a balance between fostering technical innovation and upholding ethical, user-focused design standards. By addressing the difficulties presented by dark patterns with determination and anticipation, individuals involved may establish a gaming atmosphere that is interactive and considerate of user independence and entitlements.

Pursuing a morally upright and user-centric digital gaming environment is an ongoing process. It requires continuous watchfulness, cooperative effort, and dedication to the ongoing development of our legal and regulatory systems. This dedication guarantees that the virtual worlds we pursue for escape and amusement maintain fairness, pleasure, and unwavering adherence to our rights and preferences.

REFERENCES

Business Standard. (2022, February 22). India to have 1 billion smartphone users by 2026: Deloitte report. *Business Standard.* www.business-standard.com/article/current-affairs/india-to-have-1-billion-smartphone-users-by-2026-deloitte-report-12202220099 6_1.html

California Privacy Rights Act (2020), from https://thecpra.org/

Children's Online Privacy Protection Rule (n.d.), www.ftc.gov/ogc/coppa1.htm

Cooper, D., Choi, S. J., Valat, D., & Meneses, A. O. (2023, January 31). *The EU Stance on Dark Patterns.* COVINGTON. www.insideprivacy.com/eu-data-protection/the-eu-sta nce-on-dark-patterns/

Federal Trade Commission Act, incorporating U.S. SAFE WEB Act amendments of 2006. (n.d.).

Feuer. (2022, December 21). *Wrapping Up 2022 with a Huge (Epic) Fortnite Privacy Case.* ESRB Privacy Certified. www.esrb.org/privacy-certified-blog/wrapping-up-2022-with-a-huge-epic-fortnite-privacy-case/

Goodstein, S. A. (2021). When the Cat's Away: Techlash, Loot Boxes, and Regulating "Dark Patterns" in the Video Game Industry's Monetization Strategies. *University of Colorado Law Revie, 92*(1), 285. https://scholar.law.colorado.edu/lawreview/vol92/iss1/6

Khan. (2023, February 16). Here's how much data Indians consume in a month on average. *The Hindu.* www.thehindu.com/sci-tech/technology/heres-how-much-data-indians-cons ume-in-a-month-on-average/article66516419.ece

Kumar, B., & Panwar, S. (2023, December 5). Navigating Deception: Dissecting the Implications of India's Guidelines on "Dark Patterns." *The Wire.* https://thewire.in/rig hts/india-guidelines-dark-patterns-implications

Maier, M., & Harr, R. (2020). Dark Design Patterns: An End-User Perspective. *Human Technology, 16*(2), 170–199. https://doi.org/10.17011/ht/urn.202008245641

Thiess, H. R.-L., & Dimov, V. (2023, February 7). *FTC vs. Epic Games: Illegal Dark Patterns?* Lexology. www.lexology.com/library/detail.aspx?g=7e9ab476-0cff-4ebf-a070-396b3 860f853

VIDEO: Fischer Highlights Bipartisan Legislation to Prohibit "Dark Patterns" at Data Privacy Hearing. (2019, May 1). [Video]. United States Senator Deb Fischer for Nebraska. www.fischer.senate.gov/public/index.cfm/2019/5/fischer-highlights-bipartisan-legislation-to-prohibit-dark-patterns-at-data-privacy-hearing

Zagal, J. P., Björk, S., & Lewis, C. (2013). *Dark Patterns in the Design of Games.* Foundations of Digital Games Conference, FDG 2013, May 14-17, Chania, Greece. www.fdg2013.org/program/papers/paper06_zagal_etal.pdf

16 Navigating the Legal Landscape of Online Gaming in India

Precedence, Regulations, and Future Perspectives

Nishant Sheokand and Suhasini Rao

16.1 INTRODUCTION

The legal landscape of gaming in India stands at a crossroads, marked by a delicate balance between the traditional framework established by the Public Gambling Act, 1867 (the PGA) and the evolving dynamics of online gaming. In the complex interplay of state jurisdictions, conflicting regulations, and emerging technologies, the clarity and coherence in gaming laws are notably lacking.

The Information Technology (Intermediary Guidelines and Digital Media Ethics Code) Amendment Rules, 2023 (IT Amendment Rules 2023), add a layer of complexity to the gaming framework. The longstanding reliance on the exception granted to "Games of Skill" under the Public Gambling Act has fuelled a thriving gaming industry, especially in games like rummy, poker, and fantasy sports. The applicability of the IT Rules to the gaming sector raises pertinent questions, given the historical autonomy granted to states in legislating on gambling matters.

The confusion is further compounded by the Ministry of Electronics and Information Technology's (MeitY) role as the nodal ministry and the imposition of the IT Rules. The dichotomy between state autonomy and central oversight adds another dimension to the regulatory conundrum. The gaming industry is growing exponentially, and therefore, the regulations that control it are struggling to keep up. There is a lack of clear regulations and guidelines that cover all the different types of online games. In 2021, the government promulgated the Information Technology (Intermediary Guidelines and Digital Media Ethics Code) Rules, 2021 (IT Rules 2021), but the industry is uncertain in its reception of these regulations, especially for gaming. This has led to frequent intervention by various High Courts, especially to determine which kind of games are acceptable as games of skill and which do not qualify as such. This has further complicated the legal landscape of online gaming in India. It is important to note the distinction between skill-based games and games based purely on chance. This distinction affects whether these games are legal or not,

DOI: 10.1201/9781032624204-17

how much tax they pay, and what rules they need to follow. In this complicated situation, there are many challenges. Furthermore, according to the EY FICCI Report of 2023, making sure players are safe and play responsibly is really important because of the accessibility of online games, especially in India where the number of India's online gamers is expected to reach 53.8 crore by FY28E.

This chapter will focus on the historical perspective, current regulatory framework, and future possibilities for online gaming in India. It will critically analyse IT Rules, 2021 and the IT Amendment Rules, 2023, along with pronouncements of the courts, and industry trends. This chapter further delves into the legal foundations that govern gaming in India, with a specific focus on their impact on online gaming. By scrutinizing pivotal cases such as *Chamarbaugwala, All India Gaming Federation, K.R. Lakshmanan v. Tamil Nadu, and Dominance Games, Junglee Games, Varun Gumber*, the legal landscape is examined, particularly in distinguishing between games of skill and games of chance. These cases have played a crucial role in providing clarity on the legality of games like poker and rummy.

16.2 HISTORICAL PERSPECTIVE: PRECEDENCE OF GAMING LAWS IN INDIA

16.2.1 Definition of Gaming

Online gaming includes simple pre-installed games such as Snakes to e-sports like FIFA. Digital gaming and gambling have remained a grey area in India for a long time. Indian law classifies gaming into two broad categories which are "Game of chance" and "Game of skill." There are various legislations enacted by Centre as well as States for gaming activities such as the PGA, which do not address online or virtual gaming because such activities did not exist at the time of its enactment. After independence, the Constitution of India has granted the individual states the authority to draft and enact laws which are related to gaming. Consequently, different states have varying laws governing gaming, with some allowing specific gaming categories, while others impose strict limitations or complete prohibitions on a wide variety of games.

The Supreme Court has ruled that games of skill are lawful games which can be termed as "commercial activities." These activities are protected under Indian Constitution's Article 19 (1) (g). In many states, "skill-based gaming" is partially safeguarded from gambling laws. Also, the licensed on-ground operations for gaming activities are permitted in a state like Goa, while regulatory frameworks for the online gambling industry have been established in states such as Nagaland, Sikkim, and Meghalaya.

The principal regulatory framework governing gaming is the PGA 1867. Notably, this legislation does not draw distinctions between online and offline gambling. While the PGA 1867 doesn't explicitly define "gambling" or "gaming," the Supreme Court of India[1] has interpreted "gambling" as the act of paying money for a chance to win a prize determined by accident or chance, or games where skill is not the predominant factor.

The PGA 1867 creates an exception for games of pure skill, basically exempting it from its ambit and application. Notably, the passage highlights that neither the state gambling or gaming legislation nor the PGA 1867 defines the term "mere skill" or further clarifies the principles which are consistent with games of skill.

Under prevailing gaming laws, the terms "gambling" or "gaming" are defined as the act of wagering or betting, involving money or items with monetary value. The state of Telangana specifically characterizes "gaming" as playing a game for the purpose of winning prizes, whether in money or other forms, encompassing activities like *mutka*, *satta*, or online gaming.

It is essential to recognize that the interpretation of gaming may vary depending on state jurisdiction and specific legislation in question. A majority of gaming laws were formulated before the internet era, primarily aimed at regulating gambling activities in physical establishments known as "gaming houses" or "common gaming houses." However, over the course of time, the stance has been clarified by several High Courts, evolving with time and the advent of online gaming.

16.2.2 Game of Skill v. Game of Chance

In the context of Indian law, a crucial distinction is drawn between "Games of skill" and "Games of chance." Games of skill are characterized by their dependence on the player's knowledge, experience, expertise, abilities, and skill. In sharp contrast, "Games of chance" rely on randomness and luck, diminishing the significance of the player's skill, knowledge, or experience. The outcomes of these games are intricately linked to fortuitous events, limiting the influence of players over the results.

A significant moment in Indian jurisprudence is marked by the landmark judgement of the Hon'ble Supreme Court in *K.R. Lakshmanan v. Tamil Nadu* (1996). This judgement distinctly separates a game of chance from a game of skill by assessing the predominance of chance over skill. The Supreme Court addressed the legality of betting on horse racing. The court concluded that horse racing, unlike other forms of gambling, involves a significant element of skill. The judges emphasized that the outcome of a horse race depends on various factors such as the training received by the horse and its rider (jockey), pedigree of the horse, nature of the race, and the health of the horse. Due to these factors, the court ruled that horse racing should not be considered a mere game of chance and, therefore, should not be classified as illegal gambling. This decision clarified the legal standing of horse racing, distinguishing it from other forms of betting and establishing it as a game of skill rather than pure chance.

The legal foundations for gaming and gambling in India find their roots in the landmark case of *State of Bombay v. Chamarbaugwala* (1957). In this case, the Supreme Court established a distinction between games of skill and games of chance. The court ruled that games requiring a significant level of skill would not be classified as gambling. The court provided a definition for skill-based games, stating that competitions where success relies on a substantial degree of skill are not considered gambling. Even if there is some element of chance, if a game is predominantly a game of skill, it would be categorized as a game of mere skill. As a result, games primarily based on skill were exempted from the definition of gambling and were not subject to prohibition. This decision clarified the legal status of skill-based games in contrast to those predominantly reliant on chance. This distinction was reiterated in *K.R. Lakshmanan v. State of Tamil Nadu* (1996), defining a game of skill as one where success depends on the player's superior knowledge, training, attention, experience, and adroitness.

Examining significant case laws on gambling, the definition of "Gambling" from *K.R. Lakshman's* case (1996) and Black's Law Dictionary is explored, emphasizing the elements of chance, consideration, and reward. A "Game of chance" is described as reliant on random chance, making it unpredictable and violative of Section 30 of the Indian Contract Act, 1872. In contrast, a "Game of skill" relies on mental or physical skill, promoting exploration of capabilities. In *All India Gaming Federation v. State of Karnataka* (2021), the High Court expressed the view that games of chance lack constitutional protection as they may be deemed criminal acts. In contrast, games of skill are inherently treated differently. The High Court of Karnataka determined that if the primary requisites of an online game involve skill, judgement, or knowledge, it does not qualify as "gambling," irrespective of whether there are stakes or bets involved. This underscores the importance of skill-based elements in differentiating between constitutionally protected activities and those that may be considered as gambling and subject to legal restrictions. Furthermore, in the case of *All India Gaming Federation v. Union of India* (2022), the Hon'ble Court declared the Amendment Act of 2021 to Karnataka Police Act, 1963 (KPA) as violative of Article 14 of the Indian Constitution because it failed to distinguish between "games of skill" and "games of chance." The court noted that the Amendment Act homogenized both categories without justifying this classification, contravening the doctrine of equality under Article 14. The court highlighted that the amendment contradicted the KPA 1963, which recognized the difference between skill and chance games. Furthermore, the court rejected the state's claim of competence under Entry 26 of the State List, stating that a blanket ban on skill games contradicted the constitutional protection of legitimate activities under Article 19(1)(g). The court concluded that the absolute embargo on all games of skill was disproportionate and, therefore, violated the Constitution on the grounds of "manifest arbitrariness."

Poker and rummy were also scrutinized. *Dominance Games Private Limited v. State of Gujarat* (2018) suggested poker as historically a game of chance, currently under adjudication. However, *Indian Poker Association v. State of West Bengal* (2015) deems poker beyond the scope of gaming or gambling. Judgements like *Chitravathi Sports Club v. Govt. of Karnataka* (2012) and *R. Shankar Creation Association v. State of Karnataka* (2012) classify poker as a game of skill, a stance reiterated in *Junglee Games India Private Limited v. State of Tamil Nadu* (2021). Favourable judgements on rummy are explored, including the Supreme Court's observation in *State of Andhra Pradesh v. K. Satyanarayana* (1968). In this case, the Supreme Court made a crucial distinction regarding the card game of rummy, recognizing it as a game of skill rather than one based purely on chance. This classification applies regardless of the specific format, venue, or stakes involved. The verdict is significant in the context of state enactments on betting and gambling, particularly those that govern the PGA 1867. However, certain states like Assam, Gujarat, Nagaland, Odisha, Sikkim, and Telangana have imposed restrictions on playing games with cash stakes, and they do not make exceptions for games of skill and chance. As a result, residents of these states are currently not permitted to engage in such activities. Recent cases, like *Head Digital Works Private Limited v. State of Kerala* (2021) strike down bans on online rummy as arbitrary and violative of fundamental rights.

Fantasy sports, a product of technological advancements, are examined. *Varun Gumber v. Union Territory of Chandigarh* (2017) (Dream 11 judgement) establishes that fantasy sports require skill, not amounting to gambling. The High Court of Punjab and Haryana determined that fantasy sports, such as those offered by Dream11, do not qualify as gambling. The court emphasized that, akin to other skill-based games, participating in fantasy sports requires significant experience and training. Users with a deeper understanding of the game's strategies, dynamics, and operational nuances demonstrate a heightened level of skill, influencing their success in predicting outcomes. The court concluded that engaging in fantasy sports is not a form of gambling but rather a business activity protected under Article 19(1)(g) of the Constitution, which guarantees the right to practice any profession or occupation. Bombay and Rajasthan High Courts in *Gurdeep Singh Sachar v. Union of India* (2019) and *Ravindra Singh Chaudhary v. Union of India* (2019) concur, stating that fantasy sports' outcomes depend on skill, not chance. Multiple Supreme Court orders affirm fantasy sports as a game of skill, free from the categorization of gambling or wagering.

16.3 CURRENT REGULATORY FRAMEWORK FOR ONLINE GAMING IN INDIA

Historically, the PGA 1867, adopted by many states, served as a broad regulatory framework, distinguishing between games of chance (prohibited) and games of skill (exempt). However, the decentralized nature of betting and gambling laws, being primarily a state subject, resulted in varied regulations across different states. While the judiciary has consistently upheld the constitutionality of games of skill, some states have amended laws to include these games, leading to legal battles. Notably, states like Tamil Nadu attempted to ban rummy and poker, only to have the Madras High Court lift the ban, recognizing them as games of skill. Amidst various state-level bans, the recent online gaming rules aim to bring clarity to the industry.

In a strategic move, the Government of India amended the Allocation of Business Rules in December 2022, placing "online gaming" under the Ministry of Electronics and Information Technology ("MeitY"). Subsequently, on April 6, 2023, MeitY notified the online gaming rules, providing a responsible and accountable regulatory framework for online gaming intermediaries. Furthermore, the regulatory landscape for skill-based online gaming in India has evolved significantly, with the central government introducing online gaming rules *"Information Technology (Intermediary Guidelines and Digital Media Ethics Code) Amendment Rules, 2023"* in April 2023. This initiative aims to establish a clear and self-governance framework for the skill-based gaming sub-segment, addressing the industry's prior regulatory challenges due to the absence of a uniform framework.

16.3.1 Key Provisions of Online Gaming Rules

The IT Rules 2023 introduced new definitions related to online gaming, addressing key concepts in the industry. The key definitions are as follows:

1. Online Game (Rule 2q(a)): Described as a game offered on the internet, accessible by a user through a computer resource or an intermediary. The rule further defines related concepts such as the internet, deposit, and winnings. It covers both online real money games and those that are not real money games.
2. Online Gaming Intermediary (Rule 2q(b)): Defined as any intermediary enabling users to access one or more online games. This term applies to entities offering users access to multiple online games.
3. Online Real Money Games (Rule 2q(d)): Described as an online game where a user makes a deposit in cash or kind with the expectation of earning winnings. The definition of winnings includes any prize, in cash or kind, distributed or intended to be distributed based on user performance and game rules. However, it excludes games involving wagering or betting.
4. Permissible Online Game (Rule 2q(e)): Defined as a permissible online real money game or any other online game that is not an online real money game.
5. Permissible Online Real Money Game (Rule 2q(f)): Described as an online real money game verified by an online gaming self-regulatory body under rule 4A.

These new definitions aim to clarify and enhance the understanding of terms compared to the IT Rules, of 2021, addressing previous irregularities in the regulatory framework. These rules also address user safety through a robust grievance redressal mechanism, including the establishment of a grievance appellate committee and the appointment of compliance officers. Additionally, the rules mandate self-regulation through the formation of self-regulatory bodies (SRBs) to verify and oversee online gaming intermediaries, ensuring the organization of permissible online real money games.

16.3.2 Taxation Landscape

Building on these regulatory measures, the Ministry of Finance, in the Finance Act, 2023, proposed taxation on income from online gaming. Specific provisions in the Income Tax Act, 1961 now address the taxation of "net winnings" from online gaming, differentiating it from traditional gambling and betting. However, a critical analysis of the recent amendments reveals certain lacunae. The rules lack clear definitions for "wagering" and "betting," leaving this determination to SRBs and potentially leading to discretionary powers. Foreign investment concerns persist, with ambiguity in the definition of an "online gaming intermediary," creating uncertainties for platforms hosting third-party games.

In terms of taxation, the Income Tax Act imposes a 30% tax on income from online gaming, with withholding obligations for players. The Goods and Services Tax (GST) is applicable to activities related to betting, gambling, and online gaming, with distinctions between games of chance and skill. Enforceability of wagering contracts is limited in India due to the Contract Act, which considers agreements categorized as "wagers" void and unenforceable. In India, GST is imposed on activities falling under the definition of "supply." Lottery, betting, or gambling activities are considered actionable claims and are treated as the "supply of goods," subject to a 28% GST on the entire bet amount. However, actionable claims related to games of skill are exempt from GST. Services like admission to entertainment events or access to casinos are taxable at a 28% rate.

For online platforms providing services through the internet, especially those automated and reliant on information technology, they fall under the category of "online information and database access or retrieval services" (OIDAR), which includes online gaming. The tax rate for OIDAR services is 28% for games of chance (betting/gambling) and 18% for games of skill. This tax is applied to the service fee or commission charged by gaming operators.

Regarding the enforceability of gambling debts, the Contract Act governs contractual matters. Section 30 of the Contract Act deems agreements categorized as "wagers" void, explicitly stating that no legal action can be taken to recover anything claimed to be won through a wager. Consequently, in India, gambling debts, in general, cannot be enforced.

The GST structure in India categorizes goods and services into different tax slabs, aiming to promote social welfare. The four schedules include nil, 5%, 12% and 18%, and 28% tax slabs, each applied based on the nature of goods and services.

In online gaming, the deposit is classified into gross gaming revenue (GGR) and the prize pool. The current GST rate for online gaming is 18%. However, recent proposals from the GST Council suggest raising the rate to 28%, treating online gaming on par with lottery, betting, gambling, and casinos. The Group of Ministers (GoM) proposed taxing online gaming at 28% on the full value of the consideration, including contest entry fees. This is a departure from the existing taxation model, which applies GST only to the GGR, representing the portion charged by the gaming company. The GoM has drawn on court judgements, treating online gaming as a game of chance, overlooking the skill element involved. It can be argued that it violates Article 14 of the Constitution. The proposed GST rate increase on online gaming may discourage the public from engaging in activities with no negative societal consequences, such as chess, football, or fantasy sports, impacting the modern economy's growth potential.

Various courts of the country, such as the High Court of Karnataka, have differentiated online gaming as games of skill rather than chance, challenging the uniform taxation approach proposed by policymakers. In *Gameskraft Technologies Private Limited v. Directorate General of Goods Services Tax Intelligence* (2022), the High Court of Karnataka clarified the distinction between online rummy and activities like betting, gambling, lottery, and betting. The court acknowledged that while an element of chance exists in these games, the crucial factor is the predominance of skill. In games like rummy, where memorization and strategic card play are essential, skill plays a significant role. The court concluded that there is a clear distinction between games of skill and games of chance. It referred to the All India Gaming Federation case, stating that games of skill, whether played online or physically, with or without stakes, are not considered a "supply" under Section 7(2) of the CGST Act,

2017, read with Schedule III of the IT Act. The court emphasized that online rummy is distinct and categorized the prize pool money as an actionable claim. Notably, the court ruled that GST should only be charged on contest entry fees at a rate of 18%.

In another case, the High Court of Madras, in *Junglee Games India Private Limited. v. State of Tamil Nadu* (2021) declared Part II of the Tamil Nadu Gaming and Police Laws (Amendment) Act, 2021, as ultra vires the Constitution. This amendment, seeking to prohibit various games on online platforms regardless of skill involvement, was struck down. The court, recognizing the skill-based nature of online gaming, safeguarded it under Article 19 (1) (g) of the Constitution.

Moreover, the Supreme Court, in *Skill Lotto Solutions Private Limited v. Union of India* (2020), clarified that in lotteries, where luck dominates and skill is absent, the entire lottery ticket is subject to tax. The courts consistently emphasize the importance of skill in distinguishing between games of skill and games of chance in online gaming scenarios.

16.4 CONCLUSION AND WAY FORWARD

The complex legal landscape of online gaming in India reflects a delicate balance between historical precedents, evolving regulations, and technological advancements. The clash between traditional laws like the PGA 1867 and the dynamic nature of online gaming has led to ambiguity and inconsistency in regulatory frameworks. The recent introduction of the Information Technology (Intermediary Guidelines and Digital Media Ethics Code) Amendment Rules, 2023 has added layers of complexity, challenging the established norms for the gaming industry.

The distinction between "Games of Skill" and "Games of Chance" remains a pivotal factor, with landmark judgements such as *K.R. Lakshmanan v. Tamil Nadu* and *State of Bombay v. Chamarbaugwala* providing legal foundations. The judiciary's recognition of games like poker and rummy as skill-based has played a crucial role in shaping the legal narrative, offering clarity amid the regulatory chaos.

The 2023 amendments and the establishment of the Ministry of Electronics and Information Technology (MeitY) as the nodal authority represent a paradigm shift in governance. The Online Gaming Rules aim to provide a comprehensive regulatory framework, addressing the challenges faced by the industry. However, concerns regarding taxation, foreign investment, and the definition of online gaming intermediaries persist, requiring further refinement for a more robust regulatory environment. The evolving taxation landscape, as outlined in the Finance Act of 2023, introduces a nuanced approach to taxing online gaming income. While attempting to address issues related to online gaming, such as GST rates and the classification of skill-based activities, the proposed changes raise questions about fairness, enforcement, and the potential impact on the industry's growth.

As we navigate this intricate legal journey, it is evident that a balance must be struck between fostering a responsible gaming environment and encouraging the industry's growth. Striking this balance requires continuous dialogue between regulatory bodies, the gaming industry, and legal experts. The judiciary's role in interpreting and refining the legal framework will remain crucial in establishing a clear path forward for online gaming in India.

Moving forward in the rapidly evolving landscape of online gaming in India, it is imperative to streamline regulatory frameworks for a unified legal structure across states. Harmonizing regulations will bring much-needed clarity and consistency, fostering an environment conducive to both industry growth and responsible gaming practices. Collaboration between the gaming industry and regulatory bodies is essential, emphasizing the importance of open communication channels to enhance understanding and craft effective regulations. Additionally, a nuanced approach to taxation policies, especially considering the proposed increase in GST rates, is crucial. Striking a balance that acknowledges the skill element in gaming activities is necessary to sustain a thriving gaming ecosystem. Ongoing judicial guidance remains paramount as technology and industry trends evolve, ensuring the maintenance of clarity and coherence in gaming laws.

Public awareness initiatives, highlighting responsible gaming practices and the distinction between skill-based and chance-based games, contribute to fostering a conscientious gaming community. The regulatory approach must adapt to technological advancements, including the integration of e-sports into traditional sports and updates to the Information Technology Act. To address challenges posed by high GST rates, a proposed approach involves levying GST only on the gross gaming revenue (GGR) while treating the prize pool amount as an actionable claim, aligning with the skill-based nature of online gaming and preventing adverse effects on industry growth.

NOTE

1 *K. R. Lakshmanan v. State of Tamil Nadu*, (Supreme Court of India 1996). 2 SCC 226.

REFERENCES

All India Gaming Federation v. State of Karnataka, (2022). WP 18703/2021.

Chitravathi Sports Club v. Government of Karnataka, (2012). WP 23926 of 2012.

Dominance Games Private Limited v. State of Gujarat, (2017). *(2018) 1 GLR 801.*

FICCI. (2023). Windows of opportunity: India's media & entertainment sector – maximizing across segments. In EY. Ernst & Young LLP, FICCI. https://assets.ey.com/content/dam/ey-sites/ey-com/en_in/topics/media-and-entertainment/2023/04/ey-ficci-report.pdf

Gameskraft Technologies Private Limited v. Directorate General of Goods Services Tax Intelligence (2023). Writ Petition No. 19570 of 2022.

Gurdeep Singh Sachar v. Union of India (2019). PIL (Cr) 16 of 2019.

Head Digital Works Private Limited v. State of Kerala (2021). W.P. 7785, 7851, 7853 and 8440 of 2021.

Indian Contract Act, Section 30 (1872).

Indian Poker Association v. State of West Bengal (2019). W.P. 13728 of 2015.

Junglee Games India Private Limited. v. State of Tamil Nadu (2021). 2021 (8) TMI 1377.

K. R. Lakshmanan v. State of Tamil Nadu (1996). (1996) 2 SCC 226.

Public Gambling Act, (1867). (The PGA).

R Shankar Creation Association v. State of Karnataka (2012). W.P. 16622 of 2012, decision dated 4 June 2012.

Ravindra Singh Chaudhary v. Union of India (2020). SLP Diary No. 43346/2019.

Skill Lotto Solutions Private Limited v. Union of India (2020). 2020 (43) G.S.T.L. 289 (S.C.).
State of Andhra Pradesh v. K. Satyanarayana and Others (1967), AIR 1968 SC 825.
State of Bombay v. R. M. D. Chamarbaugwala (1957), (1957) SCR 874.
Tamil Nadu Gaming and Police Laws (Amendment) Act, Part II (2021).
The Central Goods and Services Tax Act, Section 7(2) (2017).
The Constitution of India, 1950, Article 19 (1) (g).
The Information Technology (Intermediary Guidelines and Digital Media Ethics Code) Rules, (2021). (IT Rules 2021).
The Information Technology (Intermediary Guidelines and Digital Media Ethics Code) Amendment Rules, (2023). (IT Amendment Rules 2023).
Varun Gumber v. Union Territory of Chandigarh and Others (2017), W.P. 7559 of 2017.

17 Do E-Sports Broadcasts Infringe Videogame Copyright?

Sarath Ninan Mathew

17.1 INTRODUCTION

E-Sports, as commonly understood, is the competitive playing of videogames often in league-based tournament formats (Greenspan & Dimita, 2022, p. 46; Hamari & Sjöblom, 2017, p. 211; McTee, 2014, p. 2). These tournaments are typically broadcast over the internet to millions of fans. E-Sports broadcasts follow the format of conventional sports tournaments with multiple camera views, commentators providing continuous running commentary, and a production team to curate the broadcast video. Most videogames used in E-Sports are designed such as to encourage the broadcasting of the gameplay. The games allow spectators to toggle between player Point of Views or to access freehand any portion of the gameplay area as the spectator desires. E-Sports broadcasters use these features to create the gameplay video. The gameplay video is overlaid with various graphics, animations, running commentary, and interposing shots of physical camera feed of audience, interviews etcetera to generate the final broadcast video. However, most of the focus in an E-Sports broadcast remains on the gameplay video as viewers are primarily interested in watching the game being played out (e.g., International Esports Federation, 2023).

While some E-Sports tournaments are organised by the studios that created the videogames, many others are organised by third parties. Empirical studies undertaken on videogame End User Licence Agreements show that videogame companies do not normally allow third parties to host E-Sports tournaments using their videogames (Thomas, 2023, 'Where the user works as, or for, a corporate entity' section); i.e., according to videogame studios, using videogames in E-Sports requires a special licence. In this chapter, I seek to understand whether a third party organised and broadcasted E-Sports tournament without the consent of the videogame studio infringes any copyrights associated with the videogame under the Copyright Act (1957).

I divide my analysis into four parts. The first part gives a brief overview of E-Sports, including its history and how it situates within the larger online gaming ecosystem. The second part gives a very brief overview of Indian copyright laws. The third part considers in detail the various copyrights present in videogames. Having covered the foundational blocks in the previous parts, the fourth part analyses whether unauthorised E-Sports broadcasts infringe videogame copyright.

DOI: 10.1201/9781032624204-18

Some recent literature in India considers copyright in videogames and its effect on E-Sports broadcasts; I touch upon these works during the course of the chapter. Generally, copyright aspects of E-Sports have been most studied in the United States of America (Burk, 2013; Holden & Schuster, 2020; Kelly & Sigmon, 2018). Recently, there has also been some research on this in the United Kingdom (Ninan Mathew, 2022; Thomas, 2020) and the European Union (Sztobryn, 2021).

17.2 UNDERSTANDING E-SPORTS

The E-Sports market has been growing at a very fast pace over the past two decades. A popular global games market analyst estimated $1.38 billion (INR 11,500 crore approximately) global revenues from the E-Sports industry in 2022 (Newzoo, 2022, p. 7). Another industry analyst estimates the global E-Sports market in 2023 at $1.64 billion (INR 13,600 crore approximately) and the 2022 revenue generated by E-Sports in India specifically at $89.17 million or INR 743 crore approximately (Statistia, 2023, pp. 3, 6). However, there is variation between industry reports on the estimations of revenue generated by E-Sports in India. More conservative reports estimate revenues for 2022 to be $22 million or INR 183 crore approximately (Banerjee, 2023). Even taking the lower figure, it is clear that E-Sports is commercially established in India. The Government of India recognised this by bringing E-Sports within the regulatory ambit of the Central Ministry of Youth Affairs and Sports as 'part of multi-sport events' (Gazette Notification S.O. 6062(E), 2022, § 2(ii)).

E-Sports can be regarded conceptually as a subset of online gaming. Section 2(1)(qa) of the Information Technology (Intermediary Guidelines and Digital Media Ethics Code) Rules (2021) define online games as games 'offered on the internet'. This is a very broad definition. It has the potential to include a wide variety of games such as basic puzzle games like Sudoku or crossword; games conventionally played with real money such as poker or rummy; online adaptations of boardgames such as chess, ludo, or monopoly; and modern videogames such as PubG and League of Legends. Each of these games satisfy the statutory definition if they are offered to play over the internet.

Competitive playing of all online games does not fall within the ambit of E-Sports as the term is conventionally understood. E-Sports is played using videogames. It is difficult to point out any singular aspect that distinguishes videogames from the larger bucket of online games. The Oxford English Dictionary (2023b) defines videogames as "a game played by electronically manipulating images produced by a computer program on a monitor or other display". All online games technically fall within this ambit. For example, online chess is also played by manipulating the images of chess pieces produced by the chess software's computer program. However, online chess is not conventionally understood as a videogame and playing online chess is not conventionally regarded as E-Sports.

E-Sports industry analysts often define E-Sports as competitive playing of videogames necessarily including league-based tournaments (Newzoo, 2022, p. 15; Statistia, n.d., Market Definition tab). However, this is not a watertight compartmentalisation as games like online chess and online poker can also develop tournaments in league-based architecture. An alternate way to differentiate E-Sports and videogames from other online games is that videogames necessarily test the players on aspects such as reaction time and hand-eye coordination. We can call this the mechanical aspect of playing a videogame. While game knowledge is an asset to E-Sports athletes, dexterity with game mechanics is also a necessary requirement for E-Sports. This is the reason for E-Sports athletes having earlier retirement ages than typical chess players or poker players, and for their developing physical injuries similar to ones suffered by conventional sports athletes (Llorens, 2017, p. 468; Robinson, 2018, p. 294; Thomas, 2020, p. 962). Neither of these aspects are present for competitive online games such as chess, poker, or rummy.

E-Sports is constantly evolving. There are calls from within the industry for including games like chess within the definition of E-Sports (Taylor-Hill, 2022). However, there are equally powerful voices that advocate maintaining a strict separation between E-Sports and competitive playing of other online games (Suji, 2021). For the moment, Government of India supports the latter position since online games are regulated by Central Ministry of Electronics and Information Technology while E-Sports is under the ambit of the Central Ministry of Youth Affairs and Sports (Gazette Notification S.O. 6062(E), 2022, § 2).

Having understood the scope of E-Sports, I conclude this part by briefly noting the historical evolution of E-Sports and especially instances of prior litigation. E-Sports owes most of its origins to the United States of America and South Korea. In the United States, the first videogame tournament was held in Stanford University's Artificial Intelligence Laboratory on 19 October 1972. In 1982, E-Sports was broadcast on US television with the show, Starcade. The show featured players battling it out in successive bouts of various arcade games under timed formats attempting to beat each other's high scores. Modern E-Sports of the nature described in the Introduction section of this chapter arose from large videogame tournaments organised in the 1990s in both South Korea and the United States. The Red Annihilation Quake Tournament of 1997 hosted in the USA and the World Cyber Games hosted in early 2000s in South Korea were integral events in shaping up the modern E-Sports industry (Holden, Edelman, & Baker II, 2020, pp. 513–519; Jin, 2000, pp. 3730–3736; Taylor, 2012, pp. 3–10).

There are a few documented instances of disputes between videogame creators and third-party tournament hosts who used the videogames to host E-Sports tournaments. The most famous of these was in 2007 in relation to Korean eSports Association [KeSPA] using the videogame StarCraft owned by the studio, Blizzard Entertainment. Blizzard sued KeSPA in response to the latter fixing an exclusive broadcaster for its tournaments without obtaining authorisation from Blizzard. The suit was filed based on Blizzard's copyright in StarCraft. The case was settled out of court with KeSPA agreeing to not host any StarCraft tournaments in the future (Thomas, 2020, pp. 971–972). Recently, Dimita, Lee, and MacDonald (2022, pp. 176, 177, 181) noted a Chinese High Court decision where again a videogame creator was able to use its copyright to stop an E-Sports tournament held without its permission.

With this context, we can now explore how Indian copyright laws deal with this issue.

17.3 INDIAN COPYRIGHT LAWS

Copyright aims to incentivise the increased production of creative works by rewarding authors with a time-limited monopoly over their creations (Bently et al., 2022, pp. 43–44). In India, copyright is purely a statutory right. This means that there can be no copyright except as provided in the Copyright Act (1957, § 16) (*Entertainment Network (India) Ltd. v. Super Cassette Industries Ltd.*, 2008, para. 39).

Indian copyright laws protect three categories of works – (a) original literary, dramatic, musical, and artistic works; (b) cinematograph films; and (c) sound recordings (Copyright Act, 1957, § 13(1)). The exact rights granted by copyright depends on the category of the work. Typically, it includes rights such as the exclusive right to reproduce or make copies of the work, distribute copies of the work, perform the work, or communicate the work to a public (Copyright Act, 1957, § 14). Copyright owners can license or assign their copyright for monetary consideration (Copyright Act, 1957, §§ 30, 18). This is how copyright performs its incentivising function.

If any person without the authority of the copyright owner undertakes an activity that has been reserved exclusively for the copyright owner, such person infringes copyright (Copyright Act, 1957, § 51(a)(i)). The copyright owner can petition the court for remedies, including injunctions and damages in response to a copyright infringement (Copyright Act, 1957, § 55).

17.4 COPYRIGHT IN VIDEOGAMES

In *Sony Computer Entertainment v. Harmeet Singh* (2012, para. 4), the Delhi High Court granted an interim injunction against jail-breaking the Sony PlayStation. The order indicates that the honourable judge was *prima facie* convinced that there is atleast some level of copyright protection associated with videogames. Since this was an interim order, it contained no detailed analysis on the copyright protection of Sony videogames. I am not aware of any other judgement in India that specifically considers videogame copyright. Consequently, we must analyse copyright in videogames without any direct judicial reasoning to fall back upon.

Videogames are intrinsically creative products. They contain various distinct elements. First, they require computer programming to make the videogame fulfil its role as an interactive product. Videogames also have a library of art files. These can include graphical representations of characters and weapons, still images used in the background such as trees or traffic signs, and larger video files called cut scenes that are used generally for advancing the story line in narrative videogames. The story itself in narrative videogames is another instance of a creative work in videogames. Modern videogames also have a large amount of sound files which can include both background music as well as background sounds such as weapons firing or sounds of animals and birds.

Each of the abovementioned works are independently copyrightable in India. The computer code is protectible as a literary work; graphics and other still images are artistic works; the story line is a literary work; background music is a musical work; and the cut scenes and underlying sounds in the scenes constitute cinematograph films. The literary, artistic, and musical works are copyrightable only if they are original. However, originality does not imply novelty or excessive creativity. Derivative works require a flavour of creativity. Non-derivative works such as the artwork and code used in videogames are original as long as the author did not copy the work. Originality in this context only means that the work originates from the author. This is satisfied when the author exercises labour, skill, or judgement in producing the works (*Eastern Book Company v. D.B. Modak*, 2007, paras. 21, 32; *Syndicate of the Press of the University of Cambridge v. B.D. Bhandari*, 2011, paras. 17–19). Modern videogames, especially those typically used in E-Sports, are multi-billion dollar productions where a lot of skill, labour, and judgement by multiple creators goes into the production of each component (cf. *Bright Lifecare Pvt. Ltd. v. Vini Cosmetics Pvt. Ltd.*, 2022, para. 32). In the rare case that some component of a videogame is copied from another source and not created by the development team, that part will not enjoy copyright protection. However, as a matter of norm, all the artwork, music, and code used in videogames are independently copyright protected.

Distributive protection in relation to the component works of a composite work is the norm in Indian copyright law. We recognise separate copyright in songs in traditional movie films (*Indian Performing Right Society Ltd. v. Eastern Indian Motion Picture Association*, 1977, paras. 15, 23). Similarly, the lyrics and music are both independently protected in a song (*Saregama India Ltd. v. Viacom 18 Motion Pictures*, 2013, para. 9). Consequently, the distributive protection for various elements in a videogame follows logically from how we look at other composite works. Distributive protection of videogame components is acknowledged in existing Indian literature on this topic (Bhardwaj, 2022, 'Copyright Protection' section; Hashimy, 2022, pp. 7–9; Pooja, 2022–2023, p. 1; Sehgal & Arora, n.d., 'Copyright Law' section; Vallianeth, 2014) and is also recognised in an informative/non-legal note published by the Ministry of Electronics and Information Technology (2015, 'Q. How are Multimedia Products protected?' section).

Mere ideas or themes used in videogames are not protected, as copyright protects only expressions and not ideas (*RG Anand v. Delux Films*, 1978, para. 45; *Rediff.com India Ltd. v. E-Eighteen.com Ltd.*, 2013, para. 47). Thus, while the design features used by a videogame developer in representing a particular gun may be protected, the idea of using guns as weapons cannot be protected. Further, protection to expression is denied if there are only limited ways in expressing a particular idea. This is called the merger doctrine (*Dr. Reckeweg & Co. Gmbh. v. Adven Biotech Pvt. Ltd*, 2008, para. 30; *Emergent Genetics India Pvt. Ltd. v. Shailendra Shivam*, 2011, para. 29). There is precedent of 'merger' being used to disallow protection to the artistic layout of the game board used in the popular boardgame, 'Scrabble' (*Mattel, Inc. v. Jayant Agarwalla*, 2008, para. 27). The reasoning used by the court in that case is likely to affect copyright protection for simple online games such as chess but is unlikely to influence copyright on videogames used in E-Sports that typically showcase complex graphics.

The most complex question in videogame copyright is whether a videogame as a whole is protectible as a cinematograph film. Section 2(f) of the Copyright Act (1957) defines cinematograph films as "any work of visual recording" and mentions that 'cinematograph' refers to works produced by "any process analogous to cinematography". Section 2(xxa) defines visual recording as "recording in any medium, by any method including the storing of it by any electronic means, or moving images or of the representations thereof, from which they can be perceived, reproduced or communicated by any method".

Existing literature on videogame copyright agrees that there are no Indian court cases that have specifically looked at whether videogames can be considered a cinematograph work (Hashimy, 2022, p. 15; Wadhwa, 2016). In my research, I have not been able to find any judgement which analyses the Section 2(f) definition. Possibly, the explanation is that Indian cases on cinematograph films are in the context of conventional feature films such that the courts have never had to test the contours of the statutory definition of cinematograph films.

There are two key differences between conventional films and videogames. *First*, videogames are animated, and conventional films are shot on a camera. The statutory definition of cinematograph films states that the word cinematograph means works produced by processes analogous to cinematography. The Oxford English Dictionary (2023a) defines cinematography as the "art or technique of camera-work in filmmaking". Animations do not involve camera work per se. However, it is likely to be seen as a process *analogous* to cinematography. An expansive rather than a restrictive understanding of the phrase, 'analogous to cinematography' is to be preferred considering the very wide definition of 'visual recording' analysed in the next paragraph. This claim is bolstered by a recent Delhi High Court order which mentions that the animated movies, 'Spider Man Across the Spiderverse' and 'Spider Man Into the Spiderverse' are copyrighted films (*Sony Pictures Animation Inc. v. Flixhd.Cc*, 2023, para. 11). Consequently, videogames being animated products does not take away from their being classified as cinematograph films.

Second, videogames are interactive products while conventional films have no capability for audience to modify the movie by interacting with it. In an earlier piece, I considered the interactivity of videogames as a bar to its classification as films under UK copyright law and concluded that interactivity poses no problems for classification as films (Ninan Mathew, 2022, p. 733). Similar to the UK statute, Section 2(xxa) of the Indian Copyright Act (1957) repeatedly uses phrases such as 'any means', 'any medium', and 'any method'. The provision is drafted very widely, and the only requirement seems to be that visual recordings be capable of generating moving images. The courts of Australia, South Africa, and the United States have held that interactivity is not a bar to recognising videogames as films in their jurisdictions when interpreting provisions that were arguably drafted more narrowly than the Indian provision (*Galaxy Electronics Pty. Ltd. v. Sega Enterprises Ltd.*, 1997, p. 20; *Golden China TV Game Centre v. Nintendo Co. Ltd.*, 1996; *Stern Electronics, Inc. v. Kaufman*, 1982, pp. 855–856). Finally, a 2019 Chinese High Court decision, *NetEase v Guangzhou Huaduo* considers the motion picture produced by videogames as created by "a process analogous to cinematography" (Zhao, 2021, 'Case background' section).

Consequently, it is my argument that videogames are cinematograph films under Indian copyright law.

17.5 ARE UNAUTHORISED E-SPORTS BROADCASTS INFRINGING?

The Supreme Court of India has clarified that any person wishing to deal with a copyrighted cinematograph film has to take permission only from the owner of the film copyright and not the owner(s) of individual copyrighted works within the cinematograph film (*Indian Performing Right Society Ltd. v. Eastern Indian Motion Picture Association*, 1977, paras. 15, 21).[1] E-Sports broadcasts use the videogame directly and do not cut out independent parts from it. Consequently, it is the film copyright over the videogame and not the copyright over the constituent parts of the videogame that is relevant to the question of whether unauthorised E-Sports broadcasts are infringing of the underlying videogame.

The standard for copyright infringement in films, as pointed out by the Delhi High Court in *MRF Ltd. v. Metro Tyres Ltd.* (2019, para. 80), is whether a substantial portion of the film content is copied in the allegedly infringing work. There is some disagreement between the High Courts on whether remaking a film without copying the physical recording of the earlier film can constitute infringement (cf. *MRF Ltd. v. Metro Tyres Ltd.*, 2019, paras. 86–88; *Shree Venkatesh Films Pvt. Ltd v. Vipul Amrutlal Shah*, 2009, paras. 26–27 with *Star India Pvt. Ltd. v Leo Burnett (India) Pvt. Ltd.*, 2002, para. 6; *Thiagarajan Kumararaja v. Capital Film Works (India) Pvt. Ltd.*, 2017, para. 28). The disagreement centres on whether originality as a concept is included in a films' conception. However, there is no cause to believe that the High Courts also disagree on whether substantial copying is necessary for infringement of film copyright. The reference to 'substantial part' in Section 14 of the Copyright Act (1957) applies equally to all classes of works, including cinematograph films. Consequently, we must check whether E-Sports broadcasts substantially copy from the videogames that is being played.

The Supreme Court explained 'substantial copying' in *RG Anand v Delux Films* (1978). Though the case was decided under the earlier Copyright Act (1911), it has been consistently followed by various High Courts as laying down the correct position regarding infringement under the prevailing 1957 Act (*Barbara Taylor Bradford v. Sahara Media Entertainment Ltd.*, 2003, paras. 62–66; *Divya Sood v. Renu Bajaj*, 2009, paras. 10–11; *K.S. Gita v. Vision Time India Pvt. Ltd.*, 2010, paras. 13–14). The Supreme Court gave the standard that the surest and safest test for infringement is if the audience having seen both the works "gets an unmistakable impression that the subsequent work appears to be copy of the original". (*RG Anand v Delux Films*, 1978, para. 46).

E-Sports broadcast viewers are likely not to feel that an E-Sports broadcast in its entirety is a copy of the videogame. There are sufficient dissimilarities between a videogame and the E-Sports broadcast. An E-Sports broadcast is an entertainment product similar to a conventional sports broadcast; it showcases the gameplay and bolsters that with commentary and original graphical inputs like animations of statistics, etcetera. A videogame is an interactive product that is meant to be played by its users. They provide different user experiences. E-Sports broadcasts provide only a passive viewing experience while videogames allow the user to actively participate. In this sense, they cannot be considered copies of each other under a strict *RG Anand* standard (See *Star India Pvt. Ltd. v Leo Burnett (India) Pvt. Ltd.*, 2002, para. 7).

However, *RG Anand* was in the context of a film being alleged to be the copy of a play. The court evolved the test of 'appearing to be a copy of the original' in response to the defendant's claim that the similarities between the play and the film were on account of both works being based out of common themes/ideas which are unprotectible. The facts of E-Sports are different. The copying by the E-Sports tournament organisers is not of the underlying ideas or themes used in videogames but directly the exact content of the copyrighted videogame. In such case of direct copying, there is no cause for applying the 'appearing to be a copy of the original' test. In the case of such direct copying, the appropriate standard is 'de-minimis'. If a defendant directly takes more than de-minimis quantity of copyrighted materials from a work, then there is substantial similarity between the defendant's work and the copyrighted work. This was confirmed by the Delhi High Court in *India TV Independent News Service v Yashraj Films* [*India TV*] (2012, para. 24).

The infringement question then devolves to whether E-Sports broadcasts take more than de-minimis quantity of copyrighted videogame materials. *India TV* (2012, para. 56) proposes a five-factor test to identify de-minimis taking. The factors are: '(i) the size and type of the harm, (ii) the cost of adjudication, (iii) the purpose of the violated legal obligation, (iv) the effect on the legal rights of third parties, and (v) the intent of the wrongdoer'.

The size and type of harm is likely to favour a finding that tournament organisers take more than de-minimis amount. In *India TV* (2012, paras. 57, 59), the taking was found to be under de-minimis, but the taking in the case was only five words from a song of five stanzas in one cause of action and singing extracts each under one minute from nine songs in the second cause of action. E-Sports broadcasts focus on the gameplay for most of their run time. Since tournaments can be multiple hours in length, there can be hours of continuous infringement of the videogames' artistic works and sound recordings in an E-Sports broadcast. This constitutes significant harm.

The cost of adjudication factor checks whether the damages that are likely to be awarded or the valuation of the rights being violated is worth the cost of adjudication. There is not much visibility on how videogame companies license out their games presently. A 2022 WIPO Report notes that atleast some videogame companies do charge fees for allowing their games to be used in E-Sports (Greenspan & Dimita, 2022, p. 48). There is no mention in this report on how much money is charged in these licences, and I was not able to find this information anywhere publicly available. Even in the absence of specific figures, the fact situation of E-Sports is different from the *India TV* case. In *India TV* (2012, para. 57), the plaintiffs conceded that they would not charge any money for the specific use taken by the defendant and would charge only 10,000 rupees if the use were commercial. This concession had to be given largely because the quantity of material taken by the defendant was exceedingly small. As observed in the previous paragraph, a large amount of copyrighted material is taken in the case of E-Sports and therefore videogame companies can legitimately claim that they seek damages greater than the cost of adjudication. This conclusion is further bolstered from the case, *Super Cassettes Industries Ltd. v. Shreya Broadcasting Pvt. Ltd.* (2019, para. 14.6) where for 500 minutes of broadcasting infringing materials, compensatory damages of INR 21,00,600 was deemed reasonable by the court and the claim of de-minimis was denied.

Under the third factor, the defendant's purpose in *India TV* (2012, para. 57) was purely generating awareness amongst the public regarding corruption and had no profit-making motive. E-Sports tournaments are commercial events conducted for the purpose of generating revenue for the players, teams, organisers, and sponsors. Commerciality of use was found to be a 'critically significant' factor weighing against the defendant in de-minimis analysis by the Bombay High Court (*Shemaroo Entertainment Ltd. v. News Nation Network Pvt. Ltd.*, 2022, paras. 32, 33). Consequently, the third factor suggests that E-Sports broadcasts take more than de-minimis amount.

Under the fourth factor, unauthorised E-Sports broadcasts can cause third-party harm. Some videogame studios enter into exclusive licences with third parties for organising or broadcasting tournaments using their videogames (Comerford, 2012, pp. 630–633). Unauthorised broadcasts endanger the contractual rights of these third parties.

The fifth factor is the only factor that favours E-Sports tournament organisers. In *India TV* (2012, paras. 57, 60), with respect to the first cause of action, the court noted that the intention of the defendant was to create a new advertisement rather than appropriating the work of the plaintiff. In the second cause of action, the defendant's intention was again to conduct an interview rather than appropriating the plaintiff's work. Similarly, in E-Sports, the organisers intend to conduct an E-Sports tournament rather than appropriate the videogame's components as their own. Relatedly, mirroring the facts in *India TV* (2012, para. 57, 60), the audience of the E-Sports broadcast would remember the program for the skill showcased by the players rather than the beauty of the artistic work in the videogame. Having acknowledged this, the situation even under the fifth factor is not as supportive of a finding of de-minimis as it was in *India TV*. An empirical study of End User Licence Agreements of videogames used in E-Sports tournaments notes that using the game for E-Sports is a prohibited activity under the Agreements (Thomas, 2023, 'Where the user works as, or for, a corporate entity' section). Considering this, it is more doubtful in the case of E-Sports to state that tournament organisers do not intend to appropriate the copyrighted work. Thus, even the fifth factor can only be said to be weakly supporting a finding of de-minimis.

Considering that four out of the five factors regard E-Sports broadcasts as taking more than a de-minimis amount from videogames, it is likely that E-Sports broadcasts are substantially similar to the videogames being used in them. Independent from the case law discussed above, there is a possible argument that E-Sports broadcasts only *use* videogame contents and does not necessarily *copy* them. This argument is not explored further because E-Sports broadcasts typically have archived copies that are made available on platforms such as YouTube and Twitch for on-demand viewing. Therefore, E-Sports broadcasts do make permanent copies in addition to using the copyrighted videogame content.

The analysis in this part suggests that unauthorised E-Sports broadcasts are infringing under Section 51(a)(i) of the Copyright Act (1957).

17.6 CONCLUSION

This chapter made the following findings/arguments.

1. E-Sports in India is best understood as a distinct subset of online gaming.
2. Videogames used in E-Sports broadcasts enjoy copyright protection in the artworks, music, and computer code. They also constitute a cinematograph film. The ideas and themes used in videogames are not copyright protected.
3. E-Sports broadcasts, unless authorised by videogame studios, constitute infringement of the videogame's copyright under Section 51(a)(i) of the Copyright Act (1957).

This chapter aimed to set a foundation for the study of various aspects of Indian copyright regulation of the E-Sports industry. The chapter is by no means comprehensive or exhaustive of all the questions that can be asked in this area. A finding that E-Sports broadcasts are infringing under Section 51 raises the immediate question whether the broadcasts can still exist as fair use under Section 52. If E-Sports broadcasts are fair use, then we must ask whether the broadcasts can claim copyright in their own right as derivative works. There is also the question of whether various stakeholders in the industry such as E-Sports commentators and E-Sports players can claim either authorship rights or performance rights over providing commentary on the game and playing the game, respectively.

Over the recent years, some of these questions are being considered by researchers (Dahiya, 2023; Venkatesan, 2020). None of the questions can be said to be conclusively answered as this is not a field with direct judicial precedent. Further, each of these questions has a policy-oriented dimension as well. For example, this chapter argued that videogames should be treated as cinematograph films. The argument was made purely in a doctrinal capacity looking at the statutory language and limited case law available. A policy-based handling of the same question would look at whether treating videogames as films is actually required for producing more videogames and retaining videogame quality; it could also check whether protection of videogames as cinematograph films produces chilling effects in downstream User Generated Content industry to which E-Sports also belongs.

Thus, there is a large scope for academic research over copyright regulation in E-Sports industry. Such research will serve two functions. First, it will provide much needed clarity to the stakeholders in the industry on what their legal rights are. Such clarity can increase investment in the industry and further accelerate growth. Second, in investigating copyright in videogames, copyright researchers encounter a valuable opportunity to polish our first principles on copyright law and being to ask larger questions as to whether copyright laws in their current formulation still work in the context of new age creativity.

ACKNOWLEDGMENTS

I would like to thank professors Anirban Mazumder, Lovely Dasgupta, and Shameek Sen for their helpful comments on this draft. I also thank Professor Dev Gangjee, my DPhil supervisor, for his helpful comments on various iterations of many ideas presented in this chapter. Any omissions or mistakes remain my own.

NOTE

1 Post the 2012 Amendment, royalty must be shared equally between authors of underlying work and film copyright owner for non-theatrical use (Copyright Act, 1957, § 19(9)).

REFERENCES

Banerjee, S. (2023, May 9). *India's esports industry made $22.3 million in revenue in 2022.* Talk Esport. www.talkesport.com/news/esports/india-esports-industry-22-3-million-revenue-2022/

Barbara Taylor Bradford v. Sahara Media Entertainment Ltd., 2004 (28) PTC 474 (Cal), MANU/WB/0106/2003 (Calcutta High Court, 2003).

Bently, L., Sherman B., Gangjee D., & Johnson P. (2022). *Intellectual Property Law* (6th ed.). Oxford University Press.

Bhardwaj, A. (2022, March 3). *Copyright Examination of Video Game Laws of India vs. World: A Comparative Analysis.* Lexlife India. https://lexlife.in/2022/03/03/copyright-examination-of-video-game-laws-of-india-vs-world-a-comparative-analysis/

Bright Lifecare Pvt. Ltd. v. Vini Cosmetics Pvt. Ltd., 2022 (92) PTC 135 (Del), MANU/DE/2352/2022 (Delhi High Court, 2022).

Burk, D. L. (2013). Owning E-Sports: Proprietary Rights in Professional Computer Gaming. *University of Pennsylvania Law Review*, 161(6), 1535–1578.

Comerford, S. (2012). International Intellectual Property Rights and the Future of Global E-Sports. *Brooklyn Journal of International Law*, 37(2), 623–648.

Copyright Act, Act No. 14 (1957 & rev. 2012). www.indiacode.nic.in/handle/123456789/1367?sam_handle=123456789/1362

Copyright Act, Chapter 46 (1911, December 16). www.legislation.gov.uk/ukpga/Geo5/1-2/46/contents/enacted

Dahiya, G. (2023). Locating Legality of Video Game Streaming in Indian Copyright Act. *Nyaayshastra Law Review*, 4(1), 1–14.

Dimita, G., Lee, Y. H., & Macdonald, M. (2022). *Copyright Infringement in the Video Game Industry.* WIPO Advisory Committee on Enforcement WIPO/ACE/15/4 Fifteenth Session Geneva, August 31 to September 2, 2022. www.wipo.int/edocs/mdocs/enforcement/en/wipo_ace_15/wipo_ace_15_4.pdf

Divya Sood v. Renu Bajaj, 2011 (45) PTC 307 (Del), MANU/DE/0215/2011 (Delhi High Court, 2009).

Dr. Reckeweg & Co. Gmbh. v. Adven Biotech Pvt. Ltd, (2008) 38 PTC 308, 2008 SCC OnLine Del 1741 (Delhi High Court, 2008).

Eastern Book Company v. D. B. Modak, (2008) 1 SCC 1, 2007 SCC OnLine SC 1513 (Supreme Court of India, 2007).

Emergent Genetics India Pvt. Ltd. v. Shailendra Shivam, (2011) 47 PTC 494, 2011 SCC OnLine Del 3188 (Delhi High Court, 2011).

Entertainment Network (India) Ltd. v. Super Cassette Industries Ltd., 2008 (37) PTC 353 (SC), MANU/SC/2179/2008 (Supreme Court of India, 2008).

Galaxy Electronics Pty. Ltd. v. Sega Enterprises Ltd., (1997) 75 F. C. R. 8 (Federal Court of Australia, 1997).

Gazette Notification, S. O. 6062(E) (2022, December 23). https://cabsec.gov.in/writereaddata/allocationbusinessrule/amendment/english/1_Upload_3515.pdf

Golden China TV Game Centre v. Nintendo Co. Ltd., [1996] ZASCA 103, MANU/SASC/0003/1996 (Supreme Court of Appeal of South Africa, 1996).

Greenspan, D., & Dimita, G. (2022). *Mastering the Game: Business and Legal Issues for Video Game Developers*. World Intellectual Property Organization. https://doi.org/10.34667/tind.45851

Hamari, J., & Sjöblom, M. (2017). What Is eSports and Why Do People Watch It?. *Internet Research*, 27(2), 211–232. https://doi.org/10.1108/IntR-04-2016-0085

Hashimy, S. Q. (2022). Protection of Videogames under Indian and the United States of America's Copyright Law. *Indian Journal of Law and Legal Research*, 4(2). https://dx.doi.org/10.2139/ssrn.4138875

Holden, J., & Schuster, M. (2020). Copyright and Joint Authorship as a Disruption of the Video Game Streaming Industry. *Columbia Business Law Review*, 2020(3), 942–999.

Holden, J. T., Edelman, M., & Baker II, T. A. (2020). A Short Treatise on Esports and the Law: How America Regulates Its Next National Passtime. *University of Illinois Law Review*, 2020(2), 509–582.

India TV Independent News Service v Yashraj Films, 2013 (53) PTC 586 (Del), MANU/DE/3928/2012 (Delhi High Court, 2012).

Indian Performing Right Society Ltd. v. Eastern Indian Motion Picture Association, (1977) 2 Supreme Court Cases 820 (Supreme Court of India, 1977).

Information Technology (Intermediary Guidelines and Digital Media Ethics Code) Rules (2021 & rev. 2023). www.meity.gov.in/writereaddata/files/Information%20Technology%20%28Intermediary%20Guidelines%20and%20Digital%20Media%20Ethics%20Code%29%20Rules%2C%202021%20%28updated%2006.04.2023%29-.pdf

International Esports Federation. (2023, September 3). *Live: DOTA2 – Grand Final | IESF World Esports Championship* [Video]. YouTube. www.youtube.com/watch?v=f89ARxHK9-M

Jin, D. Y. (2000). Historiography of Korean Esports: Perspectives on Spectatorship. *International Journal of Communication*, 14, 3727–3745.

K. S. Gita v. Vision Time India Pvt. Ltd., 2011 (45) PTC 393 (Mad), MANU/TN/0202/2010 (Madras High Court, 2010).

Kelly, S. M., & Sigmon, K. A. (2018). The Key to Key Presses: eSports Game Input Streaming and Copyright Protection. *Interactive Entertainment Law Review*, 1(1), 2–16.

Llorens, M. R. (2017). eSport Gaming: The Rise of a New Sports Practice. *Sports, Ethics and Philosophy*, 11(4), 464–476. https://doi.org/10.1080/17511321.2017.1318947

Mattel, Inc. v. Jayant Agarwalla, 2008 (38) PTC 416 (Del), MANU/DE/1378/2008 (Delhi High Court, 2008).

McTee, M. (2014). E-Sports: More than Just a Fad. *Oklahoma Journal of Law and Technology*, 10, 1–27.

Ministry of Electronics and Information Technology. (2015). *Copyright*. Retrieved November 30, 2023, from www.meity.gov.in/content/copyright

MRF Ltd. v. Metro Tyres Ltd., 2019 (79) PTC368 (Del), MANU/DE/2037/2019 (Delhi High Court, 2019).

Newzoo. (2022). *Global Esports & Live Streaming Market Report: Free Version*. https://newzoo.com/resources/trend-reports/newzoo-global-esports-live-streaming-market-report-2022-free-version

Ninan Mathew, S. (2022). Establishing Copyright in Esport Streams under UK Law. *European Intellectual Property Review*, 44(12), 731–742.

Oxford English Dictionary. (2023a, September). *Cinematography*. https://doi.org/10.1093/OED/2073084060

Oxford English Dictionary. (2023b, September). *Video game*. https://doi.org/10.1093/OED/5546735918

Pooja. (2022–2023). Protection of Videogames under the Copyright Act. *Indian Journal of Law and Legal Research*, 4(6), 1–5.

R.G. Anand v. Delux Films, 1978 4 Supreme Court Cases 118 (Supreme Court of India, 1978).

Rediff.com India Ltd. v. E-Eighteen.com Ltd., (2013) 202 DLT 657, 2013 SCC OnLine Del 2747 (Delhi High Court, 2013).

Robinson, N. (2018). From Arcades to Online: Updating Copyright to Accommodate Video Game Streaming. *North Carolina Journal of Law & Technology*, 20(2), 286–330.

Saregama India Ltd. v. Viacom 18 Motion Pictures, 2013 (2) CLJ (CAL) 124, MANU/WB/0064/2013 (Calcutta High Court, 2013).

Sehgal, V., & Arora, D. (n.d.). *Status of copyright protection for video games in India*. Lexology. www.lexology.com/library/detail.aspx?g=19946c7c-c158-4a9b-9486-abfe84c94f69

Shemaroo Entertainment Ltd. v. News Nation Network Pvt. Ltd., 2023 (94) PTC 326 (Bom), MANU/MH/1482/2022 (Bombay High Court, 2022).

Shree Venkatesh Films Pvt. Ltd v. Vipul Amrutlal Shah, MANU/WB/1465/2009 (Calcutta High Cort, 2009).

Sony Computer Entertainment v. Harmeet Singh, 2012 (51) PTC 419 (Del), MANU/DE/6129/2012 (Delhi High Court, 2012).

Sony Pictures Animation Inc. v. Flixhd.Cc, MANU/DEOR/122100/2023 (Delhi High Court, 2023).

Star India Pvt. Ltd. v Leo Burnett (India) Pvt. Ltd., 2003 (27) PTC 81 (Bom), MANU/MH/1030/2002 (Bombay High Court, 2002).

Statistia. (2023). *eSports in India*. www.statista.com/study/115392/esports-in-india/

Statistia. (n.d.). *Esports – Worldwide*. Retrieved November 30, 2023, from www.statista.com/outlook/amo/esports/worldwide

Stern Electronics, Inc. v. Kaufman, 669 F.2d 852 (United States Court of Appeals 2nd Circuit, 1982).

Suji, L. (2021, July 15). *How Esports Is Different from Fantasy Gaming and Real Money Gaming – Lokesh Suji, Director, ESFI and Vice President, AESF*. Press Reader. www.pressreader.com/india/my-mobile/20210715/281543703927353

Super Cassettes Industries Ltd. v. Shreya Broadcasting Pvt. Ltd., 2019 (80) PTC 551 (Del), MANU/DE/0754/2019 (Delhi High Court, 2019).

Syndicate of the Press of the University of Cambridge v. B. D. Bhandari, (2011) 47 PTC 244 (DB) 2011, 2011 SCC OnLine Del 3215 (Supreme Court of India, 2011).

Sztobryn, K. (2021). In Search of Answers to Questions about Electronic Sports and Copyright. *GRUR International*, 70(3), 237–244. https://doi.org/10.1093/grurint/ikaa192

Taylor, T. L. (2012). *Raising the Stakes: E-Sports and the Professionalization of Computer Gaming*. MIT Press.

Taylor-Hill, G. (2022, June 20). *Exploring the Surprising Rise of Chess Esports*. Esports.net. www.esports.net/news/chess-esports-growth/

Thiagarajan Kumararaja v. Capital Film Works (India) Pvt. Ltd., 2018 (73) PTC 365 (Mad), MANU/TN/3844/2017 (Madras High Court, 2017).

Thomas, A. (2020). A Question of (e)Sports: An Answer from Copyright. *Journal of Intellectual Property Law & Practice*, 15(12), 960–975. https://doi.org/10.1093/jiplp/jpaa157

Thomas, A. (2023). Merit and Monetisation: A Study of Video Game User-Generated Content Policies. *Internet Policy Review*, 12(1). https://doi.org/10.14763/2023.1.1689

Vallianeth, T. (2014, January 29). *Copyright Aspects in Open World Gaming*. SpicyIP. https://spicyip.com/2014/01/guest-post-copyright-aspects-in-open-world-gaming.html

Venkatesan, V. (2020, December 5). *Mitigating IPR Conflicts under Sports Law: An Analysis of the E-Sports Industry*. Extra-Cover: The Sports Law Blog of India. www.extra-cover.org/post/mitigating-ipr-conflicts-under-sports-law-an-analysis-of-the-esports-industry

Wadhwa, R. (2016, September 13). *Copyright Aspects in Videogames*. LexisNexis India. http://lexisnexisindia.blogspot.com/2016/09/copyright-aspects-in-videogames.html

Zhao, J. (2021, February 28). *China: Court Rules on Copyright Infringement Involving Online Games and Live Streaming*. Asia IP. https://asiaiplaw.com/article/china-court-rules-on-copyright-infringement-involving-online-games-and-live-streaming

18 Player Image Rights and Online Gaming

Decoding the Game

Prakhar Maheshwari and Bissheesh Roy

18.1 INTRODUCTION

In the realm of modern sports, an athlete's image is as significant as their on-field prowess. Today, sports in India has evolved into a professional industry, wherein athletes/players are cultivating a personal brand that extends far beyond the sports arena. Over the last few years, there has been a noticeable shift in how an athlete is perceived by the public and the value attributed to their image. For instance, the likes of Michael Jordan, David Beckham, Usain Bolt, and Virat Kohli have turned from being athletes to global icons.

This is due to a culmination of certain factors. Firstly, the advent of social media platforms has provided all athletes direct access to their fans all over the world, wherein they can interact with their fans in a more personal manner, leveraging their individual brand for creating a strong social impact. Secondly, an enhanced private brand for athletes leads to corporates recognising the immense potential of collaborating with athletes, as their images are synonymous with trust, excellence, and dependability, making them coveted brand-ambassadors. Furthermore, athletes are now transcending sports to become cultural icons because of their growing influence that goes beyond entertainment, making them role models for their various aspects of life going beyond their performance on-field. To illustrate, Nike collaborated with Michael Jordan to create the iconic 'Air Jordan'.

Given the seismic change in the perception and worth of an athlete's image, it is pertinent to understand the components that encompass an athlete's image as it is multifaceted and broadens their spectrum of reach. It includes their personality, iconic celebrations, public persona, social impact, endorsements, off-field activities, media coverage, and interactions with fans, and players are carefully cultivating this image as it affects their marketability, influence, and success both within and outside the realm of sports. In the recent past, Gareth Bale has obtained a trademark for his popular goal celebration, as this helps build his own personal brand for enhancing his personal wealth.

In wake of the Indian sporting industry undergoing a remarkable revolution which has seen a surge in commercial interests, brand endorsements, and digital visibility of athletes, it is crucial to understand the nuances of a players' image rights in India. This chapter embarks on a comprehensive exploration of the legal framework surrounding

DOI: 10.1201/9781032624204-19

player image rights in India, given the growing commercial significance of such rights in modern sports. The chapter evaluates the lack of statutory recognition for a sportsperson to protect their image rights and raises a question on the need for a specific statute for governing and regulating player image rights, as the existing statutes tend to cater to artists and the protection of their rights. It also alludes to the fact that intellectual property laws in India do not specifically protect the rights of athletes in the same way they protect the rights of performers or artists. For instance, the Indian copyright laws primarily safeguard artistic works, literary works, music, films, and other creative expressions. Athletes/sportspersons may not fall directly under this category unless they have specific creative works or expressions that qualify for copyright protection, such as books they have authored, artwork they have created, or certain promotional materials. Furthermore, they also may not be classified as 'performers' under the statute. Given this ambiguity in the Indian legal framework, athletes often rely on contractual agreements to protect their image and prevent any unauthorised commercial exploitation, which may not be adequate in an evolving sporting ecosystem.

18.2 LEGAL AND JUDICIAL FRAMEWORK

The authors in the chapter delve into the existing legal landscape governing player image rights, i.e. 'right to publicity'. At the outset, it is pivotal to understand the relevant intellectual property law framework in India: (i) the Copyright Act, 1957 primarily deals with intellectual property rights and indirectly protects publicity rights by granting the creator of a work exclusive rights over the commercial use of their creations, which may include photographs or other visual representations of individuals; and (ii) the Trademark Act, 1999 prohibits the unauthorised use of an individual's name or likeness in a manner that could cause confusion or deceive the public regarding the source of goods or services. The Design Act, 2000 deals with designs, shapes, etc. while the Patents Act, 1970 deals with scientific inventions.

While these existing statutes intend to protect intellectual property rights, there is no statute explicitly governing the image rights of players. When these image rights are used by players and celebrities, these are called 'right to publicity'. This right to publicity is premised on the fundamental right to privacy under the Indian Constitution and has evolved over various judgements in the Indian courts that have held that the right to privacy includes the right to control one's image, likeness, and personal information (Luthra & Bakru, n.d.).

One of the earliest cases which recognised the right to publicity in India is the *ICC Development (International) Ltd. vs. Arvee Enterprises and Ors.* (2003) case before the Delhi High Court in 2003. The defendants in this case ran a promotional campaign wherein the winner of the campaign would get World Cup tickets. The plaintiffs argued that in the absence of any agreement between the parties, the defendants could not run such a campaign as all publicity rights in the event (in this case the World Cup) lied with the plaintiff. The Court held that publicity rights are only vested in individuals and events and corporations like the plaintiff cannot claim such rights

(*ICC Development (International) Ltd. vs. Arvee Enterprises and Ors.*, 2003). The Court held:

> 14. The right of publicity has evolved from the right of privacy and can inhere only in an individual or in any indicia of an individual's personality like his name, personality trait, signature, voice, etc. An individual may acquire the right of publicity by virtue of his association with an event, sport, movie, etc. However, that right does not inhere in the event in question, that made the individual famous, nor in the corporation that has brought about the organization of the event. Any effort to take away the right of publicity from the individuals, to the organiser {non-human entity} of the event would be vocative of Articles 19 and 21 of the Constitution of India. No persona can be monopolised. The right of Publicity vests in an individual and he alone is entitled to profit from it. For example if any entity, was to use Kapil Dev or Sachin Tendulkar's name/persona/indicia in connection with the 'World Cup' without their authorisation, they would have a valid and enforceable cause of action.
>
> (*ICC Development (International) Ltd. vs. Arvee Enterprises and Ors.*, 2003) (emphasis supplied)

In another case before the Delhi High Court in 2010, *D.M. Entertainment Pvt. Ltd. vs. Baby Gift House and Ors* (2010), where the defendant was in the business of selling dolls which were able to sing a few lines of famous songs of Daler Mehndi (whose organisation is the plaintiff in this matter), the Court held:

> 14. The right of publicity can, in a jurisprudential sense, be located with the individual's right and autonomy to permit or not permit the commercial exploitation of his likeness or some attributes of his personality.
>
> (*D.M. Entertainment (P) Ltd. v. Baby Gift House*, 2010)

However, the Court added that:

> 14. … In a free and democratic society, where every individual's right to free speech is assured, the over emphasis on a famous person's publicity rights can tend to chill the exercise of such invaluable democratic right. Thus, for instance, caricature, lampooning, parodies and the like, which may tend to highlight some aspects of the individual's personality traits, may not constitute infringement of such individual's right to publicity. If it were held otherwise, an entire genre of expression would be unavailable to the general public. Such caricature, lampooning or parody may be expressed in a variety of ways, i.e. cartoons in newspapers, mime, theatre, even films, songs, etc. Such forms of expression cannot be held to amount to commercial exploitation, per se.
>
> (*D.M. Entertainment (P) Ltd. v. Baby Gift House*, 2010)

In yet another case before the Delhi High Court, the Court, in the matter of *Titan Industries Limited vs. M/s Ramkumar Jewellers* (2012), held that there are two basic elements for infringing the right of publicity: (i) the aggrieved party owns an enforceable right in the persona of a human being; and (ii) such celebrity must be identifiable (*Titan Industries Limited vs. M/s Ramkumar Jewellers*, 2012). The Court further added that "*Infringement of right of publicity requires no proof of falsity, confusion, or deception, especially when the celebrity is identifiable*" (*Titan Industries Limited vs. M/s Ramkumar Jewellers*, 2012).

The same position was taken by the Madras High Court in the matter of *Shivaji Rao Gaikwad v. Varsha Productions* (2015). The defendants had produced a show which had the name 'Rajnikanth' and thereby infringing upon the publicity rights of the plaintiff. In this case too, the Court held that as the celebrity was identifiable, the publicity rights were violated and no proof of falsity, confusion or deception was required (*Shivaji Rao Gaikwad v. Varsha Productions*, 2015).

As we can see from the above judgements, the right of publicity evolved through the years to mean that if there is a celebrity who is identifiable, they will enjoy publicity rights. If any entity uses such a celebrity's publicity rights – like his image, likeness, well-known alias, etc. – to showcase their product or service, such usage will be violative of that celebrity's right to publicity (*Shivaji Rao Gaikwad v. Varsha Productions*, 2015). Furthermore, it is not required to prove that such an association would or would not cause confusion or deception in the mind of the customer who is consuming such a product. The Delhi High Court in the *D.M. Entertainment* case, however, drew out certain exceptions like caricatures, lampooning, and parody (*D.M. Entertainment (P) Ltd. v. Baby Gift House*, 2010).

The extent of this right to publicity was once again discussed in a recent order of the Delhi High Court.

In April 2023, the Delhi High Court passed an order ('**Order**') which dealt with the use of player images and other attributes on online fantasy sports ('**OFS**') platforms without the permission or approval of the relevant player. At the outset, it is clarified that the Order did not delve into the merits of the case and was only with respect to an interim application seeking permanent injunction. While the High Court rejected the interim application, it made certain significant observations regarding the use of a celebrity's attributes. Before we analyse the Order, the facts of the matter are as follows:

A subsidiary of the popular online fantasy platform Dream11, Digital Collectibles Pte Ltd. ('**Plaintiff No. 1**'), contracted with certain cricket players ('**Players**') to use their names, images, statistics, and other aspects of their personality ('**Attributes**') in the form of 'Digital Player Cards' for Plaintiff No.1's platform 'Rario'. These 'Digital Player Cards' function as 'Non-Fungible Tokens' or 'NFTs', and using this blockchain technology, Rario aims to market its 'Digital Player Cards' as original and authentic. These 'Digital Player Cards' are then bought, sold, and traded on 'Rario' by the users.

Another giant in the online fantasy business, Galactus Funware Technology Pvt. Ltd. or 'MPL' ('**Defendant No.1**') has a mobile application by the name 'Striker' which also provides a platform to trade 'Digital Player Cards' which includes certain attributes like images (it is to be noted that real images of the cricketers are not used and only original artworks depicting the cricketers is used) and names of various players. The 'Digital Player Cards' on Striker also run on NFT technology, but Striker and MPL did not obtain approval from the players to use their images and names.

Aggrieved by the unauthorised use of the images and names, the Plaintiff No.1 and the players ('**Plaintiffs**') filed a suit before the High Court of Delhi against Defendant No.1 and Striker ('**Defendants**') along with an interim application seeking permanent injunction against the defendants from using the player attributes.

The Plaintiffs and the defendants primarily argued on the point regarding the extent to which the right to publicity is recognised in India. Both the parties acknowledged the fact that no statute directly governs the publicity rights and cited various judgements to advance their submissions.

The Court, *inter alia*, made the following significant observation:

> 53. In the absence of a specific legislation, the right to publicity cannot be an absolute right in India.
>
> ...
>
> 55. In view of the discussion above, in my opinion, the violation of the right of publicity in India has to be considered on the touchstone of the common law wrong of passing off, as also weighed against the 'right to freedom of speech and expression' enshrined under Article 19(1)(a) of the Constitution.
>
> ...
>
> In my considered view, the very same principles that are applied in the case of passing off, will have to be applied for determining infringement of the right of publicity.
>
> ...
>
> The right of publicity cannot be infringed merely on the basis of a celebrity being identified or the defendant making commercial gain.
>
> (*Digital Collectibles (P) Ltd and Ors. v. Galactis Funware Technology Private Limited and Anr*, 2023) (emphasis supplied)

18.3 CRITICAL ANALYSIS OF THE ORDER

The Order has therefore arrived at, *inter alia*, three significant conclusions:

1. <u>Freedom of Speech vs. Right of Publicity</u> – Right of publicity is not an absolute right and has limitations. Even if the right to publicity were to be recognised in statute, it will always be subservient to Article 19(1) of the Constitution (*Digital Collectibles (P) Ltd and Ors. v. Galactis Funware Technology Private Limited and Anr,* 2023).

The Order, specifically with respect to the use of the attributes on the OFS platform, held that since the platforms used publicly available information – like player images and statistics – the use of such images and statistics will not infringe upon the right to publicity of the players, and the same will be protected under Article 19(1)(a) of the Indian Constitution, even if some commercial gain was made out by using the images and statistics.

With respect to the above, we are in full consonance with the finding of the Delhi High Court which has correctly identified that the right of publicity cannot be absolute even if it were to be statutorily recognised. There is no denying that having rigorous laws in favour of publicity rights would, in some way, stifle the free speech guaranteed under the Constitution of India. A curtailed or subjective right of publicity instead of an absolute right of publicity would definitely enable creativity amongst artists, comedians, performers, etc. to freely showcase their work without the sword of judicial action hanging over their heads.

To further this point, we would like to highlight a Delhi High Court matter – *Tata Sons Limited vs. Greenpeace International & Anr* (2011), otherwise known as the Turtles vs. Tata case. In this case, the joint venture of the petitioner, i.e., Tata, was awarded a concession to build and operate a port in Odisha and the petitioner had obtained all environmental clearances for its project. However, Greenpeace India (defendant no. 2) believed that the proposed project posed a serious risk to the eco-system of Olive Ridley Turtles that nest and breed near its vicinity.

As part of the campaign to raise awareness regarding the project and its possible impact on the Turtles, Greenpeace India launched an online game called 'Turtles vs. Tata', which was modelled after the Pac-Man game, where Pac-Man is replaced by a Turtle. The objective of the 'Turtles vs. Tata' game was that the Turtle had to collect the eggs and eat all the dots before being caught up by the four ghosts, who were made of the 'T' logo of Tata, which is a registered trademark. Aggrieved by the game and campaign of Greenpeace India, Tata filed a suit along with an interim application before the Delhi High Court alleging defamation and infringement of the registered trademark(s) of Tata and therefore praying for an injunction against the use of its name and trademarks.

While the decision of the court with respect to defamation is not relevant to this chapter, it is necessary to consider the ruling with respect to the trademark part of the suit. The Delhi High Court in this matter refused to grant an injunction to Tata holding that the use of the registered logo was within the defendant's right to freedom of speech. The Delhi High Court held that the use of the logo was a clear case of satire and that such expressions will be protected (*Tata Sons Limited vs. Greenpeace International & Anr,* 2011). Furthermore, the logo was not used for commercial benefit or for a competitive advantage but only to raise awareness regarding the turtles (*Tata Sons Limited vs. Greenpeace International & Anr,* 2011). It is therefore pertinent to note that even though the logo was a protected trademark, such protection would not supersede the right to freedom of speech and expression which includes parody.

2. <u>Test of Viewer Confusion</u>: A violation of the right of publicity will occur only if it is proved that the identity or image of a celebrity is used to mislead potential customers into believing that the particular celebrity is endorsing the product or service (*Digital Collectibles (P) Ltd and Ors. v. Galactis Funware Technology Private Limited and Anr,* 2023).

This observation made by the Delhi High Court is significant because it takes a different view in terms of dealing with the right to publicity with respect to endorsements. Various precedents in India have previously taken the position that the "*infringement of right of publicity requires no proof of falsity, confusion, or deception, especially when the celebrity is identifiable*" (*Titan Industries Limited vs. M/s Ramkumar Jewellers,* 2012). This Order limits the infringement of the right to publicity to specifically those instances where endorsements by a particular celebrity or a player can be made out. The Delhi High Court was of the opinion that since digital cards for several players were used by the defendants, it was unlikely that a customer would associate the platform with a particular player.

Miss Nina R. Nariman in her article '*A Cause Célébre: Publicity Rights in India*' has in detail advocated for tailoring of the publicity rights in a defined scope (Nariman, 2022). Miss Nariman opines that, to achieve the dual object of protecting the publicity rights and also ensuring that the same do not trample on freedom of speech, the 'test of viewer confusion' may be applied (Nariman, 2022). The test of confusion is essentially to view each case of using publicity rights of celebrities and to examine whether the use of such attributes of the celebrity would be considered as endorsement by the said celebrity by a reasonable man.

To further clarify the 'test of viewer confusion', we may apply this test to the *Digital Collectibles* matter. In such a scenario, an OFS platform need not require authorisation from players to have their digital cards; however, any kind of advertisement – whether broadcasted or simply within the mobile or web app of the platform – which depicts such player endorsing the said app would require explicit authorisation from such player. This is because for a reasonable man, such an advertisement would lead to the assumption that the player endorses the platform.

However, when it comes to online gaming and player image rights, the 'test of viewer confusion' alone would not suffice the objective of protecting the publicity rights of players. This brings us to the third significant observation by the Delhi High Court.

3. Commercial Gain: Merely because a commercial gain is being carried out using the identity of a celebrity, it cannot be said that the right of publicity has been violated (*Digital Collectibles (P) Ltd and Ors. v. Galactis Funware Technology Private Limited and Anr,* 2023).

The Delhi High Court held "*The right of publicity cannot be infringed merely on the basis of a celebrity being identified or the defendant making commercial gain*". It therefore sets out that even if the two conditions – (i) player identifiability and (ii) commercial gain – are met, it may still not be enough to make out a case of violation of a player's right to publicity. In our opinion, this aspect of the Order is a restrictive view in nature due to the absence of any legislation regarding the publicity rights. In online gaming, we see several companies floating their products wherein they use the various attributes of the players to enhance their products which gives them a competitive advantage and thereby make a commercial gain. While the use of images by an online fantasy platform may not have an impact on the popularity of the platform, the various online console and mobile games are popular due to the use of various attributes of the players be it their images, likeness, mannerisms, or even iconic celebrations.

We must acknowledge that online sports games owe their popularity, at least in part, to the players who have popularised the sport and created a culture around their sports. Therefore, in our view, especially with respect to online gaming, if any entity earns commercial gain using the attributes of a player, where such attribute has been used to enhance its product in gaming, such action would be unfair on players who are the rightful owners of those attributes and thus a specific statute requires to be enacted which evaluates such circumstances in order to ensure equitable treatment to all.

18.4 CONCLUSION

In summary, we understand that as the sporting industry is undergoing an evolution, players are cultivating their own brand in order to create a position for themselves in contemporary pop culture like any artist or performer. Amidst this transformation, the need for understanding and protecting player image rights have emerged as a critical focal point for our legal framework.

The current legal framework in India recognises the uniqueness of an artist and instils safeguards to protect their image rights and interests. However, in the absence of a robust legal framework, to protect their interests athletes often employ contractual agreements to safeguard their image and commercial rights which are not adequate in present times. It is imperative that we recognise that an athlete has a much shorter shelf life than any artist or professional and thus there is a need to ensure that appropriate measures are undertaken to protect an athlete's image rights.

As is evident from the above cited cases, the high courts have been inconsistent in their findings and thus issues concerning player image rights remain and no finality on the same has been achieved. Even with respect to judicial precedence, the various findings have come from the high courts, and there are no rulings by the apex court which could provide clarity on the aspect of publicity rights. Particularly for the online fantasy gaming sector, clarity on legal rights is crucial as we have seen that subsequent to the Order, there has been a sense of uncertainty for the entities operating in the sector as it is impacting their future course of action with respect to its operations, as the ambiguity in laws is hindering prospective investments, and this will eventually severely effect the growth of the sector as a whole.

An athlete may only be able to find a legal recourse if any resemblance of his or her attributes violates a legal right and thus there is an ardent need to formulate a specific statue for protection of player image rights. The statute may delve deeper into the certain aspects of a player's personality that can be protected and also setting forth reasonable restrictions on the exercise of their rights. The enactment of a specific statute would provide much needed clarity to the online gaming sector which continues to be in its nascent stages. Furthermore, the statute so enacted would also be required to be periodically reviewed in order to address relevant concerns that may arise due to the vast technological advancements like artificial intelligence and deepfakes.

REFERENCES

D.M. Entertainment (P) Ltd. v. Baby Gift House (2010), SCC OnLine Del 4790.

Digital Collectibles (P) Ltd and Ors. v. Galactis Funware Technology Private Limited and Anr (2023), SCC OnLine Del 2306, para 55.

ICC Development (International) Ltd. v. Arvee Enterprises (2003), SCC OnLine Del 2: (2003) 26 PTC 245.

Luthra, S. K., & Bakru, V. (n.d.). Publicity Rights and the Right to Privacy in India... *National Law School of India Review*, 31(1). https://repository.nls.ac.in/cgi/viewcontent.cgi?article=1259&context=nlsir

Nariman, N. R. (2022, January 24). *A Cause Célèbre: Publicity Rights in India*. SCC Online Blog. www.scconline.com/blog/post/2022/01/24/a-cause-celebre-publicity-rights-in-india/

Shivaji Rao Gaikwad v. Varsha Productions (2015), SCC OnLine Mad 158: (2015) 1 LW 701.

Tata Sons Limited v. Greenpeace International & Anr (2011), SCC OnLine Del 466.

Titan Industries Limited v. M/s Ramkumar Jewellers (2012), SCC OnLine Del 2382: (2012) 50 PTC 486.

19 Copyrightability of Digital Player Cards in Online Fantasy Sports

A Conundrum in the Indian Copyright Law

Atish Chakraborty and Ishaan Vohra

19.1 INTRODUCTION

Online fantasy sports gaming provides a platform for real-life sportspersons to compete on virtual playing fields. The COVID-19 pandemic witnessed a sharp rise in the Indian online fantasy gaming sector and has reflected no signs of a slowdown thereafter. This sphere of fantasy sports is now not only limited to creating teams and scoring the highest points but also includes leveraging of digital collectibles which has now become the new currency of trade in this arena. Digital collectibles are unique and limited edition virtual items that use blockchain technology to generate non-fungible tokens whose ownership is freely transferable (Levy, 2023). There usually exists an element of digitised visual art which are used more often than not as trading cards. These cards at present have become very popular on the online fantasy sports platforms.

Before we delve further, it is imperative for us to understand how digital player cards (hereinafter referred to as 'DPCs') function. For instance, if a user buys and collects a digital card of Virat Kohli and he plays exceptionally well in the ongoing World Cup, the market value of the card experiences appreciation. Consequently, the user can trade the same card on the online fantasy platform. However, the primary issue that arises for these online fantasy sports platforms is exclusivity and copyrightability of their player cards. The cards contain, including but not limited to, player names, images and statistics, which are all available in the public domain. Additionally, this issue of copyrightability clashes with the personality rights of the sportspersons. The Delhi High Court, in a recent judgement of *Digital Collectibles Pte Ltd. v. Galactus Funware Technology Pvt. Ltd.* (hereinafter referred to as '*Digital Collectibles*'), addresses these issues faced by online fantasy sports platforms (*Digital Collectibles Pte Ltd. v. Galactus Funware Technology Pvt. Ltd.*, CS(COMM) 108/2023).

 DOI: 10.1201/9781032624204-20

Hence, through this chapter, we shall analyse the Delhi High Court judgement in detail, deconstructing it to understand the rationale given by the court to allow the use of player attributes for commercial gain. Thereafter, we will discuss the copyrightability of the DPCs, which would address questions like whether a player's statistical information and image is copyrightable, thus calling for licensing by these fantasy platforms. Furthermore, we shall analyse the position taken by the Delhi High Court on the publicity rights of the sportspersons in the *Digital Collectibles* case in light of the set precedents. Furthermore, we shall delve into a global perspective as to how digital player cards are protected in jurisdictions such as the United States, Australia and Europe where the jurisprudence in this regard has experienced humongous development. Finally, we conclude with our findings on the best practices that can be undertaken going forward in light of the arguments presented in the earlier sections.

19.2 ANALYSING THE DIGITAL COLLECTIBLES PTE LTD. V. GALACTUS FUNWARE TECHNOLOGY PVT. LTD. JUDGEMENT

19.2.1 Background

Cricket is one of the most sought-after sports in India. Both the plaintiffs and the defendants deal in the business of DPCs of cricketing personalities. The plaintiffs, run by the name of 'Rario', which provide an online marketplace where users can trade licensed collectibles of sportspersons for real money. The DPCs contain photographs and names of players along with other statistical identifiers, also known as 'Player Attributes'. The plaintiffs entered into service agreements with the sports personalities, which authorise and license them to use photographs, names and other attributes exclusively. The trading value of the DPCs depends not only on the player's performance in real life but also on the supply-demand of the playing cards of the said player.

On the flip side, the defendants run by the name of 'Striker Club' (hereinafter referred to as 'Striker'), a platform where users form fantasy teams with their favourite cricketers' playing cards compete with other users. The DPCs on the Striker platform displayed graphic works of the cricketer images and other player attributes. Striker allows users with DPCs to alter their teams by trading their players for real money with other users. The trading value of the DPCs is intrinsically linked to the real-world performance of the players.

19.2.2 Arguments

Rario contended that it had spent more than 148 crores on obtaining licensing and authorisations from players, including Shivam Mavi, Arshdeep Singh, Mohammed Siraj and Umran Malik (Vaideya, 2023). Furthermore, they argued that Sriker was illegally using player identifiers leading to unjust enrichment, unlawful interference with the economic interest of Rario and unfair competition.

Striker contented that the DPCs are primarily an entry requirement to compete with their fantasy team on the platform. Additionally, it employed artists to create original caricatures of the cricketers. As per the terms of use of Striker, each card is an original artwork as defined under the Copyright Act of 1957. With respect to the names and statistics, the defendants claimed that the information which was being used is available in the public domain. It is a well-established principle that facts available in the public domain cannot be copyrighted (*Feist Publications, Inc. v. Rural Tel. Serv. Co.*, 1991) (hereinafter referred to as *'Feist'*).

Rario, in its reply, argued that the users can trade on the platform without playing the fantasy game. They can use the platform as a trading marketplace for their NFT-enabled playing cards. Moreover, the value is directly derived from the player marks and attributes which essentially isn't a feature of the artwork. As a result, Rario submitted that the defendants are unlawfully gaining profits from the trade of the DPCs without proper licensing and authorisation from the cricketers. Striker, separately, in an interview, responded that even if they take Rario's argument at their best-case scenario and assume that a user would purchase the card solely for its bragging rights, the value of the card would not go up until the user plays the fantasy game as the value also depends on the in-game features like experience points and health points.

19.2.3 Judgement

The single-judge bench of the Delhi High Court presided over by Hon'ble Justice Amit Bansal delivered the judgement on this matter. After perusing multiple judgements rendered by the US and the UK Courts, the court held that the right to publicity is not an absolute right as there is no statutory basis for the same in India. In the United States, states like California, Illinois, Indiana among others have codified the right to publicity as a statutory right (McCarthy, 2015). As a result, in India, the right of publicity has to be considered the touchstone of common law wrong of passing off along with the violation of the fundamental right of freedom of speech and expression.

Passing off, in case of publicity rights, refers to the image or any identifiable attributes of a celebrity which are used to promote a service or product without their express authorisation. It pertains to infringement of rights of a celebrity where consumers are misled to believe that the celebrity is actually endorsing the service or the product. The Court also delved into the elements which need to be satisfied in order to establish that it is a case of passing off. In the words of Hon'ble Justice Amit Bansal, "*...there has to be misappropriation of goodwill or reputation of a celebrity in selling a good/service. The right of publicity cannot be infringed merely on the basis of a celebrity being identified or defendant making commercial gain...*". The Court observed that Article 19 of the Indian Constitution allows online fantasy sports platforms to use the player's names and attributes, even if it is done for commercial gain, as it is not for the purpose of identification (Nariman, 2021). Furthermore, Striker distinguished themselves through their original artwork and did not use actual images of the players.

Moreover, the court also held that Rario cannot have exclusivity over the player's name, images and other identifiable attributes because they are available in the public domain. The Court did not note any difference between a normal fantasy game and a fantasy game enabled by DPCs. Finally, the Court did not grant any injunction against Striker in light of the above reasoning.

19.3 CAN DIGITAL PLAYER CARDS BE GRANTED PROTECTION UNDER COPYRIGHT LAW?

The *Digital Collectibles* judgement took a hard stance on the scope of public domain while weighing it with the exclusivity argument. Essentially, the term '*public domain*' can be defined as encompassing intellectual elements whose copyright protection has lapsed due to expiration of the term of protection. Thus, the concept of public domain is the inverse of copyright protection, thereby propagating a negative right. This negative approach is not regulated and is rarely even discussed in statutes. The elements of public domain are not subject to any law or rules. As a result, protection of the elements of public domain becomes very onerous.

Furthermore, in the recent times, public domain has been replaced by terms such as 'open content' and 'commons' in order to insist on the free use of the public domain materials (Dusollier, 2011). As a result, it has become even more pertinent to make the distinction between free use and free access. Once the copyrighted work is in the public domain, upon the expiry of the term, it is free to be used by anyone. No one can control the reproduction, public communication or public dissemination of the work. While if we see public access or free access works, it has a prerequisite of gaining material access to the material before it can be used for any purpose (Dusollier, 2011). However, it has to be emphasised that everything that is publicly accessible is not always in the public domain. For instance, the Creative Commons project promoted the concept of open knowledge allowing for copyrighted work to be available to the public through licensing (Creative Commons, n.d.). Thus, it might be publicly accessible, but it would not be available for free use under the public domain.

A similar fact situation was seen in the *C.B.C. Distribution and Marketing Inc. v. Major League Baseball Advanced Media* (hereinafter parties referred as '*MLB*' and '*CBC*') [*C.B.C. Distribution and Marketing Inc. v. Major League Baseball Advanced Media*, L.P., 443 F. Supp. 2d 1077 (E.D. Mo. 2006)]. In this case, *MLB* claimed that even if the performance statistics are in the public domain, for all purposes of commercial gain they had exclusive license over the statistics. While *CBC* who was offering online fantasy gaming services for the league used those performance statistics. However, the US Supreme Court sided with the *CBC* deciding that no one can claim ownership over works in the public domain. Hence, this can be corresponded with ruling in the *Digital Collectibles* case.

19.3.1 Whether Graphic Works of Images Available in Public Domain Bars Copyright Claim?

Striker employed independent artists to design its DPCs. It represented the contentious cricketers with their signature moves through graphic works. The Terms of Service of Striker states that these works of art are original and the company owns their respective copyright, though it relies on the standard of originality laid down in the *University of London Press* case which is the most preliminary criteria to grant copyright protection (*University of London Press v. University Tutorial Press*, 1916). However, the standard of originality is completely different in case of visual works. Courts have for long acknowledged the need for copyright protection of graphic works. In the case of *Bleistein v. Lithographing Co.*, Justice Holmes as his Lordship then was, said that in case of pictorial illustrations, if the expression is not copied, then the standard of originality is met (*Bleistein v. Donaldson Lithographing Co.*, 1903). This standard of originality was termed to be too generalised. Moreover, the *Fiest* standard of minimal level of creativity did not offer any guidance for future courts to decide upon originality. However, an end-product approach is adopted thereafter which builds further on modicum of creativity for graphic works (Williams, 2008). The end-product approach focussed on indications of creativity in the final product rather than the methods employed by the author to create the work.

In the graphic design case of *Meade*, the US Federal Claims Court dealt with the infringement of heart-shaped picture of earth (*Meade v. United States*, 1992). The Court held that illustration could not be granted copyright protection because it was an idea, and even if it was an expression, it existed in the public domain. The originality in the design was non-existent in the finished work. Hence, if we consider Striker, we find that, it was working upon public domain images with signature moves of cricketers, and thus, it can be argued that the independent artist who were working on public domain images did not meet the originality standard for their graphic works and are thereby not copyrightable.

19.3.2 Whether Player Statistics on DPCs Can Be Given Exclusivity?

The primary question even before addressing the exclusivity over player attributes is whether copyright protection can be granted for sports statistics. These statistics are essentially factual compilations of data available in the public domain with limited copyright protection (Massari, 2005–2006). However, no one can claim originality with respect to facts. Furthermore, there can be no authorship claim over the sports statistics, although factual compilations may be granted copyright protection for the selection, arrangement or presentation of the underlying facts (Schatz et al., 1991). While different jurisdictions have adopted different standards, in India, the case of *Eastern Book Company v. D.B. Modak* (hereinafter referred to as '*D.B.* Modak') was the landmark case that dealt with copyrightability of derivative work from public domain (*Eastern Book Company v. D.B. Modak*, (2008) 1 SCC 1). The Court established a novel criterion known as 'transformative standard', which states that derivative works or compilations must exhibit substantial variation from the pre-existing work in the public domain. The variation should not be of the same garden variety but a unique expression.

Concurrently, the *D.B. Modak* judgement refers to the modicum of creativity as a requirement of originality. While this degree of creativity does not rise to novelty or non-obviousness but a minimal degree of creativity, this standard derives its origin from the US decision in *Feist,* which holds that the more originality and creativity that is evidenced in selection and arrangement, the stronger the copyright protection. Hence, it can be said that copyright protection can be granted over the selection and arrangement of the sports data compilations if they satisfy the substantial variation and minimal degree of creativity requirements.

While there can be no authorship claim over sports statistics or player attributes, there can always be claims of ownership. The commercial use of statistics finds its basis in the 'quasi-property' right in accordance with the *hot news doctrine* (Prabhu & Shroff, 2018). The US Supreme Court, in *INS*, devised the *hot news doctrine* to protect written material or information generated through live televised events that might have a commercial value for a limited timeframe (*International News Service v. Associated Press*, 1918). Thereafter, such information would move into the public domain for free use. The doctrine stems from the Lockean theory of labour which propounds that one who is investing enough labour, skill and capital should reap the benefits (Chatterjee, 2020). Furthermore, the Delhi High Court applied the hot news doctrine in the case of *Star India*. Here, the Court upheld the Star India's exclusive media rights agreement where only they were entitled to use the ball-by-ball updates before it entered into the public domain (*Star India Pvt. Ltd. v. Piyush Agarwal*, 2013). But, this position was later reversed by the division bench on the ground that there cannot be any exclusive rights claimed over match information that comprised of mere facts. This judgement applies *pari materia* in the context of online fantasy sports games. Since if protection is granted by applying the hot news doctrine, it will result in monopolising the rights over player names and statistics that are mere facts that are accessible in public domain. Furthermore, if this doctrine is applied, it would run against the trite law that expressly disregards any exclusivity to mere facts.

19.3.3 Whether Personality Rights Can Be Said to Have Been Infringed When OFS Platform Use Images and Player Statistics Available in the Public Domain?

The scope of intellectual property rights protection in fantasy leagues extends beyond just statistics and images, as there are also concerns regarding the infringement of players' personality rights within these competitions. Personality rights encompass various aspects, such as public image, character, nickname, professional trajectory and traits, among other elements (Nariman, 2021). The notion of personality rights is considered to be derived from the Right to Privacy as expressed by Hon'ble Justice Sanjay Kishan Kaul in *Justice K.S. Puttaswamy (Retd.) v. Union of India*. He elevated the right of control over one's personality from a common law right to a fundamental right (*Justice K.S. Puttaswamy (Retd.) v. Union of India*, (2017) 10 SCC 1). In furtherance of this judgement, every citizen has a right to control how their life or persona is portrayed to the world (Luthra & Bakhru, 2019). Thus, it means that one has the right to control the commercial use of their identity and prohibit any unauthorised use of other such elements.

However, if personality rights have risen to the level of fundamental rights, there would certainly exist a conflict with the fundamental right of freedom to speech and expression. The Delhi High Court dealt with this issue in the case of *Anil Kapoor v. Simply Life India*. The Court was dealing with a situation where the actor's persona was being exploited for commercial benefit using his images, age old dialogues among other elements available in the public domain (*Anil Kapoor v. Simply Life*

India, 2023). The defendants were even using defamatory images generated using artificial intelligence to make commercial gains. The Court held that the right of endorsement of a celebrity would be a major source of income for them which cannot be destroyed by unlawful dissemination of their face or attributes of their persona without lawful authorisation. It recognised such a right within Article 21 of right to livelihood and right to privacy within a social structure.

Similarly, the Minnesota Court also held that unauthorised production of a board game with over 500 player names and their statistics violated the publicity rights of the players (*Uhlaender v. Henricksen*, 1970). The use of player names and characteristics in a board game is very similar to that in an online fantasy sports game. The reason behind the same is very simple: the marketability of the platform depends solely on the use of player names and their statistics. Thus, they derive direct benefit from using that information available in the public domain, but actually, these information are owned by the sportspersons.

Hence, in the *Digital Collectibles* case, the Court in our opinion has erred in considering that the purpose of using player information by the online fantasy platforms was not for identification. It is obvious that the NFT-enabled digital card trading platforms garner attention of the users and raise the demand for their platform by attracting users through the player's names and attributes. The users choose a platform over the others since they believe they can own their favourite cricketer's DPC and can trade that for another famous cricketer's DPC later. Thus, if no such incentive is allowed to be kept by online fantasy sports platforms, it may result in eventually rendering online fantasy sports redundant.

19.4 PROTECTION OF DIGITAL PLAYER CARDS UNDER COPYRIGHT LAW: A GLOBAL PERSPECTIVE

There has been an increasing utilisation as well as commercialisation of sports players as well as their performance data; the legal status with respect to ownership continues to remain a subject of contention even today. We shall delve into the positions in the United States, Australia and Europe to understand the approach adopted by them over the years and if there are some learnings that India can profitably rely on while formulating the legal framework in this regard.

19.4.1 United States

Most sporting event owners in the United States have tried to seek exclusivity over their respective events but only with limited success. In a catena of cases in this regard [*National Basketball Association v. Motorola Inc.*, 105 F.3d 841 (2d Cir. 1997); *National Football League (NFL) v. Governor of the State of Delaware*, 435 F. Supp. 1372, 1378 (D. Del. 1977); *C.B.C Distribution and Marketing Inc. v. Major League Baseball Advanced Media, L.P.*, 443 F. Supp. 2d 1077 (E.D. Mo. 2006)], the Courts have reiterated the ratio of *Feist*, wherein it has been observed that originality is a prerequisite of copyright protection and a mere compilation of facts cannot be copyrighted. They can only become protectable if they are "*selected, coordinated or arranged in such a way that the resulting work as a whole constitutes an original work of authorship*". Thus, even in case of raw data pertaining to sporting events like player names or statistics, they cannot be copyrighted under the prevailing copyright law and third parties cannot be prevented from collecting such data and using them commercially for online fantasy sports gaming.

19.4.2 Australia

In Australia, there exists a heterogenous regime for protecting data relating to sports. The betting industry is governed by the state laws allowing event owners to negotiate a contractual arrangement as a condition to use information for their offerings. In event of a lack of specific legislations, the event owners rely on established proprietary rights to safeguard event-related data (Frodl, 2015). However, with respect to utilisation of data relating to sports outside the betting industry, the courts in Australia do not provide any legal protection to the activities of a sporting event. But, copyright protection in Australia does not require a work to be innovative and also affords protection to mere compilations. This follows the sweat of the brow standard which is evident from umpteen rulings and intends to reward the quantity of effort, provided that the work in question represents the independent application of knowledge, skill or labour and judgement (*Desktop Marketing Systems Proprietary Ltd v. Telstra Corp*, [2002] FCAFC 112). But, in the recent years, the courts have differed in their approach and have observed that "*copyright does not protect mere facts or information*" but it only protects "*the particular form of expression of such information, namely the words, figures and symbols in which it is expressed, and the selection and arrangement of that information*" (*IceTV Proprietary Ltd v. Nine Network Australia Proprietary Ltd*, (2009) HCA 14). Furthermore, the Courts have also observed that substantial expense and labour in collating information cannot suffice for claiming copyright, but it is imperative for the authors to establish their input, both financial and intellectual, towards the particular expression of the idea and the originality resulting in the compilation as a result thereof. This view has also been followed in subsequent decisions (*Telstra Corp Ltd v. Phone Directories Co Pty Ltd*, [2010] FCA 44).

Thus, in Australia, at present, protecting raw data pertaining to sporting events like player names or statistics is difficult. Since they are mere facts and information. and in light of the recent pronouncements, collation and structured assembling too will not render it copyrightable even though some special knowledge or skills are invested by the event owner in assembling such data.

19.4.3 Europe

As per the current law in the European Union and its member states, any sporting event does not qualify for protection under their respective intellectual property laws. Since the sporting events cannot be treated as an original intellectual creation of the author, they cannot be treated as 'intellectual creations' within the meaning of their Copyright Directive. Furthermore, the European Union does not afford any other form of protection under their intellectual property regime (Frodl, 2015). The only possible recourse thus could have been sought under the Data Directive, 1996. While the

Directive does not expressly exclude copyrightability in databases, it expressly states that databases can only be protected through copyright if by the virtue of selection or method of arrangement of their content can be said to constitute an original expression of the author's creative freedom. However, such determination is not based on the use of skill or labour in setting up the database but is dependent on originality and creativity. The collation of raw data pertaining to sporting events like player names or statistics does not involve any of the parameters, thereby excluding any protection as a database under the Directive.

19.5 CONCLUSION AND RECOMMENDATIONS

The rapid growth of online fantasy sports platforms has raised pressing yet open-ended legal challenges in the intellectual property law regimes globally in their quest to find appropriate protection by law. There is a set position for copyrightability of statistical information but its application in the online fantasy sports arena still continues to be a conundrum even in the present day not only in India but also globally. The Courts have to strive to achieve the perfect balance between exclusivity and the free use of public domain material. The *Digital Collectibles* judgement explores the world of possibilities while providing critical insights into these issues, but the judgement suffers from some abnormalities with respect to disregard for publicity rights due to use of information from the public domain. Thus, given the growing popularity of such offerings by multiple online gaming platforms, there lies an urgent need to enact a robust legislative framework in India. Furthermore, it is imperative that it is devised as a *sui generis* model for protection of personality rights of celebrities and sportspersons as a means to sustain and promote the online gaming industry.

REFERENCES

Anil Kapoor v. Simply Life India. CS(COMM) 652/2023.

C.B.C Distribution and Marketing Inc. v. Major League Baseball Advanced Media, L.P. 443 F. Supp. 2d 1077 (E.D. Mo. 2006).

Chatterjee, M. (2020). Lockean Copyright versus Lockean Property. *Journal of Legal Analysis*, *12*, 141–145. https://doi.org/10.1093/jla/laaa002

Desktop Marketing Systems Proprietary Ltd v. Telstra Corp, [2002] FCAFC 112.

Digital Collectibles Pte. Ltd. v. Galactus Funware Pvt. Ltd., CS(COMM) 108/2023.

Dusollier, S. (2011, March 4). Scoping Study on Copyright and Related Rights and the Public Domain. In *Committee on Development and Intellectual Property (CDIP)* (CDIP/7/INF/2). World Intellectual Property Organisation. www.wipo.int/publications/en/details.jsp?id =4143&plang=EN

Eastern Book Company v. D.B. Modak. (2008) 1 SCC 1.

Feist Publications, Inc. v. Rural Tel. Serv. Co., 499 U.S. 340 (1991).

Frodl, C. (2015). Commercialization of Sports Data: Rights of Event Owners over Information and Statistics Generated about Their Sports Events. *Marquette Sports Law Review*, *66*, 55–90. https://scholarship.law.marquette.edu/sportslaw/vol26/iss1/5/

IceTV Proprietary Ltd v. Nine Network Australia Proprietary Ltd. (2009) HCA 14.

International News Service v. Associated Press. 248 U.S. 215 (1918).

Justice K.S. Puttaswamy (Retd.) v. Union of India. (2017) 10 SCC 1.

Levy, A. (2023, November 20). Investing in Digital Collectibles. *The Motley Fool*. www.fool.com/investing/stock-market/market-sectors/financials/non-fungible-tokens/digital-collectibles/

Luthra, S. K., & Bhakhru, V. (2019). Publicity Rights and the Right to Privacy in India. *National Law School of India Review*, *31*(1), 126. https://repository.nls.ac.in/nlsir/vol31/iss1/

Massari, M. G. (2005–2006). When Fantasy Meets Reality: The Clash between On-Line Fantasy Sports Providers and Intellectual Property Rights. *Harvard Journal of Law & Technology*, *19*, 446–466.

McCarthy, J. T. (2015, January 1). *The Rights of Publicity & Privacy*. http://books.google.ie/books?id=md8NzQEACAAJ&dq=The+Rights+of+Publicity+%26+Privacy&hl=&cd=4&source=gbs_api

Nariman, N. (2021). A Cause Célébre: Publicity Rights in India. *SCC Online*. (2021) 6 SCC J-1 from www.scconline.com/blog/post/2022/01/24/a-cause-celebre-publicity-rights-in-india/

National Basketball Association v. Motorola Inc. 105 F.3d 841 (2d Cir. 1997).

National Football League (NFL) v. Governor of the State of Delaware, 435 F. Supp. 1372, 1378 (D. Del. 1977).

Prabhu, A., & Shroff, R. (2018). Use of Third Party Intellectual Property in Fantasy Sports Games. *The Sports Law and Policy Centre*, 27–44. https://csri.co.in/wp-content/uploads/2022/08/Fantasy-Sports_Legality_India_Report.pdf

Schatz, J. et al. (1991). What's Mine Is Yours? The Dilemma of a Factual Compilation. *University of Dayton Law Review*, *17*, 423.

Star India Private Limited v. Piyush Agarwal. 2013 SCC Online Del 1030.

Telstra Corp Ltd v. Phone Directories Co Pty Ltd. [2010] FCA 44.

Uhlaender v. Henricksen. 316 F. Supp. 1277 (D. Minn. 1970).

University of London Press v. University Tutorial Press. [1916] 2 Ch 601.

Vaideya, J. (2023, May 5). Rario v. Striker: the battle over athlete personality rights in Web3 World. *The Playbook*. https://theplaybook.thesignal.co/p/rario-striker-nft-fantasy-sports

Williams, K. (2008, October). Disparity in Copyright Protection: Focus on the Finished Image Ignores the Art in the Details. *American University Law Review*, *58*(1), 169. https://core.ac.uk/display/235402908?utm_source=pdf&utm_medium=banner&utm_campaign=pdf-decoration-v1

20 Navigating Legal and Operational Uncertainty Around Advertisement of Online Games

Varun Ramdas

20.1 INTRODUCTION

Several offshore betting and gambling companies advertise and make illegal and unsafe applications available in India. Advertisements conceal that applications involve betting and instead highlight how consumers can become rich by spending money on their services (Mishra, 2022). They operate from foreign jurisdictions and encourage users to participate in games of chance for stakes, which is illegal in India. Offshore betting and gambling applications are fly-by-night operations that masquerade as games of skill in their advertisements. They violate several Indian laws like the Foreign Exchange Management Act, 1999 and the Prevention of Money Laundering Act, 2002 and expose consumers to psychological and financial risks like addiction and financial loss (Mishra, 2022). On the other hand, there are online real money games (RMGs) where users make deposits in cash or kind, with the expectation of earning winnings on that deposit. The Ministry of Electronics and Information Technology (MeitY) published the Information Technology (Intermediary Guidelines and Digital Media Ethics Code) Amendment Rules, 2023 (The 2023 Rules) on 6 April 2023. The Rules impose several obligations on online gaming intermediaries, including a self-regulatory body (SRB) led verification mechanism for RMGs. The IT Rules also create a due diligence obligation on all intermediaries to ensure that they do not advertise illegal betting and gambling applications. The delayed implementation of the 2023 Rules, lack of a clear legal standard to distinguish online games of skill and chance, ambiguity around the enforceability of advisories against betting advertisements, and the surrogate nature of betting advertisements has allowed illegal betting and gambling applications to continue their operations in India.

The Indian government sees online gaming as a sunrise segment with great potential for domestic value generation. The segment grew at a Compound Annual Growth Rate (CAGR) of 28% over the past three years to reach INR 16,428 in FY23 (EY-FICCI, 2023). India also has the second highest number of gamers in the world after China at 42.5 crores, and the number is expected to steadily increase over the coming years (EY, 2023). RMGs are at the forefront of this. They form 82.8% of the online

DOI: 10.1201/9781032624204-21

gaming market (FY23), and almost 30% of gaming startups in India have RMG offerings (EY, 2023).

It is imperative to continue efforts to legitimise the industry and provide policy and regulatory conditions that enable it to effectively contribute towards the digital economy's growth. At the same time, efforts to weed out illegal betting and gambling applications that cause user harms and losses to exchequer revenues must continue. Self-regulation was a positive first step to find a good balance between the two objectives: growth of the industry and protection of users from harmful online environments. However, MeitY has not implemented the Rules (Barik, 2023). Given the high-risk nature of unsafe betting and gambling applications, the government may need to take a stronger position like a government-led registration mechanism in this case.

In the absence of legal uncertainty and a clear mechanism to distinguish legitimate RMGs, consumers cannot easily distinguish between illegal gambling and real money online gaming. In common parlance and advertisements, online games, e-sports, betting, and fantasy sports are used interchangeably, which leads to confusion around legality. Print, digital, and TV advertisers are unable to distinguish between illegal advertisements and advertisements for RMGs. As stated above, several betting and gambling applications which are illegal in India advertise themselves as fantasy games in surrogate advertisements. Government institutions have tried to address the issue. The Ministry of Information and Broadcasting (MIB), the Central Consumer Protection Authority (CCPA), and the Advertisement Standards Council of India (ASCI) have issued several advisories to stop advertisements of illegal betting and gambling applications, and MeitY has issued orders to block several foreign-based gaming applications under Section 69A of the Information Technology Act citing national security threats as the reason (Shukla, 2023). However, ASCI's annual audit from FY 2022–23 showed that 92% of gaming advertisements did not adhere to ASCI advisories (ASCI, 2023).

This chapter looks at regulatory and operational issues with advertising online games. Guardrails to curb illegal advertisements of betting applications are imperative given the financial and psychological harms they cause users. Effective implementation of the IT Rules remain a concern because social media companies, e-commerce services, and other online intermediaries are unable to distinguish between legal RMGs and surrogate advertisements of offshore betting entities in the absence of a clear legal demarcation between the two. Online RMGs that contribute to India's digital economy runs the risk of being clubbed with illegal betting and gambling applications.

A self-regulatory certification mechanism was an effective measure to address the issue because advertisers can then demand certification marks before they onboard advertisements. However, direct government intervention to register online games may become necessary in the future. Simultaneously, SRBs could work with advertisers and the government to develop industry standards for advertising. Advertising practices in other countries target harms like exposure of children to harmful advertisements and encouragement of responsible online behaviour, but it is pertinent to note that the legal frameworks in these countries are very clear in their definition of betting and gambling and adopt measures proportionate to identified risks.

20.2 LEGAL AND OPERATIONAL CONCERNS

The first parameter that qualifies an activity as betting or gambling is the involvement of monetary stakes. If a game is played for monetary stakes, the second parameter, i.e. whether a game is one of skill or chance decides its legal status. Engaging in or facilitating betting or gambling is illegal under the Public Gambling Act, 1867. Most states in India prohibit 'games of chance played for monetary stakes, except for a few exceptions like Nagaland, Meghalaya, Sikkim, and Goa that permit such games if the operator has a licence'. Section 12 of the Public Gambling Act carves out an exception for 'game of mere skill', on which the prohibition is not applicable, and leaves out regulation of skill-based games from its purview. Some Indian states prohibit 'games of skill' played for monetary stakes as well, and they have tried to bring about changes in their laws to enforce this in the past few years.

Indian courts had developed standards to distinguish between skill versus chance and decide the permissibility of games before online games became a reality in India. In *State of Bombay v. R.M.D. Chamarbaugwala* (1957) and *State of A.P. v. K. Satyanarayana* (1968), the Supreme Court distinguished games based on their nature as games of skill or games of chance.

'Mere skill' includes games where success depends on a substantial degree of skill. The court clarified that even if the game involves an element of chance, it will not be considered gambling if there is a preponderance of skill over chance (*State of Bombay vs. R.M.D. Chamarbaugwala*, 1957). The preponderance test has since been used to differentiate games like fantasy sports (*Chandresh Sankhla v. The State of Rajasthan*, 2020), poker (*Indian Poker Association v. State of Karnataka*, 2013), and rummy (*Gameskraft Technologies (P) Ltd. v. Directorate General of Goods Services Tax Intelligence*, 2023) as games of skill. RMGs in India offer these games to consumers.

Indian courts reiterated the skill vs. chance standard in the context of online games in *Gameskraft Technologies (P) Ltd. v. Directorate General of Goods Services Tax Intelligence* (2023). Notably, the judgement notes that monetary stakes do not transform a game of skill into a game of chance. The Karnataka High Court (*All India Gaming Federation v. State of Karnataka*, 2022) and the Madras High Court (*Junglee Games India Private Limited v. The State of Tamil Nadu*, 2021) have struck down state legislations that prohibited online skill games for money as gambling.

The 2023 IT Rules only create a classification based on monetary stakes and creates two categories – online games and RMGs, without addressing the skill vs. chance question. Consequently, several legal and operational concerns surface. The IT Rules apply throughout India, but state-level laws prohibit online games of skill that involve monetary stakes. RMG companies must therefore ensure that their offerings are not available in a particular state, which requires operational modifications and technical measures like geo-blocking. From the economy's perspective, different rules for the same online service in different states fragments India's digital market.

The differential legal treatment that applies to games of skill versus games of chance and money deposits by users in online games lies at the heart of the distinction that advertisers must make while onboarding advertisements. Offshore betting and gambling applications pose a threat to the legitimate RMG industry in India. The offshore betting and gambling market is estimated to be worth INR 6000 crores in India with an average growth of 27% (Laghate, 2022). The offshore betting market drives 25–30 billion dollars away from the gaming industry (Bose, 2022) and adversely affects the industry's prospects in India both in direct monetary terms and indirectly by taking advantage of the legal lacuna and putting up surrogate advertisements. MeitY has issued blocking orders under Section 69A of the Information Technology Act, 2000 several times against offshore betting applications (Shukla, 2023), and the MIB has issued advisories against betting and gambling applications.

However, in the absence of a clear legal standard to distinguish them from legal RMGs, advertisers are unable to effectively follow government advisories. They can either choose not to onboard any advertisements by online games which would lead to significant revenue loss or advertise all gaming applications and risk sanction. An audit report by the ASCI suggests that advertisers are choosing the latter. ASCI's annual audit from FY 2022–23 showed that 92% of gaming advertisements did not adhere to ASCI advisories (ASCI, 2023).

20.3 ONLINE GAME ADVERTISING REGULATION LANDSCAPE BEFORE THE IT RULES

Several legislations and rules govern advertising in India. First, the medium of advertisement has specific advertising laws. The Advertising Code under the Cable Television Networks (Regulation) Rules regulates advertisements on television, and the Norms for Journalist Conduct by the Press Council of India governs print media. The Consumer Protection Act, 2019 created and empowered the CCPA of India to oversee and regulate misleading advertisements. Subject-specific laws like the Cigarettes and other Tobacco Products (Prohibition of Advertisements and Regulation of Trade and Commerce, Production, Supply and Distribution) Act, 2005, the Drugs and Cosmetics Act, 1940, and the Arms Act, 1959 prohibit advertisements of substances considered harmful to society.

Online gaming advertisements are covered under Rule 3(b)(x) of the 2023 Rules and administered by the Ministry of Information and Broadcasting as per the Allocation of Business Rules, 1961. There is no specific law that prohibits betting and gambling like tobacco and alcohol, even though the state considers the activity harmful to society. CCPA, MIB, and ASCI advisories prohibit them. The MIB has issued four advisories against the advertising of illegal online gaming advertisements and their surrogates and noted their spike during sporting events, and the CCPA has issued one. The Ministry has issued notices to advertisers and asked them to refrain from advertising specific websites to Indian users (ET Bureau, 2022). However, MIB's provenance to issue such advisories and enforce them remained a concern, until July 2023.

On July 28, 2023, the Cabinet Secretariat amended the Second Schedule of the Government of India (Allocation of Business) Rules, 1961 (AoBR), and brought online content publishers within the MIB's purview. Entry 22A and Entry 22B of the Second Schedule of the AoBR empowers MIB to regulate Over-the-Top platforms. Entry 22C explicitly includes online advertisements under the Ministry's purview. The amendments address enforceability concerns with MIB advisories on online advertisements.

ASCI first issued guidelines on RMG advertisements in November 2020 following the proliferation of advertisements during popular sporting events like the Indian Premier League. The Guidelines prohibited betting and gambling advertisements and laid down standards for RMG advertising. It said that advertisements should not depict people below the age of 18 playing 'Online Gaming for real income winnings'. The Guidelines also specify that it should not suggest that online games are an income-generating option or an alternative employment option. Advertisements should also present disclaimers by print/static and audio/video means to intimate about risks and habit-forming tendencies of RMGs. The Guidelines apply to all RMGs. The MIB referred to ASCI Guidelines and issued an advisory to print, television, and digital media in December the same year. At the time, the Ministry did not have jurisdiction over digital media.

In June 2022, MIB issued an advisory which stated that

> Advertisements of online betting are misleading and do not seem to be in strict conformity with the advertisement-related statutes, norms and regulations. In light of the same and taking into account the larger public interest involved, the print and electronic media is advised to refrain from publishing advertisements of online betting platforms.

Enforceability of the advisory was an issue because the Ministry did not refer to the statutes it would take action under.

MIB issued another advisory along the same lines and referred to the advisory from June in October 2022. The latest advisory restated that promotional content and advertisements of betting platforms continue to be advertised on news and OTT platforms despite the earlier advisory. The advisory highlighted that online offshore betting platforms have started using news websites as a surrogate product to advertise betting platforms on digital media. MIB clarified that betting and gambling is an illegal activity in most parts of India, and hence, advertisements of online offshore betting and gambling platforms are prohibited. The Ministry recommended that online news websites and OTT platforms should refrain from broadcasting advertisements of online betting platforms and/or their surrogate news websites or any such product/service depicting these platforms in a surrogate manner. It is pertinent to note that these advisories precede the 2023 IT Rules, and there was no common understanding on what separated legal online gaming platforms from offshore betting and gambling. On the one hand, MIB did not have the powers to seek compliance with these advisories, except in the case of TV advertisements. Second, there was no legal standard to distinguish between illegal platforms and legitimate RMGs.

20.4 THE 2023 MEITY RULES

MeitY intended to differentiate between offshore betting and gambling applications and RMGs with the 2023 IT Rules. The Rules published on 6 April 2023 sought to clarify the legal status of online games in India that are not in the nature of wagering, betting, and gambling. The Rules classify four categories of online games – online games, online RMGs, permissible online games, and permissible online RMGs. Any game offered on the internet that users access through an intermediary or a computer resource is an online game as per the definition in Rule 2(ii)(qa). Online games that users access by making a cash or kind deposit and expect winnings are online RMGs in Rule 2(ii)(qd). All online games are permissible, but RMGs become permissible after an SRB verifies them.

MeitY will register SRBs after they vet parameters like the composition of their Governing Board, financial capacity, track record of responsible gaming, and their incorporation documents like Memorandum and Articles of Association. SRBs perform two key functions – member registration and game verification. Online RMGs must register with SRBs to become permissible, and only SRB members can apply for game verification. SRBs will verify games based on their compliance with the law if they do not involve wagering on outcomes. In effect, the Rules empower SRBs to restrict illegal offshore entities from obtaining certification marks.

The certification mark is a reliable marker of a game's legality and advertisers can seek an SRB verification mark as part of their due diligence before onboarding advertisements of online games. Under Rule 3(b)(x), intermediaries must ensure that they do not host advertisements or surrogate advertisements of online games that are not permitted in India or of the online gaming intermediary (OGI) that makes the game available. In effect, intermediaries can only host advertisements of verified OGIs and RMGs.

However, the Ministry is yet to notify an SRB and implement the 2023 Rules. Reports suggest that the government is rethinking the approach it took in the 2023 Rules. In the absence of this framework, offshore betting and gambling websites and applications continue to advertise and offer unsafe online spaces to users. As for advertisers, they do not have a reliable standard to differentiate advertisements and act against offshore betting and gambling entities, even though the government has issued multiple advisories to this effect. If MeitY implements the 2023 Rules, online advertisers can seek SRB verification as a pre-requisite to advertising and include representations on online RMGs' compliance with SRB standards from the OGI in their contracts.

The MIB issued an advisory on the same day that MeitY published the 2023 IT Rules and referred to its earlier advisories from 2022. The Ministry restated that news publishers and online platforms were flouting advertisement-related statutes, norms, and regulations and referred to the Consumer Protection Act, 2019, the Press Council Act, 1978, and Information Technology (Intermediary Guidelines and Digital Media Ethics Code) Rules, 2021. The advisory said that it had been issued as a warning to follow earlier advisories by the Ministry, failing which MIB could take action against defaulters.

The CCPA issued an advisory on 6 March 2024 and expanded the scope of liability for advertising a betting or gambling application. The advisory referred to Clause 9 of the Guidelines for Prevention of Misleading Advertisements and Endorsements for Misleading Advertisements, 2022 issued by the CCPA under the Consumer Protection Act, 2019. Clause 9 prohibits and penalises any advertisement that is prohibited under any law, and the advisory clarified its applicability to betting and gambling advertisements. The advisory clearly states that the consumer protection authority can take action against advertisers, intermediaries, social media services, and all stakeholders involved in advertising an illegal betting and gambling application. The advisory clarifies the enforceability and liability of illegal advertisements but does not clarify the main issue, i.e. a standard to differentiate legal from illegal advertisements.

20.5 GLOBAL PRACTICE ON REGULATION OF BETTING AND GAMBLING ADVERTISEMENTS

Betting and gambling are legal in several countries, and they do not consider games of skill played for monetary stakes as gambling. Advertisement regulations focus on gambling and try to create safer online environments for gambling so we cannot transpose practices to the Indian scenario as is. We can analyse principles and the regulatory approach in other countries and modify them for the Indian context.

20.5.1 EU

In the European Union (EU), there are three distinct approaches to online gambling advertisements. Italy for example adopts a strict approach towards betting and gambling advertisements and does not distinguish games that involve money winnings from betting and gambling. Article 9 of Italy's Dignity Decree 2019 prohibits any form of indirect or relative advertising of games or bets with money winnings or gambling at *sports, cultural, or artistic events, television or radio broadcasts, daily and periodical press, in publications general, billboards, and computer, digital, telematic channels, social media* (Apa & Foco, 2019). Italy brought in the ban on both RMG equivalents and betting and gambling, based on research that suggested that 3% of the Italian population suffered from harms related to gambling (Adele Minutillo, 2021).

Other countries in the EU adopt less restrictive measures proportionate to the risks of betting and gambling advertisements. Belgium bans gambling advertisements 15 minutes before or after programming for children, in public posters, and targeted advertisements. The Belgian government's aim is to restrict children's exposure to gambling advertisements and does not extend its application to cover RMGs. In June 2023, the Belgian government announced a plan to ban all forms of direct advertising by 2023 and give sporting organisations time till 2027 to end sponsorship agreements with betting and gambling companies (Strauss, 2023).

Germany has adopted the least restrictive approach to online gambling advertisements. The Interstate Treaty on Advertising 2021 bans advertisements to at-risk groups specifically like people who have a history of mental health issues linked to gambling (Clifford Chance, 2021). Further, Germany has also adopted a balanced approach towards gambling adverts on print, radio, and the internet and prohibits advertisements of online casinos, poker, and virtual slot operators from 9 am to 6 pm. Germany also prohibits advertisements that involve active match officials and athletes. Interestingly, the 2021 Treaty removes the prohibition on public games of chance and migrates them to a licensing regime subject to following risk minimisation measures like adopting measures to prevent minors' exposure to gambling advertisements.

Malta and Gibraltar are popular gaming destinations and have detailed regulations on several aspects of gambling. They have laws that specify principles and mandatory and voluntary standards on several aspects, including advertising. Standard certification by audit organisations for voluntary standards signal an entity's compliance with essential requirements under regulatory frameworks (Pelkmans, 1987). Standards are initiated and developed jointly by professional and industry associations and societies. The market drives the development and adoption of standards. Since they are developed organically in a voluntary environment, they reflect market demand and emerging technological needs (Cargill, 2017).

20.5.2 USA

The United States Supreme Court overturned the Professional and Amateur Sports Protection Act (PASPA) in *Murphy vs. NCAA* (2018) and removed the federal-level prohibition on states from authorising and regulating sports wagering systems, including advertisements. It is pertinent to note that the PASPA prohibited sports wagering, betting, and gambling which is different from RMGs. Betting, wagering, and gambling through online games is prohibited in India as well, but the absence of the SRB mechanisms under the 2023 IT Rules diminishes the ability to distinguish between permissible online RMGs and betting, wagering, and gambling applications in practice.

There are limited restrictions specifically on advertising betting and gambling in the United States because of the judgement. Some states like Colorado (under Rule 9 of Sports Betting Regulations, 1 CCR 207-2, Department of Revenue, State of Colorado) stipulate that advertisements must clearly specify the legal age for gambling in advertisements and include information on how gamblers can seek help in case of addiction and a helpline number. The Federal Trade Commission's Truth in Advertising Laws prohibit misleading advertisements, like the CCPA's role in India. Further, the American Gaming Association, an industry body, has a 'Responsible Marketing Code for Sports Wagering' for traditional and digital marketing and advertising. As per the Code, the Association members adhere to standards and practices that look to address risks of exposing children to gambling and adopt mitigation strategies like providing helpline numbers.

The Marketing Code also adopts other key restrictions on advertising. Messages that guarantee financial, social, or personal success suggest that actors or influencers in advertisements are under 21, suggest that it is low-risk or risk-free, and imply or suggest any other illegal activity are all prohibited as per the voluntary code. Digital advertisements must also follow the code and additionally ensure an age-confirmation mechanism to prevent those under 21 years of age from viewing the advertisement.

20.5.3 UK

In the United Kingdom, the Committees of Advertising Practice (CAP) regulates and issues codes of conduct for advertising, and the Advertising Standards Authority (ASA) enforces the code. Like in India and the USA, misleading ads are sanctioned in the United Kingdom. Additionally, a specific code of conduct on gambling

(Advertising Guidance on gambling) prohibits advertising targeted at children by prohibiting actors or influencers under the age of 25 from endorsing gambling applications and prescriptions like alluding values like toughness and gambling as a rite of passage in advertisements.

20.5.4 Australia

Online casino gaming and poker are prohibited in Australia. Fantasy sports and games of skill are not regulated in Australia, and operators mainly function from Australia's Northern Territory. The House of Representatives Standing Committee on Social Policy and Legal Affairs released a report titled "You Win Some, You Lose More" following an inquiry into online gambling and harm. The report suggested a phased ban on online gambling advertising (Commonwealth of Australia, 2023). Currently, gambling advertisements are subject to several restrictions at the territorial, state, and national level like compulsory responsible gambling messages along with advertisements and penalties for inducing people to open betting accounts or partake in betting in any manner. With the aim of restricting children's exposure to betting and gambling advertisements, Australia also prohibits betting and gambling advertisements during sports broadcasts. Misleading and deceptive advertisements are penalised in Australia like in other jurisdictions mentioned above.

The following key points appear from the above analysis of advertising regulations in other countries.

- Countries seek to restrict misleading advertisements, children's exposure to betting and gambling advertisements, advertisement exposure to people who suffer from gambling addiction.
- Several countries allow only licensed entities to operate and advertise, which would in effect weed out illegal offshore fly-by-night operators that create unsafe online environments for users.
- Casual games and RMGs based on skill are treated separately from betting and gambling in most jurisdictions, except Italy which includes games that involve money winnings in the same category as betting and gambling, for advertisement regulation.
- Countries rely on industry standards for advertising and specify principles and enforcement mechanisms within the law. Market-led standard setting organically leads industry towards compliance and reduces the government's regulatory burden.

20.6 CONCLUSION

The key question that Indian policymakers need to consider is the harms they are trying to address with a regulatory framework for online games and restrictions on advertisements. Exposing users to a harmful and unsafe online environment on platforms operated by offshore betting and gambling, children's exposure to money-based games, and misleading advertisements that induce customers through deceptive advertisement campaigns that promise personal and financial success are the main risks that online gaming advertisements seek to restrict. It is pertinent to note that these harms arise primarily from betting and gambling, which is illegal in India.

At the same time, legitimate online RMGs continue to get caught in regulations that seek to address harm from offshore entities. To address this, the immediate government imperative should be to notify SRBs and start implementing the 2023 IT Rules to ensure a safe reliable gaming ecosystem that protects users from harm and illegal offshore offerings. Like in other countries, legitimisation through registration could be an effective strategy for advertisers to distinguish permissible ads from illegal applications. SRBs can encourage responsible gaming practices, register online games and intermediaries, address consumer grievances, and evolve responsible advertising practices that members must follow, like the AGA in the United States. To conclude, a registration mechanism and industry-led standard setting and enforcement are the two key imperatives for effective oversight over RMG advertising in India.

REFERENCES

Adele Minutillo, L. M. (2021). Gambling prevalence in Italy: main findings on epidemiological study in the Italian population aged 18 and over. *Minerva Forensic Medicine*, 1, 29–41.

All India Gaming Federation v. State of Karnataka, 2022 SCC OnLine Kar 435 (DB) (Karnataka High Court 2022).

Apa, E., & Foco, E. (2019, May 5). *Portolano Cavallo*. Retrieved from Portolano Cavallo: https://portolano.it/en/newsletter/portolano-cavallo-inform-digital-ip/italian-communications-authority-issues-new-guidelines-softening-the-restrictions-on-gambling-and-betting-advertisements-provided-by-the-decreto-dignita

ASCI. (2023). *ASCI Annual Complaints Report 2022–23*. Mumbai: Advertising Standards Council of India.

Barik, S. (2023, November 25). Citing betting concerns, GoM set to tighten online gaming rules. *The Indian Express*.

Bose, S. (2022, October 12). How offshore betting sites are laughing all the way to the bank. *Moneycontrol*.

Cargill, L. H. (2017). *Setting Standards for Industry: Comparing the Emerging Chinese Standardization System and the Current US System*. Honolulu: East-West Center.

Chandresh Sankhla v. The State of Rajasthan, SCC Online Raj 264 (Rajasthan High Court 2020).

Clifford Chance. (2021, July). *New German Interstate Treaty on Gambling Entered into Effect*. Retrieved from www.cliffordchance.com/content/dam/cliffordchance/briefings/2021/07/new-german-interstate-treaty-on-gambling-entered-into-effect.pdf

Commonwealth of Australia. (2023). *You Win Some, You Lose More*. Canberra: Parliament of Australia.

ET Bureau. (2022, December 7). MIB asks Google to comply with advisory against online betting ads. *The Economic Times*.

EY. (2023). *New Frontiers: Navigating the Evolving Landscape for Online Gaming in India*. Mumbai: EY.

EY-FICCI. (2023). *Windows of Opportunity*. Mumbai: EY-FICCI.

Gameskraft Technologies (P) Ltd. v. Directorate General of Goods Services Tax Intelligence, 2023 SCC OnLine Kar 18 (Karnataka High Court 2023).

Indian Poker Association v. State of Karnataka, WPA No. 39167 to 39169 (Karnataka High Court October 8, 2013).

Junglee Games India Private Limited v. The State of Tamil Nadu, W.P. No. 18022 of 2020 (Madras High Court August 3, 2021).

Laghate, G. (2022, April 12). Indians flock to offshore betting sites in absence of legal platforms in the country. *The Economic Times*.

Mishra, P. (2022). *Offshore Online Betting and Gambling in India: A Risk Assessment*. New Delhi: ESYA Centre.

Murphy v. NCAA, No. 16-476, 584 U.S. ___ (2018) (United States Supreme Court May 24, 2018).

Pelkmans, J. (1987). The new approach to technical harmonization and standardization. *Journal of Common Market Studies*, 1, 249–269.

Rana. (2023, April 10). *Lexology*. Retrieved from New Online Gaming Regulatory Regime Bans Wagering Apps-India: https://lexology.com/library/detail.aspx?g=2d97da66-e4e9-4935-846b-82019e5f286e

Shukla, A. (2023, December 11). India's government blocked 174 betting and gambling sites. *The Economic Times*.

State of A.P. v. K Satyanarayana, AIR 1968 SC 825 (Supreme Court of India 1968).

State of Bombay vs. R.M.D. Chamarbaugwala, AIR 1957 SC 699 (Supreme Court of India 1957).

Strauss, M. (2023, March 9). Belgium bans gambling advertising from July 1. *Reuters*.

21 Gender Dynamics in Online Gaming

Exploring Participation and Representation in India

Anjali Yadav

21.1 INTRODUCTION

The evolution of digital gaming has been propelled by rapid shifts in consumer preferences, new business models, and technological advancements. Key milestones, like the advent of the initial digital games in the 1950s and the arrival of computers and video game consoles, laid the groundwork for a profound transformation within the gaming industry. These early games, featuring straightforward gameplay and basic graphics, ran on mainframe computers and were primarily crafted for instructional and research purposes. Despite their simplicity, these trailblazers paved the way for developing more intricate games in the following decades.

The 1970s and 1980s saw the surge in popularity of arcade games such as Pong and Space Invaders, presenting players with more sophisticated graphics and engaging gameplay. The introduction of coin-operated gaming played a pivotal role, propelling the triumph of arcade games. Subsequently, this success spurred the creation of home video game systems like the Atari 2600, bringing the thrill of the arcade experience directly into people's homes.

The 1980s witnessed the ascendance of home consoles, exemplified by the Atari 2600 and the Nintendo Entertainment System, enabling players to immerse themselves in gaming from the comfort of their homes. The 1990s ushered in the era of PC gaming, fuelled by the growing popularity of personal computers and the advent of 3D graphics technology. This period marked a significant turning point in digital gaming, with the introduction of 3D-capable consoles such as the Sony PlayStation and the Nintendo 64, providing a platform for more realistic graphics and immersive gameplay. The proliferation of the internet further revolutionised gaming, introducing real-time online multiplayer experiences.

The 2000s witnessed the rise of mobile gaming, driven by the widespread adoption of smartphones and the establishment of mobile gaming platforms like the App Store and Google Play. This era brought about a surge in mobile games, including casual games that could be enjoyed while moving (Karun, 2023).

As the gaming industry consolidates, games undergo significant technological and audience evolution. The advent of digital technology and widespread internet

DOI: 10.1201/9781032624204-22

accessibility has transformed online gaming into a pervasive cultural phenomenon. This virtual realm's global expansion necessitates a closer examination of the nuanced dynamics shaping the experiences of diverse user groups, particularly in gender.

Initially reliant on consoles and arcades, electronic games were predominantly played by boys. However, the technology connected to gaming has evolved, fostering a broader understanding of both genders and encompassing diverse age groups. The multifaceted nature of gender dynamics in the evolving landscape of online gaming in India encompasses participation patterns, gender representation within gaming spaces, and the impact of socio-cultural norms on gaming behaviour.

Research indicates that despite an increasingly diverse player base, persistent gender-related stereotypes impact women's participation and the portrayal of female characters in games (Beasley & Standley, 2002; Consalvo, 2012). While online gaming offers opportunities for global interaction, traditional gender norms continue to influence various aspects of gameplay, from character design to social interactions between players.

The competitive nature of online games fosters an environment where traits like dominance and control are highly valued. It can lead to behavioural shifts, with some female players adopting aggressive behaviours in response to societal expectations. Conversely, male players might shy away from openly expressing their emotions, driven by a concern about being perceived as vulnerable. At the same time, there has been noticeable headway recently as some developers strive for more varied character representations and diverse player demographics.

Nevertheless, persistent disparities underline the need for ongoing efforts involving individual gamers, developers, publishers, educators, and regulatory bodies on various fronts. This study takes a deep dive into the gender dynamics within online gaming in India, zeroing in on participation and representation. Its goal is to shed light on the social and cultural threads weaving through the gaming community, pinpointing trends, preferences, and challenges. Grasping these dynamics becomes pivotal for policymakers to carve out a gaming landscape that is not only safer but also more enjoyable, fostering diversity and user protection.

In scrutinising the intricacies of participation and representation, the research aims to unravel nuanced insights into the factors influencing individuals across the gender spectrum in the rapidly expanding universe of online gaming in India.

21.2 PARTICIPATION IN ONLINE GAMING

In recent years, online gaming has experienced a remarkable surge in popularity in India, propelled by high-speed internet connectivity and affordable smartphones (Kumar, 2021). This technological evolution not only expanded gaming accessibility but also fostered the development of a robust gaming ecosystem. The online gaming market in India has seen substantial revenue growth, with a projected rate of 22.1% between 2020 and 2025. Various factors, like increased disposable income, changing lifestyles, and the rise of esports, contribute to this upward trend. The COVID-19 pandemic and ensuing lockdowns further accelerated online gaming growth as people sought entertainment and social interaction during isolation. This phenomenon not only presents opportunities for economic growth but also spurs job creation in areas like game development, design, and esports management. Overall, the burgeoning popularity of online gaming in India is driven by technological advancements and evolving consumer preferences, positioning it as a lucrative industry with significant growth potential.

Research by Lopez-Fernandez, Williams, and Kuss (2019) reveals intriguing insights into the gender dynamics of Indian gamers. The gaming population in India is predominantly male, aligning with the global perception of gaming as a predominantly male-dominated activity. However, the gradual narrowing of the gender gap is noteworthy, indicating a rising number of female gamers in India. This gender distribution complexity extends to gaming platforms and genres, with female gamers leaning towards mobile gaming while male counterparts prefer console and PC gaming. Socio-cultural factors and platform availability contribute to this dynamic gender disparity in gaming preferences.

Despite the growing popularity of online gaming, persistent barriers impede women's full participation. Bergstrom highlights these barriers, ranging from toxic and hostile environments within gaming spaces to gender-based discrimination and harassment. The prevalence of a male-dominated space perpetuates harmful stereotypes, creating an unwelcoming atmosphere for women. Lack of representation and diversity in game development exacerbates the issue, as games often cater to a male audience, featuring hypersexualised female characters and reinforcing stereotypes. The absence of female role models and mentors further hinders women's involvement, contributing to their underrepresentation in online gaming.

Addressing the cultural factors influencing gender-specific participation, a critical analysis of *Computers in Human Behavior* emphasises the role of traditional gender norms and societal expectations (Su et al., 2020). Cultural beliefs around femininity may discourage girls and women from engaging in gaming, perpetuating the perception that it is a masculine activity. Societal pressures and gender stereotypes additionally limit girls' access to gaming platforms and dissuade them from pursuing gaming as a hobby or career. The study advocates for interventions challenging these cultural factors to promote gender equality in online gaming.

The intersection of social and economic factors impacting women's involvement in online gaming is a focal point of a systematic review by Sublette and Mullan (2012). Traditional gender roles and societal norms discourage women from participating in perceived male-dominated activities like video games. This societal pressure, coupled with the lack of representation and inclusivity in gaming spaces, is a barrier for women entering the online gaming community. Financial considerations, such as the price of gaming accessories and memberships, further restrict women's access to online gaming platforms. To advance gender equality in the gaming business, the authors stress the significance of removing these social and financial barriers. They call for more accessible and reasonably priced gaming environments that enable women to participate actively in online gaming communities.

21.3 REPRESENTATION IN ONLINE GAMING

The evolution of gender representation in online gaming characters has been a fascinating journey across time, illuminated by an in-depth historical analysis carried out by Waddell, Ivory, and Conde (2015). Their research highlights a noticeable shift from traditional and stereotypical depictions to more inclusive and diverse representations. In the early days of gaming, female characters were often confined to roles that were hypersexualised or distressed, reinforcing conventional gender norms. However, as the gaming industry progressed, embracing inclusivity and social awareness, we witnessed the emergence of empowering portrayals of women as strong, independent individuals. This transformation is credited to the increased presence of women in the gaming industry, a growing social consciousness, and a demand for more inclusive content. The evolution of gender representation in online gaming characters reflects broader societal changes and an ongoing commitment to gender equality.

Delving into the impact of stereotypes and gender roles in online gaming characters, a study by LK Kaye, CE Gresty, and N Stubbs-Ennis (2017) emphasises their potential influence on player perceptions and attitudes. The research reveals that stereotypical portrayals reinforce traditional gender norms, with female characters often hypersexualised and male characters portrayed as dominant. Beyond mirroring societal gender inequalities, these stereotypes can shape real-life attitudes and behaviours, potentially marginalising women in the gaming community. The study underscores the importance of game developers critically examining and challenging these stereotypes, fostering gender equality and cultivating a more inclusive gaming experience.

Recent years have witnessed a heightened interest in examining gender representation in online gaming characters, exemplified by a study titled "Gender Equality in Online Gaming Characters: An Exploration of Recent Studies" by Naidoo, Coleman, and Guyo (2020). The researchers argue that addressing gender equality in online gaming is crucial, with implications for players and the industry. Despite persistent gender imbalances in character portrayals, the study advocates for challenging existing stereotypes to create a gaming environment that is more inclusive and diverse. Recognising the potential benefits of such inclusivity, the study calls for further research and action to rectify gender inequality in online gaming characters.

In an insightful article published in *Educational Technology*, GT Richard (2017) emphasises the pivotal role of gender representation in games and its impact on gender diversity. The article highlights the historical bias towards male characters in video games, perpetuating stereotypes and contributing to the underrepresentation of women in gaming. To foster gender inclusivity and encourage more women to participate, Richard suggests increasing the visibility and diversity of female characters in games. This research underscores the necessity of addressing gender representation to cultivate a more inclusive gaming environment.

The influence of stereotypes in shaping gaming culture and participation across genders is underscored by Paaßen, Morgenroth, and Stratemeyer (2016). Their study illuminates the deep-seated stereotypes ingrained in the gaming community, negatively impacting women and perpetuating a hypermasculine gaming culture. Negative stereotypes, such as perceiving women as less skilled, lead to exclusionary practices and a hostile gaming environment. Similarly, stereotypes imposed on men reinforce aggressive and dominant behaviour, creating challenges for those who deviate from these norms. This emphasises the profound impact of stereotypes on gender participation, perpetuating inequality and shaping the gaming landscape.

A study by Williams, Martins, Consalvo, and Ivory (2009) reinforces the significant role of gender portrayals in shaping gender inclusivity in games. The research indicates that video games often reinforce traditional gender stereotypes, depicting males as powerful and females as sexualised and submissive. These portrayals contribute to the marginalisation of women in gaming spaces, fostering a hostile environment. Exposure to such gender portrayals in games can influence players' real-world attitudes, emphasising the urgency of promoting diverse and inclusive gender representations to challenge stereotypical notions and foster a more inclusive gaming culture.

21.4 ONLINE GAMING CULTURE IN INDIA

Tushya, Chhabra, and Abraham (2023) explored the social dynamics thriving within India's online gaming community. The authors illuminated the remarkable growth of the gaming industry, particularly in multiplayer online games, underlining its role as a dynamic platform for social interaction. Within this virtual realm, diverse players converge to form communities, engaging in various activities that transcend the boundaries of the digital world. The study unveiled the concept of "fandom" within the gaming community, where players forge emotional connections with the game and fellow gamers. This profound sense of belonging fosters robust social interactions and friendships, creating bonds beyond the virtual landscape.

Delving into the cultural fabric, the study underscored how Indian gaming communities prioritise teamwork and cooperation, mirroring the collectivist values ingrained in the culture. However, the research does not shy away from addressing challenges, such as gender representation issues and toxic behaviours, that the online gaming community in India grapples with. This comprehensive analysis provides valuable insights into the distinctive characteristics and hurdles faced by this vibrant and growing community.

Research findings spotlight female gamers' unique challenges within predominantly male online gaming communities. These challenges, as illuminated by studies, unveil a landscape marred by sexism, online harassment, and threats directed at female gamers. The impact of such experiences on the mental well-being and gaming journey of women underscores the urgency of tackling toxicity and fostering respectful behaviour within these communities. The research further highlighted the existence of gender biases and stereotypes hindering the acceptance and recognition of female gamers. This amplifies the call for enhanced representation and visibility, challenging and dismantling gender stereotypes to create a gaming environment that embraces diversity and inclusivity.

Against the backdrop of significant growth and popularity within the Indian online gaming community, Brewer, Romine, and Taylor's (2020) insights present compelling implications and recommendations. A key emphasis is placed on creating a safe and welcoming environment through stringent moderation policies, discouraging hate speech, harassment, and discrimination. The need for diversity is stressed, urging active encouragement and support for individuals from marginalised groups to participate in gaming activities. Game developers are encouraged to contribute by creating culturally diverse games, ensuring everyone feels represented and included. Additionally, community events and tournaments promoting inclusivity are seen as catalysts to bring people together and cultivate a shared sense of belonging.

Examining the portrayal of gender identity within online gaming, A. Pulos's (2023) study dives into the complex dynamics that often reinforce traditional gender norms and perpetuate a male-dominated culture. The study calls for a critical examination of gender dynamics within online gaming to comprehend its impact on players' experiences, aiming to address issues of gender inequality and discrimination in these virtual spaces.

The deep-rooted issue of gender stereotypes and the challenges gamers face in virtual worlds is highlighted by Choi, Chung, and Kim (2012). Their research underscored the pervasive nature of gender stereotypes within the gaming community, manifesting in the portrayal of female characters as overly sexualised or weak. These stereotypes contribute to the marginalisation and exclusion of female gamers, fostering a hostile environment that reinforces the misconception that gaming is exclusively for men. The study advocates for promoting inclusivity and diversity in virtual worlds, challenging gender stereotypes embedded in gaming culture.

Exploring the psychological effects of online gaming on self-perception and gender identity, Leménager et al. (2014) shed light on the transformative potential of prolonged engagement in virtual environments. The immersive nature of online gaming, allowing individuals to shape and customise their avatars, blurs the lines between virtual and real-world self-perception. The study also underscored how gender stereotypes perpetuated in these environments can influence individuals' perception of their own gender identity, either reinforcing or challenging existing norms. The intricate interplay between online gaming and self-perception requires further exploration to unravel its complex implications.

21.5 THE LEGAL JURISPRUDENCE AND REGULATIONS

The Indian Copyright Act, 1957, and Trademarks Act, 1999 protect game developer's and publishers' rights, while the Consumer Protection Act, 1986, and Information Technology (Intermediary Guidelines) Rules, 2011 provide consumer protection and regulate online conduct. The Information Technology Act of 2000 empowers the government to handle digital content and prosecute cybercrime. The Information Technology Act is a comprehensive law in India that deals with various aspects of electronic commerce and online activities. While these laws do not explicitly address gender dynamics in gaming, they provide a legal framework for addressing issues related to online harassment, cyberbullying, and other offences that might occur in online gaming spaces. The Ministry of Electronics and Information Technology and CERT-In monitor and control the digital gaming industry. Sections of the IPC related to offences like defamation, harassment, and threats could potentially be invoked in cases where gender-based issues arise in online gaming.

The National Commission for Women (NCW) is tasked with promoting and protecting the interests of women. While it may not directly relate to online gaming, the NCW could play a role in advocating for women's rights and investigating cases of harassment or discrimination.

21.6 THE WAY FORWARD

India boasts the world's largest youth population and is rapidly ascending to the forefront of the gaming industry. Fuelled by this spirit and building on the successes of its preceding editions, IGS 2023 unfolded in tandem with IETF 2023. Within a single venue, the event showcased technological innovation, the latest games crafted by independent developers, animations, gamification of products and services, eSport, virtual reality (VR), gaming zones, start-ups, skill development, digital India, and Made in India. Many young individuals are drawn to the gaming industry as a means of livelihood due to the abundance of employment opportunities. Future strides in the Indian gaming sector will be steered by technologies like artificial intelligence (AI), VR, and the metaverse, playing a crucial role in fostering the country's creative economy.

According to experts, the gaming sector will be pivotal in our efforts to harness resources and cultivate start-ups, scalability, and entrepreneurial opportunities. Therefore, ensuring a secure competitive environment for all participants is essential, encompassing protocols to prevent cheating and mistreatment. Striving to replicate the positive aspects of offline play in online settings while recognising the behavioural and mindset differences between online and offline gaming is crucial. Promoting healthy competition among teams, irrespective of gender, and striving for gender diversity in team composition encourages collaboration and teamwork.

Recognising the challenges female gamers may encounter in the gaming community, including toxicity and objectification, it's crucial to take proactive steps to address these issues. Some measures that can allow female gamers to compete in male-dominated games involve reassuring them that it is feasible to compete and excel in such environments. Organising tournaments exclusively for female gamers creates a secure and inclusive atmosphere, allowing them to compete confidently against other female players. Collectively, these actions contribute to fostering a more inclusive and supportive gaming landscape.

REFERENCES

Beasley, B., & Standley, T. C. (2002). Shirts vs. skins: Clothing as an indicator of gender role stereotyping in video games. *Mass Communication & Society*, 5(3), 279–293.

Brewer, J., Romine, M., & Taylor, T. L. (2020). Inclusion at scale: Deploying a community-driven moderation intervention on Twitch. *DIS '20: Proceedings of the 2020 ACM Designing Interactive Systems Conference.* https://dl.acm.org/doi/10.1145/3357236.3395514

Choi, G., Chung, H., & Kim, Y. (2012). Are stereotypes relative to gender usage applicable to virtual worlds? *International Journal of Human-Computer Interaction*. https://www.tandfonline.com/doi/abs/10.1080/10447318.2011.601973

Consalvo, M. (2012). Confronting toxic gamer culture: A challenge for feminist game studies scholars. *Ada: A Journal of Gender, New Media, and Technology*. https://doi.org/10.7264/N35M63M4

Karun, S. (2023). The digital gaming revolution: An analysis of current trends, issues, and future prospects. *Russian Law Journal*, XI(1)(18). https://doi.org/10.52783/rlj.v11i1.288

Kaye, L. K., Gresty, C. E., & Stubbs-Ennis, N. (2017). Exploring stereotypical perceptions of female players in digital gaming contexts. *Cyberpsychology, Behavior, and Social Networking*, 20(12), 740–745.

Kumar, K. (2021). Growth trends in India's gaming industry. *International Journal of Social Science and Economic Research*, 06(07). https://ijsser.org/2021files/ijsser_06__164.pdf

Leménager, T., Dieter, J., Hill, H. et al. (2014). Neurobiological correlates of physical self-concept and self-identification with avatars in addicted Massively Multiplayer Online Role-Playing Games players. *Addictive Behaviors*. https://www.sciencedirect.com/science/article/abs/pii/S0306460314002287

Lopez-Fernandez, O., Williams, A. J., & Kuss, D. J. (2019). Measuring female gaming: Gamer profile, predictors, prevalence, and characteristics from psychological and gender perspectives. *Frontiers in Psychology*. https://www.ncbi.nlm.nih.gov/pmc/articles/PMC6498967/

Naidoo, R., Coleman, K., & Guyo, C. (2020). Exploring gender discursive struggles about social inclusion in an online gaming community. *Information Technology & People*, 33(2), 576–601.

Paaßen, B., Morgenroth, T., & Stratemeyer, M. (2016). What is a true gamer? The male gamer stereotype and the marginalisation of women in video game culture. https://core.ac.uk/download/pdf/211855666.pdf

Pulos, A. (2023). Confronting heteronormativity in online games: A critical discourse analysis of LGBTQ sexuality in World of Warcraft. *Games and Culture*. https://journals.sagepub.com/doi/10.1177/00332941231153798

Richard, G. T. (2017). Video games, gender, diversity, and learning as cultural practice: Implications for equitable learning and computing participation through games. *Educational Technology*, 57(2), 26–43. https://eric.ed.gov/?id=EJ1137584

Tushya, Chhabra, D., & Abraham, B. (2023). Social networking or social isolation? A systematic review on socio-relational outcomes for members of online gaming communities. *Sage Journals*. https://journals.sagepub.com/doi/10.1177/15554120231201760#:~:text=The%20study's%20results%20suggest%20that,social%20capital%2C%20and%20social%20skills

Waddell, T. F., & Ivory, J. D. (2015). It's not easy trying to be one of the guys: The effect of avatar attractiveness, avatar sex, and user sex on the success of help-seeking requests in an online game. *Journal of Broadcasting & Electronic Media*, 59(1), 112–129. https://doi.org/10.1080/08838151.2014.998221

Williams, D., Martins, N., Consalvo, M., & Ivory, J. (2009). The virtual census: Representations of gender, race, and age in video games. *New Media & Society*. https://ocw.metu.edu.tr/mod/resource/view.php?id=1334

22 Child's Consent in Online Gaming Click-Wrap Agreements and Its Intersection with Privacy

Mili Gupta and Gagneet Singh

21.1 INTRODUCTION

With increased number of online gamers, click-wrap agreements have been one of the prominent online contracts for the gaming industry with an ease of obtaining consent where a user consents to the terms and condition of a gaming website or application by clicking on the "I agree" checkbox. With regard to the consumption of online gaming, the KPMG report states that only 18 percent of the total age groups of 5–14 have been engaged in online gaming. It has been estimated that more online gamers under the age of 18 will be added by 2025 to the existing gaming population in India. A child, i.e., minor, to play an online game has to enter into a click-wrap agreement with the online gaming platform, and click-wrap agreements are valid e-contracts with an exception that a minor cannot enter into any contract even though it being click-wrap because of his incompetency to contract as provided under section 11 of the Indian Contract Act, 1872.

21.2 CHILD'S CAPACITY TO GAMING CLICK-WRAP AGREEMENT

A child as per law is not capable to enter into contract but can be capable in certain circumstances just for his benefit. Section 30 of Partnership Act, 1932 states that a minor can be admitted as a partner only for his benefits and shall not be personally held liable. In order to arrive at a conclusion as to the capacity of the child to enter into a gaming click-wrap agreement, it becomes important to underline the definition of Child and Minor as per the Contract Law. Indian Contract Act, 1872 neither defines Child nor Minor. Section 11 only states "*Every person is competent to contract who is of the age of majority*". It implies that both minor and child be considered as person. The importance of minor contracts was largely reduced when the majority age was reduced from twenty-one to eighteen because of long-term transactions. The General principle is that if a transaction is carried out by the minor, he cannot undo it unless the transaction is of a nature which could have been withdrawn by an adult (Furmston, 2012).

DOI: 10.1201/9781032624204-23

One of the research projects had concluded that a user shall be deemed to have assented to the browse-wrap agreement if the following conditions are satisfied. Firstly, the user has been provided with adequate notice of the proposed terms. For a child consenting to click-wrap agreement, how can he be expected to be aware of the notice and understand the consequences of it. Secondly, the user avails the opportunity of reviewing the terms. A child who cannot understand cannot review it (Kunz et al., 2003).

21.2.1 Revisiting Section 11 of Indian Contract Act, 1872

Section 11 makes it clear that a child cannot enter into an agreement because he or she is an individual below the age of 18 years. UN Convention on Rights of Child defines a child as a human being below 18 years of age (General Assembly, 1990, p. 2). However, the contract law provides an alternative to the minor for his incapacity in allowing the guardian to enter into contract on his behalf (Bhore, 22, p. 3). Both Hindu Minority and Guardianship Act, 1956, and Guardian and Wards Act, 1890 define a guardian, but the former is religious specific and the latter is uniformly applicable to all. According to both legislations, guardian is defined as "*a person having the care of the person of a minor or of his property or of both his person and property*". In the judgment of *Sri Kakulam Subrahmanyam v. Kurra Subba Rao* (1948), the privy council emphasized on the concept of entering into a contract by a guardian on behalf of the minor. The Court stated that a contract can be enforced against a minor if the "*The contract is one which it is within the competence of the guardian to enter into on his behalf so as to bind him by it*".

This implies that a guardian entering into a gaming click-wrap agreement for a minor should also hold competency as per Section 11 of Indian Contract Act, 1872. The court also stated that if the contract is for the benefit of the minor, it can be enforced. An analysis that can be drawn from this judgment is that a guardian entering into a gaming click-wrap agreement for a minor is for the benefit of the minor. Whether a sort of entertainment can be considered as a benefit of the minor needs to be looked upon. Several studies have shown that playing online games results in the development of cognitive skills such as problem-solving and decision making. (Maurya, 2023). Video games did not seem to pose harm for most domains of children's psychosocial development (Lobel et al., 2017, p. 895). The criteria in the said judgment appear to be satisfactory as the online gaming click-wrap agreement though might be entered into by a minor but is presumed to be entered into by a guardian. The same shall be construed as an agreement that is entered into by the guardian for the benefit of the minor and such entering into agreement was for the minor's benefit.

21.2.2 Identification of Contracting Party: Child or Parent

With the statistical reports, it is evident that children are the most involved age category in online gaming. As per Section 10 A of Information Technology Act, 2000: legal validity of e-contracts is accorded which means that click-wrap agreements fall within the ambit of contract legality. In such a contract, the person consenting to the click-wrap agreement should be a major. In case of online gaming applications, if the parent of child consents to the "I agree" button in the click-wrap agreement, then the contracting party is identified as parent. If the contracting party to the click-wrap agreement of online gaming application is the child who is well-versed with the installation and usage of gaming application, the presumption would always be that the parent is a contracting party to the click-wrap agreement even if the child has entered into the gaming click-wrap agreement. A critical analysis of the available data shows that out of the total online gaming individuals, 45 percent fall below the age category of 24 years, 42 percent fall between the age category of 25 and 40 years, and 13 percent fall above age category of 40 years. Majority of online gaming players are under the age of 24 years, but there has been a decrease of 14 percent in 2021 from 59 to 45 percent as compared to 2016. The number of internet users in India is set to surpass one billion in 2023 while the number of online gaming users in India is also projected to grow from 481 million users in 2022 to 657 million users in 2025 (Murthy, 2022).

Parents do restrict their children not to use their mobile phones for playing games. Mobile phone service providers offer parental control services which limit the content children can access via internet to content suitable for under 18s (Ofcom, 2020). For identification of contracting party, the gaming application should inculcate a practice of including a checkbox for revealing of identity stating whether he or she is a parent or child. The point is game platforms should include a checkbox to confirm that the person installing and using the application is a parent or a child. Can a child create a Gmail ID through which he can prove that he is above the age of 18 years as click-wrap agreements of gaming platforms cannot verify age? Most of the installation of gaming application is done only with the existence of a Google account which is very easy to create and subject to mis-use. Even Google states that a guardian can create a Google account for a child below 13 years for the reason that children get access to Google products like Chrome, Gmail, etc. (Google, 2024). It is interesting to note that the Reserve Bank of India has allowed children above the age of 10 years to open a bank account independently. Earlier, a child was authorized to open a bank account only with the consent of guardian (Economic Bureau, 2014). If most of the social networking sites have specified minimum age criteria as 13 years, then the entering into click-wrap agreements by the children into social networking sites appears to be against law as specification of minimum age by social networking platforms on their own on one hand and pre-determined age criteria by law on the other hand. If your child has a profile on a social networking site, they will likely access it on their mobile phone. For those sites that are aimed at younger children, parental consent and confirmation of the child's age will usually be required (Denham CBE, Wood, 2022).

21.3 COLLECTION OF CHILD'S PERSONAL INFORMATION THROUGH GAMING CLICK-WRAP AGREEMENT

The privacy of children especially in online games has an inter-connection with click-wrap agreements as both go simultaneously hand in hand. The legality of gaming click-wrap agreement entered into by a child and the collection of child's personal data through the gaming click-wrap agreement remains debatable. A child incapable of entering into contract is a child incapable of giving consent for processing his data to be used by online gaming platforms. Parental consent for both the scenarios has been preferred mostly, but lack of age verification is a major drawback.

21.3.1 Requirement of Parental Consent

Even though gaming click-wrap agreement and submission of children's data for processing aim at securing parental consent, age disparity is point of concern. Indian Contract Act, 1872 states that a person should be of 18 years age to enter into contract, and if not, then a parent or guardian can enter into contract for benefit of the minor. The GDPR data protection law stipulates that an individual above the age of 16 years is capable of giving personal data for processing, and if below 16 years, parental consent becomes mandatory. Recently in India, an Aadhaar-based consent mechanism has been proposed by the government under the new data protection rules which shall enable all online platforms to verify parental consent for those below 18 years (Desk, 2023). A government ID is encrypted in such a form where no other personal information except name and age is shared with the gaming company to verify that the individual is matching with their eligibility requirements.

A law was passed by Utah which mandated social media entities to provide the access of contents and interactions to a parent made by a child under 18 years of age. Arkansas passed a law which banned that a child under 18 years will not be allowed to access social media platform without parental consent (Bryant, 2023). The laws so promulgated shall not be effective until and unless a mechanism of age verification is derived out. For this, Arkansas law also provides that social media companies to verify the age of users through third-party vendors prior to allowing the access to platform. The proposal of age verification through third-party vendors may enable the gaming platform to identify the age of users, but such verifications demand the use of technologies such as facial scan and biometric data and would make it difficult (Bryant, 2023).

Drum said "every single website platform, with very limited exceptions" should anticipate children will access their sites and design with that in mind.

21.3.2 Age-Verification Process

Knowing the age of users is a key component in creating a safe online experience (Denham CBE, Wood, 2022). The age-verification process includes age verification or self-declaration. Age verification through self-declaration would be deemed appropriate as it will enable the gaming platforms to identify whether the beneficiary is a parent or a child. A clause should be added in the online click-wrap agreement reading that "*person consenting to this agreement is adult and any case of wilful misrepresentation shall not confer any right to the user for demanding the performance of obligations arising thereof*". In 2021, Tencent became the first game company to pilot face recognition authentication technology, plugging the loopholes of identity fraud by deploying face recognition technology in its games. According to the data disclosed by Tencent, from January 17th to February 15th, 2022, during the winter vacation, an average of 7.92 million game accounts that have been authenticated as minors with their real names were intercepted when they tried to log in to Tencent games during non-playable periods ("Children's game recharge and refund disputes are frequent: how to strengthen real-name authentication", 2022). A privacy-by-design approach emphasizes on carrying out identification of underaged players by online gaming companies first and then informing a child regarding his or her privacy rights. Informing a child and understanding of child that how the collected data is used and for what purposes is difficult.

21.3.3 Unauthorized Information Disclosure to Gaming Platforms

A child is not bound to disclose any information to any online gaming entity. Any data of child so collected by any gaming platform shall not be construed as data collected with consent. The child data has to be collected only after complying with data protection principles.

21.4 ONLINE GAMING PLATFORMS AND THEIR GDPR COMPLIANCE ON COLLECTION OF CHILD'S PERSONAL DATA

21.4.1 Article 8 GDPR

There have been irregularities in conforming to the age as data collection age and contract entering age have huge variances. Article 8 of GDPR expressly mentions that the processing of child's data shall be deemed lawful provided that the child is above the age of 16 years, and where the child is below the age of 16 years, the consent should be authorized through parental responsibility (General Data Protection Regulation, 2016). The age of entering into click-wrap agreement is 18, whereas the age of giving data for processing is 16 years. In the online gaming click-wrap agreement, the consent for processing child's personal data is given through the click-wrap agreement and when the consent so obtained for the click-wrap agreement is not deemed to be valid, then the consent for data collection shall not hold any legal validity. Consent for the click-wrap agreement comes first while the consent for processing child's data comes second.

21.4.2 Data Protection Principles and Online Gaming

21.4.2.1 Data Processing

What kind of personal information do gaming companies collect through online gaming? The answer is everything from names, addresses, credit card information for billing purposes, email and IP addresses, feedback rankings from others, digital images, and personalized profiles. You often need to provide personal information to access gaming services. To create an online account, gaming companies often require your name, mailing address, email address, and date of birth. They may also ask for and store payment information for in-game purchases. Companies often automatically collect some geographical information to offer you the closest server as well as players in similar time zones to play with. For online gambling games, gamers will also be asked to confirm they are of legal gambling age. To wager actual money, gamers will also need to make a deposit and provide financial information to arrange for payment. Similarly, some games ask permission to access your device's camera, microphone, or location data in order for the game to function properly. It may be appropriate to allow access while playing, but you should have the ability to turn off access when not.

21.4.2.2 Data Collection

Online gaming platforms do collect the data of their users, and the users should be aware of the sensitive information that the gaming platforms collect. The sensitive information includes geolocation and list of contacts from mobile device. When a child is not competent to contract, how can he consent to collection of data. Further, if a child is not aware of the data that he is sharing with the gaming platform, then his privacy is of utmost importance to be preserved. The privacy policy of online gaming platforms needs to be revisited by checking out whose data is collected through whose consent. A question that arises is whether it is possible or permissible under the Contract law that one person consents to the agreement entered into and the other performs the obligations. In gaming contracts, a parent or a guardian enters into the gaming click-wrap agreement and the child performs the obligation of using the application. A child is considered to be incompetent under the contract as he or she is not aware of the consequences of entering into contract; likewise, a child is not aware of the consequences of sharing his personal data and such data is easily shared by a child.

21.4.2.3 Data Minimalization

There are certain games that can be played online by turning on a video camera (Tamarkin, 2020). Such games can infringe the privacy of children which the children are not aware of. When data protection authority of several countries emphasizes on data protection of children in several places like online education, then the data protection authorities owe a responsibility of issuing advisories to children who play games. Advertisements and awareness programs pertaining to internet usage should also be issued to children. Prevention of Sexual Harassment at Workplace Act, 2013 states that the employer should conduct training sessions from time to time for its employees. Similarly, educational institutions, including higher educational institutions, should conduct awareness sessions for children regarding the usage of their personal data while accessing online gaming platforms. During Covid-19, Hungarian data protection authority issued guidelines to the schools which focused on the data minimization principle of data protection. The authority stated in its notification that schools should direct students not to turn on their video cameras while attending online classes as background information assists in data profiling.

21.4.2.4 Storage Limitation

The storage limitation principle focuses on the aspect that if a gaming entity collects any information, then it has to provide the information as till when the data will be stored. Any gaming platform which collects children's data should not store and retain the user's personal data. The data so collected might be relevant for age verification and doesn't require for processing.

21.5 CHILD'S PRIVACY IN INDIAN E-GAMING APPLICATIONS VIS-A-VIS OTHER JURISDICTIONS

As of the third quarter of 2022, roughly 80 percent of internet users surveyed in India played video games on their smartphones. On the other hand, approximately 45 percent of internet users played video games on laptops or desktops. In comparison to reports from the previous year, the preference for these devices saw a slight decline while the share of internet users gaming on media streaming devices and virtual reality headsets increased (Basuroy, 2023).

21.5.1 European Union (European Commission)

Recital 38 of EU GDPR calls for a special protection of children's data. Children are unaware of risks associated with the processing of their personal data. The special protection should be conferred particularly from marketing or creating user profiles of children for marketing ("Recital 38 Special protection of children's personal data", 2020). Any collection of children's personal data should be in a clear and plain language, making it easy for children to understand. The Consent of parent or guardian has to be obtained for the online services availed by a child. This includes online music downloading platforms and online purchase of games. Parental consent for a child below the age of 16 years and no parental consent above 16 years. EU Digital Services Act requires that all online platforms that can be accessed by a minor to ensure a high level of privacy when they access their services.

21.5.2 Canada (Office of Privacy Commissioner, Canada)

Gaming companies in Canada have to obtain meaningful consent from players if personal information is being collected, used, or disclosed. The Office of Privacy Commissioner, Canada, believes that children aged below 13 can provide consent but not a valid consent. If the gaming companies believe that the child is below 13, they need to request for a consent from parent of child (Gaming and personal information: playing with privacy, 2019). However, age verification remains a persistent issue. Most of the gaming click-wrap agreements include a clause that they don't hold any responsibility if the personal information is transferred to a third party and further if such transferred information is processed in other countries by a third party. When most of the online gamers are not aware of the fact that gaming companies disclose personal information to third parties, then considering a child is too far. Some gaming platforms do not have a privacy policy that follows the principle of storage limitation. The policies don't state out as to time for which a data will be retained by a gaming company.

21.5.3 United States (Children's Online Privacy Protection Rule – COPPA)

In the United States, the Children's Online Privacy Protection Act has been in picture since 2000, and it makes illegal for online service providing entities, including gaming companies, to collect the information of children below the age of 13 years without parental consent. Recently, the Federal Trade Commission (FTC) of America had proposed to bring revisions in the Act. Businesses would have to get parents' separate verifiable consent to disclose information to third parties, including third-party advertisers. Operators using kids' information to send these push notifications would also be required to flag that use in their COPPA-required direct and online notices. This would ensure parents are aware of, and must consent to, the companies' use of nudges. The FTC also wants operators to post their data retention policy for children's personal information.

21.6 PROPOSED PRIVACY MODEL

There are issues revolving about protecting the privacy rights of children in online gaming. Firstly, the online gaming service provider has to consider the age-verification process for identifying whether the child is having access to their platform or not. Secondly, after identification that a child is accessing their online platform, a responsibility to be casted upon gaming platform to inform the users, i.e., children regarding their privacy rights. Thirdly, informing them about the data being used by the online gaming provider.

Step 1: An authority directing that all companies should include age-verification method by a tick-box option when a gaming application is downloaded. The tick-box option should state parent or child.

Step 2: If the tick-box option states that the individual entering into a click-wrap agreement is a child, then the verification can be carried out by the online gaming platform with the help of third-party authentication. The same would require a biometric or use of facial recognition technology but would be a tedious process for every user to follow.

Step 3: Upon verification, the individual can be allowed to access the gaming platform, and it would be easy to determine the contracting party.

21.7 UNICEF RECOMMENDATIONS FOR ONLINE GAMING PLATFORMS

The recommendations of UNICEF call for all the companies to respect the child rights. These guidelines will help the platforms, game developers, publishers, etc. The fundamental aspects involve the special protection to children playing games under 18 years of age. The recommendations read that child rights like all human rights are inalienable and universal, and keeping in view, the ineffectiveness of the current age-verification mechanism, the companies should consider the fact that children play their games and it is the responsibility of a company to protect the privacy of children. It implies that the privacy regulations for a child need to be complied along with the incentive to a child to lie about his age to enable him in playing the online game of interest. Then, the companies should create a privacy model where the companies can create games that shall not collect data for children under the age of 18 years. It can be concluded that digital consent age be divided into two categories: digital consent under the age of 18 years and digital consent above the age of 18 years. The former shall not involve the collection of personal data while the latter shall only involve the collection of personal data.

21.8 CONCLUSION AND SUGGESTIONS

This chapter addresses the concerns of the online gaming industry in India with due reference to policy making and its implementation. Children are playing online games using the electronic device of their parents, and this may pose pertinent issues in the near future to decide contractual liabilities arising out of click-wrap agreements. Online gaming click-wrap agreements have legal validity according to Information Technology Act, 2000 in India and are e-contract as well according to the contract law of different jurisdictions. The present framework is that the online gaming platforms can claim exemption from any liability in case of money paid by minors using their parents' device stating that the game behavior and identity used for authentication was that of an adult. Not only the privacy of children playing online games is a concern, but evolving consumer disputes where the minors have been found using the device of parents for registering online gaming accounts by paying hefty amounts, thereby leading to consumer disputes over refunds. Lack of parental control and supervision is also an issue which has been left highly ignored, and gaming companies should focus on face recognition because of real-person authentication and not for real-name authentication which is highly abused. Certain data or information such as chat content, game time, and nick-names to some extent can be used by an online gaming company to determine whether it is a minor or adult playing the online game. With reference to chat content, when intermediaries like WhatsApp concerning the user privacy state that chats and calls are end-to-end encrypted, then the observation and access to gaming chat content between two children, two adults, and a child and an adult will lead to privacy violation. Further, the principle of necessity and legality will be violated if the facial recognition technique is implemented as it involves storage, processing, and transmission of facial information. To suspect underaged players, if the online gaming platforms do not store the facial recognition data by complying with the data protection principle of storage limitation, the risks would be low. It is apparent that such issues demand for a specific legislation concerning the age-verification mechanism and its mis-use in online gaming purchases, online purchase of goods, etc. with some obligation to be casted upon gaming platforms. In case of conflicting interests between a child and online gaming entities, a child is given due legal protection, and the gaming platforms earn huge revenue only because it is played by minors.

REFERENCES

Basuroy. (2023, March 28). *Preferred devices of internet users who play video games in India as of 3rd quarter 2022*. Statista. www.statista.com/statistics/1266239/india-preferred-devices-of-internet-users-playing-video-games/

Bhore. (2022). Contracts Entered into By Guardians on Behalf of Minors: An Exception to the General Legislation. *Indian Journal of Law and Legal Research*, *4*(6), 3. www.ijllr.com/post/contracts-entered-into-by-guardians-on-behalf-of-minors-an-exception-to-the-general-legislation

Bryant. (2023, April 25). *The 'big shift' around children's privacy*. IAPP. https://iapp.org/news/a/the-big-shift-around-childrens-privacy/

Data protection trends in children's online gaming. (2022, September 12). IAPP.

Denham CBE, Wood. (2022, September 12). *Data protection trends in children's online gaming*. IAPP. https://iapp.org/news/a/data-protection-trends-in-childrens-online-gaming/

Desk. (2023, December 17). New data protection rules propose Aadhaar-based consent framework for children to access online platforms. *Deccan Herald*. www.deccanherald.com/india/new-data-protection-rules-propose-aadhaar-based-consent-framework-for-children-to-access-online-platforms-2814797

Economic Bureau. (2014, May 7). Minors above 10 years can operate accounts, ATMs: RBI. *The Indian Express*. https://indianexpress.com/article/business/business-others/minors-above-10-years-can-operate-accounts-atms-rbi/

European Commission. (n.d.). *Can personal data about children be collected?* European Commission. https://commission.europa.eu/law/law-topic/data-protection/reform/rights-citizens/how-my-personal-data-protected/can-personal-data-about-children-be-collected_en

Furmston. (2012). *Law of Contract* (16th ed.). Oxford University Press.

GDPR.EU. (2020). *Recital 38 Special protection of children's personal data*. GDPR.EU. https://gdpr.eu/recital-38-special-protection-of-childrens-personal-data/

General Assembly. (1990). *Convention on the Rights of the Child* (General Assembly resolution 44/25). United Nations. www.ohchr.org/en/instruments-mechanisms/instruments/convention-rights-child

General Data Protection Regulation (679). (2016). European Union. https://gdpr-info.eu/art-8-gdpr/

Google. (2024). *Create a Google Account for your child*. https://support.google.com/families/answer/7103338?hl=en

Guardian and Wards Act, 1890, s.4

Indian Contract Act, 1872, s.11.

Kunz, C. L., Ottaviani, J., Ziff, E. D., Moringiello, J. M., Porter, K., and Debrow, J. (2003). Browse-Wrap Agreements: Validity of Implied Assent in Electronic Form Agreements. *The Business Lawyer*, *59*(1). https://ssrn.com/abstract=1640185

Lobel, A., Engels, R. C. M. E., Stone, L. L., Burk, W. J., and Granic, I. (2017). Video Gaming and Children's Psychosocial Wellbeing: A Longitudinal Study. *Journal of Youth and Adolescence*, *46*(4), 895. https://doi.org/10.1007/s10964-017-0646-z

Maurya. (2023, May 8). *The Impacts of Online Gaming on Children's Behaviour*. Digital Gyan. https://digitalgyan.org/impact-of-online-gaming-on-children/

Narayan Murthy. (2022, June 9). Gamers nation. India – a nation of gamers. *Business Line*. www.thehindubusinessline.com/data-stories/data-focus/india-proves-to-be-a-nation-of-gamers-as-numbers-spike/article65482841.ece

Ofcom. (2020, October 28). *Parental controls for mobile phones*. www.ofcom.org.uk/tv-radio-and-on-demand/advice-for-consumers/television/protecting-children/advice-guides-for-parents/parental-controls-for-mobile-phones

Office of the Privacy Commissioner of Canada. (2019). *Gaming and personal information: playing with privacy*. Office of the Privacy Commissioner of Canada. www.priv.gc.ca/en/privacy-topics/technology/mobile-and-digital-devices/digital-devices/gd_gc_201905/

Sri Kakulam Subrahmanyam v. Kurra Subba Rao, (1948) 50 BOM LR 646

Tamarkin. (2020, April 8). *6 Ways to Play Games via Video Chat Since Just Talking Is Getting Old*. SELF. www.self.com/story/video-chat-games

Teller Report. (2022, October 11). Children's game recharge and refund disputes are frequent: how to strengthen real-name authentication. *Teller Report*. www.tellerreport.com/news/2022-11-11-children-s-game-recharge-and-refund-disputes-are-frequent--how-to-strengthen-real-name-authentication.S1fVa7Moro.html

UNICEF. (2020). *Online Gaming and Children's Rights: Recommendations for the Online Gaming Industry on Assessing Impact on Children*. UNICEF. https://sites.unicef.org/csr/css/Recommendations_for_Online_Gaming_Industry.pdf

23 Responsible and Ethical Framework for Online Gaming
A Shared Responsibility

Kriti Singh and Kazim Rizvi

23.1 INTRODUCTION

In 2023, the global online gaming market reached a remarkable $175.8 billion and is projected to grow to $304.48 billion by 2027 [2023]. This sector, growing at a 4.3% compound annual growth rate (CAGR), boasted over 3.13 billion players globally in 2023 (EY India, 2023). India stands out with a 28% CAGR, hosting 425 million players and ranking as the second-largest market after China (EY India, 2023).

This translated into a market value of approximately USD 1.9 billion (INR 16,428 crore) in FY23. With investments exceeding USD 2.7 billion (INR 22,931 crore), the sector is poised to draw significant foreign investment and generate numerous job opportunities (EY India, 2023). Beyond its economic impact, the online gaming sector, which encompasses skill-based games, is poised to contribute substantially to the digital landscape. It is at the forefront of adopting new technologies such as AR/VR and driving innovations in areas like esports and live streaming, thus shaping the future of digital entertainment. India exemplifies this trend with over 568 million gamers. The rise of online and mobile gaming platforms has significantly fuelled digital adoption and economic growth.

23.1.1 Driving Diversity and Inclusion

The online gaming sector in India is experiencing a significant demographic shift that sets it apart. Traditionally perceived as a male-dominated field, recent reports show that women constitute 41% of the gaming community (Lumikai, 2023). Moreover, 66% of gamers come from non-metro areas, underscoring the democratisation of gaming experiences across diverse demographics.

However, this rapid growth introduces new challenges and complexities, sparking more nuanced discussions about responsible gaming. With an increasingly diverse and expanding player base, the emphasis on safe and responsible gaming practices has become more critical than ever.

 DOI: 10.1201/9781032624204-24

23.1.2 A Double-Edged Sword

While the sector showcases tremendous economic potential, it is crucial to acknowledge its prospective drawbacks. The harms associated with online gaming are becoming increasingly evident. Excessive gaming can result in addiction, social isolation, and even physical health problems (Mohammad et al., 2023).

The World Health Organization in 2019 officially included "online gaming disorder" as a behavioural addiction under the International Classification of Diseases (ICD-11).

It defines it

> as a pattern of gaming behaviour ("digital-gaming" or "video-gaming") characterised by impaired control over gaming, increasing priority given to gaming over other activities to the extent that gaming takes precedence over other interests and daily activities, and continuation or escalation of gaming despite the occurrence of negative consequences. For gaming disorder to be diagnosed, the behaviour pattern must be of sufficient severity to result in significant impairment in personal, family, social, educational, occupational or other important areas of functioning and would normally have been evident for at least 12 months.
>
> (WHO, n.d.)

The Indian Journal of Community Medicine and Public Health reported in 2020 that approximately 3.5% of Indian adolescents suffer from internet gaming disorder (IGD), a rate that is 0.5% higher than the global average. The study highlighted that variations in age, gender, socio-economic status, and the widespread availability of smartphones with internet access significantly contribute to the risk of developing IGD. These findings underscore the need for targeted interventions to address these risk factors within the Indian context (Undavalli et al., 2020).

The National Institute of Mental Health and Neurosciences established the Service for Healthy Use of Technology Clinic, the first of its kind in India, to assist individuals struggling with tech-based addictions. The clinic has been witnessing a surge in cases involving school children and young adults addicted to gaming. Primarily, this clinic focuses on helping adolescents aged 14–18 who are grappling with excessive use of mobile and other digital games. This initiative underscores the growing concern over gaming addiction and the need for specialised support services (Travasso, 2014).

While there is a lot of literature to show the impact of online gaming on mental health among adolescents and adults in other parts of the world – in India, there is a lack of concrete research establishing the relationship between online games of skill and addiction among users. However, anecdotal evidence for increasing addiction among users, specifically platforms providing online games of chance, is mounting (Bhat & Punit, 2023).

The financial risks associated with online gaming deserve close scrutiny. These risks disproportionately impact vulnerable groups with limited financial literacy, such as minors, young adults, and individuals.

Additionally, a lack of transparency and inadequate regulation in the sector has paved the way for unfair practices and predatory behaviour by unauthorised platforms.

Survey reports have revealed that a staggering 75% of Indian gamers have experienced cyber threats on their gaming accounts (ORF, n.d.), highlighting the urgent need for enhanced security measures and regulatory oversight in the online gaming industry. The advancement of technology has led to a blurring of the lines between skill and chance games, which can confuse users. This confusion can be exploited by unscrupulous operators who misclassify their games as skill-based when they are, in fact, heavily reliant on chance.

23.1.3 Need for Responsible Gaming Practices

To tackle these challenges, implementing responsible gaming practices is crucial for maintaining a sustainable online gaming ecosystem. Such practices protect users, foster trust, and ensure the industry's long-term viability. A collaborative approach is vital, requiring industry stakeholders to embrace their responsibilities and help build societal trust within a responsible gaming framework. The online gaming industry can contribute to a sustainable and prosperous future by committing to ethical conduct. Simultaneously, the government can balance economic growth, welfare, and governance by implementing clear and enforceable regulations. This partnership will strengthen the foundation of the online gaming sector and safeguard all participants.

To implement this, a standardised mechanism should be developed that acknowledges the motivations of stakeholders involved and the heterogeneity of business models and services within the online gaming sector while emphasising the collective responsibility of all stakeholders to prioritise user protection and economic growth. The said mechanism should have a comprehensive set of principles and practices that aim to address the potential harms associated with online gaming, such as addiction, financial integrity issues, and unfair practices. The Indian government, under the amended IT Rules, addresses these concerns by placing the onus on platforms and self-regulatory bodies to ensure additional safeguard obligations. However, a uniform, consultative, and collaborative approach to tackle prospective harms effectively is necessary. This will enable a positive shift in societal perception and instil confidence in consumers, the government, and investors alike.

23.2 STAKEHOLDER MOTIVES TOWARDS RESPONSIBLE GAMING

"Responsible Gaming," while traditionally linked to gambling, encompasses a broader ambition – to build a secure and supportive gaming environment for all (Griffiths & Woods, 2008). It encompasses a comprehensive set of policies and measures designed to protect vulnerable individuals, prevent underage access to pay-to-play games, implement safety measures against cyber and financial threats, provide accurate information, and ensure ethical and responsible advertising practices. These strategies should be developed through collaboration between stakeholders in the gaming ecosystem, including government and industry leaders, leveraging their expertise to ensure safe play while minimising potential harm. This collaborative approach aims to create a secure gaming environment that supports fair play and the well-being of all players (GamCare, 2022).

In this case, India is in a unique position where, on the one hand, the online gaming sector is thriving, and on the other, a uniform central law to regulate the sector is yet to be established. This presents a setback because the lack of central regulation and dissonance in state-level legislation for online gaming (excluding gambling and betting) has led to ambiguity. The inconsistency in legal definitions, including fundamental differentiation between online gaming and gambling or betting since the latter is a state subject, has resulted in consumer protection challenges.

However, this also presents an opportunity to develop a comprehensive definition of responsible gaming and implement uniform practices that consider the cultural and contextual needs of all states and the country. To realise this aim and to navigate the concerns emerging from the fast-paced technological advancements, it is necessary to undertake a "whole-of-society approach" to responsible gaming. This approach requires a more profound understanding of the associated harms, harmonising the roles and responsibilities of each stakeholder group and ensuring a proportionate shared responsibility for creating a safe and equitable digital environment (Shreya & Saxena, 2023).

It is, therefore, pertinent to first study the socio-economic motivations of the stakeholders involved in the implementation and the priorities for undertaking responsible gaming initiatives, discussed below. Users, platforms, and governments are this ecosystem's core stakeholder groups. Other critical stakeholder groups are the medical and welfare fraternity, academia, which provides expertise and resources dealing with the impact of online gaming and the legal and civil society organisations that contribute to the legal and regulatory policy landscape. This understanding would help synergise the efforts of all stakeholder groups and develop a cohesive, standardised approach that fosters a sustainable online gaming ecosystem.

23.2.1 Users

The primary goal for most users of online gaming platforms is entertainment and recreation. However, these platforms also serve as a professional arena for the growing community of seasoned players with experience and expertise. They use them as outlets to participate actively or express their strategies in games, such as in fantasy sports, where they select members to form teams or in esports competitions. Nevertheless, attitudes towards responsible gaming practices vary significantly among users, influenced by factors such as age, cultural background, gaming habits, and individual risk profiles. This diversity makes it challenging to implement a one-size-fits-all approach to responsible gaming that effectively addresses the needs and perceptions of all players. Users are the nucleus of the online gaming sector. India boasts the second-largest online gaming user base globally, highlighting the importance of considering factors like age, income level, and access to technology. It is thus essential to understand their motivations to play and the level of awareness of responsible gaming practices to develop targeted initiatives that resonate with different user segments.

23.2.2 Online Gaming Platforms

While commercial interests inevitably play a role in platform-driven responsible gaming practices, it is essential to recognise that these motivations are often multifaceted. Platforms engage in responsible gaming practices, such as know your customer (KYC) and tax obligations, location verification, privacy policies, etc., not just to protect their bottom line but also to cultivate a positive brand image, ensure user trust, comply with regulations, and potentially contribute to overall player well-being.

The effectiveness of these measures will be reflected in the platform's user retention rate. Users who feel informed, protected, and valued are likely to stay engaged with a platform longer, which translates into sustainable business growth for the platform.

Understanding the multifaceted motivations of platform-driven responsible gaming practices would enable a collaborative environment where user protection and industry growth are prioritised. This would pave the way for a future where responsible gaming practices are not just a compliance requirement but a core value driving a thriving and sustainable online gaming industry in India.

23.2.3 Medical and Clinical Fraternity

Driven by a clinical understanding of potential harm, medical professionals closely examine the accessibility, availability, and societal attitudes towards various game formats since they witness the consequences among patients firsthand. This concern may lead them to advocate for stricter regulations or limitations on specific games, particularly those with a high potential for addiction or negative impacts on mental health, to safeguard public well-being.

Historically, the narrative surrounding responsible gaming was dominated by a medicalised view (Blaszczynski et al., 2004) because of focused research on gambling and its associated harms. Gambling problems were seen as an illness with little agency attributed to users. This "disease model" offered limited solutions, often failing to empower users to navigate potential risks.

However, with innovation and the introduction of skill-based gaming formats in recent years, responsible gaming has witnessed a crucial shift as a dynamic field of research within academia and civil society, distinct from research on gambling addiction. The proliferation of online gaming, distinct from betting and gambling, with options like esports, fantasy sports, and casual games, has triggered a societal reevaluation of these activities. These emerging formats are perceived as more inclusive and appealing as opposed to the stigma associated with traditional gambling or games of chance. As a result, studies now look at different aspects of responsible gaming and models that can be adopted throughout the lifecycle of the online gaming ecosystem.

Based on empirical research and anecdotal evidence, their professional opinions empower users to make informed choices about their online gaming habits. The involvement of the medical fraternity would strengthen the foundations of the responsible gaming framework, which would provide a medical perspective on not just how to address the symptoms but also lend an understanding of the identification of underlying causes and factors that may contribute towards the negative impact of online gaming.

23.2.4 Academia and Civil Society

Academic research studies and civil societies are vital alongside the medical fraternity. Researchers critically analyse the interplay between player behaviour and the risks associated with specific gaming formats, including video games. Many scientific studies have also evaluated the difference between skill games and games of chance. By analysing factors such as the interplay of user behaviour and game mechanics, researchers actively test and develop interventions to mitigate potential harm. Based on scientific research and/or data-driven insights, they advocated for effective interventions, which may include technical responsible gaming measures such as in-game prompts based on time spent by the user, limiting spending or measures to be taken by the developers and non-technical measures such as providing educational tools, support for at-risk users, and so on.

On the other hand, civil society organisations are driven by the motivation to champion the cause of user rights, including digital rights in online gaming and a safer digital environment. These organisations, often based on medical and academic insights, advocate for balanced policies and regulations that protect users from exploitation, unfair practices, and potential harm and promote the sector's innovation and growth. Civil society organisations also focus on conducting media literacy training, providing educational resources and promoting financial and digital literacy. These organisations act as a binding force to uphold the stakeholders' accountability and help each group navigate the complex socio-economic and regulatory environment.

23.2.5 Governments

The regulatory landscape for online gaming presents a complex challenge, particularly in India, where the billion-dollar industry offers tax revenue opportunities. The knowledge-to-action gap, where impactful research struggles to translate into real-world practices, highlights the crucial role of governments in bridging the gap by using research findings in effective regulations. However, the socio-political pressures have led to the introduction of prescriptive measures under the IT Rules, which address immediate concerns but lack long-term effectiveness. Moreover, the blanket 28% GST on online gaming deposits, applied through an amendment that conflates it with betting and gambling, creates a confusing and divergent regulatory landscape that hinders a comprehensive and balanced approach to responsible gaming.

The online gaming sector has the potential to fuel economic growth through job creation, foreign investment, support to ancillary industries, promotion of emerging technologies, and tax revenue. However, this potential can only be fully realised in an environment that fosters user trust, minimises associated risks, and incentivises industry growth through uniform regulatory policies.

Understanding the government's motivations and socio-economic objectives in ensuring responsible gaming would help converge the priorities of all the stakeholder groups involved into a unifying comprehensive policy framework.

This comprehensive framework requires conceptual clarity and consensus (Blaszczynski et al., 2004) among the stakeholders for the effective development and implementation of a responsible gaming regime.

23.3 NEED FOR CONVERGENT VIEW ON RESPONSIBLE GAMING

As detailed above, "responsible gaming" encompasses a variety of perspectives and can be interpreted differently by various stakeholders within the online gaming ecosystem. It is essential to achieve conceptual clarity and define responsible gaming to align with the needs and understandings of all involved parties to implement effective policies and ensure player well-being.

Further discussion is needed on key concepts, such as the definition of "harmful" gaming. Stakeholders may have differing views on what constitutes excessive or problematic gaming behaviour. For example, gaming operators may focus on addiction because it affects their sustainability. In contrast, government entities and medical practitioners might be more concerned with the consequences like financial losses, social isolation, or mental health impacts. This diversity of concerns underscores the need for a comprehensive, inclusive approach to defining and managing responsible gaming.

23.3.1 Outlining Responsibilities and Effective Tools

Another important consideration is determining who is responsible for promoting responsible gaming. This responsibility is often debated, with governments, operators, researchers, and players having different views on their roles and obligations. Additionally, what constitutes effective interventions? There is no universal solution to prevent gaming-related harm. Effective strategies must be customised to fit specific player demographics, game formats, and risk factors. Moreover, keeping up with the ever-evolving landscape of online gaming and its constant innovations poses a significant challenge.

Simultaneously, technological advancements have enhanced the tools available to foster responsible gaming initiatives. Unlike traditional or offline environments, the online setting offers greater control over the gaming environment. This includes modifying the aesthetics and auditory effects of the game, altering gameplay characteristics such as speed and duration, and providing players with tools for setting limits on spending and gaming time. It also involves offering behavioural feedback, such as alerts when a player's behaviour changes significantly over time and instant access to online support services. Furthermore, online platforms can educate players through engaging and animated vignettes that integrate seamlessly into the gaming experience, making learning about responsible gaming informative and enjoyable (Wood & Griffiths, 2014).

23.3.2 Need for a Standardised Approach

However, before developing strategies to mitigate the harms, it is imperative to have a standardised approach towards identification, laying out terminologies and definitions of risks and harms. It is essential to understand that technological innovation is at the cusp of transitioning to Web 3.0, which demands a globalised approach that considers a more nuanced and stakeholder-inclusive definition of responsible gaming and moves beyond just being a social responsibility.

To achieve this and bridge the conceptual gap, a few key principles that should encompass responsible gaming include player protection, informed choices, ethical gaming environment, and shared responsibility.

23.4 PRINCIPLES OF RESPONSIBLE GAMING

The partnership between the government and operators should leverage the government's regulatory authority with the operators' deep understanding of player behaviour. Such collaboration further builds trust and confidence among players, ensuring their safety and well-being. This encompasses physical, mental, financial, and social well-being. It includes preventing addiction, minimising financial losses, promoting healthy gaming habits, and protecting vulnerable players.

A comprehensive, responsible gaming framework should be envisaged based on a few core principles. This includes preventive measures to identify and address potential risks. This moves beyond the reactionary to a more risk-based approach. Furthermore, providing information and tools to educate users is essential to promote informed choices. This would empower users to utilise these tools effectively to play responsibly. Establishing safeguards to protect vulnerable players, such as minors, from potential harm is vital to address some of the concerns. Consequently, the effectiveness of these principles lies in maintaining communication and transparency between all stakeholders, including users, platforms, and the government, to foster a safe and sustainable online gaming ecosystem.

23.4.1 Informed Choice

Players should have access to transparent information about game mechanics, the risks associated with excessive play, and resources to support responsible gaming practices. This transparency is crucial for facilitating informed choices. The core idea is that the decision to play is a personal choice, and making informed decisions requires access to comprehensive information. This trend towards granting consumers greater autonomy to make informed decisions is evident across various sectors. It can be seen in practices such as providing detailed product ingredient lists and disclosing potential risks in financial investments (Wood & Griffiths, 2014). This approach enhances player safety and supports a fair and transparent gaming environment.

23.4.2 Player Protection

Online gaming platforms are responsible for implementing effective player protection measures to facilitate informed choices. This involves deploying tools and providing detailed information about game mechanics, game format, the criteria for selecting winners, disclosures related to pay-ins and payouts, tax compliance, data collection purposes, and certifications for random number generation (RNG) and anti-bot technologies (Voluntary Code of Ethics, 2023). Adopting such measures safeguards players and fosters a more sustainable business environment.

Adequate player protection also requires precise and targeted communication. Messages must be clear, transparent, and fair. Equally important is the strategic placement of these messages; they must target the right audience at the right time to avoid message fatigue and ensure the content resonates with the intended recipients. This approach promotes a safer, risk-minimised gaming environment and helps distinguish legitimate platforms from offshore betting and gambling sites. This clarity is crucial, as it aids players in distinguishing between legally permissible online games and those that are not. This differentiation is key to maintaining trust and ensuring compliance within the gaming ecosystem.

23.4.3 Ethical Game Design

Effective responsible gaming necessitates creating awareness and integrating ethical practices throughout the game lifecycle, from conceptualisation to deployment. Games should be designed with ethical principles and privacy-enhancing measures embedded from the start. This approach involves more than just avoiding harmful elements; it includes the fundamental integration of ethical design principles that prioritise privacy and steer clear of manipulative mechanics. One innovative aspect of this approach is "ethical gaming," which is deliberately designed to encourage ethical thinking and foster attitudes such as empathy (Farber & Schrier, 2017).

This involves training both new and seasoned game developers to inherently design games and gameplay that are ethical in nature. Moreover, developers, educators, and trainers can use game features to enhance players' ethical decision-making and promote positive values like social justice, equality, and environmentalism (prosocial gaming).

Another critical component is responsible gamification. While it can effectively engage users, this technique can lead to ethical concerns if used solely to increase engagement and playtime, with some scholars labelling it "exploitationware" due to the potential misalignment between user interests and provider incentives (Deterding et al., 2011). To address these concerns, it is crucial to ensure participant autonomy, allowing users to opt-out at any time and maintain control over their participation. Securing voluntary participation and informed consent is vital before implementing gamified elements.

Additionally, it is vital to encourage participants to reflect on their engagement and motivations within gamified systems. Ensuring system transparency and fairness is equally essential; gamification rules and algorithms should be transparent to ensure fair treatment for all participants.

From a design perspective, integrating prosocial elements such as empathy and positive portrayals of women, along with collaborative gameplay, can help mitigate player aggression and compulsiveness issues, fostering ethical thinking and instilling positive values in players. This holistic approach enhances the gaming experience and contributes to developing a responsible and ethical gaming ecosystem.

23.4.4 Role of Research

The research community, thus, plays a vital role in this process by evaluating the effectiveness of responsible gaming strategies, including gamification techniques, through rigorous studies with defined objectives. This research can inform and guide policymakers in their oversight role, helping them oversee predatory practices' prevention and fostering a culture of responsible game design and development through outcome-based frameworks. This shift, in turn, empowers operators to innovate within defined ethical boundaries, focusing on desired outcomes like preventing underage engagement and minimising addictive behaviours. For example, regulations might mandate responsible advertising practices without dictating specific ad content, allowing operators to determine effective methods for avoiding targeting minors.

23.4.5 Ethical Impact Assessment Framework

Additionally, a periodic Ethical Impact Assessment (EIA) framework (Bajpai et al., 2021) becomes crucial with the increasing integration of AI-based algorithms in online gaming platforms. This proactive approach can help platforms understand the potential ethical implications of their AI systems and game design choices, fostering responsible practices and building user trust. This assessment can be conducted periodically during design and development to identify potential ethical issues early on to allow corrective measures to be implemented before deployment and post-launch to continuously assess the evolving impact of AI algorithms to reveal unforeseen consequences and necessitate further adjustments.

The EIA framework could involve the following key questions:

- Actors involved and affected: Who are the players, developers, operators, and other stakeholders impacted by the AI algorithms? What are their values, interests, and potential vulnerabilities?
- Legal and regulatory framework: Do existing laws and regulations adequately address the ethical implications of AI in gaming? Are there gaps or ambiguities that must be addressed?
- Contextual values and interests: How do the gaming community's and platform-specific values and interests influence the ethical considerations surrounding AI implementation?

Gaming platforms can reap numerous benefits by identifying and addressing ethical issues early on. They can boost their credibility by demonstrating a proactive approach to AI ethics, built on trust and transparency with users and investors. This leads to valuable insights and data that can be used to enhance user experience. Mitigating potential harm from AI algorithms creates a safer and more enjoyable environment for everyone. Additionally, by setting clear ethical boundaries for AI development, platforms can encourage responsible innovation and avoid unintended consequences. For instance, an EIA could analyse the moral implications of AI-driven loot boxes, considering issues like fairness, transparency, and the potential for gambling addiction. This would allow platforms to ensure a balanced and responsible approach to monetisation.

Similarly, an EIA could assess AI-powered matchmaking algorithms to ensure they don't exacerbate discrimination or bias against specific player demographics. This, in turn, promotes responsible innovation within the industry. Platforms encourage responsible practices and prevent unintended consequences by setting ethical boundaries for AI development. By integrating regular EIAs into the development and operation of online games, platforms can take a proactive stance on AI ethics. This commitment to responsible innovation builds trust, protects players, and contributes to a more sustainable and enjoyable gaming ecosystem.

Responsible gaming is not a singular act or policy but requires a multifaceted approach with shared responsibility that weaves together well-being, informed choices, and ethical practices. By addressing the issue of conceptual clarity and fostering collaboration among stakeholders, a more comprehensive and practical approach can be developed to promote responsible gaming practices within the online gaming ecosystem.

23.5 A SHARED RESPONSIBILITY

Regulators face a challenge in balancing an open market with player protection. Striking the right balance between encouraging competition and promoting responsible gaming practices requires careful consideration. Collaboration between regulators, operators, users, and the technical expertise of the research and health community can pave the way for a thriving industry built on trust and player well-being.

Achieving this and a shared understanding of responsible gaming among stakeholders requires ongoing dialogue, collaboration, and research. This can be facilitated through open communication and knowledge sharing through regular dialogue between stakeholders that can help bridge the gap in understanding and identify areas of common ground.

Developing standardised definitions and frameworks is the next step to establishing clear and consistent responsible gaming frameworks to help guide implementation and measure progress. Even for the thriving startup community in India, a standardised code of conduct can ensure consistent player protection across the industry. This code should prioritise clear, transparent, and fair practices without stifling innovation. Such proactive measures will benefit all stakeholders, fostering a responsible and ethical gaming ecosystem.

23.5.1 Research and Civil Society

The policy decisions should be further informed by research evidence on the effectiveness of different interventions and approaches. Here, academia and civil society can enable access to the latest innovations and research findings on gaming platforms and provide direction to the policymakers to ensure that responsible gaming initiatives continue to provide their players with a low-impact, enjoyable gaming experience. Educational resources and tools can help players make informed choices about their gaming behaviour and manage risks. Ongoing research is needed to understand the evolving nature of online gaming and develop practical solutions to emerging challenges.

23.5.2 Gaming Platforms

Platforms are responsible for implementing robust player protection measures, even without formal regulation. These include avoiding celebrity endorsements that appeal to minors, adhering to age verification protocols, and setting responsible spending limits.

23.5.3 Government

Adopting these measures protects players and creates a more sustainable business environment. However, in the context of gambling, such as Canada's online gaming regulation, global examples demonstrate the importance of player protection in fostering a sustainable and responsible industry. Regulation can then build upon this to ensure fair practices through independent testing, timely payouts, and robust data protection measures, minimising risks of harm and promoting responsible gaming habits.

Regulatory approaches have also evolved from prescriptive rules to outcome-based frameworks. This shift empowers operators to innovate within defined boundaries, focusing on achieving desired outcomes like preventing underage gambling or minimising addictive behaviours. For instance, regulations might mandate responsible advertising practices without dictating specific ad content, leaving operators to determine effective methods to avoid targeting minors.

23.6 CONCLUSION

The ever-evolving landscape of technology and gaming practices demands a dynamic approach to responsible gaming. While traditional partnerships between users, platforms, and governments at the local level remain essential, the complexities of the global internet necessitate a paradigm shift. To effectively address the challenges of today's online gaming landscape, there is a need to transcend borders and adopt global cooperation to tackle shared challenges and forge a more secure and protective environment for all users worldwide.

Sharing knowledge and strategies across countries can allow for adoption of practical solutions and the constant improvement of responsible gaming practices. Additionally, establishing consistent standards for player protection, data privacy, and ethical design will ensure a level playing field for all stakeholders, regardless of location. Collective efforts can further pool resources to tackle complex issues like money laundering, fraud, and player safeguarding, leading to more efficient and impactful interventions.

India has the opportunity to lead global cooperation on an online gaming regime that moves towards a progressive form of regulation that protects consumers while ensuring optimal growth and innovation. This will help India set an example for other countries and those looking to regulate this space or enhance existing responsible gaming regimes.

REFERENCES

Bajpai, H., Shreya, S., Pande, T., & Vats, A. (2021). Response to Niti Aayog's Draft on Responsible Ai for All. In Kazim Rizvi (Ed.), *The Dialogue*. https://thedialogue.co/wp-content/uploads/2020/09/Responsible-AI-for-All-Submission_NITI-Aayog_-The-Dialogue-1.pdf

Bhat, A., & Punit, I. S. (2023, April 18). Fantasy sports apps are driving a surge in gambling addiction in India. Rest of World. https://restofworld.org/2022/fantasy-sports-apps-are-driving-a-surge-in-gambling-addiction-in-india

Blaszczynski, A., Ladouceur, R., & Shaffer, H. J. (2004). A Science-Based Framework for Responsible Gambling: The Reno Model. *Journal of Gambling Studies*, 20(3), 301–317. https://doi.org/10.1023/b:jogs.0000040281.49444.e2

Deterding, S., Dixon, D., Khaled, R., & Nacke, L. (2011). "From game design elements to gamefulness: Defining "gamification"", Proceedings of the 15th International Academic MindTrek Conference on Envisioning Future Media Environments – MindTrek '11, ACM, pp. 9–11.

EY India. (2023, December 8). New frontiers: Navigating the evolving landscape for online gaming in India. Retrieved July 28, 2024, from www.ey.com/en_in/media-entertainment/new-frontiers-navigating-the-evolving-landscape-for-online-gaming-in-india

Farber, M., & Schrier, K. (2017). "The limits and strengths of using digital games as 'empathy machines'" UNESCO/MGIEP Working Paper Series, India.

GamCare. (2022, April 12). What is 'Responsible Gambling'? – GamCare. www.gamcare.org.uk/news-and-blog/blog/what-is-responsible-gambling/

Gaming Market Size, Share & Growth Revenues [2030]. (2023). Fortune Business Insights. www.fortunebusinessinsights.com/gaming-market-105730

Griffiths, M. D., & Woods, R. T. A. (2008). Responsible Gaming and Best Practice: How Can Academics Help? *Casino & Gaming International*, 4(1), 107–112. NTU IRep. https://irep.ntu.ac.uk/id/eprint/19776/1/200169_6558%20Griffiths%20Publisher.pdf

Lumikai. (2023, November 2). Indian gaming industry poised for strong growth: Projected to reach $7.5 Bn by FY28. Lumikai. www.lumikai.com/post/indian-gaming-industry-poised-for-strong-growth-projected-to-reach-7-5-bn-by-fy28

Ministry of Electronics and Information Technology Notification. (2023, April 6). MeitY. Retrieved December 2, 2023, from www.meity.gov.in/writereaddata/files/244980-Gazette%20Notification%20for%20IT%20Amendment%20Rules%2C%202023-%20relating%20to%20online%20gaming%20%26%20false%20information%20about%20Govt.%20business.pdf

Mohammad, S., Jan, R. A., & Alsaedi, S. L. (2023). Symptoms, Mechanisms, and Treatments of Video Game Addiction. *Cureus*, 15(3), e36957. https://doi.org/10.7759/cureus.36957

ORF. (n.d.). Cybersecurity threats in online gaming: Learnings for India. orfonline.org. www.orfonline.org/research/cybersecurity-threats-in-online-gaming-learnings-for-india#:~:text=At%20the%20same%20time%2C%20Indian,cyberattack%20on%20their%20gaming%20accoun

Shreya, S., & Saxena, G. (2023, October). Policy Framework – #BreakTheSIlO: Streamlining gender safety in the digital space. thedialogue.co. https://thedialogue.co/wp-content/uploads/2023/10/BreaktheSilo-Policy-Framework.pdf

Travasso, C. (2014). India Opens Clinic to Help People "Addicted" to Mobile Phones and Video Games. *BMJ*, 349, g4439. https://doi.org10.1136/bmj.g4439

Undavalli, V. K., Rani, G. S., & Kumar, J. R. (2020). Prevalence of Internet Gaming Disorder in India: A Technological Hazard Among Adolescents. *International Journal of Community Medicine and Public Health*, 7(2), 688. https://doi.org/10.18203/2394-6040.ijcmph20200450

Voluntary Code of Ethics. (2023, December). https://fifs.in/. https://fifs.in/wp-content/uploads/2023/12/Voluntary-Code-of-Ethics-for-Online-Gaming-Intermediariess.pdf

WHO. (n.d.). Addictive behaviours: Gaming disorder. www.who.int/news-room/questions-and-answers/item/addictive-behaviours-gaming-disorder

Wood, R. T. A., & Griffiths, M. D. (2014). Putting Responsible Gambling, Theory and Research into Practice: Introducing the Responsible Gambling Review. *Responsible Gambling Review*, 1(1), 1–5. NTU IRep. https://irep.ntu.ac.uk/id/eprint/26043/1/221352_2937.pdf

24 A Comparative Study of the GGR and Turnover Models of Taxing Online Gaming

Meyyappan Nagappan, Eeshan Sonak, and Saranya Ravindran

24.1 INTRODUCTION

The taxation regime of online gaming in India underwent a slew of changes in 2023, the most notable of which is the application of a 28% turnover tax on the industry (Sinha, 2023). Previously, online skill gaming was treated as an OIDAR service and taxed at 18% on the commissions earned by gaming platforms under a gross gaming revenue ("GGR") taxation model (Service Tax Rules, 1994). In furtherance of the GST Council's decision, key definitions in the Central Goods and Services Tax Act, 2017 ("CGST Act") were amended, enabling the taxation of online gaming platforms as suppliers of bets. Rule 31B was notified under the Central Goods and Service Tax Rules, 2017 ("CGST Rules"), requiring the taxable base to be calculated upon the total amount deposited with the supplier, whether used or not.

This chapter discusses the experiences of various jurisdictions in implementing such a tax and compares the relative success of the turnover and GGR models. While skill and chance-based gaming used to be treated differently in India, it is essential to caveat here that definitions of games of skill and chance vary across jurisdictions, and many states lack such a classification. For the purpose of comparing the turnover and GGR models, it is assumed that a tax having punitive effects when applied to games of chance would have similar effects if applied to games of skill, and vice-versa, as long as the levy itself is imposed similarly.

24.2 TURNOVER MODEL

24.2.1 Turning Away from Turnover Taxes

A turnover model calculates taxes based on the entire transaction value, including the prize pool, even though most of this amount is distributed back to players as winnings. As the Karnataka High Court notes, this is akin to taxing a stock broker on the entire amount received to purchase securities rather than on the commission

DOI: 10.1201/9781032624204-25

they earn (Bangalore Turf Club, 2021). This results in gaming operators paying far more taxes than their commissions, paving the way for gray markets. This is why, for instance, Delta Corp has been subject to a tax notice six times its market capitalization (Maloo & Kumar, 2023) and why the vast majority of countries have been unable to implement a turnover tax successfully.

For example, in Austria, experts have noted that the levy on casinos is "way too high to survive in a competitive environment" (Häberling, 2012). A report submitted to the Polish Ministry of Finance recorded that Poland's tax resulted in severe restrictions on operators' ability to sustain their business. It proposed a shift to a GGR tax (Vixio, 2021). Only 2 of the 20 sports betting platforms are profitable, and several entities operate using unlicensed and unregulated websites. It is, therefore, no surprise that Poland, as a result of having one of the highest levies on betting in the European Union (EU), also has one of the lowest channelization rates of betting operators (European Gaming & Betting Association, 2021).

Similarly, Germany's tax led to two of the largest operators immediately pulling out of the German market (Weir, 2012). The move was sharply criticized, with analysts predicting the spread of unregulated online gaming markets in Germany (Spitz et al., 2023), and even noting how German exits are an example of countries banning exchanges indirectly using punitive turnover taxes (Blitz, 2012) by making it impossible to run a profitable business (Goodley, 2011).

Portugal's tax also resulted in low channelization rates, with only 52% of players playing on regulated sites. As of 2018, there were only four sports betting licenses granted by the Serviço de Regulação e Inspeção de Jogos ("SRIJ"), Portugal's regulatory agency. BetClic, one of Portugal's major players, also announced that its taxes constituted 66% of its revenues, necessitating reconsidering its decision to stay in the market (Wood, 2018). This has led to talks in Portugal to move to a 25% tax on online gaming levied on the GGR as an alternative (IGaming Business, 2018). Portugal would not be the first European nation to make this transition. Originally, Italy had imposed a turnover tax for all platforms. However, to allow for the growth of the gaming industry, it shifted to a GGR tax in 2010 at 20% for casino games (Millar, 2012). Faced with similar concerns of low channelization and gray markets, the United Kingdom and France also shifted from a turnover to a GGR model over the past two decades.

The United Kingdom levied a 6.75% turnover tax until 2001 which was replaced with a 15% tax on GGR. The levy was further amended in 2014 to make consumption the point of supply to tax offshore bookmakers. The amendments caused unlicensed bookmakers and offshore intermediaries to relocate to the regulated market in the United Kingdom, given they no longer had to pay punitive taxes beyond their revenues and could enjoy the marketing opportunities a legal market offered. Despite a reduction in the overall base at which the tax was levied, the 15% GGR increased gaming turnover by over 35%, encouraged more investments into the sector, and resulted in a notable increase in the revenue collected by the state, exemplifying the benefits of a GGR model (Deloitte, 2023).

The French experience is even more telling. Up until 2020, France taxed poker at 2% of stakes and sports betting at 7.5% of the wagers made (Häberling, 2012). A 2016 report by the Court of Auditors noted that the high tax resulted in lower turnovers and tax revenues than expected. KPMG also attributed the low revenue to the overly burdensome tax, which decreased competition between operators and lowered the market value of the entire industry. KPMG compared this with Italy, concluding that over time, Italy's 20% GGR tax would result in a turnover four times that of France (Millar, 2012). In 2016, L'Autorité de Régulation des Jeux En Ligne ("ARJEL"), the French gaming regulator, published a report that among the 11 operators offering poker, nine had never made a profit since the regulation was started in 2010, with over half of the licensees exiting the market (Wood, 2018). This prompted the French Senate to shift to a GGR tax model in 2020, to ensure that the industry could meaningfully contribute to national revenues (Deloitte, 2023). Consequently, France presently applies a GGR tax of 19.9% on horse race betting, 33.8% on sports betting, and 36.7% for online poker. However, these rates are still excessive, making the French market continue to be unattractive (International Betting Integrity Association et al., 2021).

24.2.2 Low Rates, High Turnovers: Successful Implementation of the Turnover Tax

Despite the numerous examples of the turnover model's lack of success, it continues to be desirable for its efficiency from an administrative standpoint (Millar, 2012). Since a turnover tax is applied solely on the deposit amount, transaction costs can be reduced by collecting the tax in advance rather than at each bet or after completion of the game. However, to mitigate against an unlicensed market for gaming due to punitive taxes, the rate at which the turnover tax is applied becomes crucial. To successfully implement a turnover model, the tax rate must be significantly lower than what would have been applied under a GGR model.

For instance, even an 8% turnover tax in Portugal corresponded to around 60% of the GGR. This is usually why, in jurisdictions with a turnover tax and an operative gaming industry such as Malta and Belize, the rates are very low. In Italy, horse betting is taxed under a turnover model (Häberling, 2012). In 2017, Italy recorded tax revenues of over €10 billion (USD 10.91 billion) from its turnover tax, marking an overall increase in revenue between 2006 and 2017. Interestingly, during this period, the tax rate on turnover decreased from 19% in 2016 to 10% in 2017 (Gandullia & Leporatti, 2019).

Similar results were also seen in Ireland. Until 1986, the betting duty was levied at 20%, which led to widespread evasion and was described by the Commission on Taxation's report as "irresponsible." Ireland responded by reducing the rate to 10%. While revenue initially declined, it recovered over a few years due to growth in the industry. The rate of tax was progressively reduced over the years, until in 2006, it was changed from 2% to 1% turnover tax. That year, the government collected €54.3 million in revenue (USD 59.23 million), up from €45.8 million (USD 49.96 million) the previous year (Colm McCarthy and Associates, 2017). This further shows that turnover taxes if implemented at a low rate of less than 2% can show better returns than an ambitious rate of a turnover tax.

However, even a 5% tax in Germany and a 6.75% levy in the United Kingdom were unsustainable when levied on the turnover of an operator. When Cyprus was considering a 3% turnover tax for online betting, a KPMG study recommended that the tax instead be applied on GGR (Cyprus Mail, 2012). Therefore, even though a low turnover rate is certainly preferable to a higher rate, its desirability compared to a GGR tax is still debatable. The next section focuses on the various rates at which GGR is levied and compares the effects such taxes have had on the legal gaming market, its growth, and revenue collection across states.

24.3 GGR TAX: A BET THAT PAYS

As noted, the GGR model applies the tax on the commission received by operators, much like most taxes levied on commission-based services. Apart from being in line with the CGST Act as held in Gameskraft (Gameskraft Technologies, 2023), this makes the tax viable in contrast to a turnover model.

24.3.1 Low Rates: 5%–15%

The Philippines's tax is expected to generate 144 billion pesos (USD 2.60 billion) in annual taxes (Morales, 2021). The low tax combined with the 2008 liberalization of the industry has resulted in rapid growth in the industry, with the number of Philippine Amusement and Gaming Corp (PAGCOR) operated and licensed casinos steadily increasing and revenue shooting up from 41.63 billion pesos (USD 0.75 billion) in 2008 to 152.46 billion pesos (USD 2.73 billion) in 2017 (International Monetary Fund, 2018). Similar results were also seen in Nevada (Yakowicz, 2022) and Singapore, where the low rate has attracted some of the biggest global operators such as Riot Games and Ubisoft. Singapore's online gaming market is also expected to grow significantly, at a yearly rate of 14.29%, with a projected revenue of USD 253 million by 2023 (Lim, 2023).

In South Korea, locals are only allowed to place bets on Kangwon Land and not on other operators in the state, which are reserved for foreigners. However, in 2022 alone, Kangwon Land recorded a total revenue of KRW 1.22 trillion (USD 940 million) (Statista, 2023a). The casino sector's market size is the second biggest in the Asia-Pacific region (Global Data, 2022) and is expected to grow by around 7.36% between 2022 and 2027 (Statista, 2023b). The online gaming market has also been steadily increasing, including Vegas-based Caesar's Palace, Singapore's OUE Ltd., and Hong Kong's Lippo Ltd., entering the South Korean casino industry (Lee et al., 2014). This shows that a low 5%–15% tax rate would attract global investments in the gaming industry and generate growth. However, such a rate might be too low for countries that seek to gain more revenue from the sector.

Additionally, we would further argue that gaming taxes ought not to be distortive in nature. Online skill gaming is not a sin good, with over half a decade of Indian jurisprudence differentiating games of chances as res extra commercium (immoral activities) from skill gaming as regular trade (Jaimon & Sengupta, 2023). Professional gamers treat gaming as an active source of livelihood, with gaming viewed as merely another form of entertainment. Hence, there is no justification to tax online gaming at the 28% sin rate. However, we are also not arguing that they should be actively incentivized to promote business in online gaming. A levy on gaming should be treated along the same lines as any other service and should neither be punitive nor concessionary.

24.3.2 Moderate Range: 15%–25%

In Columbia, the first online gaming licenses were officially issued in 2017, and gaming revenues have steadily increased since. Columbia witnessed a 76% increase in revenue in 2019 compared to its 2015 levels, in addition to the gaming industry having generated thousands of jobs (IGaming Businesses, 2020). Similarly, in Spain, the GGR was reduced from 25% to 20% in 2018 to attract unlicensed operators into the legal market (Panousi, 2018). This proved successful with channelization rates of operators going up from 71% in 2017 to 76% in 2019 (International Betting Integrity Association et al., 2021).

Lastly, since 2019, Sweden has approved over 87 license applications with a 91% channelizing rate (International Betting Integrity Association et al., 2021). Thus, as predicted by the Copenhagen Report (Copenhagen Economics, 2016), a GGR tax applied at around 20% results in high channelizing rates and increased revenues, without incentivizing widespread evasion and gray markets. The next section further highlights that many jurisdictions have also applied a higher tax rate on the GGR with varying success.

24.3.3 Intermediate Range: 30%–50%

In Slovenia, the cumulative rates (Ministry of Finance, Slovenia, 2022) applied to gaming is quite high, resulting in low growth of the industry. Between 2001 and 2008, while there was an increase in revenue due to the liberalization of the sector, there was subsequently low growth and a decline in revenues from 2009 to 2016 (Andrej et al., 2019).

In 2017, when Kenya increased its gambling tax to 35% from the 7.5% previously applied, the President noted that the amendment was to "discourage Kenyans, and especially the youth, in directing their focus on betting, lottery and gaming activities" (IGaming Business, 2017). Some operators also exited the market, arguing that this was an additional burden to the 35% corporate tax they were already paying (Business Today, 2019). SportPesa, the leading sports betting platform which also backs the Kenyan Premier League, withdrew support from local sports clubs in opposition to the tax. Analysts have predicted the closure of many operators due to unsustainability (Dahir, 2017), but the effect of the increased tax is yet to be analyzed.

In contrast, Macau continues to have a strong gaming industry and sizable revenues from it, despite levying a 35% GGR tax and a few additional levies (Ho et al., 2023). For instance, in 2023, Macau collected over USD 5.68 billion in taxes from the gaming industry in the first 9 months until September, a 200.7% rise compared with the previous year, primarily due to the COVID restrictions in place. From 2012 to 2017, Macau generated over USD 70 billion in taxes from casinos, making it one of the largest gambling centers in the world (Master, 2017). US investments in Macau's gambling industry exceed USD 24 billion, and prior to the pandemic, Macau's revenues were seven times higher than Las Vegas's (US Department of State, 2023).

In conclusion, while rates of 30% and above generate opposition to the tax, they are not as unviable as a turnover tax. Additionally, at such high rates, other regulatory systems, such as the extent of a liberal market for gaming, cost of license fees, and other corporate tax rates, also play a crucial role in the extent of growth of the gaming sector. While the results of the 30%–40% range are unclear, it is reasonably evident that tax rates above 50% would lead to low revenues and channelization rates, as evidenced in the following case study of Hong Kong.

24.3.4 High Range: Above 50%

The Hong Kong Jockey Club is the only body authorized to offer sports betting (The Government of the Hong Kong Special Administrative Region Press Releases, Betting Duty). This has also been burdened with additional taxes, which are expected to result in significant losses to the entity (Kang-Chung & Kong, 2023). The high rate and a tightly restricted market have resulted in an illegal market estimated at over HK $12 billion (USD 1.54 billion) annually, primarily through offshore operations from Macau (Fraser, 2014). While around HK $36 billion (USD 4.61 billion) in legal gambling revenues were reported during 2015–16 (Tessler et al., 2017), the revenue that could be accrued by reducing taxes and having a more open policy to gaming would be substantial.

24.4 CONCLUSION

While global comparisons of the tax applied to online gaming are available, this chapter aimed to go beyond a tabulation of the taxes applied to analyze the effects of such taxes on the gaming market. In this process, it is also important to note that comparisons are more challenging to draw, given that countries often impose different taxes based on the nature of the game (the most common model being to apply a turnover tax on sports betting, with a GGR on other forms of gaming) and different rates within these taxes, based on the scale and kind of game being played. Thus, any comparison is bound to have shortfalls due to the inherent complexities involved in this area.

While we have drawn out the impacts of different rates across countries, a more detailed study to determine the appropriate rate of tax should be conducted. Nevertheless, an overview of global comparisons weighs in favor of a GGR taxation model and certainly against India's high turnover tax across skill and chance-based gaming that no other country has imposed. The highest recorded turnover tax in this chapter is Austria's at 16%, which had detrimental impacts on the market. Various studies, including the Copenhagen Report and the submissions by the Deputy Finance Minister of Poland, conclude that even a GGR tax that exceeds 20%–25% is counter-productive. Applying not just a much higher rate at 28% but also levying it on the face value of bets only paves the way for a gray market, where platforms neither contribute to the state's revenue nor can any negative externalities from gaming be regulated.

In conclusion, a blind imposition of a high tax on a high taxable base does not (and often has not) translate to high tax revenues. A comparison of Denmark's revenues with France's under a turnover tax makes the loss accrued from a turnover tax apparent. Denmark imposes a 20% tax on GGR, while France previously imposed an 8.8% turnover tax on stakes. Consequently, owing to high gambling volumes, Denmark enjoyed higher revenues amounting to around €186 million (USD 202.93 million) in 2013, while France received €79 million (USD 86.19 million) in revenue, less than half of Denmark's collection (Lycka, 2014). India must take a cue from these experiences when deciding its gaming tax.

REFERENCES

Andrej, R., Iva, B., Ana, S., & Darko, L. (2019). How Important Is Gambling in National GDP: Case Study from Austria, Croatia, Italy and Slovenia. *Economics, Sciendo*, *7*(1), 31–49. https://doi.org/10.2478/eoik-2019-0004

Bangalore Turf Club Ltd. v. Karnataka 2021 SCC OnLine Kar 12607.

Blitz, R. (2012, November 7). Betfair exits from Germany over tax. *The Financial Times*. www.ft.com/content/2ebb3c88-28e5-11e2-9591-00144feabdc0

Business Today. (2019, November 28). Current State of Online Gambling in Kenya. Business Today. https://businesstoday.co.ke/current-state-of-online-gambling-in-kenya/

Central Goods and Services Tax (Third Amendment) Rules, 2023, inserted by Notification No. 51/2023-Central Tax dated 29-09-2023.

Colm McCarthy and Associates. (2017, May). *The Taxation of Betting in Ireland*. https://assets.gov.ie/25570/56e3b53d2c8f4078bac8a60222062dd1.pdf

Cyprus Mail Archive. (2012, May 7). *Change in taxation suggestions would net government more money*. Cyprus Mail Archive. https://archive.cyprus-mail.com/2012/03/07/change-in-taxation-suggestions-would-net-government-more-money/

Dahir, L. A. (2017, June 26). *Kenya thinks a five-fold tax hike on its betting sector can deter child gambling*. https://qz.com/africa/1014567/sportspesa-will-pull-sponsorship-of-kenyan-sports-teams-over-over-tax-hike

Deloitte. (2023, July). *GST on Online Gaming: Analysing the effect of the tax rate and value of supply on tax revenues*. www2.deloitte.com/content/dam/Deloitte/in/Documents/tax/in-tax-GST-on-online-gaming-06.07-noexp.pdf

European Gaming & Betting Association. (2021, November 2). *Poland: EGBA Supports Changes to the Tax Base for Online Sports Betting*. www2.deloitte.com/content/dam/Deloitte/in/Documents/tax/in-tax-GST-on-online-gaming-06.07-noexp.pdf

Fraser, N. (2014, June 8). Hong Kong punters splash out HK $500b on illegal sports betting. *South China Morning Post*. www.scmp.com/news/hong-kong/hong-kong-economy/article/3210345/controversial-proposal-raise-taxes-betting-hong-kong-be-given-prudent-consideration-minister-says

Gameskraft Technologies (P) Ltd. v. Directorate General of Goods Services Tax Intelligence, 2023 SCC OnLine Kar 18.

Gandullia, L., & Leporatti, L. (2019, July 18). Distributional Effects of Gambling Taxes: Empirical Evidence from Italy. *The Journal of Economic Inequality*, *17*, 565–590. https://doi.org/10.1007/s10888-019-09423-9

Global Data. (2022, November). Market Size of the Casino Industry in South Korea (2017–2021, $ Billion). www.globaldata.com/data-insights/travel-and-tourism/market-size-of-the-casino-industry-in-south-korea/

Goodley, S. (2011, April 6). Newly merged Bwin.party rocked by German betting tax proposals. *Guardian*. www.theguardian.com/business/2011/apr/06/bwin-party-rocked-by-german-betting-tax

Häberling, G. (2012). Internet gambling policy in Europe. In Williams, R.J., Wood, R.T. & Parke, J (Eds.), *Routledge International Handbook of Internet Gambling* (pp. 294–295). Routledge.

IGaming Business. (2017, June 16). Kenya operators to face new 35% gambling tax. https://igamingbusiness.com/casino-games/kenya-operators-to-face-new-35-gambling-tax/

IGaming Business. (2018, October 17). *Portugal mulls 25% tax rate for online operators.* https://igamingbusiness.com/casino-games/portugal-mulls-25-tax-rate-for-online-operators/

IGaming Business. (2020, November 2). Colombia collects COP 2.8tn in gaming taxes since 2015. https://igamingbusiness.com/finance/colombia-collects-cop2-8tn-in-gaming-taxes-since-2015/

International Betting Integrity Association & H2 Gambling Capital. (2021, June). *An Optimum Betting Market: A Regulatory, Fiscal & Integrity Assessment.* www.egba.eu/uploads/2021/06/An-Optimum-Betting-Market-A-Regulatory-Fiscal-and-Integrity-Assessment-1.pdf

International Monetary Fund. (2018, October 24). *Estimating Casino Revenues and Transfers for the Philippine Balance of Payments Statistics.* www.imf.org/external/pubs/ft/bop/2018/pdf/18-23.pdf

Jaimon, D., & Sengupta, A. (2023, October 19). Constitutionality of Uniform Taxation of Online Real Money Gaming in the light of the Gameskraft Case. *Indconlawphil.* https://indconlawphil.wordpress.com/2023/10/19/guest-post-constitutionality-of-uniform-taxation-of-online-real-money-gaming-in-the-light-of-the-gameskraft-case/

Kang-Chung, N., & Kong, H. (2023, February 15). Controversial proposal to raise taxes on betting in Hong Kong to be given prudent consideration, minister says. *South China Morning Post.* www.scmp.com/news/hong-kong/hong-kong-economy/article/3210345/controversial-proposal-raise-taxes-betting-hong-kong-be-given-prudent-consideration-minister-says.

Lim, N. (2023, November 16). Taking a Leap into the Online Gaming Landscape of Singapore. *Tsingapore.* www.tsingapore.com/article/taking-a-leap-into-the-online-gaming-landscape-of-singapore/

Lycka, M. (2014). Lawyering in the online gambling sector: Part 2 – Non-legal aspects of the in-house. *International In-House Counsel Journal*, *7*(28), 1–8. www.iicj.net/subscribersonly/14september/iicj2sept-management-martinlycka-betfair-uk.pdf

Maloo, M., & Kumar, S. (2023, October 16). Delta Corp shares hit 3-year low after tax demands rise to Rs 23,200 crore: A timeline of events so far. *CNBC.* www.cnbctv18.com/market/delta-corp-share-price-gst-demand-23000-crore-timeline-of-events-market-cap-q2-results-18059391.htm

Master, F. (2017, September 12). Macau's unused billions: Booming casino taxes sit in government coffers. *Reuters.* www.reuters.com/article/us-macau-economy/macaus-unused-billions-booming-casino-taxes-sit-in-government-coffers-idUSKCN1BN0H3/

Millar, S. I. (2012). Taxation of Regulated Internet Gambling. *California Tax Lawyer*, *21*(3), 4–24 www.taylorlaw.com/assets/docs/3162_001.pdf.

Ministry of Finance, Slovenia. (2022, May). *Taxation in Slovenia 2022.* www.gov.si/assets/ministrstva/MF/Davcni-direktorat/Taxation-in-Slovenia-2022-v-anglescini.pdf

Morales, J. N. (2021, February 08). Philippine lawmakers pass bill to tax online gambling firms. *Reuters.* www.reuters.com/article/philippines-gambling-idUSL1N2KE1GN/

Panousi, V. (2018, October 05). EGBA response to Greek Ministry of Finance consultation on the opening of the online gambling market. *European Gaming & Betting Association.* www.egba.eu/uploads/2018/12/181029-Memo-on-Greek-consultation-and-EGBA-response.pdf

Service Tax Rules, 1994, 2(1)(ccd)(xiv).

Sinha, S. (2023, August 09). Cabinet okays bill to bring clarity on 28% GST rate for online gaming, casinos, horse racing. *The Hindu Business Line.* www.thehindubusinessline.com/news/cabinet-okays-bill-to-clarify-gst-rate-for-online-gaming-casinos-horse-racing/article67175815.ece

Spitz, M., Hofmann, J., Straimer, N., & Herpich, R. (2023, May 29). In review: licensing and taxation of gambling activities in Germany. *Lexology*. www.lexology.com/library/detail.aspx?g=a8a13639-f52e-49f0-b2ec-a2c60606d4e7

Statista. (2023a, October 18). Revenue of Kangwon Land Casino in Gangwon, South Korea from 2012 to 2022. www.statista.com/statistics/695410/south-korea-kangwon-land-casino-revenue/

Statista. (2023b, October). Casino Games – South Korea. www.statista.com/outlook/dmo/app/games/casino-games/south-korea

Tessler, A., Beyrouty, E. K., & Crapnell, N. (2017, December 02). An exploratory study of illegal gamblers in Hong Kong. *Asian Journal of Gambling Issues and Public health*, *7*(1), 1. doi:10.1186/s40405-017-0030-7

The Association of Online Gambling Operators (BOS) (2016, September 26). *Licensing system for online gambling: Which tax-rate yields both high channelization and high tax revenues?* Copenhagen Economics. https://copenhageneconomics.com/wp-content/uploads/2021/12/copenhagen-economics-2016-licensing-system-for-online-gambling.pdf

The Government of the Hong Kong Special Administrative Region, Press Releases. (2023, February 15). LCQ6: Betting Duty. www.info.gov.hk/gia/general/202302/15/P2023021500272.htm

US Department of State. (2023). *2023 Investment Climate Statements: Macau.* www.state.gov/reports/2023-investment-climate-statements/macau/

Vixio. (2021, October 19). Polish Ombudsman Wants to Overhaul Gambling Tax. www.vixio.com/insights/gc-polish-ombudsman-wants-overhaul-gambling-tax#:~:text=In%20his%20report%2C%20Raczkowski%20said,to%2065%20percent%20GGR%20tax%E2%80%9D.

Weir, K. (2012, November 07). UPDATE 2-Betfair Pulls Back from Germany over Gambling Tax. *Reuters.* https://jp.reuters.com/article/betfair-germany/update-2-betfair-pulls-back-from-germany-over-gambling-tax-idUKL5E8M730B20121107

Wood, J. (2018, March 08). A Look at Portugal's First Full Year of Regulated Sports Betting, and Lessons for the US Market. *LegalSportsReport.* www.legalsportsreport.com/18956/portugal-sports-betting-lessons/

Yakowicz, W. (2022, January 27). Nevada Hits All-Time Record of $13.4 Billion in Gambling Revenue in 2021. *Forbes.* www.forbes.com/sites/willyakowicz/2022/01/27/nevada-hits-all-time-record-of-134-billion-in-gambling-revenue-in-2021/?sh=19e47360168b

25 GST and Online Gaming Sector

A Taxing Saga

Sudipta Bhattacharjee and Arjyadeep Roy

INTRODUCTION

The online gaming sector in India, by all accounts, has a massive potential to contribute significantly to the overall economic growth of the country. However, GST and regulatory issues in the last couple of years have cast a shadow on this sector. In this chapter, we will discuss the GST issues affecting the sector, at length.

But before going into GST, it is pertinent to understand that the entire online gaming industry can broadly be bifurcated into the following segments:

a. Casual gaming – This primarily pertains to playing casual games over an electronic medium and does not involve players staking any monetary amount.
b. Real money gaming – These forms of gameplays involve players playing skill-based games against each other by staking a monetary amount. In India, most of the real money gaming platforms pertain to traditional skill-based games such as rummy, poker, chess, fantasy games, and ludo.
c. Real money gambling – These forms of gameplays involve players playing games of chance against each other/against the online platform by staking a monetary amount. Such platforms have been legally allowed only in a few states (like Goa and Sikkim).
d. E-sports (or competitive video gaming) – This primarily comprises of online sports wherein individuals or teams participate in a variety of online games with audience viewing such games. A few popular games under this category are Counter-Strike, Fortnite, Valorant, Battlegrounds Mobile India (earlier known as PUBG), etc. As per a news report from *Mint*[1] – "*In 2022, the Indian government officially recognized Esports as a sport, placing it on an equal footing with mainstream sports like cricket and football. In the same year, Esports debuted as an official medal sport at the Asian Games and as a pilot event at the Commonwealth Games.*"

Of these segments, it is (b) and (c) above [especially (b)] that has borne the brunt of aggressive GST investigations, including the biggest ever tax demand in India (Of Rs 21,000 crores/around US$2.6 billion, faced by Gameskraft Technologies which was quashed by the Karnataka High Court in May 2023).

DOI: 10.1201/9781032624204-26

It is pertinent to note here that the physical casino segment has also been subjected to GST investigations on similar lines as online real money gambling platforms.

In light of the foregoing, this chapter focuses on the nuances surrounding the online real money gaming and gambling segments and the GST disputes pertaining to the sector.

In this regard, it is relevant to start the discussion with the constitutional position qua 'betting and gambling' because what the GST authorities have essentially been trying to achieve is to levy GST on both (b) and (c) categories by treating them as 'betting and gambling'.

The 101st Constitutional Amendment Act, 2016 (**'CAA'**) ushered in a new era of indirect taxation in as much as GST was introduced as a single levy for taxing goods and services and it subsumed various other indirect levies. The constitutional position pre and post the implementation of the CAA is discussed hereunder:

TAXATION OF 'BETTING AND GAMBLING' PRIOR TO CAA

a. The term 'betting and gambling' prior to the implementation of the CAA was mentioned at two places of the Constitution of India, 1950 (**'COI'**). Entry 34[2] of List II of the COI pertained to 'betting and gambling' whereas Entry 62[3] of List II provided for levy of tax on 'betting and gambling'.
b. Prior to the implementation of CAA, in relation to 'betting and gambling' – the States had powers to make laws vis-à-vis two aspects: (i) regulate 'betting and gambling' and (ii) levy tax on 'betting and gambling'.

TAXATION OF 'BETTING AND GAMBLING' AFTER CAA

a. Post the implementation of CAA, the Central Goods and Services Tax Act, 2017 (**'CGST Act'**), Integrated Goods and Services Tax Act, 2017 (**'IGST Act'**), and Central Goods and Services Tax Rules, 2017 (**'CGST Rules'**) were enacted. The COI also underwent a significant change.
b. Entry 62[4] posted its amendment after the implementation of CAA was amended and the power of the States to levy tax on 'betting and gambling' was omitted.
c. Additionally, new constitutional provisions were also added which gave simultaneous taxing power to the Center and the States. Article 246A[5] of the COI was a newly added provision which provided for levy of GST on the 'supply' of goods and services to both the States and the Center.
d. In accordance with Article 246A, the CGST Act was enacted. Section 7 thereof provides for the scope of supply. The taxable event under the CGST Act is 'supply', i.e., only when an activity qualifies as a 'supply' – can it be said that there is a taxable event. In addition to Section 7, the CGST Act contains three schedules – Schedule III of the CGST Act contains those activities which were not to be treated as either supply of goods or as supply of services, i.e., they were altogether outside the ambit of the GST.
e. Entry 6 of Schedule III prior to its amendment on 1 October 2023 read as 'actionable claim other than lottery betting and gambling'. The purport of

Entry 6 therefore implied that 'actionable claims' were outside the ambit of GST. However, if such 'actionable claims' pertained to 'lottery, betting, and gambling' – such 'actionable claims' were within the scope of levy of GST.

f. Due reference needs to be made to Rule 31A(3) of the CGST Rules too, which provides for the valuation mechanism. Rule 31A was inserted into the GST framework with effect from 25 January 2018 after the recommendation of the Goods and Services Tax Council (**'GST Council'**) in its 25th meeting in 2018. This provision states that "*value of supply of actionable claim in the form of chance to win in betting, gambling or horse racing in a race club shall be 100% of the face value of the bet*".

Therefore, the following points can be inferred vis a vis the taxability of 'betting and gambling' in terms of the constitutional position and GST laws:

- Prior to the implementation of the CAA and GST regime, States had the power to levy tax on 'betting and gambling' under Entry 62 of List II of the COI.
- Post the CAA, vide Article 246A of the COI, the Center and the States have been given the simultaneous power to levy GST on supply of goods and services.
- Schedule III of the CGST Act exempts all forms of actionable claims from the levy of GST apart from actionable claims attributable to 'betting and gambling'.
- The value of supply under GST in case of 'betting and gambling' is construed to be 100% of the face value of the bet.
- It can therefore be inferred that the power which vested with the States under Entry 62 of List II of the COI prior to the GST regime has been engrafted in Section 7 read with Schedule III of the CGST Act.

INTERPRETATION OF THE TERM 'BETTING AND GAMBLING'

In the foregoing context, the important question that arises is in relation to the interpretation of the term 'betting and gambling'.

In this regard, it is relevant to note that judicially, the term as appearing in Entry 34 and Entry 62 of List II of the COI has been interpreted to only mean 'games of chance' and it has been categorically held that 'game of skill' is a separate class altogether and cannot be clubbed with 'betting and gambling'.

Few of the judicial precedents which have discussed this aspect are as below:

a. *State of Bombay v R.M.D Chamarbaugwala* (**'RMDC-I'**)[6] – While interpreting the validity of a State Act in relation to regulation of prize competitions under Entry 34 of List II, the Hon'ble Supreme Court held that if even a scintilla of skill was required for success, the competition could not be regarded as that of a gambling nature and could not be regulated under Entry 34 of List II of the COI. Therefore, in essence, the Hon'ble Supreme Court was of the view that Entry 34 encompasses within its fold only those activities which are primarily 'game of chance' – ergo in the nature of 'betting and gambling'.

b. *R.M.D. Chamarbaugwala v Union of India & Ors* (**'RMDC-II'**)[7] – In this case as well, the Hon'ble Court was dealing with validity of a statute in terms of Entry 34 of List II of COI. The Hon'ble Supreme Court categorically held that competitions that involve substantial amount of skill are business activities and protected under Article 19(1)(g) of the COI and form a separate class from 'gambling' activities in which the element of chance is preponderant.

c. *All India Gaming Federation v State of Karnataka* (**'AIGF'**)[8] – In this case, the Hon'ble High Court was seized of the validity of a State enactment dealing with regulation of online gaming activities. Tracing the interpretation accorded to the term 'betting and gambling' – the Hon'ble High Court reinforced the view that Entry 34 takes within its fold only those games which qualify as 'game of chance' and activities which are predominantly 'skill-based' cannot be regulated under Entry 34.
d. *Junglee Games Private Limited v State of Tamil Nadu*[9] – This case was also dealing with the validity of an enactment which governed activities which were primarily skill-based. The Hon'ble Court held that the term 'betting and gambling' appearing in Entry 34 of List II of the COI can only be interpreted to mean 'game of chance' and hence 'game of skill' being a separate class altogether cannot be regulated under Entry 34.

The consistent judicial position for the last several decades therefore has been that the term 'betting and gambling' can only mean 'game of chance', and 'game of skill' being altogether a separate class cannot be equated with 'betting and gambling'.

While the aforesaid precedents were interpreting the term in context of Entry 34 of List II of the COI, the same meaning ought to also be given to the term as was appearing in Entry 62 of List II – as has been held by the Hon'ble Supreme Court in the case of *State of Karnataka v State of Meghalaya.*[10] Accordingly, it emerges that the term 'betting and gambling' in context of Entry 34 and Entry 62 can only be interpreted to mean 'game of chance'. Since the power to levy GST on 'betting and gambling' can be traced back to the erstwhile Entry 62 of List II of the COI, it would be reasonable to conclude that even in the context of GST laws, the term 'betting and gambling' can only connote 'game of chance' and not 'game of skill'.

EARLY BEGINNINGS IN GST LAWS

GST laws were introduced with effect from 1 July 2017. Prior to that, the taxing power in relation to 'betting and gambling' was a part of the State list as discussed above. It is also apt to note that prior to the enactment of the GST laws, the service tax regime did not tax 'betting and gambling'. It formed a part of the negative list[11] meaning thereby that it was not subjected to service tax.

With the implementation of the GST regime, simultaneous taxing powers to Center and States were granted vide Article 246A. At the initial stages of GST, the issue pertaining to levy of GST on online gaming *per se* did not attract much attention unlike what it has now snowballed into. While the taxability of online gaming was being discussed in the GST Council meetings, the issue gained significant momentum post the search and seizure operations against Gameskraft Technologies Private Limited (**'GTPL'**). However, few of the important landmarks which ultimately led to the impasse is discussed hereunder:

a. The GST Council in its 25th meeting on 18 January 2018 suggested for incorporation of Rule 31A(3) in the CGST Rules.
b. Subsequently, Rule 31A(3) was inserted with effect from 25 January 2018. While the primary reason behind incorporation of the provision was with respect to valuation of horse-racing activities, the actual text also provided for valuation of 'betting and gambling'.
c. Similarly, Entry 229 was also inserted in the rate notification for goods[12] Notification No. 1/2017 – Central Tax (Rate) dated 28 June 2017 (**'Notification No. 1'**) which provided that 'actionable claim in the form of chance to win in betting, gambling' shall be taxed at 28%.
d. The entire online real money gaming industry however had adopted a position that since they are mere online intermediaries facilitating players playing games of skill online against each other, their activities are more in the nature of services and classifiable under Entry 22 of Notification No. 11/2017 – Central Tax (Rate) dated 28 June 2017 (**'Notification No. 11'**). Accordingly, GST at the rate of 18% was being deposited only on the Platform Fee, i.e., on the actual consideration received by them.

Parallelly, as stated above, the taxability of online gaming was being deliberated before the GST Council and to that extent, the GST Council formed a Group of Ministers (**'GoM'**).

Vide order dated 24 May 2021, the terms of reference of the GoM were finalized which inter-alia included deciding about the valuation mechanism to be adopted for the online gaming sector.[13]

The GoM deliberated for a period of more than three years and remained inconclusive. Finally, the GST Council ultimately took a decision in its 50th and 51st meetings in July and August 2023, respectively, regarding the taxability of the online gaming sector – this is discussed in the later part of this chapter.

The GST Department, till about 2021, did not raise any significant objection on the practice of the sector in discharging GST at the rate of 18% on only the Platform Fee. But all that changed in November 2021 with the investigation against Gameskraft/GTPL.

GTPL CASE AND THE BEGINNING OF A NEVER-ENDING SAGA

a. The proceedings against GTPL commenced with a search and seizure operation in November 2021 by the Directorate General of Goods and Services Tax Intelligence (**'DGGSTI'**).
b. Initially, it was not clear as to what is the alleged contravention on the part of GTPL. However, the search and seizure proceeding led to provisional attachment of bank accounts of GTPL which was challenged before the Hon'ble Karnataka High Court.[14] The Hon'ble High Court vide its order dated 3 December 2021 was pleased to grant interim relief to GTPL inasmuch as the bank accounts were allowed to be operated for normal business activities.
c. The investigation continued wherein voluminous amounts of information, data, and records were submitted. Statements of various officials of GTPL, including their founders, were recorded on multiple occasions.

d. It was only somewhere around June 2022 that the Department in one of its affidavits for the first time disclosed that GTPL is being investigated on the issue of underpaying GST in relation to 'betting and gambling'.
e. In the first week of September 2022, GTPL was issued an intimation notice under the CGST Act whereby a staggering demand of approximately INR 21,000 crores was raised on account of evasion of GST. The core allegation which could be deciphered from the intimation notice[15] was that GTPL was involved in the supply of 'actionable claim' in the form of chance to win in 'betting' and should have accordingly discharged GST at the rate of 28% on the entire amounts staked with it in terms of Rule 31A(3) of the CGST Rules read with Entry 229 of Notification No. 1.
f. Despite there being a stay on the intimation notice proceedings, the Department on the very same day of the said stay order, i.e., 25 September 2022 issued the show cause notice whereby the demand of INR 21,000 crores was reiterated along with imposition of personal penalty.
g. GTPL challenged the show cause notice before the Hon'ble High Court which ultimately led to the Hon'ble High Court passing its judgment on 11 May 2023.[16]

KEY ARGUMENT OF THE DEPARTMENT AND THE CONCLUSION REACHED BY THE HON'BLE HIGH COURT

The core argument of the Department was that even in a 'game of skill', if any monetary stakes are involved, it partakes the character of 'betting and gambling' and the underlying nature of the game pales into insignificance. The core issue therefore was whether a 'game of skill' played with stakes remains a 'game of skill' or does it qualify as 'betting and gambling' – therefore being taxable under Rule 31A(3) of the CGST Rules.

The Hon'ble High Court, after examining the judicial precedents in a detailed manner, completely rejected the above argument of the GST authorities and set aside the show cause notice, thereby reiterating a long settled legal proposition that a 'game of skill' even if played with monetary stakes remains a 'game of skill' and cannot be categorized or taxed as 'betting and gambling'.

Separately, from this GST litigation, a bunch of PILs were filed against online fantasy games platform Dream11 across the country which led to several High Court orders: some of which are discussed below. While these were not in the context of GST directly, these precedents also effectively reiterate the proposition that a 'game of skill' even if played with monetary stakes remains a 'game of skill' and cannot be categorized or taxed as 'betting and gambling'.

KEY JUDICIAL PRECEDENTS IN THE CONTEXT OF ONLINE FANTASY GAMES

Cases	Particulars
Varun Gumber v Union Territory of Chandigarh[a]	This was a petition filed before the Hon'ble Punjab & Haryana High Court wherein the issue was whether fantasy games such as Dream 11 qualify as 'gambling' under the Public Gambling Act. The Hon'ble High Court after thoroughly examining the nature of the gameplay held that fantasy games are 'game of skill' and thus cannot qualify as 'gambling'.

Cases	Particulars
	The special leave petition[b] against the same has been dismissed and the review petition[c] against the said dismissal has also been rejected by the Hon'ble Supreme Court.
Gurdeep Singh Sachar[d]	This case before the Hon'ble Bombay High Court also pertained to online fantasy games being of gambling nature.
	The Hon'ble Bombay High Court after following the ratio in the case of Varun Gumber (supra) held that online fantasy games are 'game of skill' and thus cannot qualify as 'gambling'.[e]
Chandresh[f]	This case was also concerned with the nature of online fantasy games such as Dream 11. The Hon'ble Rajasthan High Court held that such games are of 'game of skill' as held in Varun Gumber (supra) and thus cannot qualify as 'gambling'.
	SLP against the same was also dismissed vide order dated 30 July 2021.

Notes: [a]*Varun Gumber v. Union Territory of Chandigarh*, (High Court of Punjab and Haryana April 18, 2017). 2017 SCC OnLine P&H 5372.

[b] Order dated 15 September 2017 in Diary Number 27511 of 2017.

[c] Order dated 9 November 2022 in Review Petition (Civil) Diary No. 5195 of 2022.

[d] *Gurdeep Singh Sachar v Union of India*, (High Court of Bombay April 30, 2019). 2019 (30) GSTL 441 (Bom).

[e] Four SLPs were filed before the Hon'ble Supreme Court- (i) Vide order dated 4 October 2019, SLP Diary Number No. 35191 of 2019 filed by Varun Gumber was dismissed, (ii) Vide order dated 13 December 2019, SLP Diary Number 43346 of 2019 filed by Gurdeep Singh Sachar was dismissed, (iii) Vide order dated 13 December 2019, SLP Diary Number 41362 of 2019 filed by Union of India was allowed to file a review before the Hon'ble Bombay High Court only qua the GST issue and (iv) Vide order dated 6 March 2020, stay on the judgment was granted qua SLP Diary Number 42282 of 2019 filed by State of Maharashtra.

[f] *Chandesh Shankla v State of Rajasthan & Ors*, (High Court of Rajasthan February 14, 2020). DBCWP No. 6653 of 2019.

AMENDMENTS MADE TO THE GST FRAMEWORK WITH EFFECT FROM 1 OCTOBER 2023 AND TENABILITY OF THE GST DEPARTMENT'S POSITION IN LIGHT OF THE SAME

As discussed above, the Hon'ble Karnataka High Court comprehensively rejected the arguments of the GST Department in the Gameskraft matter.

Post the same, the GST Council (which had been deliberating on the issue for close to three years) ultimately decided against the industry position in its 50th meeting and recommended for taxing the online gaming companies on the full-face value of the bets at the rate of 28%, notwithstanding the fact that the GoM formed for this purpose remained inconclusive. In the 51st meeting, this was changed to ensure that the 28% GST is levied only on the initial amount deposited by the players and not on the winnings amounts redeployed for gameplays by the players.

Large-scale amendments were made to the GST statutes, rules, and notifications since then, as summarized below:

Existing provision	Amendments made	Our view
	CGST Amendment Act	
Schedule III: Activities or Transactions which shall be treated neither as a Supply of Goods nor a Supply of Services 6. Actionable claims, other than lottery, betting and gambling.	Schedule III: Activities or Transactions which shall be treated neither as a Supply of Goods nor a Supply of Services 6. Actionable claims, other than specified actionable claims.	Originally, activities or transactions in actionable claims with the exception of lottery, betting and gambling were kept outside the scope of GST. The GST authorities tried to tax 'online gaming' under 'betting and gambling'. However, having failed to do so, the law has now been amended to bring all 'specified actionable claims' within GST, which now specifically includes 'online money gaming' as a category of taxable actionable claim.
No corresponding provision	(102A) 'specified actionable claim' means the actionable claim involved in or by way of— (i) betting; (ii) casinos; (iii) gambling; (iv) horse racing; (v) lottery; or (vi) online money gaming	
No corresponding provision	(80A) 'online gaming' means offering of a game on the internet or an electronic network and includes online money gaming	The Parliament has, for the first time, included and defined the concept of 'online gaming' and 'online money gaming' under GST laws
No corresponding provision	(80B) online money gaming' means online gaming in which players pay or deposit money or money's worth, including virtual digital assets, in the expectation of winning money or money's worth, including virtual digital assets, in any event including game, scheme, competition or any other activity or process, whether or not its outcome or performance is based on skill, chance or both and whether the same is permissible or otherwise under any other law for the time being in force	

(105) 'supplier' in relation to any goods or services or both, shall mean the person supplying the said goods or services or both and shall include an agent acting as such on behalf of such supplier in relation to the goods or services or both supplied	(105) 'supplier' in relation to any goods or services or both, shall mean the person supplying the said goods or services or both and shall include an agent acting as such on behalf of such supplier in relation to the goods or services or both supplied; Provided that a person who organizes or arranges, directly or indirectly, supply of specified actionable claims, including a person who owns, operates or manages digital or electronic platform for such supply, shall be deemed to be a supplier of such actionable claims, whether such actionable claims are supplied by him or through him and whether consideration in money or money's worth, including virtual digital assets, for supply of such actionable claims is paid or conveyed to him or through him or placed at his disposal in any manner, and all the provisions of this Act shall apply to such supplier of specified actionable claims, as if he is the supplier liable to pay the tax in relation to the supply of such actionable claims.	Online real money gaming companies' have consistently emphasized the fact that they are not involved in supplying an 'actionable claim in the nature of chance to win'; instead, it is the players / users who supply such 'actionable claim' to each other. To overcome this fundamental factual argument, the Legislature has now amended the definition of the term 'supplier' by introducing a deeming fiction in the said definition. As per the deeming fiction 'online gaming companies' will be deemed to be the 'supplier' of 'actionable claims' (in the nature of chance to win). The Legislature has thus enhanced the concept of 'supplier' itself as envisaged under the CGST Act, in order to widen the taxable base to levy GST on 'online gaming companies' as 'suppliers' of 'actionable claim'. This would apply for online gambling companies too.
	CGST Amendment Rules	
No corresponding provision	31B. Value of supply in case of online gaming including online money gaming.– Notwithstanding anything contained in this chapter, the value of supply of online gaming, including supply of actionable claims involved in online money gaming, shall be the total amount paid or payable to or deposited with the supplier by way of money or money's worth, including virtual digital assets, by or on behalf of the player:	The valuation mechanism has been prescribed for the first time in relation to online gaming/gambling (another Rule 31C has also been added for casinos). As per the valuation mechanism, only the initial deposits can be taxed, and redeployment of winnings does not form a part of the taxable value.

(*Continued*)

Existing provision	Amendments made	Our view
	Provided that any amount returned or refunded by the supplier to the player for any reasons whatsoever, including player not using the amount paid or deposited with the supplier for participating in any event, shall not be deductible from the value of supply of online money gaming. Explanation.- For the purpose of Rule 31B and Rule 31C, any amount received by the player by winning any event, including game, scheme, competition or any other activity or process, which is used for playing by the said player in a further event without withdrawing, shall not be considered as the amount paid to or deposited with the supplier by or on behalf of the said player.	
Integrated Goods and Services Tax (Amendment) Act, 2023		
Section 2(17) of the Integrated Goods and Services Tax Act, 2017 (**'IGST Act'**): (17) online information and database access or retrieval services means services whose delivery is mediated by information technology over the internet or an electronic network and the nature of which renders their supply impossible to ensure in the absence of information technology and includes electronic services such as,—	(17) online information and database access or retrieval services means services whose delivery is mediated by information technology over the internet or an electronic network and the nature of which renders their supply impossible to ensure in the absence of information technology and includes electronic services such as,— (i)… (ii)… (iii)… (viii) online gaming, excluding the online money gaming as defined in clause (80B) of Section 2 of the Central Goods and Services Tax Act, 2017 (12 of 2017.)	Section 2(17) of the IGST Act categorizes online gaming as OIDAR *services*, i.e., it is categorized as a supply of service. However, online money gaming is excluded from the same. 'Online money gaming' in turn is defined to mean 'online gaming' involving monetary stakes under Section 2(80B) of the CGST Act. 'Online gaming' is therefore the genus and 'online money gaming' is therefore the specie. It is surprising that the specie (ie., online money gaming) is being treated in a different manner (ie., as goods) from the genus (ie., 'online gaming', which has been defined as a 'service' since 2017).

(i)… (ii)… (iii)… (viii) online gaming		
Notification No. 72/2023 – Customs (NT) dated 30th September 2023		
No corresponding provision – no HSN code was earlier provided for supply of actionable claims	9807 – Specified actionable claim 9807 60 00 – Actionable claim involved in or by way of online money gaming	Mentioning of HSN classification on invoices has always been a mandate under the GST laws. However, HSN for online gaming has been introduced for the first time which shows that the online gaming companies could not have been involved in supply of 'actionable claim' before 1 October 2023.
Notification No. 12/2023- Central Tax (Rate) dated 19-10-2023		
Entry 34: Heading 9996 (Recreational, cultural and sporting services) (v) Gambling	Entry has been omitted.	Before this amendment 'gambling' was recognized as a service. Accordingly, as per 'Scheme of Classification of Services' 'betting and gambling' was recognized as a 'service' under tariff service code 999692. However, this entry has now been omitted.

The substantive amendments that have been made to the framework with effect from 1 October 2023 strengthen the case of online gaming companies that the GST position adopted in the past period by them was in accordance with law. While the nature of the amendments, i.e., whether they are prospective or clarificatory in nature, is yet to be clear; as a settled principle of law, it can be stated that these substantive amendments can only be treated to be prospective. The validity of these amendments has already been challenged before the Hon'ble Allahabad High Court.[17] Further, the GST Council in its 51st meeting has also acknowledged that the entire framework would be reviewed after a period of six months, which shows that the legal position is far from being settled.

CURRENT STATUS OF DISPUTES AGAINST ONLINE GAMING/ GAMBLING COMPANIES AND THE WAY FORWARD

The Department went in appeal against the judgment of the Hon'ble Karnataka High Court in GTPL's case before the Hon'ble Supreme Court. The Hon'ble Supreme Court vide order dated 6 September 2023 stayed the judgment and has posted the matter for further hearing.[18] The very fact that the Department chose to file an appeal is puzzling on account of the following reasons:

a. Purely from a legal perspective, the Hon'ble High Court merely followed judicial discipline and adhered to the position of law that has been settled by the Hon'ble Supreme Court since 1957, reiterated several times by various courts and re-emphasized in 1996 when a prohibition on horse racing (and staking money thereon) was struck down by the Supreme Court since the same is a game of skill (in Lakshmanan's case).
b. Given the fact that the Government itself has made substantive amendments to the GST framework with effect from 1 October 2023, the rationale of litigating for the past period does not seem to make sense legally.
c. Further, one also has to be cognizant of the ramifications that may arise in a scenario where the Department ultimately succeeds. This would lead to recovery actions not only against GTPL but also against the similarly situated online gaming companies. As a matter of fact, these gaming companies do not have the revenue to discharge the GST liability since the entire staked amount is not retained by them. This will only lead to complete liquidation (since none of them would be in a position to pay GST of a quantum which is several times their total revenue earned) of all these companies, thousands of job losses, sinking of thousands of crores in investments (in such companies) and last but not the least, a massive blow to investor sentiment qua India.

One of the outcomes on account of the stay granted by the Hon'ble Supreme Court has been that the Department has gone on to issue show cause notices to other online gaming/gambling companies as well, all over India. These notices have also been challenged before the Hon'ble High Courts of the respective States – favorable interim orders have also been received from various High Courts. Apart from the arguments on 'game of skill' versus 'game of chance', additional arguments vis-à-vis the constitutional validity of Section 15(5) of the CGST Act and Rule 31A(3) of the CGST Rules have also been framed to hit at the very genesis of the issue. The arguments are further supported by the fact that new amendments have been made which shows that for the past period, demands are bad in law.

In this context, various players in the casino industry have also received notices and approached the respective High Courts challenging the demand raised against them.

Recently, vide order dated 5 April 2024, the Supreme Court of India has transferred to itself 27 cases pending before 9 different High Courts on the issue of GST on gaming – it is possible that a final position may emerge in this regard from the Supreme Court of India in 2024 itself.

CONCLUDING THOUGHTS

While the ultimate resolution on this matter would be reached before the Hon'ble Supreme Court, one sincerely hopes that better sense prevails and at least for past period, the demands are dropped to achieve a modern and equitable tax regime consistent with our decades of constitutional jurisprudence, the human right to earn by using one's skills as enshrined in our Constitution and the global best practices.

NOTES

1 Sheth, A., & Patel, V. (2023, April 13). *Esports needs key growth drivers to flourish in India.* Mint. www.livemint.com/opinion/columns/indias-esports-industry-set-to-become-a-1-100-crore-industry-by-2025-with-potential-for-11-000-jobs-government-recognition-and-infrastructure-support-critical-for-growth-11681403128002.html
2 The Constitution of India, Seventh Schedule, List 2, Entry 34 – Betting.
3 *Ibid*, Entry 62 – Taxes on luxuries, including taxes on entertainments, amusements, betting and gambling.
4 *Ibid*, Entry 62, post 101St Constitutional Amendment Act – Taxes on entertainments and amusements to the extent levied and collected by a Panchayat or a Municipality or a Regional Council or a District Council".
5 *Ibid*, Article 246A – Special provision with respect to goods and services tax – (1) Notwithstanding anything contained in articles 246 and 254, Parliament, and, subject to clause (2), the Legislature of every State, have power to make laws with respect to goods and services tax imposed by the Union or by such State.
6 *State of Bombay v R.M.D Chamarbaugwala*, (Supreme Court of India April 9, 1957). AIR 1957 SC 699.
7 *R.M.D. Chamarbaugwala v Union of India & Ors*, (Supreme Court of India April 9, 1957). AIR 1957 SC 628.
8 *All India Gaming Federation v State of Karnataka*, (High Court of Karnataka February 14, 2022). 2022 SCC OnLine Kar 435.

9 *Junglee Games Private Limited v State of Tamil Nadu*, (High Court of Madras August 3, 2021). 2021 SCC OnLine Mad 2762.
10 *State of Karnataka v State of Meghalaya*, (Supreme Court of India March 23, 2022). CA No. 10466-10476 of 2011.
11 Finance Act, 1994, 66D(i) (1994). Negative list of services – (i) betting, gambling or lottery.
12 Notification No. 1/2017 - Central Tax (Rate), (2017). Since 'actionable claims' fall under the definition of 'goods' under GST.
13 The terms of reference provided for the following: (a) to examine the issue of valuation of services provided by casinos, race course, and online gaming portals and taxability of certain transactions in a casino, with reference to the current legal provisions and orders of Courts on related matters; (b) to examine whether any change is required in the legal provisions to adopt any betters means of valuation of these services; (c) to examine the administration of such valuation provision if any alternative means of valuation is recommended; and (d) to examine the impact on other similarly placed services like lottery.
14 *Gameskraft Technologies v. DGGSTI*, (High Court of Karnataka December 3, 2021). WP No. 22010 of 2021.
15 The intimation notice issued was also immediately challenged before the Hon'ble Karnataka High Court in WP No. 18304 of 2022.
16 WP No. 19570 of 2022 was filed before the Hon'ble High Court to challenge the show cause notice issued to GTPL. Separate writs were preferred for challenging the imposition of personal penalty.
17 *Kamal Mishra and Associates Pvt. Ltd. v Union of India & Ors*, (High Court of Allahabad). Writ Tax No. 1257 of 2023.
18 Tentatively, the matter is likely to be listed on 15 December 2023, prior to which the parties will have to complete their pleadings and written submissions.

REFERENCES

All India Gaming Federation v State of Karnataka, (High Court of Karnataka February 14, 2022). 2022 SCC OnLine Kar 435.

Chandesh Shankla v State of Rajasthan & Ors, (High Court of Rajasthan February 14, 2020). DBCWP No. 6653 of 2019.

Finance Act, 1994, 66D(i) (1994).

Gameskraft Technologies v. DGGSTI, (High Court of Karnataka December 3, 2021). WP No. 22010 of 2021.

Gurdeep Singh Sachar v Union of India, (High Court of Bombay April 30, 2019). 2019 (30) GSTL 441 (Bom).

Junglee Games Private Limited v State of Tamil Nadu, (High Court of Madras August 3, 2021). 2021 SCC OnLine Mad 2762.

Kamal Mishra and Associates Pvt. Ltd. v Union of India & Ors, (High Court of Allahabad). Writ Tax No. 1257 of 2023.

Notification No. 1/2017 – Central Tax (Rate), (2017).

R.M.D. Chamarbaugwala v Union of India & Ors, (Supreme Court of India April 9, 1957). AIR 1957 SC 628.

Sheth, A., & Patel, V. (2023, April 13). Esports needs key growth drivers to flourish in India. Mint. www.livemint.com/opinion/columns/indias-esports-industry-set-to-become-a-1-100-crore-industry-by-2025-with-potential-for-11-000-jobs-government-recognition-and-infrastructure-support-critical-for-growth-11681403128002.html

State of Bombay v R.M.D Chamarbaugwala, (Supreme Court of India April 9, 1957). AIR 1957 SC 699.

State of Karnataka v State of Meghalaya, (Supreme Court of India March 23, 2022). CA No. 10466-10476 of 2011.

The Constitution of India.

Varun Gumber v. Union Territory of Chandigarh, (High Court of Punjab and Haryana April 18, 2017). 2017 SCC OnLine P&H 5372.

Index

Note: Endnotes are indicated by the page number followed by 'n' and the endnote number e.g., 20n1 refers to endnote 1 on page 20. Page numbers in *italic* refers to Figures.

D

H

I

J

K

L

M

N

O

P

T

U

Printed in the United States
by Baker & Taylor Publisher Services